The Babri Masjid Question, 1528–2003:

'A Matter of National Honour'

VOLUME II

edited by
A.G. NOORANI

I0809491

The Babri Masjid Question, 1528–2003:

'A Matter of National Honour'

VOLUME II

edited by
A.G. NOORANI

Tulika Books

Published by **Tulika Books**
35 A/1 (ground floor), Shahpur Jat, New Delhi 110 049, India

© This collection, A.G. Noorani 2003

First published in India 2003
Second edition (paperback) 2004
Third edition (paperback) 2014

ISBN: 978-93-82381-46-4

Printed at Chaman Offset, Delhi 110 002

To the memory of
C. RAJAGOPALACHARI
a devout Hindu, a great Indian
and a consistent champion of minority rights

Contents

List of Documents

CHAPTER VII DEMOLITION OF THE BABRI MASJID, 6 DECEMBER 1992

CHAPTER VII

Demolition of the Babri Masjid, 6 December 1992

1. News Reports on the Demolition

1a. Outrage in Ayodhya

The Babri Masjid was today razed to the ground. Hundreds of volunteers who had come here for *kar seva* stormed the disputed Ramjanmabhumi–Babri Masjid edifice and destroyed the over 450-year-old structure.

The 'Operation Demolition', which commenced at 11.50 am 20 minutes before the scheduled time for commencement of the *kar seva* as finalized by the Janmabhumi leaders lasted nearly six hours. There was no resistance whatsoever to the operation either by the organizers or the police, barring three rounds of fire into the air with no impact.

The destruction, in full view of the top brass of the BJP–VHP–RSS built up tension in the town and Faizabad and there were reports of attacks on houses of the minority community. To tackle the explosive situation curfew was being clamped in Faizabad town and the Army has been put on stand by. The CRPF, with a strength of over 120 battalions, is ready to move in any time and is awaiting instructions from New Delhi.

Hasty Retreat by Top Brass

The top brass of the combine, including Mr L.K. Advani, Dr Murli Manohar Joshi and Mr Ashok Singhal, who were present at the site in full strength beat a hasty retreat from the spot after the volunteers took charge of the complex and their feeble attempts to halt the trickle towards the disputed structure only brought a tide of volunteers.

These leaders were whisked away by RSS volunteers to the nearby venue. 300 yards away from the disputed structure, where a massive public meeting was under way. They camped there for most part of the demolition and addressed the crowd. None of the top leaders ventured anywhere near the demolition operation and photo journalists who were targets of physical attack from the crowd had to plead for their lives. Equipment of several photographers was attacked and rolls of exposed films on the 'operation demolition' destroyed. Several foreign journalists and TV crews were ordered to leave the premises.

The contingent of the Central Reserve Police Force (CRPF) present inside the structure made a token attempt to push back the initial batch of *kar sevaks* who had managed to sneak in through the 12-feet high wired steel barricade but gave up the resistance within minutes once the number of intruders swelled beyond control. As the number of attackers grew, the CRPF jawans withdrew from their positions and disappeared from the complex.

The Provincial Armed Constabulary (PAC) and the local police, which was present in big numbers around the complex, watched silently as milling crowds chanting 'Jai Sri Ram' barged into the disputed structure from all the sides. Within an hour after storming the barbed fence around the complex, the outer wall of the structure and the checkpost points of the CRPF were demolished.

Free for all

With no one to check the inflow of volunteers into the disputed structure it was a free for all. The euphoric crowd dashed into the structure from all sides with shovels, axes and whatever they could manage. In the melee, several people were injured and had to be treated for first aid. As the first batch of volunteers who had climbed on to the domes struck them with shovels the whole atmosphere got electrified with slogans of establishment of a Hindu rashtra.

The District Magistrate of Faizabad, Mr R.N. Srivastava, who was present all along at the site evaded all questions from the record number of journalists and maintained that a decision on the situation would be taken after consultations with the State Government. The Supreme Court observer, Mr Tej Shankar, could not be traced in the vicinity of the complex.

Around 1 pm, a large contingent of the Rapid Action Force of the CRPF reached very close to the complex and returned to its barracks after the District Magistrate informed the CRPF officers that the Chief Minister, Mr Kalyan Singh, has turned down the suggestion for deployment of Central forces.

Senior CRPF officers disclosed that they headed towards Ayodhya after the District Magistrate requisitioned their services on behalf of the State Government. 'But strangely when we were about to approach the temple complex, the District Magistrate told us that the Chief Minister had rejected the proposal and that we may go back. We feel betrayed', a senior officer said.

There were signs of trouble at the disputed structure since dawn and in anticipation of the worst the organizers had virtually sealed the entire complex including the 2.77-acre disputed site and the place where the *kar seva* programme was to have commenced. Besides erection of wooden barricades in three layers the task of guarding the complex was entrusted to the trained RSS volunteers. They could be seen standing on the outer walls of the disputed structure along with paramilitary forces.

First indications of what was to come in the next few hours were available as soon as Mr Advani, Dr Joshi and Mr Singhal arrived at the site around 10.45

am in a cavalcade of cars. Their arrival led to groups of Bajrang Dal and Shiv Sena volunteers surging forward to gain entry into the site where the *kar seva* programme was to commence.

The RSS volunteers tried their best to check the surging crowds but lost control of the situation around 11.30 am. Heated arguments and jostling built up tension in the air and in no time it became a wave of resentment against the organizers. What sparked off the worst was the effort by RSS volunteers to physically throw out these elements from the venue. Egged on by the crowd atop the Manas Bhawan, facing the disputed structure, they broke through the wooden barrier and surged towards the iron barricade of the disputed structure.

Then, stones began flying in the direction of the CRPF jawans inside the disputed structure. Soon a group of volunteers had climbed over the barbed fence and gained access to the CRPF post. After a minor scuffle, they rushed to plant the saffron flag. The left dome of the disputed structure was the first to be attacked. After that there was no going back for the thousands of *kar sevaks*.

Even as the intruders went about their job, leaders of the Janmabhumi movement were busy addressing an estimated gathering of a lakh people just 300 yards away from the scene at the Rama Katha Kunj. Mr Advani, could be heard telling the gathering in the afternoon to seal all approach roads to Ayodhya as the Centre forces could intervene any moment.

People in and around the complex were in a frenzied mood and greeted each other with a sense of victory. The wild mood of the crowd did give tense moments to the Rama Temple Movement leadership. However, their role was confined to appeals from time to time for discipline.

The 'operation demolition' has clearly upset the grand plans of the Temple Movement Committee on the current phase of '*kar seva*' and once the situation slipped out of control they made no effort whatsoever to undertake the announced programme of *kar seva*. The organizers had planned to engage the two lakh-odd volunteers in the cleaning operation of the platform erected on the disputed 2.77-acre plot and undertake simultaneous construction activity to the east of the site.

In preparation for the current phase of *kar seva* the organizers had mobilized a group of the religious leaders, sants and dharmacharyas on the platform. Two hours before the demolition operation the site was under saffron seize.

Within minutes after the situation turned grave the huge gathering which has come on the call of Dharma Sansad refused to heed to their advice ironically, the sadhus who were on the other side of the fence during the regime of Mr Mulayam Singh Yadav realized to their rude shock that their writ does not run any longer.

[From *The Hindu*, 7 December 1992.]

1b. Masjid razed to the ground

Frenzied Rama temple *kar sevaks* in thousands on Sunday overran the security forces and demolished the disputed shrine here prompting the Centre to swiftly dismiss the Bharatiya Janata Party (BJP) government in Uttar Pradesh and bring the State under President's rule.

According to hospital authorities in Ayodhya, four persons were killed and hundreds injured when the domes of the structure caved in. By 5 pm it was all over; nothing existed of the structure except a mass of debris. The *kar sevaks* stormed the site after closing in from all sides exactly 25 minutes before the proposed *kar seva* on the acquired 2.77-acre land was to begin.

The demolition of the disputed structure was carried out in full view of senior RSS–BJP–VHP leaders, including Lal Krishna Advani and Murli Manohar Joshi.

The decision to sack the Kalyan Singh government in Uttar Pradesh was taken in New Delhi at an emergency meeting of the Cabinet presided over by the Prime Minister, Mr P.V. Narasimha Rao. Soon after receiving reports of damage to the disputed structure, the Prime Minister made repeated appeals for peace and communal amity on the national hook-ups of Doordarshan and All India Radio.

The presidential proclamation, issued under Article 356, said a situation had arisen in which the Government of Uttar Pradesh could not be carried on in accordance with the provisions of the Constitution.

The Union Cabinet, which met at the Prime Minister's residence for two hours, reviewed the situation and recommended President's rule. The meeting expressed concern over the likely impact on the communal situation in the country resulting from the events in Ayodhya. Besides Cabinet ministers, some junior ministers, including Mr Rajesh Pilot, Mr Ajit Panja and Mr P.R. Kumaramangalam, were also present.

The Cabinet felt that priority should be to ensure that peace returned and communal harmony and law and order were maintained in the country. The Home Minister, Mr S.B. Chavan, met the President after the meeting and conveyed to him the recommendation of the Cabinet.

In Lucknow, Mr Kalyan Singh submitted his resignation to the State Governor, Mr B. Satyanarayan Reddy, five-and-a-half hour after the situation in Ayodhya got out of hand, virtually pre-empting any move for his dismissal.

Mr Kalyan Singh and his cabinet colleagues shut themselves inside the Chief Minister's Kalidas Marg residence in Lucknow immediately after reports of *kar sevaks* breaking through security barriers and storming the disputed Ayodhya shrine reached the State capital.

There was a marathon strategy session during which the Chief Minister contacted senior party leaders in Ayodhya, New Delhi and Rashtriya Swayamsevak Sangh (RSS) headquarters in Nagpur. Mr Kalyan Singh drove to the Raj Bhavan with five senior Cabinet colleagues and submitted a one-line resignation without making any recommendations. His letter merely said that his resignation should be accepted.

The Chief Minister refused to meet newspersons.

Confirming that the Chief Minister had resigned, the Governor told reporters that there were clear indications that the Uttar Pradesh government had failed to protect the disputed structure and discharge its constitutional obligations.

Earlier in the day, frenetic mobs broke the walls surrounding the structure even as the Faizabad district administration made no effort to intervene. Securitymen trooped out of the structure soon after it was stormed and watched silently as thousands went on with the levelling operation.

The situation in Ayodhya and Faizabad was explosive. Curfew was clamped on Faizabad and the army has been placed on stand-by.

Four battalions of the Rapid Action force were at one stage summoned to Ayodhya but returned by the district administration from the outskirts of the town on the plea that their presence was not required.

The Rapid Action Force, dispatched at 1 pm from Faizabad after a magistrate approached the Central Reserve Police Force (CRPF) posse, was attacked in Faizabad, but despite heavy stoning by people who took to the streets, penetrated as far as the Saket Degree College, which is two kms from the disputed site.

Mr Advani was heard ordering sealing of all entry points to Ayodhya to prevent Central forces from entering the town. This was around 2 pm when men were hammering away atop the domes of the structure.

Belligerent boys attacked mediamen, robbed them of their equipment and money and even threw cameras in the air. Wooden barricades and bonfires came up on all roads leading out of the Ayodhya and boys waved pistols and swords menacingly.

It was evident in the morning itself that the situation was going to be very different from what the BJP and Vishwa Hindu Parishad (VHP) leaders had been assuring all along. Instead of awaiting their turn for the planned *kar seva* of 12.15 pm, and joining the assembly in *Rama Katha Kunj* close to the acquired land, groups of youth milled on the road outside the structure and chanted '*mitti nahi khiskaenge, dhancha tod kar jayenge*' (We will not shift mud. We will go after breaking the structure). Some flashed pistols and others pointed to pickaxes kept in a corner at a site behind the structure. The boys kept taunting swayamsevaks and policemen on the so-called security wall around the disputed premises.

It all began at 11 am after Bajrang Dal and Shiv Sena activists had a scuffle with swayamsevaks and forced their way into the 2.77-acre land and started pelting stones of policemen outside the outer wall of the structure. The policemen scattered and that signalled the beginning of the end. Mobs closed in from all sides, clambered over fences, pulled down barricades, and armed with crowbars, pickaxes, tongs and hammers, reached the outer walls.

While the wall was being attacked, a boy somehow reached atop the left dome of the structure and after planting a saffron flag smashed the surfacers. After that all hell broke loose as people poured inside the structure premises, felling police booths and attacking every corner inside. There were thousands and there is no saying how many were injured in the scramble towards the structure.

District administration officials sipped tea and watched helplessly from their vantage point at the police control room. Securitymen, who trooped out of the structure, watched silently, some grinning and others hanging around lazily with their sticks. Only two hours after the storming, a few rounds were fired in the direction of the structure, urging them to 'join the real *kar seva*'.

Mediamen were kicked and slapped and told to save their skins. It was a crazy sight and the stunned few, who did not take part in the demolition, watched in horror and dismay the spectacle of a nation's disgrace.

The walls and the arches disappeared. The idols inside the structure, placed in December 1949, and the plaque of Mir Baqi were removed and taken away by someone. The right dome collapsed at 2.45 pm and the dome to the left caved in 15 minutes later. The massive central dome came down at 4.45 pm. Nothing now remains of the disputed structure and there is only rubble and concrete stumps at the site.

Mr Advani and Uma Bharati's appeals to come down from the structure fell and deaf ears as the frenzied mobs went hammer and tongs, with lumpen elements screaming '*Ab banega Hindu rashtra*'. (Now we will build a Hindu state). Sadhvi Rithambara's voice could be heard over the loudspeaker—whether a cassette was being played or she was physically present was not clear—urging the mobs to have another go at the structure. Later, district magistrate Ravindra Nath Srivastava turned down queries from newsmen and retorted that he was not obliged to answer questions.

While swayamsevaks maintained that the day's events were not what they had planned, *kar sevaks* said that the orders for 'Operation Demolition' were passed the previous night. Shiv Sena activists claimed their member of Parliament Moreshwar Save had a meeting with Mr Advani and Mr Ashok Singhal, the VHP chief, before showing up at the disputed site in the morning.

Ayodhya is burning and central troops are waiting for a signal from New Delhi to go in. Officials of the Central forces in Ayodhya said they had been cheated and betrayed as they had all along suspected the worst.

Faizabad is absolutely surcharged, in fact there was a blast at Behniganj in which a boy lost one of his arms and where two *kar sevaks* were allegedly abducted, and people in Ayodhya are busy sealing all entry points. There are bonfires and spirals of smoke everywhere. There is utter lawlessness. The *kar sevaks* are fortifying Ayodhya and some two lakh are present willing to take on the Central forces. Nobody here has a clue as to what can happen and everybody feels that the worst is already over.

[From *The Indian Express*, 6 December 1992.]

2. The President of India, Dr Shankar Dayal Sharma, condemns the crime and directs the Prime Minister to 'uphold the rule of law'

The following is the text of the statement issued by the Press Secretary to the President: 'The President Dr Shankar Dayal Sharma, has strongly deplored vandalism that has caused damage to the Masjid in Ayodhya and has observed that such acts are absolutely against the doctrine and practices of Hinduism and all other great religions. Those who have harmed the structure of the Masjid have caused injury to the centuries-old ethos of India nurtured and strengthened by the martyrs and great leaders of India's struggle for freedom and national reconstruction. They have violated the rule of law, the tradition of India of mutual respect of all religions, and the basic tenets and values of the Hindu way of life.'

'The President has requested the Prime Minister to initiate appropriate expeditious steps to uphold the rule of law, the maintenance of public order and protection of all law-abiding citizens. The President has appealed to the people to maintain peace and unity and cooperate with one another in curbing all anti-national elements.'

[From *The Hindu*, 7 December 1992.]

3. Report to the Citizens' Tribunal on Ayodhya

The Commission of Enquiry to the Citizens' Tribunal visited Ayodhya and Faizabad from 9 to 11 February 1993, apart from visiting Lucknow on 8, 12 and 13 February. The visits to Ayodhya and Faizabad were publicized in a local daily Hindi paper *Jan Morcha*. The commission invited witnesses to come forward to give evidence. The Commission examined 84 witnesses, met and discussed the events with various professionals, government officials, religious leaders, etc., viewed and heard video and audio cassettes and received submissions from different sources. The efforts of the Commission to obtain relevant information from the Central Government and State Government did not meet with success. There were several other persons who could give evidence, but refrained from doing so on account of fear, loyalty, etc. Despite all these handicaps, the Commission was able to gather considerable material. After deliberating over the evidence and other material obtained by them the Commission submitted their report to us. We are greatly indebted to Shri Kamala Prasad and his colleagues for the immense trouble taken by them in visiting Lucknow, Ayodhya and Faizabad, for gathering considerable relevant evidence and, finally, for an analytical, educative and excellent report. Indeed, without the assistance rendered by the Commission, the Tribunal would have found it difficult to function effectively.

In its report, the Commission discussed at length the background and the build-up that led to the events at Ayodhya on 6 December 1992, the immediate aftermath of Ayodhya, the role of the Sangh Parivar, the actions and particularly the inaction of the two governments, Central and the State, the failure of the judicial process, etc., and set forth their conclusions. The Commission stated that the evidence led them to come to the inevitable conclusion that the demolition of the Babri Masjid on 6 December 1992 was pre-meditated and the subsequent disowning of the responsibility for the demolition by the Sangh Parivar was a mere cover-up to avoid legal responsibility. The Commission found that there was a failure of the democratic institutions to uphold the Constitution and the law. The demolition took place despite the parliamentary and the legislative discussions, the orders of the High Court and the Supreme Court and the directives of the National Integration Council to the Central Government. There was considerable forewarning about the likelihood of the demolition by various observers, and by the senior counsel who appeared in the Supreme Court. But the Central Government turned a blind eye to what was expected to happen though the Central and the State intelligence bureaus must have obviously passed on detailed information to the Centre even by 26 November 1992. The Central Government was reluctant to take a decision to intervene. Timely intervention could have saved the Babri Masjid, but as it was not forthcoming, the demolition was inevitable. The BJP government which was in power at the state level, did everything in its power to remove possible hurdles to the demolition of the Babri Masjid as a prelude to the construction of Sri Rama temple. The BJP government ensured the entry of the *kar sevaks* by providing all possible facilities to them. The CPMF was kept out of the disputed site while the PAC with a reputation of communal bias was deployed in addition to the local police. The terrorizing of Muslim inhabitants which preceded the events of 6 December, was not attempted to be stopped. The CPMF was allowed to go the disputed site only in the morning of 8 December 1992, after the demolition of the Babri Masjid and the construction of the make-shift temple were complete. The Central Government was guilty of failure to discharge their constitutional obligations and they had to share the blame with the Sangh Parivar and the State Government. The media also was to be blamed in that they played down the warning signals. It appeared that they failed to gauge the gravity of the situation and to report accurately the various preparations being made by the Sangh Parivar.

The Commission further found that the leaders of the Sangh Parivar spoke in two different voices; one to mislead by stating that the disputed shrine would not be harmed and another that Sri Rama temple would be constructed at any cost at the very site of the Babri Masjid. They were openly inciting the *kar sevaks* with their statements. . . .

Ms Suman Gupta, Sub-Editor, *Jan Morcha*, stated

'On 6th I went to Ayodhya at about 10.30 am. *Bhashan* (speeches) were going on in Rama Katha Kunj. Crowds were around the security walls on all sides. Khaki-pant clothed RSS volunteers were controlling crowds near the platform and were letting in only selected people. VHP Media Centre (Director) had issued pink passes for the press—they were being checked and only then were journalists allowed inside. Volunteers were stopping people. This was not being done by the police. At 11.55 am some *kar sevaks*, about two dozen from the front of the disputed structure broke the volunteers' cordon and, after breaking the barricades, entered the inner complex where the mosque was and started breaking it. Some people with *bhagwa dhwaj* (saffron flag) . . . first also waved them around. Just before the people climbed on the mosque Ashok Singhal came from behind Rama Katha Kunj and up onto the platform. The moment he climbed the platform, the *kar sevaks* started stoning the structure. More people started climbing the structure, including the RSS volunteers with khaki-half pants, and breaking the structure. People had iron rods and other wooden *dandas* to begin with. A lot of *kar sevaks* climbed from behind—ropes were used. Also, *gayti, phavra* and *belcha, hathoras*, all these were produced there and were used. Then after about ten minutes of this climbing, the journalists, actually first the photographers and video men were attacked. I had a camera with me. When I started trying to take photographs (in fact I had just taken one) I was attacked by 3–4 *kar sevaks*—they pushed me on a pile of bricks and snatched at my camera—I tried to hide my camera and clutched it near my chest. There were about 30–40 policemen near me (alongside me) but they didn't help me. A woman *kar sevak* also tried to snatch my camera, but I resisted. Two *kar sevaks* caught hold of me and dropped me towards the back of 'Janmasthan'. I asked for water as I fainted but though about 100 PAC and CRPF were standing nearby and heard me shouting for water, they did not do anything. One PAC man pointed toward a *nala* and shouted '*pani hai tho*'. When I bent down to drink, the PAC made a threatening sound and the *kar sevaks* left me and ran. I took shelter for a short while in a home and then came out with a boy from that house. I had asked him to accompany me to Dorahi Kuan where my press car was. The moment I reached the road a crowd of *kar sevaks* surrounded me/us. They shouted at the boy, '*tum patrakar liye ja raho ho*'. While they were arguing I ran when I was only about 50 feet from the car about fifteen *kar sevaks* with *trishuls*, *gayti*, knife, etc., ran after me and caught me—they put a sort of knife at my chest and twisted my face and said, 'Give me the film otherwise you will be killed'. They attacked my bag and threw my camera. Two men (later I learnt they were drivers) stopped them and I again ran and hid in Jugal Kishore's house till 4 pm.'

Ms Ruchira Gupta of *Business India*

'I reached Ayodhya on 6 December at 11 o'clock in Rama Katha Kunj. We had driven down straight from Lucknow. I went with three other journalists Swapan Dasgupta, Chandan Mitra and Suman Chatterjee of *Ananda Bazar Patrika* and we went inside Rama Katha Kunj to the BJP camp office from the terrace of which all the leaders were giving speeches on the mike. I was allowed to go up to the terrace when most of the other journalists were not being allowed to go upstairs, because I had accompanied two other journalists—Swapan Dasgupta and Chandan Mitra—who knew Mr Advani very well.

'While going through the crowd we feared a lot of hostility because the crowd seemed to be against the press. They were calling us *angrej ki aulad, Babar ki aulad*. I had a photographer with me, Diwan Mehra who was carrying the camera. We somehow managed to go up to the terrace of Rama Katha Kunj. When we were there, Pramod Mahajan was at the mike making a speech. We could not clearly hear what he was saying except that he was saying something about the structure that '*Hum is laye ayae hai ki Babri Masjid ko hatana hai yehan se*' and just when we saw two people climb on top of the dome, he stopped speaking. He stepped away and said I don't want to speak any more and Advani went up to him to continue speaking he said no, 'I don't want to talk'. Then he went up to Uma Bharati, who was also on the terrace. She refused. Some people brought a harmonium in front of the mike and they tried to play the harmonium and *bhajans*, etc. The mike failed by that time, the electric wire had been cut off. After about half an hour, the mike was restored and Vijaya Raje Scindia went up to the mike to speak. However, Uma Bharati first spoke saying to the people 'don't climb on top of the dome; it is not the time. You might get hurt, we have a plan, follow our plan'. This is what she was saying but no one seemed to listen to her and more and more people climbed on top of the domes. Then Vijaya Raje Scindia took the mike and she started saying that 'you know we are supposed to be a disciplined party, what kind of Rama Bhakts are you. We do have a plan in mind. Don't do anything at random.' But no one listed to them. But at one point we felt that people had begun to climb down from the domes, and Advani even told us that 'look I have a disciplined party, we told them to come down, they came down, we tell them to go up, they go up.' After that people had begun to climb down from the domes. Some people came with bricks, etc., to the terrace of Rama Katha Kunj and they kept showing that there was a Pali inscription on the bricks, etc., and there was B.L. Sharma, an MP, who hugged someone who came with one brick and said you are doing a very brave and courageous act for India and after that Sadhvi Rithambara went from person to person because it was quite evident that the structure had been broken, there had been bricks chipped away from the structures, I heard Rithambara saying that. Then she went to talk to Advani. Advani took Sheshadri aside and went to a corner on the terrace. I couldn't hear what they were saying. I tried to follow them but they were talking in whispers. They spoke after which Advani went downstairs, I followed him. He went into a room, but I wasn't allowed to go inside the room with him.

But I was told that he was talking to Kalyan Singh on the phone. And by this time, two domes had come down. I went back upstairs when Advani went back upstairs and somehow the mood had changed on the terrace by then, because people seemed to be for the demolition, and there was Guru Paramanand and there was also some photographer who had been telling Acharya Dharmendra that 'you know people are being attacked. Why don't you do something about it?' He never said anything. In fact, just as we had come on the terrace after Pramod Mahajan and Uma Bharati and Vijaya Raje Scindia had spoken. Acharya

Dharmendra also spoke once and he had told crowds not to let anyone take photographs after the mikes had been restored. I heard it distinctly. I can't tell you the exact sequence of events because things were happening very fast and I was not wearing a watch. After Advani came back and all this happened, two domes had come down and my photographer also came back. He had gone to the domes and he had been taking photographs there. He said that his camera had been snatched away and his roles had been taken away. And there were some policemen who said, 'no, no, just give your roll and run away. We can't do anything to save you.' Then we decided to go because we knew that in about an hour or two, the last dome would also come down. So, I convinced the other journalists on the terrace to let us go and have a last look at the structure. Chandan Mitra, Swapan Dasgupta and Suman Chatterjee, all three agreed, and Pramod Mahajan, Secretary accompanied us. The four of us walked to where the structure was. Most of it was rubble by then and there was a kind of trench which was being dug all around the structure. So we had to climb down a little bit and up through the trench to go. When we reached the trench the hostility was so evident that Swapan and Suman decided not to go inside the domes. Chandan wanted to go inside. He told me to wait. He told me not to come inside. He went in. I waited for five minutes, and he didn't come back. I thought that anyway I will go and have a look as time was very short. So, I climbed on to the platform where the structure was, went in and I could see that people with yellow bands who were pushing people aside who were not *kar sevaks*, and people had ironrods in their hands. There was a kind of fencing, around the structure, they were swinging the iron rods in their hands.

'There were hacking away with that. They were also using stones to constantly hack away because very little of the structure was left by then. I went inside. There was a kind of broken wall with a slight arch. I walked through it and went inside and there was a huge crowd absolutely body to body so we had to really squeeze past these people. Pramod Mahajan, Secretary, had disappeared by then. I went in. At that point, someone screamed 'no, no! Musalman hai' and they began to attack me. Then someone decided that they would not try to strike me, because they were not really beating me, there was no one to beat anyone or anything. They decided that they wouldn't do it inside the structure, but outside. I was dragged out, pushed down the trench and the two journalists who were with me sent some other *kar sevaks* who were with them, who accompanied us from the terrace of the BJP camp office. They came down. There was a tussle between the yellow banded *kar sevaks* and these other *kar sevaks* and one of these was hit on the head, and was bleeding. He also injured his leg but had managed to pull me out. I went back to Rama Katha Kunj. I spoke to Advani, I spoke to Pramod Mahajan. I told Mahajan what was happening to the structure. Pramod Mahajan said that 'forget about this, we will talk about this in Delhi. Tell me how much time is left for the rest of the dome to come down.' I was not interested in that so again I gave up trying to talk with them. Advani also, of course, just ignored me. We were waiting for the last dome to come down. Sadhvi

Rithambara was on the mike by then. She was screaming. There was a minister from Rajasthan who had resigned to join the *kar seva*. He came and told me, 'See if I do the right thing, God is on my side. That is why we are able to accomplish this.' Pramod Mahajan again came back to me and said, 'Finally I feel that the *tirth* (a religious journey) which began two years ago is complete now.' And Vijaya Raje Scindia hugged Uma Bharati and said: 'Finally now my eyes can rest in peace.' There was sugar being distributed on the terrace. Someone came, in fact, one of the policemen came, and gave me some sugar then. I said that I don't want it. Advani said, 'Look, there are other people eating *prasad*, can't you see!' He pointed to some crowd who were eating something sweet and I saw one of his NSG guards clapping. There was chaos on the terrace, not joy. The Kotharis, the parents of the boys who had died during the last *kar seva* of 1990, came on the terrace. B.L. Sharma went and touched their feet and people were walking in and touching their feet. We waited for about two or three hours on the terrace even after the dome came down. Two or three hours because we were not sure about the reaction of the crowds. I saw some other journalists; an Englishman, or American, was bleeding. Manoj Raghuvanshi and other journalists came. Raghuvanshi hugged Ashok Singhal and congratulated him. Then after two hours we walked down. We could not see any policemen who were against it at all. Finally, we were walking towards our car we went down and Chandan Mitra went and talked to L.K. Advani. We even asked L.K. Advani for help. But he said, 'No I am going to stay back tonight because I have to supervise certain operations'. We walked out, we met a lady constable on the way and she said to go very carefully since the crowd was very hostile. While I was on the terrace itself, I saw some shops and houses burning. I asked one of the *kar sevaks* on the terrace, 'So whose houses are there'. He said that those were Muslim houses. I asked again that who was burning them. He said that it was basically being burnt by the Muslims themselves because they want compensation. Once I heard Advani on the mike (this was after the second dome had fallen, and the third dome had not fallen) telling *kar sevaks* 'please block the roads, don't let the CRPF come, put tyres, whatever you have but don't let the CRPF come because there could be a Jallianwala Bagh here'. That is about it. That is what I witnessed that day.

'On 5 December, I met the U.P. Governor in Lucknow and I told him that I had been to Ayodhya earlier. I had been following Advani before that also, on his tour of U.P. when he went on collecting *kar sevaks* to Ayodhya and I told the Governor that the crowd were very enthusiastic and it didn't seem as if it could be curbed. So he told me that Atal Behari Vajpayee had promised him that the crowds would not break any law and he said that the RSS cadre was very disciplined; 'we have given them all identity cards so you can rest assured that no law would be broken.' Besides that, during Advani's rally all over U.P. when I followed him, he kept saying that we are not going to Ayodhya just to sing *bhajans* or *kirtans*. We are going there with a purpose. We are going to use bricks and shovels. He kept saying that all through his rallies. But when I went and asked him what do you mean by bricks and shovels and what do you (mean by saying) that *bhajans* and *kirtans* will not be sung? Does that mean that you going to break the law?

He said, 'there are ways and ways, you don't know about it'. 'But you have to clarify it'. At least Advani did seem a little puzzled in the beginning.

Did they appear to be in the dark?

I don't know (whether) Pramod Mahajan was in the dark but L.K. Advani certainly may not have known the plan to tell you. That's the impression I got.

Did you see Advani?

I didn't see him wringing his hands. That women must have seen that, I didn't see Advani wringing his hands.

We didn't know till we left the '*Manch*'. We knew when we reached Lucknow. We didn't know that on the terrace. We kept hearing the rumour that Kalyan Singh is going to resign when Advani went down and spoke to him on the phone.

'What I said is Rithambara said that now the government is going to go in any case. So why should they let the structure remain? And there seems to have been some element of planning on it, because from the terrace I saw that all the women who were near the site of the structure suddenly being told to leave in a line. And they all walked out and I asked the leaders why were they being led away from there. Then they said, 'no, no, no, forget about it. Don't ask any questions'. 'So there seems to have been some element of plan. That is all I can say. I can't be really sure about who knew about it and who didn't. B.L. Sharma seemed to know about it. He went there, came back with the idols wrapped up in a kind of cloth. He saw me taking a picture of it. He said, 'no, no, don't take it. We are going to keep away the idols somewhere'. So there was an element of involvement in what was happening.

At what stage (were) the idols removed?

This is in the afternoon between 2 and 3.

Before the demolition?

No, not before the demolition started. Everything was going on simultaneously. It was not. . . .

Did it appear well-planned?

They did it very efficiently. They climbed on top of the domes. Two or three boys climbed up first. They had ropes with them. They went up and let down the ropes. Other people climbed them very fast within half an hour or forty five minutes, it turned to about 60–70 then 200. They did have some implements with them. Sadhus don't carry axes but they had axes when I watched them. So, they seem to have known about it. Especially, these people with yellow bands on their heads definitely knew about it and there was a kind of planning.

'After the third dome fell, when we were coming back, no this is before the third dome fell when we had visited the structure when we were coming back to the terrace, we met a *kar sevak* from Maharashtra. After I had visited the disputed structure on that terrace and we were walking back to the terrace at the Rama Katha Kunj where the BJP leaders were, we met a *kar sevak* from that site and he came and told me that he was one of the first people to climb on top of the dome.

He said he was from Baramati. His name was Talangi and he said that there had been a plan, they had rehearsed it. He was supposed to have climbed on top of the dome at 11.35 am but he decided to climb up at 11.15 am because the slogan and the music frenzied him so much that he could not wait. I forgot to mention that when I was summarizing the statement.' . . .

In the Supreme Court, not only had the Counsel for the Muslim residents of Ayodhya expressed apprehensions about what might happen, their own counsel, the Attorney General, had himself mentioned to the Court that the situation had already almost gone out of control and that any further delay might make the situation irreversible in practical terms. Having told the Court so through their Counsel, what prevented the Government of India from taking appropriate action to prevent further deterioration of the situation? The letters of the Home Minister to the Chief Minister of Uttar Pradesh indicate that the Government of India was alive to the gravity of the situation, alive to the fact that the Government of Uttar Pradesh was weakening and withdrawing the security arrangements around the Babri Masjid, and alive to the urgent need to protect the structure. From 1 December onwards, there were continuous reports streaming in from Ayodhya about the destruction of Muslim graves and Muslim property. Even then there was inaction on the part of the Government of India. The inaction on the part of the Government of India indicates a lack of direction, a lack of policy, and a lack of initiative. Where decision and action were urgently needed, there was indecision and procrastination. It was probably thought that after the floods have passed, no matter what destruction they have wrought, the stream would continue to flow as calmly as before; it was probably thought that the inevitable would happen, and it was not for mortals to prevent what was ordained; it was probably thought that the large Hindu population of Uttar Pradesh, Madhya Pradesh, Rajasthan and Himachal Pradesh, who had already voted for the BJP in the elections would be further alienated from the party in power at the Centre, if it prevented the demolition of the Masjid and the construction of the temple; or was there a sneaking, cynical sympathy for the objective of destroying the mosque and constructing a temple? History and the people alone will judge. If the recent elections to the U.P. Legislative Assembly are of any indication, the people have judged and found the Government of India guilty. For our part, we are emphatically of the view that the Government of India was guilty of culpable negligence and a willful refusal to discharge its obligation as a constitutional government. The inaction was deliberate and with full knowledge of the likely outcome. The laboured effort made in the White Paper to absolve itself by claiming that the demolition was sudden and spontaneous without any inkling as to what was about to happen is a pretence, a mere pretext, a clumsy attempt made with a view to disown responsibility.

[From *Citizens' Tribunal on Ayodhya*, Judgement and Recommendations, Justice O. Chinnappa Reddy, D.A. Desai and D.S. Tewatia, December 1993.]

4. Jyoti Basu's deposition before the Liberhan Commission

Following is the statement made by Jyoti Basu before the Liberhan Commission of inquiry:

I am happy that I have been given the opportunity to appear before the Commission. I wish to make a few points on the demolition of the Babri Masjid and reply to any queries.

There were reports that the Babri Masjid in Ayodhya may be attacked by the *kar sevaks*. The then prime minister Shri Narasimha Rao, convened the meeting of the National Integration Council on 23 November 1992. On behalf of the CPI(M), Harkishan Singh Surjeet, the general secretary, and I attended the meeting. No member of the BJP attended it. Unanimously, powers were given to Shri Narasimha Rao to take necessary measures to protect the Masjid. On our party's behalf we proposed that even Article 356 of the Constitution may be used if there was no other way to protect it, though we have been opposing its use.

Two days before the demolition, i.e., on 4 December 1992, I rang up the Prime Minister to inform him that there was apprehension that the Masjid may be attacked and hence something has to be done to protect it. The prime minister said the Working Committee of the Congress was to meet on the issue. But your lordship knows what happened.

After the U.P. government was dismissed, Shri Kalyan Singh addressed a meeting in Calcutta on 2 February 1993, as recorded by the police. The Hindi speech, along with its English translation, is also with me. I shall leave these with you. I particularly draw your attention to that part of the speech in which he speaks about the demolition of the mosque:

> 'I express before you, I did not have any repentance, nor any pangs or agony for the case, and I had a pleasure to declare it as a historic day. I can tell you, my dear friends, without the inspiration of God such a colossal job of demolition could not have been pulled off within five hours without using any explosive device. Even if we engaged a labour contractor for the same, the contractor might have taken at least one and half months time for the said purpose, including removal of huge amount of debris. You know, the birth of a new Indian era will take place with some glorious future after 6 December 1992. The demolition of the structure (though some sections of people took it for a shame for the nation) has become an affair of pride to the nation.'

In the third week of December, 1993, Surjeet and I met the prime minister and asked him why nothing was done. He said, '*How could I disbelieve a chief minister when he assured me that no harm will be done to the Masjid.*' I then presented the cassette to him and told him what I told you now. I do not know whether he heard the cassette.

The present prime minister, Shri Vajpayee met me on 20 March 1999, in Calcutta and asked me why I called the BJP barbaric and uncivilized. I said I do not normally name anybody, but I do call the demolition a barbaric act, and I asked him how did it happen and what language should I use. He said '*It was an accident and not organized*'. *I told him about Kalyan Singh's speech. He kept quiet. Now he is saying something else—'expression of national sentiment*'.

We shall await the findings of the Commission.

[From *People's Democracy*, 8 December 2002.]

5. Two eyewitness accounts of the pre-planning of the demolition

Praveen Jain

If you think the demolition of the Babri Masjid was a spontaneous one, then hear this: On Saturday afternoon a BJP Member of Parliament forewarned me of the events to follow on Sunday (6 December).

He smiled as he directed me to the spot where the *kar sevaks* were rehearsing how to bring down the 465-year old structure. The *kar sevaks,* with ropes and rods had roped a rock pile and were tugging at it from different directions. As events turned out later, this was the very manner in which the three domes of the mosque were brought down the next day.

Near the mosque, a concrete dais had been erected. Hordes of *kar sevaks* from several directions were periodically racing towards the dais. This was the run-up to Sunday afternoon.

December 6

Early on Sunday we made our way to the spot where the BJP–VHP combine was expected to carry out the 'symbolic' *kar seva.* All photographers, journalists and cameramen were directed to a *dharmashala* (Manak Bhawan). The terrace had been cleared for us.

As events moved forward Bajrang Dal activists scampered onto the terrace. Their number increased till we were outnumbered. Sensing trouble, I slipped away.

It was the sensible move, as I realized later. The journalists and camera crew who stayed back were pulled and jostled around, their movie cameras were snatched away and flung down from the terrace five floors above the ground. On the ground there were thousands of people milling around. They were all chanting '*Jai Siya Ram'.* They converged on me. Even though I was caught unawares I managed to get away from the spot. Someone in the mob snatched at my open bag. Later I realized that the *kar sevaks* had made off with Rs 2,500.

Even as the crowd chased me, its attention was caught by another hapless photographer who was literally shooting from the hip as he ran. The mob set upon him giving me a fleeting opportunity to move towards the dais where the BJP–VHP leaders were seated. On the way I met two other photographers—Nitin Rai and Pablo Bartholomew. On the spur of the moment we decided there might be safety in numbers and were glued together by fear.

By then the hordes had swarmed up the domes and they fell upon it with *trishuls* and whatever else they had their hands.

It would have been unthinkable not to get this on film, even if this was the last thing we did. Out came our cameras and we got clicking. This focussed attention on us. *Kar sevaks* armed with *trishuls* and daggers chased us. I was luckier than the other two who were nabbed, stabbed and beaten.

Later that night, journalists who managed to get away from the site told us the mosque had been turned to rubble.

December 7

Early in the day, sporting a saffron bandana printed entirely with the word Rama and wearing saffron sweaters and carrying only a minimum of photo equipment in our pockets we made our way steadily to the complex.

Kar sevaks were clearing the rubble to make way for some sort of structure. To take pictures from so near would have been suicidal. Through a small window of a house in the vicinity I squeezed the shutter six times.

I breathed freely. Not outside the house. Not in Faizabad—12 kilometers away. Not on the flight back. But at the office when the prints came out fine.

They were the pictures of Hindus giving Hinduism a bad name. I am ashamed.

[From *The Pioneer*, 8 December 1992.]

Hemant Sharma

What happened here yesterday (Ayodhya, December 6) was preplanned. The Plan to demolish the disputed structure was within the full knowledge of VHP, Bajrang Dal and *sadhu sants*. Selected cadre of the RSS were being methodically given training for the job in Rama Katha Kunj. . . .

The planning for demolition was divided into five distinct parts. . . .

For the job there were separate groups of *kar sevaks* who climbed up the disputed structure from the north and south. An RSS volunteer in uniform, standing on the watch tower just in front of the structure was directing them. He commanded the *kar sevaks* methodically with whistle and flag in hand. There was a separate group to carry away the injured *kar sevaks*. This group was already prepared with cots and vehicles before the *kar sevaks* climbed the structure. . . . Another group was given responsibility for keeping the photographers away from the whole process, and it was engaged only in beating up the cameraman and breaking their cameras. A big contingent was deployed on all roads leading to Ayodhya, preventing all others except the *kar sevaks* from reaching there

Every attempt was made also to prevent leakage of the news of what was happening in Ayodhya. Telephone lines were cut and all wires of the police control room removed. All this had taken place within 20 to 30 minutes of the attack on the structure.

Picks and shovels were kept on the spot for demolition of the structure. The first batch of *kar sevaks* moving towards the Masjid had ropes and were climbing the structure with the help of these. While they were climbing, power supply was stopped, as electric wires lay between the outer wall and the structure. After entering the disputed area, the *kar sevaks* first disconnected the CRPF's hotline. Apart from those in the district hospital, a team of doctors was also present in the Ramjanmabhumi Trust office as well. . . .

[From *Jansatta*, 8 December 1992.]

6. Police foreknowledge of the demolition

All police officers on duty in Faizabad and Ayodhya during the *kar seva* of December 1992 were aware of the fact that the disputed mosque would be attacked by the *kar sevaks* a day before it was demolished.

This statement was made by the then additional superintendent of police, Faizabad, Ms Anju Gupta, before the Liberhan Inquiry Commission probing the Babri mosque demolition case.

Ms Gupta told the commission that on 5 December 1992, the then inspector general of police, Faizabad zone, had warned officers of his departments that there was clear indication from the intelligence agencies that the disputed shrine would be attacked on December 6. However, Ms Gupta said that it would be difficult to say whether the minutes of the meeting were recorded or not.

The commission is trying to put together the events that preceded the demolition of the Babri mosque, and decide whether it was a pre-meditated act or spontaneous as suggested by the BJP leaders. If the government knew of the plans of the *kar sevaks* a day in advance as suggested, then it will be difficult for them to give excuses as to why no action was taken.

Ms Gupta told the commission that around 9 am on 6 December, she got a wireless message that some graves behind the Ved temple had been desecrated and that the *kar sevaks* were gearing up for the demolition of the Babri mosque. Narrating an eyewitness account of the demolition, Ms Gupta told the commission that around 200 *kar sevaks* sporting head bands had climbed up the three domes and were all armed with iron rods, sharp digging instruments and ropes. With such sharp implements the *kar sevaks* had managed to pull down the domes and the thick walls of the mosque within two hours of the assault, said Ms Gupta and added 'this could not have been possible without proper training and planning.'

She however added, that she had no definite knowledge whether planning to demolish the mosque or attack it had been undertaken, but the facts available indicate that this work could not have taken place without proper planning.

Ms Gupta told the commission that when Mr L.K. Advani, the BJP president, expressed his desire to go to the area to stop the *kar sevaks*, she informed the S.P.–Intelligence and the Commandant of the 15 Battalion of the Provincial Armed

Constabulary, and they discouraged her and advised her not to take him to the site. Ms Gupta said that Mr Advani was with her at the Duarti Kuan (well), which is near the disputed site and from there one could see the chaotic situation in and around the structure.

Ms Gupta told the commission that Mr Advani had in her presence said that the temple would be constructed at the very spot and the same was repeated by Mr Murli Manohar Joshi, accepting that they were pleased with the actions of the *kar sevaks*. The Bajrang Dal leader, Mr Vinay Katiyar had mocked Mr Mulayam Singh Yadav by saying over the public speaking system '*Yahan parinda par nahin maar sakta*.'

She told the commission that she was not aware of the fact whether the Supreme Court appointed observer was present or not. But argued that the way the journalists were beaten up, gives credence to the fact that the entire episode was planned. She said that she had somehow managed to save the journalists from the wrath of the frenzied *kar sevaks*. One of the journalists was Mr Nitin Rai, a photojournalist with *Sunday Magazine* and Mr Pathali Barthi Melias, a freelance journalist.

The Union Government has provided a list of 57 witnesses who will depose before the commission including the Supreme Court observer, and the then Commissioner of Faizabad.

[From *The Asian Age*, by Osama Talha, 11 May 1994.]

7. Shiv Sena's admission of pre-planning

In a surprise statement here today, the Shiv Sena MP from Maharashtra, Mr M. Sarve, admitted that demolition of the Babri mosque was pre-planned and that the *kar sevaks* had acted on instructions.

According to Mr Sarve, the decision to storm the structure was taken on Saturday night.

Meanwhile, the VHP leader, Mr Ashok Singhal, in a statement, blamed the Prime Minister and Muslim fundamentalists for yesterday's demolition. He asked the Centre to accept the Hindus' claim on the site, and their wish to build a temple on it.

[From *The Statesman*, 7 December 1992.]

8. A foreign scholar's perception

Although BJP leader, Lal Krishna Advani, who was present at the site, immediately tried to distance himself from the act of demolition, there can be little doubt that the entire event had been well planned in advance . . . the destruction of the mosque provoked immense communal violence, especially in Bombay,

Ahmedabad, Surat, and Calcutta. More than a thousand people—most of them Muslims—were killed in Bombay alone. The pogroms in Bombay were led by the Shiv Sena, a fanatic Hindu political party active in the Bombay region, which, although banned, was, according to a number of reports in English-language news media, actively supported by the Bombay police force. The participation of the police in the attacks on Muslims has also been documented in other areas, such as the east Delhi neighbourhood of Seelampur.

[From Peter van der Veer, *Religious Nationalism*, pp. 6–7.]

9. The BJP's Ruse

9a. Nikhil Chakravartty's revelations

The vandalism that brought down the Babri Masjid structure on 6 December will remain a Black Sunday in the annals of independent India. Like the insensate violence of fratricidal communalism of the partition days that culminated in Gandhiji's killing forty-four years ago, the demolition of the Babri Masjid will remain a symbol of shame for the nation, and particularly for the majority community which permitted a bunch of blackguards to pose as its guardian and get recognized as such.

While anger and anguish over this ghastly incident have overwhelmed millions in this country, there is no escape for certain elements in public life from being held responsible for this despicable act. The BJP and the RSS leaders who backed the so-called *Dharma Sansad* issuing the *fatwa* for the *kar seva* have to unequivocally own up the guilt for having collected such a huge number of people around the disputed area by whipping up raging frenzy which was beyond control. And the BJP bosses who had been campaigning in support of the *kar seva* were found to have beaten a retreat when the mob was actually demolishing the mosque—an ignominious commentary on both their capacity and courage. Those who incite a crowd and lack the guts to face and halt it are unworthy of claiming to be leaders. Their moral posture which they flaunt as part of their *Hindutva* should have the honesty to offer public apology for this shocking abdication of responsibility . . . .

In the critical days after the National Integration Council meeting on 23 November, the senior BJP–RSS leaders were working out some settlement terms with the Central Government. The terms of these negotiations, which the present writer can vouch for, were, firstly, the Babri Masjid disputed structure complex would be adequately protected until the dispute is settled by dialogue or due process of law, and the U.P. government would invite the Centre, if it is so desired, to send its force to reinforce the State Government's security arrangements. Secondly, there would be no *kar seva* in violation of law. Thirdly, the Centre would make a one-point reference to the Supreme Court under Article 143 and the Court's opinion would be accepted as binding by both the Centre and the U.P.

government as also the BJP–RSS combine. Fourthly, the Centre would express its support for expeditious disposal of the case about the disputed plot now pending before the High Court. As these terms were hammered out, an impression prevailed on the eve of December 6 that perhaps the crisis was on the way of being defused. In fact, the BJP–RSS leaders were expected to persuade the *Dharma Sansad* not to precipitate the crisis.

The question now arises whether the BJP–RSS leaders were diabolically agreeing to these terms while preparing for the demolition of the Babri Masjid; or were they themselves outstripped by the blitz attack of the mob? . . .

. . . More than once during these crisis days, the BJP spokesmen have talked about 'the majesty of law', and now they themselves connived, if not actively involved, in the blatant defiance of the Constitution. The pulling down of the Babri Masjid structure is not just a matter of religious frenzy, but the blatant assault on the rule of law and civilized conduct of public affairs. Here is the essence of their guilt.

[From *Mainstream*, 12 December 1992.]

9b. *Organizer* reveals the strategy

A tacit understanding seems to have been hammered out after a series of meetings Shri P.V. Narasimha Rao had with Shri Atal Behari Vajpayee, Shri Bhairon Singh Shekhawat and Prof. Rajendra Singh (Rajju Bhaiyya), Joint General Secretary of the RSS. Some editors who took the initiative after the controversial NIC meeting to avert a crisis played a meaningful role in convincing the Prime Minister that the Sangh Parivar's insistence on de-linking the cases pertaining to 2.77-acres acquired by the U.P. government and the disputes about the structure had considerable merit. . . .

The Sangh Parivar played its cards well in this battle of wits with the Prime Minister. The Parivar realized that Shri Rao's game-plan was to put the Parivar in confrontation with the courts which it detested. The Parivar's commitment to nationalism and institutions of parliamentary democracy being what it is, it was decided after prolonged discussions with various organizations of the Parivar to devise a strategy to confront the Centre while avoiding a clash with the judiciary. It was as part of this strategy that the U.P. government filed an affidavit in the Supreme Court assuring the latter that the government would not allow violation of the court orders. The game-plan was not to allow the Centre to pre-empt the arrival of *kar sevaks* at Ayodhya by dismissing the U.P. government and deploying paramilitary forces in and around Ayodhya. As for the threat of dismissal of the government, Shri Kalyan Singh had taken all preliminary steps and had even selected a house to which he planned to shift within hours of his dismissal.

Apprehending that this tactical move might be misconstrued by the rank and file and exploited by the Parivar's detractors, Shri L.K. Advani and Dr M.M.

Joshi were asked to set out on *yatras* commencing from Varanasi and Mathura respectively. It was a significant move on more than one count. The VHP has raised the issue of liberation of Kashi Vishwanath temple at Varanasi and Sri Krishna Janmabhumi at Mathura but the BJP had so far refrained from taking any public stand on these two prominent shrines. By launching their *yatras* from these temple towns, the BJP leaders sent signals to the quarters concerned that the party might enlarge its area of confrontation if the Centre did not allow *kar seva* at Ayodhya on 6 December.

Meanwhile orders went out to places all over the country to rush *kar sevaks* to Ayodhya to pre-empt any Central action. By December 4 when the Rao government was considering various options, more than two lakh *kar sevaks* swarmed Ramjanmabhumi making it impossible for the Centre to take any precipitate action.

The Sangh Parivar, thus, registered an impressive victory in the battle of wits as well. It also demonstrated its capacity to mobilize people in millions at short notice. The sea of humanity assembled at Ayodhya sent haywire all arrangements for stay, food and medical aid of the *kar sevaks*. The Parishad had earlier planned to have 50,000 *kar sevaks* each day for ten days beginning 6 December. In order to meet the threat posed by the Centre and presence of paramilitary forces, it assembled two lakh *kar sevaks* well before the D-Day.

[From *Organizer*, Vol. XVIV, No. 19, New Delhi, 13 December 1992.]

9c. Vajpayee's Proposal on 5 December 1992

The senior Bharatiya Janata Party leader, Mr Atal Behari Vajpayee, today suggested to the Central Government to acquire the disputed structure at Ayodhya and hand it over to the Vishwa Hindu Parishad to construct the Rama temple there. Rama was the symbol of the cultural legacy of India and the existence of India could not be imagined without Him. Construction of the Rama temple at the birthplace was to consolidate this cultural heritage, he added.

Mr Vajpayee was addressing a public meeting here on the eve of the proposed *kar seva* programme of the Vishwa Hindu Parishad and allied organizations at Ayodhya tomorrow. The two '*yatras*' undertaken by the BJP chief, Dr Murli Manohar Joshi from Mathura and the Leader of the Opposition, Mr L.K. Advani, from Varanasi also reached Lucknow this evening. The two leaders are to proceed to Ayodhya tomorrow morning to participate in the *kar seva*.

Both Mr Vajpayee and Mr Advani declared that the BJP was committed to the construction of the Rama temple at Ayodhya. Both however, added that the Uttar Pradesh government was alive to its legal and constitutional responsibility and it would always respect court orders.

Mr Advani praised the steps taken by the U.P. government in removing obstacles in the construction of the temple while not flouting legal norms. The Chief

Minister, Mr Kalyan Singh had discharged his twin responsibilities to abide by law and fulfil the party commitment for the temple construction in a meticulous manner. The opposition parties, however, opposed every step taken by the State Government in this direction and the Centre had almost planned to dismiss the U.P. government this time. Mr Advani insinuated that the Congress government at the centre had disclosed its intentions to dismiss the U.P. government to the parties opposed to the BJP on the Ayodhya issue. It was in this context that repeated threats were issued to Mr Kalyan Singh and heavy contingents of the Central forces were rushed to Uttar Pradesh.

Aware of the moves of its adversaries, the U.P. government assured the Supreme Court that it would abide by the orders. It, however, never promised to stop *kar sevaks* from coming to Ayodhya or stopping *kar seva*.

[From *The Hindu*, 6 December 1992.]

9d. General Secretary of the BJP, K.N. Govindacharya, confirms pre-planning

The general secretary of the Bharatiya Janata Party, Mr K.N. Govindacharya, today said his party had collected massive crowds in Ayodhya to foil a suspected move by the Centre to dismiss the Uttar Pradesh government and seize the disputed Babri Masjid–Ramjanmabhumi structure before 6 December. He said while the Centre's game-plan was to prove to the world that BJP was a mere paper tiger, BJP effectively foiled it by collecting huge crowds in Ayodhya.

A much-valued member of the BJP think-tank, Mr Govindacharya said this in an hour-long interview to *The Statesman*. The two-part, interview covered a wide range of subjects, from what led to the demolition and how BJP views it, to BJP's problems with the sants and mahants and how the party would treat the Muslims once in power. Mr Govindacharya's disclosure on why BJP collected crowds in Ayodhya is the first admission, even if tacit, by the party that this was done as part of a political strategy rather than in the interest of the Rama Mandir.

Mr Govindacharya's case was that had the Centre cleared the 2.77-acres of acquired land for construction, the *kar sevaks* would have confined their activities to this portion. This, he said, would have prevented the attack on the Masjid even while giving the Centre as many as two years to solve the main dispute. Mr Govindacharya admitted that since the 2.77-acres of land ran around the Masjid, the construction would have ultimately encircled it. Asked if this was not patently unjust to the Muslims, Mr Govindacharya said this could not be helped as BJP's earlier efforts to be reasonable had been spurned because of the compulsions of vote-bank politics.

Mr Govindacharya said that in 1988, his party had reconciled itself to building the temple leaving the structure as it is, but that the then Home Minister, Mr Buta Singh had shown no interest in the proposal. He said that at that time, the entire Sangh Parivar including Mr Ashok Singhal and dharmacharyas like Swami Jayendra Saraswati of the Kanchi Peetham had been willing to commit themselves to leaving the structure out of the temple plans, provided the Muslim community handed it over to them as a gesture of goodwill.

Excerpts from the interview:

Why did you collect such massive crowds in Ayodhya? Did this not violate the spirit of the Supreme Court order that the kar seva should be symbolic?

The Court is not the only institution which determines the course of events. If you view it in perspective, you would realize that the Congress (I) government was intent on breaking the sants, limiting the assemblage at Ayodhya and then seizing the structure by dismissing Kalyan Singh. Their plan was two-fold: break the *kar sevaks* and at an opportune moment dismiss Kalyan Singh and seize the structure. If they had succeeded, they would have told the public, 'see, the BJP is a paper tiger.'

So what do we do? We decided that on the one hand we will persuade the government to allow construction on 2.77-acres and on the other collect crowds to foil the dismissal plan. Actually, as early as 28 November, when the crowd strength was already 30,000, the Centre had realized that dismissal would not work. So they again called the RSS leaders, Rajju Bhaiyya, H.V. Sheshadri and Moropant Pingle for discussion. We continued negotiations but decided that we cannot trust the Centre any more and must mobilize crowds.

The sum total of your arguments don't jell. You will collect crowds and threaten the Centre and yet it cannot send in its forces until you ask for it.

We are talking of a complex situation and you cannot use a straitjacket approach. The complexity of the situation went through many twists and turns. You must understand that we kept pleading with the Centre to look at the situation from the national angle and allow *kar sevaks* to construct on the 2.77-acres. When it is a question of the lives and sentiments of millions, you cannot use a strictly legal or constitutional outlook.

But this is blackmail. Let us construct or else. . .

One view could be that it is blackmail. But the way we see it, we were being sincere and we just could not match the vileness and deception of our opponents. I feel so sad that even in situations of national distress, politicians cannot rise above petty considerations.

If you were so sincere, why did you allow VHP to announce the 6 December plan right in the middle of negotiations?

For this you must understand the dynamics of the Sangh Parivar relationships. This involves allowing all the units to function autonomously even while retaining the spirit of cooperation between them. In this situation, striking the right balance between national and parivar interests becomes a delicate task at times.

Could BJP not have dissociated itself at least from the demolition?

First, we cannot and do not want to dissociate ourselves and secondly, the equations of the Sangh Parivar relationships have to be maintained. So even if the assessment from outside is that we should have disowned it, it is not so simple.

Why did you not agree to government's suggestion on a single-point reference?

We wanted a package. But the government while wanting our commitment on the court reference, was not prepared to commit itself on the *kar seva* on 2.77-acres. We did not want to be cheated as we were earlier when Mr Kamal Nath came to us with an excellent proposal on Article 143 and then backed out of it.

But then Mr Advani wanted the words 'due process of law' inserted in the proposal so that BJP could keep its options open. Why?

From our side, we have no doubts at all about the legitimacy of our claims and demands on the temple issue. So essentially it means that if the government wants an opinion it can get it. The way we saw it, the only solution was to start construction on 2.77-acres and refer the main dispute to the apex court under Article 143. This would have given the Centre two years to solve the dispute.

Meanwhile, your temple would have encircled the mosque?

The 2.77-acres of acquired land did run around the structure and we would have eventually encircled it. If the 143 decision was in our favour, we would have included it otherwise gone in for legislation.

Where is any justice in all this for the Muslims?

Justice? There was a time in 1988 when we made an offer that if the Muslim community, in a gesture of goodwill, handed over the structure, then the leaders of the temple movement like Mr Ashok Singhal and even Swami Jayendra Saraswati would in return commit themselves to constructing the temple keeping the structure intact. But Buta Singh was not interested in it because of Muslim votes.

[From *The Statesman*, 31 December 1992.]

10. The BJP's announcement of Murli Manohar Joshi and L.K. Advani's participation in the *kar seva*

10a. Statement released by the BJP on 29 November 1992

Am emergency meeting of Bharatiya Janata Party office bearers was held on 29 November 1992 at party headquarters.

Dr Murli Manohar Joshi presided. The meeting decided that Party President Dr Joshi and party leader in Parliament Shri L.K. Advani should participate in the *kar seva* at Ayodhya on 6 December 1992.

Here is the text of the statement released at the end of the meeting.

The Ayodhya Movement is not just a plea for a temple for Sri Rama—it implies a far deeper quest for recapturing our national identity. It represents the soul of the nationalist thrust of the pre-Independence days.

The post-independence political creed of the Congress and most other political parties has come to regard everything that inspired this nation in the past as less than secular and in fact communal and even anti-national. The Ayodhya phenomenon is a massive protest against this derailment of all that inspired the freedom movement—the inspiring chant of Vande Mataram which Bankim gave the nation, the goal of Rama Rajya propounded by the Mahatma, the ideal of spiritual nationalism held out by Swami Vivekananda, the spirit of Sanatana Dharma which Shri Aurobindo described as the soul of India and the mass faith around the Ganapati festival aroused by Tilak. Thus, the quest for temple for Sri Rama at Ayodhya is the expression of a brooding national conscience that has been brooding since the partition of India and it is a symbol of the greatest national introspection of the present century.

This movement is not the culmination, but the commencement of the nationalist reassertion. The movement derives its strength no less from the peoples' commitment to nationalism than it does from the religious faith of tens of crores. An attempt to regard this movement as less than what it is will not dilute its real character. However, this movement which is the core of Indian nationalism today has to be thoughtfully and carefully guided as tremendous responsibility rests on the shoulders of the Hindus to safeguard the national interest in every possible way. All the time regard by government and the judiciary has been, and is being given, only because of this heavy responsibility that weighs on the Hindus, the movement and its leadership. But this shall not deter or detract from the objective of the movement—the construction of a Rama temple at the very place which Hindus believe to be the birth place of Rama. This is a national commitment—and, in fact, supreme national duty.

BJP is committed to the construction of the temple to make the very place adorned by Ram Lalla today as the sanctum sanctorum. Court wranglings can delay, and New Delhi can obstruct, but no one can deny this ultimately. I hope that the judiciary realizes that justice delayed is justice denied. This is precisely what is happening to Ramjanmabhumi case today.

Every hurdle to the movement whether from the government or the courts stresses rather than dilutes its importance. Great movements have always witnessed strong official resistance. And so does the Ayodhya movement. But finally, as history tells us, it is the movement and not, the State that prevails. It is only a matter of time before Rama Mandir becomes a reality. The *kar seva* on December 6 is a crucial step towards that reality.

As a symbol of the party's commitment to this great national reassertion, Dr Joshi and Shri L.K. Advani will be participating in the *kar seva* on the 6 of December 1992. They will commence their *yatra* to Ayodhya on 1 December and be there in time for the *kar seva*. Details of their programme are being worked out.

(29.11.1992)

[From *BJP Today*, 1 January 1993, p. 9.]

10b. L.K. Advani's statement on 30 November 1992

Four months back, the religious leaders of the Ayodhya movement embarked on *kar seva* at the 2.77-acres site acquired by the U.P. government. Predictably N.F., the L.F., and sections of the Congress Party raised a storm over the development, and paralyzed the proceedings of Parliament. The Prime Minister urged the BJP to intervene, and said that if only he was given some time he would sort out the tangle.

As a result of BJP's intervention, and, formally, in response to the Prime Minister's appeal, the *sadhus* and the *sants* deferred their *kar seva* for three months.

It is a matter of regret that government has failed to avail of the respite given to it. It now appears that the government never intended to use this critical time to solve the issue. Instead it set in motion moves that would make the solution difficult and even impossible. Indeed actions during the last four months have created grave doubts about government's bonafides and sincerity.

I do not propose a detailed narrative of government's hamhanded and/or devious doings during this vital interlude. But I have a public duty to tell, in brief, how the government dodged and ducked the issue and tried to distort and complicate the matters. In a nutshell, I can affirm:

- that through power brokers government has been exerting hard, though in vain, to make the *sadhus* and *sants* leading the movement disown the VHP, the RSS and the BJP.
- that, having failed in this effort, government has been assiduously trying through touts to create a cleavage among the sants themselves, though again in vain;
- that the government has been mooting diverse proposals through different emissaries, and when any such proposal elicits a positive response, the government promptly disowns responsibility for the move;
- that, worst of all, government has been, all through this period, pressurizing and signalling to Courts either to keep delaying decisions on matters pertaining to Ayodhya or to issue orders which raise legal obstacles in the way of *kar seva*.

The first step taken by the Kalyan Singh government after assumption of office in discharge of its mandate was acquisition of the complex land. But very deliberately and consciously it did not acquire the structure and the land beneath it. The acquisition order, only covered 2.77-acres outside the structure. This is the area where *shilanyas* (foundation laying) was held in 1989. This area was never a matter of public controversy. The bone of contention in Ayodhya has been the structure.

Kalyan Singh's was a far reaching move blessed by political farsight. It was a conscious attempt to delink two matters: first, commencement of temple construction and second, resolution of the dispute regarding the structure. The U.P. government categorically declared that it would resolve the second issue either by a negotiated agreement or, if that failed, by legislation.

The greatest disservice the Government of India has done is to link up the two issues. The link up is not just an accident, but seems a conscious manoeuvre to make the solution difficult.

A month back it was pointed out to the government that events were once again moving towards a confrontation because no verdict was forthcoming from the Allahabad High Court, and so Sadhus and Sants who had after much persuasion deferred *kar seva* would still not be legally free to resume *kar seva*. We proposed that the Central and State governments together approach the High Court and urge it to deliver verdict expeditiously. The Central Government's response was that they would agree to it only if the U.P. government consented to refer the dispute regarding the structure to the Supreme Court under Art. 138 (2) of the Constitution. By this link up, government has deliberately tried to enlarge the area of controversy so that a solution becomes impossible. Even now, wisdom lies in delinking the two issues, enabling construction work to be resumed in the 2.77-acres of land and then letting the U.P. government proceed with sorting out the structure dispute as it has planned.

The Ayodhya movement has thoroughly exposed the secular pretensions of the political parties in India and chiefly that of the Congress, its allies and offshoots and also of the Indian Left. The very leaders who ask in private 'where is the mosque in Ayodhya?' are the ones who testify to its existence in public.

The Defence Minister admits to the Chief Minister of U.P. that legal evidence shows that what they assert in public as a mosque is undeniably a temple but he wants a face-saving and cosmetic court order to allow the construction of the temple. Does truth require a face-saving formula?

Where the government knows what the truth is and the Constitution shows the way to settle the pending dispute by declaring the truth by law. Government has overturned even judgements, not just interim orders, by retroactive laws—in the field of tax, land acquisition and corporate laws. Such power has been conveniently extended to undo even momentous judgements of courts as in the Privy Purses case, Bank Nationalization Case, election case of Mrs Indira Gandhi and the Shahbano Case. Why cannot the Government of India muster courage to declare the truth on Ramjanmabhumi through law? No ideological inquest is needed to find the answer. It is the sordid consideration of vote banks which prevents it from doing so. It is precisely against this all consuming passion for minority votes and minority appeasement that the Ayodhya movement is directed.

By the action of the government, yet another institution, the judiciary, at the highest level, is being drawn into what is essentially a political issue and, besides, a matter of religious faith, to share the loss of credibility of the government. There are two clear trends in the judicial orders on Ayodhya: and attempt to delay the decision that would clear the legal hurdles to constructing the temple and a discernible anxiety to expedite injunctions that would stifle *kar seva*. Surprisingly this is precisely what the government wants and this is exactly what the massive public opinion detects.

The recent judicial proceedings in the Ayodhya matter have sent an unambiguous message to the Ramjanmabhumi movement that the Courts are an inadequate forum for the purpose. I am even more firmly of the view today that while the judiciary deserves extreme respect, the executive should not be allowed to use the Judiciary as an instrument to thwart the people's will. If the Judiciary today is seen as an instrument to grant what the government wants, the responsibility for that rests largely on the government. Even when the U.P. government went all out to show its deference and respect for Court orders, the GOI's ro e in the Supreme Court was all along negative and obstructionist. The insistence on judicial determination of the Ayodhya case is another name for a non-decision.

I am convinced that it is only the people who can assert themselves in this matter and provide the lead. Hence my decision to go to the people to explain to them and to alert them, even while bowing my head to them for their steadfastness.

[From *BJP Today*, 1 January 1993, pp. 10–11.]

11. Prime Minister P.V. Narasimha Rao's TV address on 7 December 1992

Fellow countrymen, I am speaking to you this evening under the grave threat that has been posed to the institution, principles and ideals on which the constitutional structure of our republic has been built. During the struggle for freedom under the leadership of Mahatma Gandhi, we had promised to ourselves an India free of exploitation, hunger and pestilence, recognizing the right of every citizens to the fruits of democracy and also his right to practice and preach his own religion without any interference. This resolve was enshrined in our Constitution and the founding fathers of our country sanctified this in the written Constitution of India.

In a country of the size and diversity like ours, it is only the concern and care for the sensibilities of each other which can ensure a smooth functioning of the institutions that we have created. This is the only way to maintain peace and harmony among the people of India. Whatever may be our differences on political, social and economic issues, they have to be acted upon keeping this wider concept in view. The delicate fabric of our nation woven around democracy and secularism is the only anchor-sheet for our country's existence.

The country has witnessed in the last few years an attempt by certain political parties who have in their pursuit of power not been able to exercise restraint and keep their actions within the limitations of propriety, law and the demands of national integration. They have used the difference revolving around the Ramjanmabhumi–Babri Masjid dispute to excite base communal passions and utilize the same for political purpose. We have pleaded together in an effort to resolve this matter amicably through peaceful negotiations.

We have gone to the fullest extent to create an atmosphere in the country which would be conducive to this effort. We have posed to all parties to the dispute ways and means to get a judicial determination to this vexed problem. I see no other way in a democratic polity to determine matters on which strong views are held on all sides.

I have personally done whatever I could to help reach a negotiated settlement or a judicial determination to this issue while all democratic and secular forces have helped in this effort. But I am said to state that the BJP, the VHP combine has not only failed to respond to my efforts but as a matter of fact have gone about deliberately to not only thwart my efforts but also to mislead the nation about my intentions. What has happened today in Ayodhya, where the Ramjanmabhumi–Babri Masjid structure has been demolished, is a matter of great shame and concern for all Indians.

Each and everyone of us want, and I have stated so repeatedly, that we must have a grand temple to Lord Rama being built at Ayodhya. As a matter of fact, people of all faiths in India were even prepared to actively help in this. The BJP–VHP combine has, however, continued to pursue a different line because they felt that is the only route to carry them on to the seats of power. This is a betrayal of the nation and a confrontation with all that is sacred to all Indians as the legacy which we have all inherited and is a part of our national ethos. A great affront has been caused to this. As the first servant of the people of India, it is not only my duty but also my mandate to ensure that all such communal forces which are out to confront the nation itself must be met resolutely. We will go to any extent to preserve and protect secularism and democratic credentials of our nation. In this onerous task I seek the support and blessings of all the citizens of this country. I would like to say very clearly that we shall no longer suffer the machiavellian tactics of the communal forces in this country.

I appeal to all those misguided people who have assembled at Ayodhya on the inspiration of persons who do not have the wellbeing of the nation at heart to disperse peacefully and let the law of the land have full sway there. It is to achieve this that my government has dismissed the Government of U.P. headed by Shri Kalyan Singh which have totally failed in its primary duty to which they pledged themselves time and again to protect the structure.

I would like to sound a note of warning to everyone who may try to help such elements who have put the peace and tranquility of the nation in jeopardy that we shall not spare any action against them in the interest of the nation. I appeal to all of you to maintain calm, peace and harmony at this grave moment of crisis. We have faced many such situations in the past and have overcome them. We shall do this again with firm determination and conviction in the rightness of our path.

Jai Hind.

[From *The Great Betrayal*, AICC publication, 1993, pp. 23–26.]

12. Statement that Prime Minister Could *Not* Make in Parliament on 7 December 1992

'On 3 December 1992, statements had been in both the Houses of Parliament on the general situation at Ayodhya in the context of the proposed *kar seva*. Since then, the developments have taken place at a fast pace.

2. The Hon'ble Members are aware of the unsparing efforts made by the Central Government to help in finding an amicable settlement of the contentious Ramjanmabhumi–Babri Masjid dispute. After my statement in Parliament on 27 July 1992, I had held wide-ranging consultation with large number of individuals and groups. These included discussions with representatives of the two sides, leaders of political parties, representatives from the media, religious leaders, and others. Even after the resumed negotiations were jeopardized by the unilateral and unfortunate call for the resumption of the *kar seva*, I made every effort to convince the leaders of the VHP and allied organizations of the unreasonableness of their stand and tried to make them agree to some acceptable solution. However, a very intransigent stand was taken by the VHP and allied organizations, and instead of cancelling or postponing the *kar seva*, preparations were started for it.

3. As the House is aware, the Hon'ble Supreme Court has also been seized of this matter. The Central Government was called by the Supreme Court to indicate the manner in which it could assist in the enforcement of its earlier orders. During the hearing, the Central Government had assured the Court that it would be prepared to give to the State Government whatever assistance is required in furtherance of the directions of the Court. We had also conveyed that the Central Government will take such action as may be directed by the Hon'ble Court to secure the enforcement of its order. The Government of Uttar Pradesh had to give an assurance and undertaking to the Court that no construction activity, either permanent or temporary, will take place or will be carried out on the acquired land and no construction machinery or construction material will move into the acquired land as long as the interim order of the High Court is in force in the writ petitions pending before it relating to the land acquisition. The State Government further submitted that the *kar seva* would be a symbolic occasion for carrying on certain religious activities and will not be allowed to be exploited for any construction activities, symbolic or otherwise. The Supreme Court also directed the State Government, as also the Central Government, to give due publicity to the fact that the proposed *kar seva* would not involve any construction activity or moving of any building material into the acquired land so that all *kar sevaks* get properly informed in this regard.

4. Even outside the Court, the Government of India repeatedly took up the matter with the Chief Minister of Uttar Pradesh requesting him to take measures to ensure that no activity is allowed that is contrary to the Court orders or derogatory of judicial authority. This concern of the Central Government was conveyed to the State Government time and again. Even in his recent letter of 3 December

1992, the Home Minister again repeated this request to the Chief Minister.

5. The security of the RJB–BM structure has been a matter of continuing concern for the Central Government. The Home Minister had taken up this matter with the Chief Minister of Uttar Pradesh on innumerable occasions through meetings, discussions, letters, etc. In recent week, alone, the Home Minister had written several letters to the Chief Minister in this regard. He had suggested to the Chief Minister that a comprehensive review of the security plan for the structure may be carried out in which the representatives of Central organizations should also be associated. However, this suggestion was not accepted by the State Government despite our repeated requests from our side. Also, particular shortcomings in the security measures taken by the State Government were pointed out to the State Government. We had also informed the Chief Minister that according to our assessment the forces deployed by the State Government for security purposes at Ayodhya would not be sufficient to meet the security requirement, especially if any untoward development takes place, or if in the environment of religious frenzy, violence breaks out. The Central Government also brought the inadequacy of security arrangements to the notice of the Supreme Court on 30 November 1992, when the Supreme Court asked the State Government to give its constructive consideration to the suggestions made by the Government of India. The Home Minister also wrote to the Chief Minister that reportedly arrangements such as food, water supply, sanitary facilities, etc. were not adequate to meet the large assembly of *kar sevaks* and, there more measures should be taken to ensure that this does not give rise to any health hazard or outbreak of epidemic.

6. The Central Government had taken the precaution of stationing Central Para Military Forces at various places in Uttar Pradesh on 24 November 1992 itself in the proximity of Ayodhya so that these could be made available at short notice if and when required by the State Government for deployment in connection with the security of the disputed structure and maintenance of law and order. As many as 195 companies of these Central Para Military Forces were stationed and they were equipped with every facility required to deal with any untoward development such as teargas, rubber bullets, plastic pellets, over 900 vehicles, etc. The Force included Mahila CRPF companies, NSG Commandoes, bomb disposal teams and sniffer dog squads. The intention was that this force should be utilized by the State Government with minimum loss of time. The Home Minister urged the Chief Minister to consider deploying the Force in connection with the security arrangements at Ayodhya. However, instead of utilizing the Force, the Chief Minister criticized our action in stationing the Force and demand its withdrawal. He went to the extent of challenging the constitutional validity of the Central Government's action. All that the State Government accepted was the service of bomb detection squads and sniffer dog squads and that too after the Central Government brought to the State Government's notice the possibility of threat by explosives to the disputed structure and urged the deployment of these squads. Despite the Chief Minister's strange and recalcitrant attitude, the Central

Para Military Forces stationed near Ayodhya were kept on total alert so as to be made available to the state authorities if and when required. The Union Home Secretary reiterated this message to the Central Para Military Forces in the morning of 6 December 1992.

7. On 6 December 1992, the initial reports from Ayodhya indicated that the situation was peaceful. About 70,000 *kar sevaks* had assembled in the Rama Katha Kunj for a public meeting to be addressed by senior leaders of the Sangh Parivar. Five hundred sadhus and sants had gathered on the foundation terrace and preparations were made for the *puja*. Between 11.45 am and 11.50 am, about 150 *kar sevaks* managed to break the cordon on the terrace and started pelting stones at the police personnel. About 1,000 *kar sevaks* broke into the RBJ–BM structure. About 80 *kar sevaks* managed to climb on the domes of the structure and commenced damaging them. Meanwhile, *kar sevaks* had damaged the outer boundary wall of the structure. By about 12.20 hrs, about 25,000 *kar sevaks* gathered in the complex while large numbers were milling around outside. At 2.40 pm, a crowd of 75,000 was still surrounding the structure of whom many were engaged in demolishing it. By the late evening of 6 December 1992 the RJB–BM structure had been totally demolished. It is also understood that the Rama Lalla idols from within were deposited with the head priest, ostensibly for safekeeping; later, the idols were reportedly re-installed and a tin shed has been erected over them.

8. According to available reports no action by the local police to prevent the damage to the RJB–BM structure was noticed. The CRPF stationed in the isolation cordon of the structure could not take effective action for want of orders from the State Government officers under whose command it was placed. The movement of additional police forces to Ayodhya was blocked by *kar sevaks* by using iron poles, over-turned trollies, etc. All the railway crossing between Ayodhya and Darshan Nagar were blocked by the *kar sevaks*.

9. Immediately on receipt of information regarding the attack by *kar sevaks* on the disputed structure the Union Home Secretary contacted the State officers and suggested that in view of the situation which seemed to be getting out of the control of the State authorities, they should use the Central Para Military Forces stationed at Faizabad and nearby places, who had already been instructed to be available to the State Government without loss of time. Subsequently, the State authorities requested three battalions of Central Para Military Forces which were made available. However, when the Force was moving from Faizabad to Ayodhya it was sent back by local magistrates stating that their orders were that no use of force should be resorted to. Later the State Government requested 50 companies of Central Para Military Forces and these were also made available. The Union Home Secretary and other senior officers in the Home Ministry kept in constant touch throughout the afternoon with the State authorities, drawing their attention to the developing situation in the RJB–BM complex and repeatedly urged immediate action for effective deployment of the para military forces. The Home Min-

ister also spoke to the Chief Minister of Uttar Pradesh on telephone more than once.

10. In the face of these developments, the Central Government recommended to the President the imposition of President's rule in the State of Uttar Pradesh and the dissolution of the State Legislative Assembly. The proclamation in this regard was issued last (Sunday) night.

11. Alert messages were sent out by the Home Ministry to all the State governments and Union Territories requesting them to take necessary measures to prevent communal disturbances in other places.

12. The developments at Ayodhya culminating in the tragic destruction of the disputed structure have brought shock and pain to all of us. It is hard to believe that any responsible State Government could behave in this manner. Ours is a federal structure and in recognition of this fact, we reposed a certain amount of trust in the commitments and assurances given repeatedly by the State Government. I regret that the State Government betrayed not only our trust but the trust of the whole nation. It also dishonoured the solemn pledges it gave before the highest Court of the land as also before a body, such as the National Integration Council, I understand that even the Hon'ble Judges of the Supreme Court during the special hearing on 6 December 1992 evening expressed shock and dismay over the total failure of the State Government in abiding by its assurances given to the Court.

13. Sir, the nation has been a witness to one of the most dastardly acts being committed since it achieved freedom, after making untold sacrifices. Those who had laid siege to the minds and conscience of the people of this country for some time mounted the final assault when they demolished the Babri Masjid in Ayodhya. This ancient land of ours has within its boundaries from centuries past, symbols and faiths which have motivated countless people belonging to different faiths and persuasions. In fact, India is recognized by this underlying pluralism of faith, religion and conviction. Every temple is sacred, every mosque is sacrosanct, every gurdwara is a source of inspiration and every church is a place for communion with God. The communal forces represented in this instant case by the BJP–VHP–RSS combine have thought fit to violate this sacred trust which every Indian holds dear and close to his heart. Every effort was made to halt this mad rush to destruction. Every political and constitutional initiative was set in motion so that we could with wisdom and tolerance reconcile the irre-concilable. This is the only way a democratic and civilized nation can function. If any set of people choose to break out of this mould and arrogate to themselves the right to do what they want in pursuit of power at any cost, the nation will have to summon the courage to meet such a threat squarely and decisively.'

[From *Muslim India*, 121, January 1993.]

13. Prime Minister P.V. Narasimha Rao promises to rebuild the demolished mosque

Panel to probe Ayodhya events

Prime Minister, P.V. Narasimha Rao today (8 December) announced that the Uttar Pradesh government would set up a Commission of Inquiry into the Ayodhya outrage and the dismissed Chief Minister Kalyan Singh would be prosecuted.

Addressing a meeting of the Congress Parliamentary party, he reiterated his government's commitment to rebuilding the demolished mosque at Ayodhya. Details regarding the manner and the agency to undertake reconstruction would be worked out.

The government was firm about rebuilding the mosque as also the construction of a Rama Mandir, after the Allahabad High Court judgement expected on 11 December.

As regards the government's decision to ban communal organizations, the Prime Minister said 'there is no other way but to ban the organizations which are guilty of opposing the rule of law and the constitution and of horrendous perfidy'.

The communal parties and organizations had exhibited total betrayal of the nation, he said, adding that the government would finalize the organizations to be banned by tomorrow.

The CPP extended its whole-hearted support to the Prime Minister for his determined resolve to uphold secularism, protect and preserve the country's unity and integrity. The CPP also endorsed the resolution condemning the dastardly and diabolical conspiracy of the BJP–VHP–RSS and Bajrang Dal combine to demolish the Babri Masjid at Ayodhya and authorizing the government to take all necessary steps required to maintain law and order and communal harmony.

Mr Narasimha Rao announced that the government had also decided to take 'very strong but very difficult decisions, such as banning communal organization and action against Uttar Pradesh government officials who were responsible for dereliction of duty resulting in the demolition of the Babri Masjid'.

Referring to the government's decision to rebuild the Babri Masjid at Ayodhya, he said that the details relating to the manner and the agency to do it would be worked out. They may encounter criticism in this regard also. 'But we are firm about rebuilding the Masjid as also the Rama Mandir.' After the judgement of the Allahabad High Court on 11 December, decision would be taken in regard to the new Rama temple at Ayodhya, he said.

The Prime Minister declared that even after the tragedy 'if we can come up with something which will be remembered as a symbol of communal unity, we would have done our duty'. He said that India was not just like any other country; but it had got civilizational dimensions and culture. The time had come now when a new message should go to the entire world from India. It would be a message of complete synthesis, a synthesis of spiritual and material aspects. He could not say when this would materialize, but said that in the years to come, it would happen.

Mr Narasimha Rao observed 'after the destruction in Ayodhya which spelt darkness, some sort of a ray of sunshine may come out. On the issue of banning communal organizations, the Prime Minister asserted that after what had happened in Ayodhya, there was no way out but to ban the organizations which were guilty of opposing the rule of law and the Constitution and of horrendous perfidy. They had exhibited total betrayal. He said that by today evening, they would finalize the organizations to be banned.

However, the Prime Minister cautioned the partymen against any backlash in some parts of the country to the banning of communal organizations. He wanted the members to be prepared for such a backlash and to minimize the effect.

The same time, they should try their best that a backlash did not occur. Knowing that they are dealing with a very 'ruthless opponent', Mr Rao said that it was time when 'absolute, unstinted unity in the party and the country is demonstrated'.

Expressing his grave concern over the demolition of the 400-year old structure in Ayodhya and some forces in the country becoming so brutalized, he said the greatest need of the hour was unity in the Congress. In its entire history, the party had never been a monolith and it had never been a party of dictatorial functioning.

'We have the courage to dissent. We have the capacity to unite.' Both these things were fully reflected in the functioning of the party.

The Prime Minister also declared that Congress and its government would never violate the rule of law and the Constitution. Their party may lose power and sit in the Opposition, but it would not do anything to belittle the Constitution given to it by its leaders.

However, the Prime Minister further warned that country was passing through difficult times and the next three or four years were going to be extremely crucial. He said if 'we blink now, events may blind us.'

He criticized the Kalyan Singh government for filing affidavits with amazing amount of self-contradictions, which were realized by the Supreme Court but after some delay.

Human Resource Development Minister Arjun Singh congratulated the Prime Minister for saving the country from a very real danger.

[From *The Hindustan Times*, 9 December 1992.]

14. A Commission of Inquiry is appointed

Ministry of Home Affairs
Notification
New Delhi, the 16 December, 1992
SO 913(E)—Whereas the Central Government is of opinion that it is necessary to appoint a Commission of Inquiry for the purpose of making an inquiry into a

definite matter of public importance, namely, the destruction of the Ramjanmabhumi–Babri Masjid structure at Ayodhya on 6 December 1992.

Now, therefore, in exercise of the powers conferred by Section 3 of the Commissions of Inquiry Act, 1952 (60 of 1952), the Central Government hereby appoints a Commission of Inquiry consisting of Justice Shri Manmohan Singh Liberhan, a sitting Judge of the High Court of Punjab and Haryana.

The Commission shall make an inquiry with respect to the following matters:

(a) The sequence of events leading to, and all the facts and circumstances relating to, the occurrences in the Ramjanmabhumi–Babri Masjid complex at Ayodhya on 6 December 1992 involving the destruction of the Ramjanmabhumi–Babri Masjid structure.

(b) The role played by the Chief Minister, Members of the Council of Ministers, officials of the Government of Uttar Pradesh and by the individuals, concerned organizations and agencies in, or in connection with, the destruction of the Ramjanmabhumi–Babri Masjid structure;

(c) The deficiencies in the security measures and other arrangements as prescribed or operated in practice by the Government of Uttar Pradesh which might have contributed to the events that took place in the Ramjanmabhumi–Babri Masjid complex, Ayodhya town and Faizabad on 6 December 1992;

(d) The sequence of events leading to, and all the facts and circumstances relating to, the assault on media persons at Ayodhya on 6 December 1992; and

(e) Any other matters related to the subject of inquiry.

The Commission shall submit its report to the Central Government as soon as possible but not later than three months.

The Commission may, if it deems fit, make interim reports to the Central Government before the date on any of the matters mentioned in paragraph 2 above.

The headquarters of the Commission shall be at Lucknow.

The Central Government is of opinion that, having regard to the nature of the inquiry to be made and other circumstances of the case, all the provisions of sub-section (2), sub-section (3), sub-section (4) and sub-section (5) of section 5 of the Commissions of Inquiry act, 1952 (60 of 1952) should be made applicable to the said Commission and the Central Government, in exercise of the powers conferred by sub-section (1) of the said section 5, hereby directs that all the provisions of the said sub-sections (2), (3), (4) and (5) of that section shall apply to the Commission.

[No. N-7103/27/92-AY-I]
Madhav Godbole, Home Secretary

[A decade and more later the Commission is yet to submit its report—Ed.]

15. Home Minister S.B. Chavan's statement in Parliament on 18 December 1992

Statement of the Home Minister in Parliament on 18 December 1992 in relation to the situation arising out of the Demolition of the Ramjanmabhumi–Babri Masjid Structure.

Honourable Members are aware of the unsparing efforts made by the Prime Minister in finding an amicable settlement of the contentious Ramjanmabhumi–Babri Masjid dispute. However, all these efforts were brought to naught by the unilateral and totally unwarranted call for the resumption of *kar seva* from the 6 December 1992 and the very intransigent stand taken by the VHP and allied organizations.

2. The Supreme Court during its proceedings also viewed the impending resumption of *kar seva* with concern and it obtained an assurance from the Government of Uttar Pradesh that no construction activity would take place or be carried out on the acquired land as long as the interim order of the High Court is in force in the Writ Petitions relating to the land acquisition pending before it. The State Government further submitted that the *kar seva* would be a symbolic occasion for carrying on certain religious activities and will not be allowed to be exploited for any constructional activity. As directed by the Supreme Court, considerable publicity was given in this respect by the Central Government but the publicity efforts of the State Government were lukewarm and half-hearted.

3. In view of the build-up of the tempo of the proposed *kar seva*, the Central Government reiterated its concern regarding the security of the RJB–BM structure to the State Government and requested it to undertake a comprehensive review of the security plan; however, this suggestion was not accepted by the State Government. The Chief Minister was also informed that in our assessment, the Force deployed by the State Government for security purpose would not be sufficient in the context of the proposed *kar seva*. In view of the developing situation, the Central Government took the precaution of stationing 195 companies of Central Para Military Forces in various locations near Ayodhya on 24 November 1992 itself so that these could be made available at short notice if and when required by the State Government for deployment in connection with the security of the disputed structure and maintenance of law and order. The Chief Minister was urged to consider deploying this Force. However, instead of utilizing it, the Chief Minister criticized the stationing of the Force and demanded its withdrawal; he also challenged the Constitutional validity of the Central Government's action. Nevertheless, the Force was kept in total readiness.

4. On 6 December 1992, initial reports from Ayodhya indicated that the situation was peaceful. However, between 11.45 and 11.50 hours about 150 *kar sevaks* suddenly broke the cordon and started pelting stone; at the police personnel. Equally suddenly, about 1000 *kar sevaks* broke into the RJB–BM structure. About

80 *kar sevaks* climbed the domes of the structure and started damaging them. At 14.40 hours, a crowd of 75,000 *kar sevaks* was surrounding the structure and many of them were engaged in demolishing it.

5. Immediately on receipt of information regarding the attack on the RJB–BM structure, the Union Home Secretary and other officers of the Home Ministry contacted various State officers and urged them that in view of the situation which seemed to be getting out of control, they should use the Central Para Military Forces. The State officers informed that they would seek the Chief Minister's orders in this regard. I also spoke to the Chief Minister, Uttar Pradesh on telephone more than once. Later, some Forces were requisitioned by the State authorities and these were made available. However, when the forces were moving from Faizabad to Ayodhya, these were sent back by the local authorities who said that their orders were that no use of force should be resorted to.

6. According to available reports, effective action was not taken by the local police. On the other hand, *kar sevaks* were allowed to block the access routes to the RJB–BM complex by using various kinds of materials such as iron poles and over turned trolleys. All the railway crossings between Ayodhya and Darshan Nagar were blocked by the *kar sevaks*. As a result of the total absence of protection by the local police and the State authorities not allowing the Central forces to reach the spot despite repeated requests from the Union Home Minister and Home Secretary the RJB–BM structure was completely demolished.

7. In the face of these developments, President's Rule was imposed and the State Legislative Assembly was dissolved on 6 December 1992. However, the situation in the RJB–BM complex was very sensitive as large numbers of *kar sevaks* were still present in Ayodhya and many of them were in a defiant or agitated mood.

8. In view of the situation, the command of the security forces decided to move the force in the night of 7 and 8 December 1992 so as to use minimum force. Action was taken accordingly and the RJB–BM area was quickly secured. The movement of *kar sevaks* out of Ayodhya was also expedited by running special trains. The situation was rapidly brought under control. To assist the Governor, three senior officers were also posted at Lucknow as Advisors.

9. The Central Government has taken several actions swiftly and firmly. These include:

1. The strongest action possible under the law has been initiated against those who incited people all over the country and brought crowds to Ayodhya and persuaded them to commit the heinous act. Cases under relevant provision of law have been registered and some arrests have also been carried out. This included leaders of various organizations and political parties involved in the events of 6 December 1992.
2. The investigation of offences connected with the demolition of the RJB–BM structure and related incidents has been entrusted to the CBI; orders in this behalf were issued on 14 December 1992.

3. Notification has been issued on 16 December 1992 for setting up of a Commission of Inquiry consisting of Justice Manmohan Singh Liberhan, a sitting Judge of the High Court of Punjab and Haryana to enquire into the matters relating to the events at Ayodhya on 6 December 1992.
4. Government has declared Rashtriya Swayam Sevak Sangh, Jamaat-e-Islami Hind, Vishwa Hindu Parishad, Islamic Sevak Sangh and Bajrang Dal as unlawful associations under the Unlawful Activities (Prevention) Act, 1967. The powers to take action under the various provisions of the Act have also been delegated to the State Govern-ments. Reports about the implementation of the orders have started flowing in.
5. The Central Government has been deeply concerned about the assault on media persons at Ayodhya on 6 December. The Commission of Inquiry which has been set up will look into this matter fully. The State Government has been asked to entrust the investigation of these cases to a separate cell headed by senior police officer of the rank of Inspector General of Police. The government has also decided that media persons whose equipment was damaged in Ayodhya would be allowed to import replacements and clear the same free of customs duty.
6. As already announced, the government will see to it that the demolished structure is rebuilt.
7. Government has decided that appropriate steps will be taken regarding the construction of a Rama temple.

10. The tragic events at Ayodhya had their reverberations on the law and order situation in many parts of the country. Alert messages had been sent out promptly by the Home Ministry to all the States and Union Territories, requesting them to take necessary measures to prevent communal disturbances. However, despite such measures, violence broke out in many places. The Army authorities had already been alerted and the States and Union Territories were informed that in case additional forces were required, they could requisition the help of the Army by contacting the local Army authorities. The Central paramilitary forces were also instructed to make available whatever help they could from the group centres, battalion headquarters and even from training institutions. In this manner, in addition to the then existing deployment of Central paramilitary forces and Army contingents, 156 companies of CPMFs were made available. The situation is now returning to normal in most of the States.

11. The State Governments have been advised to organize relief and rehabilitation to the victims of the riots immediately.

12. The National Foundation for Communal harmony has got in touch with the State Government to identify the children who have been rendered destitute and who need assistance.

13. In view of the situation that had arisen in the States of Madhya Pradesh, Rajasthan and Himachal Pradesh, President's Rule was imposed in these States

and the State Legislative Assemblies were dissolved on 15 December 1992.

14. The Allahabad High Court delivered the judgement in the writ petitions relating to the acquisition of 2.77-acres of land in RJB–BM complex on 11 December 1992. The High Court allowed the petitions and quashed the notifications for land acquisition on the ground of malafides of the State Government. The implications of this judgement are being studied. Appropriate decisions will be taken by the government regarding the land in the RJB–BM complex.

15. The developments at Ayodhya culminating in the tragic destruction of the disputed structure have brought shock and pain to all of us. It is hard to believe that any responsible State Government could have behaved in this manner. Ours is a federal structure and, in recognition of this fact, we reposed trust in the commitments and assurances given repeatedly by the State Government. We regret that the State Government betrayed not only our trust but the trust of the whole nation. It also dishonoured the solemn pledges it gave before the highest Court of the land as also before a body of eminence such as the National Integration Council. Even the Hon'ble Supreme Court in its order of the 6 December 1992 observed that it was a great pity that a constitutionally elected government could not discharge its duties in a matter of this sensitiveness and magnitude.

16. Sir, the Nation has been a witness to one of the most dastardly acts committed since it achieved freedom. The Government of India unequivocally condemns this act. Those who had spread communal poison among the people of this country for some time mounted the final assault when they demolished the Babri Masjid in Ayodhya. This ancient land of ours has been recognized by the underlying pluralism of faith, religion and convictions. Every temple is sacred, every mosque is sacrosanct, every gurudwara is a source of inspiration and every church is a place for communion with God. The communal forces represented in this instant case by the BJP–VHP–RSS combine have thought fit to violate this sacred trust which every Indian holds dear and close to his heart. Every effort was made to halt this mad rush to destruction. Every political and constitutional initiative was set in motion so that we could with wisdom and tolerance reconcile the irreconcilable. This is the only way a democratic and civilized nation can function. If any set of people choose to break out of this mould and arrogate to themselves the right to do what they want in pursuit of power at any cost, the nation will have to summon the courage to meet such a threat squarely and decisively.

17. The Central Government will stand up and face these forces, and I am sure Parliament, the political parties actuated by patriotism, and the people of India would support us. In our liberal and democratic functioning, everyone has the right to promote and practice what he thinks right. But it is not given to anyone in this country to take a stand which militates against the very basic concept and ideals of our democratic and secular polity. Unfortunately, some people and some political parties have chosen to break out of these confines and have made

determined bid to subvert the basic tenets of the nation. We shall not allow such people and organizations to continue doing this.

18. At this moment of national peril, we appeal to all sections of the House to stand united because only in this manner can we preserve and protect our Constitution as well as the future of this country.

19. To the minorities in India who live in every corner of this sacred land, we have only one message to give. The government will not and shall not default on its basic commitment to protect and preserve their rights, their lives and liberty. We will walk every extra step that is needed in fulfiling this commitment which has been given to them not only by the constitution of this country, but also by our great leaders Gandhiji, Pandit Jawaharlal Nehruji, Lal Bahadur Shastriji, Smt Indira Gandhi and Shri Rajiv Gandhi. Let no one mistake our resolve or determination under any circumstances.

16. The RSS alleges breach of understanding by P.V. Narasimha Rao

16a. Rao had agreed to Temple: RSS

The Prime Minister, Mr P.V. Narasimha Rao, and the RSS had reached a broad understanding that the 'preliminary construction' of a Rama temple would be permitted on the 2.77-acres of land acquired by the Kalyan Singh government, the organization's joint general secretary, Prof. Rajendra Singh, said.

Speaking to *The Telegraph* Prof. Singh said, 'In our discussions we reached an understanding that work could begin on this (acquired) land and the government would then try and resolve the main dispute'. The RSS had found this proposal acceptable although the government had changed its stand from time to time.

The RSS leader said the Prime Minister had agreed to this solution in the final meetings he had held with the now banned organization's leaders. This was after the government's public statement saying it was keen to link the land acquisition to the main dispute. 'The Prime Minister said if we went on with construction for a year or two on the acquired land, he would try and find a solution. We asked him for a time frame, but on this he would not commit himself.'

The RSS leader said he saw the Prime Minister as a 'well meaning, sweet-talking man, with no airs about him. But he did not seem to be an effective decision maker. The Prime Minister has been acting under pressure. I am sure he would not take the present hard line without being under pressure from within. And when you take decisions under pressure, you make mistakes.'

Prof. Singh felt the government had committed a serious mistake by dismissing the BJP state governments without any valid reason. 'The government kept saying it would not dismiss the Kalyan Singh government because it was democratic, elected government. But now the Centre has dismissed three governments on flimsy grounds', Prof. Singh said.

The RSS leader said he was also deeply disappointed with the judiciary as 'the judges seem to function as if they have nothing to do with the rest of society. If the courts had delivered a judgement before December 6, a lot of damage would have been avoided.' The courts had to realize the responsibility vested in them.

Saying the destruction of the disputed shrine was unplanned, Prof. Singh said two things were clear. 'There is no question of a Masjid being build. No one will allow that. But, more importantly, we have been saying that an excavation at the site will prove the existence of a Hindu structure.'

The RSS said a team of archaeologists should be appointed to examine the site and give its findings on whether a 'Hindu structure' existed. Such a move will solve the dispute permanently.

[From *The Telegraph*, 19 December 1992.]

16b. Onus of Betrayal

Rashtriya Swayamsevak Sangh (RSS) leader H.V. Seshadri holds Prime Minister Narasimha Rao squarely responsible for the demolition of the disputed structure in Ayodhya on December 6 as also for the violent course events have since taken. Mr Rao who really betrayed the nation, not those whom he has charged for betrayal.

Tracing the course of developments that led to the demolition and the consequent crescendo of communal violence, Mr Seshadri told ENS in an interview on Saturday, that all this had been caused by Mr Rao's inaction or weak responses. The RSS leader roundly accused the Prime Minister of having had petty political considerations and his own career prospects in mind while dealing with them.

Mr Seshadri is technically the Number Two man in the RSS hierarchy but has been effectively functioning as its supremo since its chief, Mr Balasaheb Deoras is sick. He was busy working out action plans for his outlawed organization when he answered questions.

The RSS leader came out with what sounded like a severe indictment of the Prime Minister when he said RSS/VHP/BJP leaders were in constant touch with Mr Rao till December 4. Each and every step had been discussed with him. Mr Seshadri had a meeting with the Prime Minister when no more time was sought. There was no suggestion that *kar seva* be postponed.

Mr Seshadri's allegation is sharp: 'Prime Minister was trying to drag us into legal problems, asking for all kinds of affidavits'. And, now, Mr Seshadri said, Mr Rao is showing 'panic reaction' to save his career. The RSS leader wanted him to realize that this would yield no results.

[From *Indian Express*, 13 December 1992].

17. Resolution approved by both Houses of Parliament, 16 December 1992

Text of the Resolution

'This House strongly and unequivocally condemns the desecration and demolition of the Babri Masjid at Ayodhya by and at the instigation of forces represented among others by VHP, RSS and the Bajrang Dal, which has caused communal violence in the country. Such an act of vandalism was carried out not only in violation of the orders of the Supreme Court but amounted to an attack on the secular foundations of our country.

'This House expresses its anguish at the happening and wishes to reiterate its resolve that it will ceaselessly endeavour to uphold the secular and democratic traditions of our country and for the maintenance of the rule of law.

'This House conveys its sympathies and condolences to all victims of the tragic incidents which have been caused consequent upon the sacrilege at Ayodhya and demands from the government all necessary steps to rehabilitate the affected people. It appeals to the people of the country to maintain peace and communal harmony.

[From *The Statesman*, 17 December 1992.]

18. The BJP defends the demolition, 8 December 1992

Statement released by Shri L.K. Advani

The pulling down of the disputed structure at Ayodhya was an unfortunate event. But the vicious and intemperate language in which the happening is being condemned by opponents of the Ayodhya movement is sending some very wrong signals not only to the people in India but also to the international community.

A few years back over fifty Hindu temples were destroyed in Kashmir. Apart from the BJP, no political party uttered even a single word of condemnation. So far as the Establishment is concerned, there was a deafening silence.

When in 1984, after Mrs Gandhi's assassination, more than 3000 Sikhs were murdered in cold blood by mobs organized by ruling party leaders, I do not remember anyone in authority feeling particularly upset about it.

A grim tragedy has overtaken two lakh Hindus of Kashmir. They have been uprooted from their hearths and homes and made refugees in their own country. For nearly three years now they are having to live a life of destitution and suffering. Yet, barring the BJP–RSS family, no one is bothered about their fate. Is this only because they are Hindus!

And today when an old structure which ceased to be a mosque over 50 years back is pulled down by a group of people exasperated by the tardiness of the judicial process, and the obtuseness and myopia of the executive, they are reviled by the President, the Vice-President, and political parties as betrayers of the nation, destroyers of the Constitution and what not!

It is blatant double standards such as evidenced by this tirade against the Ayodhya movement that is making the Hindus feel incensed and outraged about the pseudo-secularists.

I wish those in authority realise an even more dangerous outcome of these irresponsible outbursts. They are providing a justification and rationale to communal elements in the country to precipitate violence. In many cases, as in Bombay, the violence that has erupted is not at all Hindu–Muslim. Deaths have occurred because police have had to use force against frenzied Muslim mobs. The frenzy is the direct upshot of the vicious tirade unleashed by government, and the official media, against the *kar sevaks*.

I wish to caution government against this approach. Their pronouncements against *kar sevaks* are only strengthening the movement. But these statements certainly amount to slandering the country. This must stop forthwith.

[From *BJP Today*, 1–15 January 1993.]

19. A tabulation of Advani's statements: *The Statesman*

Varanasi, December 1: 'We do not want to destroy Masjid and make Mandir. There was never a Masjid at the Janmabhumi site. The idols of Rama are there and all we want to do is build a temple there . . . to democratically protest against wrong practices and law is an old tradition of the country . . . *kar seva* does not mean bhajans and kirtans. We will perform *kar seva* with shovels and bricks on the 2.77-acres of land acquired by the U.P. government.'

Azamgarh, 1 December: 'We want peaceful *kar seva* but the centre is creating tension.'

Mau, 2 December: 'Now *kar seva* will begin on 6 December. All *kar sevaks* will perform physical activity on the 2.77-acres in Ayodhya and not merely sing bhajans.'

Gorakhpur, 3 December, where he had described a news report quoting him as having said *kar seva* would involve use of shovels and bricks as false: 'The *kar sevaks* will be fully under control. The *kar seva* will be symbolic. I never said such a thing (about shovels and bricks being used). Yet due to this misreporting half a day's work in Parliament was lost because of the uproar this report caused.'

Public meeting in U.P., 2 December, where he exhorted people to go to Ayodhya for *kar seva*: 'Take a plunge and do not bother whether the Kalyan Singh government survives or is dismissed.'

New Delhi, 7 December: 'It (the demolition of the mosque) was unfortunate. Both I and the U.P. Chief Minister did all we could to prevent the destruction but what actually happened was we could not gauge the intensity of the people's feelings over Ayodhya. We wanted that the temple should be constructed by legal and lawful means.'

New Delhi, 8 December: 'Today, when an old structure which ceased to be a mosque over 50 years back is pulled down by a group of people exasperated by the tardiness of the judicial process and obtuseness and myopia of the executive, they are reviled by the President, the Vice-President and political parties as betrayers of the nation, destroyers of the constitution and what not. It is blatant double standards such as evidenced by this tirade against the Ayodhya movement that is making the Hindus feel incensed and outraged.'

[From *The Statesman*, 11 December 1992.]

20. *The Statesman's* rebuttal of Advani

Following is the statement issued by the Bharatiya Janata Party in response to *The Statesman* report dated 10 December:

'Shri L.K. Advani, leader of Opposition, Lok Sabha, issued a statement before being taken to Agra after his arrest on 8 December. The statement was released from the BJP Central Office on Wednesday. The statement is a rebuttal of the attempt being made by the government to pin the blame for the unfortunate events in Ayodhya on the BJP–RSS family.

'Nowhere in the statement it is stated, either directly or indirectly, that the demolition of the structure was part of the Ayodhya movement. Yet, *The Statesman* of Delhi (dated 10 December) headlined its front page lead story on the report with the words 'Demolition 'part of movement', with 'part of movement' within inverted commas. This blatant mis-statement is repeated again in the body of the report by adding that contrary to his earlier postures, Mr Advani acknowledged for the first time that the demolition of the Masjid was part of the 'Ayodhya movement', which gives a totally misleading impression that the words are quoted from the statement.

'The paper goes one step further in its issue of Friday, 11 December. The Editor-in-Chief of the paper, in his front-page column captioned "The price of honour and decency" repeats the mis-statement with the words. "The truth is out in the open. . . Mr Advani's statement made it quite clear that the demolition of the masjid was part of the temple movement". Mr Irani is a responsible Editor. It is possible that he too has been carried away by anti-Hindu frenzy that has gripped some of our more "secular" friends. But a misquote is a misquote, no matter how often it is repeated and it is sad to see even Editors of reputable newspapers putting words into mouths which never uttered them.'

Reproduced is Mr Advani's original statement

'The pulling down of the disputed structure at Ayodhya was an unfortunate event. But the vicious and intemperate language in which the happening is being condemned by opponents of the Ayodhya movement is sending some very wrong signals not only to the people in India but also to the international community.

A few years back, over fifty Hindu temples were destroyed in Kashmir. Apart from the BJP, no political party uttered even a single word of condemnation. So far as the establishment is concerned, there was a deafening silence.

'When in 1984, after Mrs Gandhi's assassination, more than 3,000 Sikhs were murdered in cold-blood by mobs organized by ruling party leaders, I do not remember any one in authority feeling particularly upset about it.

'A grim tragedy has overtaken two lakh Hindus of Kashmir. They have been uprooted from their hearths and homes and made refugees in their own country. For nearly three years now they are having to live a life of destitution and suffering. Yet, barring the BJP–RSS family, no one is bothered about their fate. Is this only because they are Hindus!

'And today, when an old structure which ceased to be a mosque over 50 years back is pulled down by a group of people exasperated by the tardiness of the judicial process, and the obtuseness and myopia of the executive, they are reviled by the President, the Vice President, and political parties as betrayers of the nation, destroyers of the Constitution and what not!

'It is blatant double standards such as evidenced by this tirade against the Ayodhya movement that is making the Hindus feel incensed and outraged about the pseudo-secularists.

'I wish those in authority realize an even more dangerous outcome of these irresponsible outbursts. They are providing a justification and rationale to communal elements in the country to precipitate violence. In many cases, as in Bombay, the violence that has erupted is not at all the Hindu-Muslim. Deaths have occurred because police have had to use force against frenzied Muslim mobs. The frenzy is the direct upshot of the vicious tirade unleashed by government, and the official media, against the *kar sevaks*.

'I wish to caution government against this approach. Their pronouncements against *kar sevaks* are only strengthening the movement. But these statements certainly amount to slandering the country. This must stop forthwith.'

The Statesman has this comment to offer:

According to the BJP rejoinder, Mr Advani's 8 December statement was a 'rebuttal of the attempt being made by the government to pin the blame for the unfortunate events in Ayodhya on the BJP–RSS family.'

There is no evidence of any rebuttal in Mr Advani's statement of the attempt by the government to blame the BJP–RSS for the Ayodhya events. Does it not stand to reason that if Mr Advani was rebutting the charge, he would have disowned the *kar sevaks* who brought the structure down? Instead, what Mr Advani does is to go on an elaborate defence of the *kar sevaks*. He even warns that any criticism of the *kar sevaks* will strengthen the Ayodhya movement.

At the outset, Mr Advani describes the 'pulling down of the disputed structure at Ayodhya' as 'an unfortunate event'. Yet, after that, far from distancing himself from the action, he goes on to explain it away saying 'when an old structure . . . is pulled down by a group of people exasperated by the tardiness of the judicial process, and the obtuseness and the myopia of the executive, they are reviled by the President, the Vice-President, and political parties. . . .'

In fact, in the very next para, Mr Advani refers to 'blatant double standards such as evidenced by this tirade against the Ayodhya movement'. As if all this is not enough evidence of his tacit embrace of the *kar sevaks*, he goes on to say that the government and the official media's 'pronouncements against the *kar sevaks* are only strengthening the movement'.

At no stage does Mr Advani attempt to separate the demolition of the mosque from the Ayodhya movement. Also, his words not only fail to condemn the *kar sevaks* and their actions, they, to all intents and purposes, justify the sevaks' actions. So although Mr Advani may not have used the exact words as mentioned in *The Statesman* story, the message spills out—both directly and indirectly—of every word of his statement: the demolition of the masjid was part of the temple movement.

[From *The Statesman*, 12 December 1992.]

21. Resolution of the BJP's National Executive on 23–24 December and after

After the unfortunate incidents of 6 December at Ayodhya, the Congress Party and the Congress government at the Centre have launched a programme of repression and untruth against all nationalist forces. It is a condemnable attempt to replicate what was done after the foul murder of Mahatma Gandhi in 1948. This deliberate programme of mis-information and dis-information, launched by the government will not succeed.

The National Executive of the Bharatiya Janata Party would like to remind the Congress, its new-found allies in the Left Parties and its old allies among communalists who have now rushed to their support, that this triple conspiracy of Congress, Communists and Communalists to keep the country divided and directionless will not succeed. 1992 is not 1948. The people of India are now wide awake to their rights and responsibilities. They are also fully aware of what the Congress and its allies have done to the country by constantly playing the politics of pandering votes.

The incidents of 6 December would have been easily avoided had the Central Government co-operated with the Government of Uttar Pradesh in trying to obtain an early decision from the Allahabad Bench of the Lucknow High Court, in the matter of the acquisition of 2.77-acre plot. Had this decision been given before 6 December, *kar seva* would have started on this tract of land and no untoward incident would have taken place. It, however, appears that the Central Government was determined to not only thwart the efforts of the leadership of Ramjanmasthan Mandir renovation but also to create other complications, so that this leadership would be compelled to confront either the Courts or the impatience of the *kar sevaks*. There was neither sincerity in the Central Government's attitude, nor any desire on its part to solve the problem in a comprehensive and satisfactory manner.

After giving the assurance of four months to the Sadhu Samaj, the Union Government did not take any action for almost half that period; it attempted to divide the leadership of that Samaj; it sent different proposals through different emissaries and ministers, and when there was a positive response to these, it retracted from them. These are among the many such incidents that took place during this period, putting a big question-mark on the dependability of this government. It is obvious that then, as now, the Congress Party and its government are more interested in keeping the matter unresolved, complicated and as a source of tension.

Accepting their moral responsibility, Shri L.K. Advani resigned as Leader of the Opposition. Similarly, Shri Kalyan Singh, the then Chief Minister of Uttar Pradesh and his government, also resigned. They acted in accordance with the highest traditions of democracy. But the Central Government, on its part, arrested Shri L.K. Advani and, hours after the resignation of Shri Kalyan Singh, they announced the dismissal of that government. This is reflective an extreme pettiness of mind in the face of an event of major proportions. A government duly elected by the people is not expected to treat another elected government in this manner.

The manner in which RSS, Vishwa Hindu Parishad and other organizations have been banned, is, not only a step riddled with illegality, it is of an action born entirely out of the frustration of the weak.

The National Executive of BJP unequivocally condemns the dismissal of the constitutionally and democratically elected governments in Madhya Pradesh, Rajasthan and Himachal Pradesh and the dissolution of these and of U.P. State Assemblies. This is a step born out of political malice and mendacity and it will be answered in no uncertain terms by the people of India.

The undemocratic and repressive measures adopted by the Congress Party at the Centre can also be seen in their attempts at arresting archaeologists in the midst of a Press Conference; in their destroying the credibility of AIR and Doordarshan; in the banning of BJP's protest meetings in Delhi, when all others are permitted to hold whatever meetings they like. And then, to compound it all, there was the mindless vendetta of arresting a veteran like Shri Atal Behari Vajpayee. We would like to forewarn the people of India that these are but the first signals of a panicky government attempting the totalitarian method.

It is most unfortunate that this government is behaving as it is because it is caught between the pincers of internal party dissentions, discord within the Cabinet and external pressures. On top of all this, to announce that a Masjid will be built at Ramjanmasthan is to betray not jut total bankruptcy of thought but also an insensitivity to the present situation that is beyond belief. Had this disputed structure not constantly and wrongly been called by the Congress Party and government and its allies as a 'masjid', the country would have been spared the protests and violence, at home and abroad, in the wake of 6 December.

The National Executive of the BJP expresses its fervent hope that even now the Muslim community will recognize the deep commitment of faith and the sentiments of the majority society on this issue. What has happened at Ramjanmasthan is the reaction to grave historical wrong and the idea is not to hurt the sentiments of anyone. Indian Muslims should not identify themselves with the excesses of invaders, just because they happened to be Muslim.

The BJP neither believes in, nor subscribes to, India ever becoming a theocratic State. The BJP reiterates its commitment to, and conviction about, equal opportunity and equal rights to all citizens of India. It implicitly believes in 'Justice for all and appeasement of none'. Wherever the BJP has been in power, it has through its conduct, amply demonstrated this belief through purposeful and responsible governance.

The National Executive of the BJP reiterates its firm commitment to judicial independence and dignity. However, the concept of a 'committed' judiciary and, of late, the methodology of some judicial appointments, has tended to politicize it. This has tended to erode the public confidence in the judiciary. BJP hopes that, in spite of these circumstances, the judiciary will assert its independence particularly when authoritarianism is sought to be justified in the name of secularism.

The National Executive treats the many anti-democratic and lawless measures adopted by the Congress Party and government as declaration of political war on the BJP and all other like-minded organizations and crores of citizens of this country. We will face this onslaught with courage and conviction. We are confident of victory because today history has made the future of India synonymous with the future of BJP—and the people of India know it in their bones. The National Executive of the BJP demands that:

(a) Immediate steps be taken to remove the impediments in the construction of Ramjanmasthan temple in Ayodhya and *puja* and *darshan* of Rama Lalla be allowed as before 6 December; a mosque may be built outside the Panch Kosi Parikrama;
(b) Dr Murli Manohar Joshi, President BJP, Shri L.K. Advani, leader of Opposition, Shri Vishnu Hari Dalmia, Shri Ashok Singhal, Shri Vinay Katiyar, Uma Shri Bharati and all other leaders and workers who have been arrested on false and fabricated charges be released;
(c) The lawless and unwarranted ban on RSS and other organizations be lifted;
(d) Elections to the four State Assemblies be held without any loss of time;
(e) This government having lost its moral authority must go back to the people at the earliest and seek a fresh mandate.

[From *BJP Today*, 1 January 1993, pp. 4–5.]

22. Memoranda submitted by the BJP to the President of India

22a. 16 December 1992

Memorandum submitted to the President by BJP Members of Parliament on 16 December 1992:

Respected Rashtrapati Ji;
You are no doubt aware of the course the events have taken in the last few weeks and which have brought this nation at cross-roads.

If the government over-reacted before 6 December, it has been over-reacting after that date. It has arrested some of the most respected leaders in the country, banned some of the most public-spirited organizations in the land and unconstitutionally dismissed BJP-ruled State Governments, dissolving their State Assemblies. The BJP, RSS and VHP have made it repeatedly and categorically clear that the demolition in Ayodhya was not part of their agenda. We wanted the sacred site peacefully and lawfully restored to the Hindus and the situation was moving in that direction when on 6 December some *kar sevaks* acted entirely on their own and attacked the structure this despite impassioned and repeated pleas of BJP, RSS and VHP leaders on the spot not to touch the structure. Indisputable recorded film and eye witness accounts of reporters who themselves were subjected to attacks by such *kar sevaks* as those who acted on their own, will confirm that those who touched the structure acted against the directives of the leaders present on the site that day.

We welcome the CBI inquiry the government has ordered and hope that such an inquiry will reveal the truth as to what happened on that fateful day. However, the government without waiting for the CBI's findings has arrested BJP, RSS and VHP leaders, which act we condemn and protest against. In the arrest of leaders and the banning of organizations the government, perhaps, hopes to cover up their failure and divert public attention from it.

Shri L.K. Advani is a senior leader of the BJP as also the Leader of the Opposition in Lok Sabha, and Dr M.M. Joshi is the President of the BJP, the main Opposition Party in the country. Arresting persons of such nature on transparently false allegations is adding insult to injury. Such actions can only be seen as an assault on our democratic institution. Even during the notorious Emergency of 1975–77, the non-Congress governments in Gujarat, Tamil Nadu and Jammu and Kashmir were not touched.

The ban on RSS and VHP is undemocratic and repressive; blaming these organizations for what happened in Ayodhya on December 6, is totally unjustified. Even the British did not blame Mahatma Gandhi for the Chauri Chaura Police Station incident in 1921 where several policemen were burnt alive.

The government is adding insult to injury and endangering peace in the future by its thoughtless announcement of re-building the 'Babri Masjid'. The government owes to hand over the Ramjanmasthan to the people of India to re-build the Rama Mandir. It is by such an over-due act alone that the people of India will be willing to build a Mosque somewhere in Ayodhya.

In the aftermath of 6 December, there should be no interference in the conduct of Darshan and Akhand Kirtan at the site where idols remain. Any shifting or stoppage of Darshan or Akhand Kirtan will be considered intolerable interference of the religious freedom of our people. The unfortunate events since 6 December, which have resulted in hundreds of deaths and several hundreds of injuries and sufferings should not be reviewed as so many Hindus killed and so many Muslims killed and so many injured. We view it at so many citizens of this country destroyed. Let the government at the Centre fashion its policies and conduct its affairs in a manner in which India can become riot-free State; we commend the functioning of BJP government in U.P. in this respect. Let the government provide adequate compensation, including free education to all bereaved families and let, in such atmosphere of tolerance Hindus restore damaged mosque and Muslims restore damaged mandirs: we look forward to a brave new era of amity in Hindu–Muslim relationship based on reality in the country.

[From *BJP Today*, 1 January 1993, p. 25.]

22b. 29 December 1992

On 29 December 1992, a BJP delegation led by Shri A.B. Vajpayee, MP, submitted the following Memorandum to the President of India:

Maha Mahim Rashtrapati Ji,
We understand that the Union Government has decided to acquire all the disputed area in Ayodhya about which title suits are pending before the Allahabad High Court and divide it between Hindus and Muslims, for the construction of a temple and a mosque, respectively. The matter concerning the area on which the disputed structure stood, is proposed to be referred to the Supreme Court by you under Article 143 for its opinion about whether a temple stood there before. If its opinion is in the affirmative, the site is to be made part of the temple area; else it is to be attached to the masjid area. The government proposes to set up two separate trusts for Mandir and Masjid.

The above scheme of things would not be acceptable to the country.

The Central Government has no right to partition Ramjanmasthan area. The Ramjanma Mandir must be built at Ramjanmasthan—with the *garbha griha* on the spot of the Rama idol, and a mosque in Ayodhya can be built anywhere outside the Panchkosi Parikrama of that Mandir.

Also it would be singularly inappropriate for the government to appoint either a temple trust or a masjid trust. The people of India will not accept either Sarkari Sadhus or Sarkari Trustees.

We had repeatedly requested the Government of India before 6 December, that it should allow *kar seva* on 2.77-acre plot and refer the disputed site matter to the Supreme Court under Article 143. Had our advice been heeded, all would have been well; there would have been no tension, no lawlessness, no violence. But government did not listen to our friendly advice. The fact that the same government is now prepared to refer the matter to the Supreme Court can only mean one thing, namely that it was not interested in solving the problem, but in creating a situation in which it could make an excuse of the same, to arrest our leaders, dismiss all the four elected BJP governments, ban the RSS, VHP, Bajrang Dal and do other lawless things. We, therefore, question the bonafides of its belated and dubious reference to the Supreme Court.

In any case the 'Archaeological Survey of the Ramayan Sites', carried on by Dr B.B. Lal, at the instance of the then Education Minister, Mr Nurul Hasan, had reported the existence of brick bases of the pillars which once belonged to an eleventh century Hindu temple. And the archaeological finds in the debris of 6 December, particularly the Sanskrit inscription in Nagri script, have only confirmed the existence of a great temple on this spot. In this situation of conclusive evidence, it is pointless to refer an archaeological matter to a law court. The Supreme Court has repeatedly held that it is not an expert in matters of economy and commerce, art and science.

We welcome the Faizabad DM's decision allowing Darshan at Ayodhya on 27 December.

We repeat that the Ramjanmasthan Mandir is a people's movement conducted by the Dharma Sansad assisted by BJP, VHP, and RSS. The government cannot decide this matter without their consent and against their will. For this it is imperative that leaders are released, so that purposeful negotiations can be held and normalcy restored to the land.

We would also request you to see to it that elections are held to the four dissolved assemblies without any loss of time so that the people can have governments of their choice.

[From *BJP Today*, 1 January 1993, p. 8.]

22c. 10 May 1993

Memorandum to President

A delegation of saints and holy men as well as VIPs from all corners of the country has called upon you. This indeed is a historic occasion. Posterity will remember the event and the deliberations that will take place will have a special significance.

We believe Your Honour is well aware that Lord Rama, the ideal of humanity, is the symbol of India's lofty culture, nationalism and highest values of life and that millions of our countrymen look forth to the renovation of the existing temple on the hallowed Ramjanmabhumi to make it a grand monument. Countless Hindus residing abroad are also keenly awaiting the auspicious day when the imposing edifice will be ready for installing Rama Lalla, when they could visit India for *darshan*.

What an irony of times/history that instead of honouring the faith of millions of compatriots certain elements are trying to put hurdles in their way. The Government of India also, rather than restraining them, has been indirectly patronizing them. The people of this country strongly feel that the Centre should reconsider its attitude and clear the way for the reconstruction of the temple.

We are here to submit a memorandum expressing these popular sentiments. Thousands of votaries of Rama visited towns and villages and obtained the citizens signatures to this memorandum. Thanks to the indefatigable volunteers' efforts, this signature campaign has been the most massive of such ventures. In fact it is a world record. There is no place in the country from where copies of the signed memorandum have not been received. People who have appended their signatures hail not only from the urban areas, towns and villages, but also from remote forests and inaccessible hill tracts. The signatories include all sections of society covering all sects, castes and classes. They represent the sentiments of people from 2,81,212 villages. It deserves to be emphasized that among the signatories are 3,97,388 Muslims and 1,19,763 Christians. These people have expressed their commitment to India's cultural legacy and fulfilled their national obligation. No doubt, they have strengthened the country's unity. We are confident the reclamation of the sacred Ramjanmabhumi would prove us memorable as the reconstruction of the Somnath temple, the inauguration of which was graced by no less a person than the then Hon'ble President of India, Dr Rajendra Prasad.

Sir, we are pleased that the hon'ble Governors of almost all States received with due respect this memorandum signed by the citizens and promised to forward the same to Your Honour. We must, however, put on record with regret that the hon'ble Governors of West Bengal, Jammu and Kashmir and Andhra Pradesh refused to meet the representatives of the Manch and personally receive the signed memorandum. We regard their action as unbecoming and injurious to the courtesy implicit in a democracy.

Mr President, Sir, in the considered opinion of this delegation the atmosphere, the very ethos of the town of Ayodhya, particularly around the area called 'Sri Ramjanmasthan' has always been infused with the spirit of Rama, thereby giving strength to the country by forming as it were its nerve centre. It is our constitutional right to preserve the cultural significance of this spot. Therefore, nothing that would be incongruous with the holy atmosphere should be allowed within the precincts of Rama's birthplace. It would be extremely unfortunate if any move to build a mosque at Ramjanmabhumi or near around comes up under the Centre's patronage. In the interest of national unity and also communal amity it is imperative that the Government of India give up any plan of building a mosque at the site.

The people of India have, with millions of signatures, implored your honour that, if at all a mosque comes up, it must be beyond the Panchkosi.

We request your honour to direct the Government of India and advise them that they should honour the democratically expressed sentiments of the country's millions of people and as early as possible remove the hurdles in the way of the temple reconstruction. The Centre can thus contribute to the preservation of Ayodhya's dignity and importance.

Jai Bharat.

Yours in the service of the nation

Sd/ Paramahansa Swami Vamdev, President, Sri Ramjanmabhumi Nyas Manch and Members of the Delegation

Names of members of the delegation who met the President of India, Dr Shankar Dayal Sharma.

1. Swami Vamdev Maharaj, leading saint and recluse, President, Sri Ramjanmabhumi Nyas Manch
2. Mahant Avaidya Nath, MP, Senior Member, SRN Manch
3. Swami Haridas Giri, President, Shri Jnanananda Peeth
4. Swami Sivanandamoorthy, well-known leading saint
5. Swami Anandabodh Saraswati, President, Sarvadeshik Arya Pratinidhi Sabha
6. Mahant Ram Prakash Das, Ramanand Sampradaya
7. Swami Aumanand, leading saint of Jammu and Kashmir
8. Smt Vijaya Raje Scindia, MP, Trustee, VHP (banned)
9. Smt Ushatai Chati, co-Convener, Rashtra Sevika Samiti
10. Prof. Rajendra Singh, Joint-General Secretary, RSS (banned)
11. Shri Dattopant Thengadi, Founder, Bharatiya Mazdoor Sangh and Bharatiya Kisan Sangh
12. Shri Nanaji Deshmukh, Founder, Deendayal Research Institute and Vice-Chancellor, Gramodaya University, Chitrakoot
13. Shri Vishnu Hari Dalmia, President, VHP (banned)
14. Shri Dau Dayal Khanna, Freedom-Fighter and ex-Minister, U.P.
15. Dr Murli Manohar Joshi, MP, President, BJP
16. Shri Lal Krishna Advani, Leader of the Opposition, Lok Sabha
17. Shri Sikandar Bakht, MP, Leader of the Opposition, Rajya Sabha
18. Shri Atal Behari Vajpayee, Senior BJP leader
19. Shri A.P. Venkateswaran, former Secretary, Ministry of External Affairs.
20. Col. Daljit Singh (Retd), noted writer
21. Dr K.K. Sastri, veteran Sanskrit scholar, leading intellectual
22. Dr Sujit Dhar, renowned cardiologist and social worker
23. Shri P.G. Gavai, ex-Lt. Governor, Delhi
24. Dr M.C. Modi, world-renowned ophthalmologist
25. Shri L.G. Havanur, ex-Minister, Karnataka State
26. Shri Kariya Munda, MP, ex-Minister of State, GOI
27. Shri Jagdev Oraon, Vice-President, Vanvasi Kalyan Ashram
28. Adv. O.M. Mathew, Vice-President, BJP, Kerala

Nos 5, 19, 25 and 27 could not reach Delhi.

Nos 6, 16, 18 and 26 could not attend as Lok Sabha was in session. However they sent a joint letter to the President conveying their full support to the memorandum.

44 Parliament House
New Delhi 110 001
May 10, 1993

To
The Hon'ble President of India

Sir, We submit herewith a memorandum signed by millions of countrymen pleading for a Rama temple at Ramjanmabhumi in Ayodhya. A mosque may be allowed beyond the Panchakoti Parikrama.

In this connection you have agreed to see a delegation at 6 pm today. The undermentioned members of the Lok Sabha were to join the delegation. But today the Lok Sabha is going to debate the resolution on impeachment of Shri Justice Ramaswami. Voting on the resolution is likely to take place after 6/7 pm. We therefore regret our inability to join the delegation. We fully endorse in the sentiment expressed in the memorandum and pray to you that you advise government to respect the people's sentiments regarding this subject.

Yours,

Sd/ Atal Behari Vajpayee — Sd/ Vi. Ra. Scindia
Sd/ Karia Munda — Sd/ Lal Advani

[From *Organizer*, 23 May 1993.]

23. Uma Bharati's ecstasy at the demolition

Kedar Jain, who took the controversial picture of Ms Uma Bharati hugging the BJP president, Dr Murli Manohar Joshi, on 6 December, reiterated that he had shot it when the demolition of the Babri Masjid was on.

Joining issue with Ms Bharati, Jain said, 'I won't know which dome was being demolished when I took the picture, but I know for a fact that the two leaders were rejoicing the destruction of the mosque.'

The BJP sanyasin, who is lodged in a jail in Uttar Pradesh, had said that the picture was taken at 11 am when she was felicitating Dr Joshi and other leaders at the Rama Katha Kunj in Ayodhya. Remarked Jain, who works for a Gwalior-based Hindi daily: 'If you look at the picture you will find that the two were certainly watching something with glee.'

While other news photographers were asked to gather in a nearby building, the intrepid young Jain managed to reach the leaders. As he shot the picture of Ms Bharati hugging the BJP president, the sanyasin in fact told him to 'send me a copy of the picture.'

The photograph was first carried by *Amar Ujala*, a Hindi daily, with a caption that the ecstatic mood of the sanyasin was captured by the photographer when the third dome of the masjid was demolished. Ms Uma Bharati, however, disclaimed this when the photograph was reproduced by a Delhi newspaper.

[From *The Telegraph*, 24 December 1992.]

24. Vajpayee's speech in the Lok Sabha on 17 December 1992

I am ready to go one step ahead and ask those *kar sevaks,* who were small in number to come forward and openly confess that they have demolished the structure and for that they are prepared to face the music. I would also like to state that there were *kar sevaks* present in a large number but they were not all involved in the demolition.

Rama temple will not be constructed by foul or unfair means. If Rama temple is constructed it would be constructed on the basis of moral strength.

. . . We would like to know who was that group, from where it came and who organized it. I repeat it again that the *kar sevaks* who took part in demolishing the structure should come forward and reveal their participation in demolition. If punishment is given they should accept it. The temple of Lord Rama cannot be built without making sacrifice. At least it will not be built in this manner.

But there are other aspects also of this issue. It was not only a structure which was demolished. There was a temple as well. '*Namaz*' was not offered in the mosque. Even the entry to the mosque was prohibited. But prayer was offered in the temple by the orders of the court.

. . . I had said in a public meeting held in Bombay in 1986 that Ayodhya issue could be solved. I had given two suggestions in this regard. First, Muslims should forsake their claim on the structure in favour of Hindus saying that they were doing so because the sentiments of Hindus were attached to this place. Hindus believe that it is the birthplace of Lord Rama and there is evidence to it. Faith is something very precious. We live in this country with you, we have to live together. If you believe that it is the birthplace of Lord Rama, we give it to you. Second suggestion was that the Hindus, after getting the structure should say that their struggle for Ramjanmabhumi has now ended. This structure now would not be demolished. *Puja* will continue to be performed there. Temple would be constructed at some other place.

. . . Now the particular state is under the control of Central Government, so Archaeological Survey of India should be asked to carry out excavations at the site with a view to determine whether earlier there existed temple or not. This dispute should be settled once for all. . . .

[From *Lok Sabha Debates*, 17 December 1992.]

25. Vajpayee's press interview on 26 December 1992, calling the mosque 'a symbol of shame' which had been 'erased'

In late December 1992, Vajpayee delivered a speech in which he declared that the Babri Masjid 'was a symbol of shame and has been erased' (*Sunday*, 27 December 1992, 2 January 1993). Such declarations require careful attention. Although there are differences in temperament and sensibility, and thus in the interpretation of events, between the various leaders of the BJP, these are of fine degree and do not justify any distinction between 'moderates' and 'hard-liners'. There exists in the party a division of labour between its leaders which enables them to attract, recruit and retain individual supporters with a variety of outlooks. Indeed, nobody left the party after 6 December, even though that day's events made some party members feel ill-at-ease.

[From Christophe Jaffrelot, *The Hindu Revivalist Movement in India*, Viking, 1993, p. 475.]

26. Murli Manohar Joshi on the demolition

In a written interview to UNI from the Matatila guest house, where he, along with Mr L.K. Advani and other leaders of BJP–VHP–RSS combine, is under detention, Dr Murli Manohar Joshi said he was not repentant over the Ayodhya incidents of 6 December.

In fact, I pay my homage to the *kar sevaks* who were killed at the site while they were performing the *kar seva*, the BJP president said.

Following are excerpts from the interview:

How do you assess the political scenario after the Ayodhya incidents?

It has brought 'Hindutva' to the centre-stage. The BJP has become the voice of resurgent nationalism. It is redefining the political ideology of every aspect of the national life—be it secularism, socialism, foreign policy or economic issues. The Hindutva concept is going to be the deciding factor. All the political parties are going to be affected by this. This would lead to the creation of a new India. This would unite the society and caste conflicts would come to an end.

The greatest contribution of the Ramjanmabhumi movement is that the debate in the country has now shifted from politics to policy.

How do you see the prospects of the BJP?

Ayodhya has brought to the fore the polarization of Indian politics between the BJP and non-BJP parties.

The people would repose their faith in the BJP. It has emerged as the only party which has the qualities for leading the nation in this hour of crisis.

I am confident that whenever the elections are held, the BJP would come to power at the Centre.

What is the main plank in the immediate future?

Building the Rama temple where the idols are installed now. The mosque should be built outside the Panchkosi Parikrama. Uninterrupted 'darshan' should be allowed to the public at the Janmasthan, immediate elections to the State assemblies of U.P., M.P., Rajasthan and Himachal Pradesh, dissolution of the Lok Sabha and fresh elections, lifting of ban on all five organizations and the restoration of democratic rights.

Do you think that the Congress would succeed in appropriating Lord Rama to its advantage?

Whatever they do or undo, Rama has come to be associated with the Hindutva movement. And Rama mandir has become the slogan of the Hindu society. Can the Congress show the courage to say in public that it is for the Rama temple at the Janmasthan?

[From *The Hindustan Times*, 1 January 1993.]

27. Advani on the demolition

Bharatiya Janata party leader, L.K. Advani told a largely attended public meeting at Naranpura in Ahmedabad at the end of his three-day visit to the State on Sunday that what happened at Ayodhya on 6 December would change the course of Indian history.

Mr Advani said he did not regret the demolition of the mosque though he was sad that day because his fervent pleas to *kar sevaks* not to damage the monument had been ignored.

Reiterating that the Rama temple would be built at the same site, Mr Advani said judicial delay and vacillation by the Prime Minister should be held responsible for the demolition. By frequent references to the disputed structure as a mosque, the Prime Minister had incited *kar sevaks* to go for the demolition.

He said he was surprised at the criticism the demolition got from the President and the Prime Minister among others. It was after all an old structure built by Babar.

He said the demolition could have been averted had the Muslims leadership listened to requests to shift the mosque to another site. He said he would have been the first to help shift the structure to a place 5 kms away from the birthplace of Lord Rama.

Although the demolition was not pre-planned it would have occurred after some time, as the BJP had planned to construct the mandir at the same place by bringing about a legislation. When the Muslims had stopped offering *namaz* they should have given up their claim on the site.

[From *The Indian Express*, 25 January 1993.]

28. Syed Shahabuddin's offer to the Prime Minister, 30 December 1992

30 December 1992

My dear Prime Minister,

I have separately sent you the statement of the Babri Masjid Movement Coordination Committee dated 28 December 1992 reacting to the 'Package' announced by the Central Government on 27 December. I am attaching a copy for ready reference. We have been discussing the matter with Members of Parliament, Leader of Muslim organizations, the Ulema and other representative figures from the Muslim community. We must report to you that the package, as it stands, is universally unacceptable.

We have also discussed the matter with several members of the Council of Ministers in order to understand the logic of the package. We were told that the uppermost objective was the commencement of the construction of a Rama Mandir on a site adjacent to that of the Babri Masjid at the earliest possible. If this is the objective, we would like to suggest for your consideration the following alternative package:

(i) All pending cases including the Title Suit should be referred to the Supreme Court under Article 138(2);

(ii) All the property-in-dispute and some adjacent land as necessary may be taken over by the Central Government for safe custody with the express intention to hold it until the final judicial verdict of a universally acceptable settlement, by an Ordinance;

(iii) The status-quo in the land taken over including the Babri Masjid site should be frozen as at the time of promulgation of the President's Rule;

(iv) The Hindu Trust should be asked to submit the site plan for the Rama temple to the government if any part of the land in disputes falls within the site plan, the Muslim community may be asked to donate it in the interest of amity and harmony;

(v) We would like to assure that the Muslim community will rise to the occasion and respond positively. This part of the property in dispute will then be outside the purview of the Supreme Court proceeding by appropriate legal action;

(vi) The Muslim community may also be offered land on the west of the Babri Masjid to build a masjid if it so wishes;

(vii) The Babri Masjid site may be disposed of in the light of the Supreme Court decision.

You will appreciate that these proposals do not envisage any form of confrontation. The Muslims are prepared to wait until the Supreme Court decision and are committed to accept it, whatever may be. The Muslims are not asking you to restore the demolished property-in-dispute, as can be rightfully claimed by them under the law of the land. The Muslims would like to assure you that they also want a solution to this problem at the earliest because it is consuming so much of their energy, which can be better utilized for constructive and developmental purposes. The Muslims would like to co-operate with you in finding a lasting solution but it must be based on law, justice and morality and safeguard their dignity.

We would request you not to let them down and revise your package plan in the light of the above submissions.

Sd./- Syed Shahabuddin

Shahabuddin clarifies stand:
'My letter to the Prime Minister of 30 December 1992, whose copies had been sent to a number of Ministers and Muslim leaders, does not amount to acceptance of the government's proposal for reconstruction of Babri Masjid at an alternative site. Indeed, in the very first paragraph I have stated that the government's proposal as it stands is universally unacceptable.

'In the course of discussions, ministers had indicated that the construction of the Mandir must immediately begin and the government must immediately allocate a site for it, and to balance it, the government, should at the same time, allocate site for an alternative masjid, while the question of the Babri Masjid site was under reference to the Supreme Court, the Muslim community has never agreed to an alternative masjid even when the Vishwa Hindu Parishad had offered a large sum for its construction at an alternative site. It was in this context that an alternative package proposed in the letter left it to the government to offer an alternative site to build a masjid if it so wished. That did not imply that the Muslim community would accept the offer.

'The burden of the last paragraph is that the Muslim community does not want any confrontation and therefore, is prepared to wait for reconstruction of Babri Masjid till final judicial verdict even though it can rightfully claim immediate fulfilment of commitment made by the Prime Minister and also the restoration of Babri Masjid in terms of the universally accepted principle of jurisprudence that a property in dispute, if deliberately destroyed or altered by one of the parties during the pendency of the suite, must be substituted.

'To sum up, the headline gives a completely baseless and erroneous interpretation of my letter to the Prime Minister of 30 December 1992.'

[From *Muslim India*, 122, February 1993.]

29. Advani on the reaction to the demolition

But the Congress stand on Ayodhya is clear. So what is the theme of the debate?

The theme revolves round the meaning of nationalism. What is to be realized is that the average Hindu today is not distressed over what happened in Ayodhya. A large section is happy. In my own article I said the whole country may have felt revulsion at the blinding of under trial prisoners in Bhagalpur. But when I visited Bhagalpur, I found that there was not only no sense of revulsion there but there was an attitude to justify—including lawyers who came out in procession in defence of what had been done by the police. I said that this only shows that when the system is inadequate to deal with problems which really bother the people and on that account the people take the law into their own hands, they do not think that they had committed a very great offence.

You had even agreed for reference under Section 143 but now the government has come to the same conclusion. What is your opinion on that?

My statement was, of course, at a point of time when the Babri Masjid Action Committee leaders themselves had said that if a judicial body gives a finding that there was a temple here earlier, we will hand over our claim. Now they have gone back upon it. So the proposal to refer it under Article 143 had a relevance to that premise. That premise is not valid now.

The recent finding in respect of that temple—particularly that stone inscription we hold, clinches the issue, gives no scope whatsoever for any doubt.

[From *Organizer*, 28 February 1993.]

30. Jaswant Singh acknowledges BJP's responsibility

Does the BJP today deny responsibility for what happened in Ayodhya on 6 December 1992?

Of course not. We have accepted our responsibility directly. The Chief Minister of U.P. resigned, everyone from Atal Behari Vajpayee to L.K. Advani to the *Sarsanghachalak*, said that this was not the right thing to happen. . .

But they were a few metres from the site of the demolition. . .

I agree, I agree with you. . .

. . .*But it could not be stopped?*

. . . It could not have. Your suggestion that even if they *could* have stopped it, they wouldn't have stopped it is incorrect. I was not there, but I have seen videotapes, conducted by curiously enough, the then defence minister Sharad Pawar. His team was recording the whole event from early morning to five o'clock. We are honest in saying, yes we are responsible, that it should not have happened. But I also believe that you cannot saddle either a party or a society or least of all a nation, with a permanent sense of guilt. An ancient country like ours cannot come to a standstill because one mistake is made.

Was the demolition a mistake?

Yes of course. It should not have happened. I mean, in the sense that the BJP was one of the participants, the BJP has direct responsibility. But what about all the others? What about the responsibility of the Babri Masjid Action Committee, the Narasimha Rao government? The central forces, the ministry of defence, who had direct access to what was taking place on a minute by minute basis? We accept our responsibility, the others create a fear about us in the minds of the minority. Only to garner their votes. This electoral exploitation of the minority is what we call fraudulent secularism.

[From *Economic Times*, 11 June 1996.]

31a. Vajpayee owns up responsibility

The Sangh is my soul
The RSS has a two-fold task before it. One is to organize the Hindus. To build a strong Hindu society, wellknit and rising above caste and other artificial differences. Some differences will persist but then variety is the spice of life. Like, we have the differences of language. We don't want to destroy this diversity. The other task is to assimilate the non-Hindu like Muslims and Christians in the mainstream. They can follow the faith of their own conviction. No one can object to it. We worship trees, stones, animals and what not. We have hundreds of ways of worshipping God. They can go where they want. But this country must be looked upon as the Motherland for them. . . .

Congress has not correctly understood the Muslim problem. They continue to carry on their policy of appeasement. But to what effect? The Muslims of this country can be treated in three ways. One is *tiraskar* which means if they will not themselves change leave them alone, reject them as our compatriots. Second is *puraskar* which is appeasement, i.e., bribe them to behave, which is being done by the Congress and others of their ilk. The third way is *parishkar* meaning to change them, that is, to restore them to the mainstream by providing them *samskaras*. We want to change them by offering them the right *samskaras*. Their religion will not be changed. They can follow their own religion. Mecca can continue to be holy for the Muslims but India should be holier than the holy for them. You can go to a mosque and offer *namaz*, you can keep the *roza*. We have no problem. But if you have to choose between Mecca or Islam and India you must choose India. All the Muslims should have this feeling: we will live and die only for this country. . . .

But we did pull down the structure in Ayodhya. In fact it was a reaction to the Muslim vote-bank. We wanted to solve this problem through negotiation and legislation. But there was no *puraskar* for *burai* (evil act). We change *burai* also with *parishkar*. Now, I think, the Hindu society has been regenerated which was the prime task of the RSS. Earlier Hindus used to bend before an invasion but not now. This change is Hindu society is worthy of welcome. So much change must have come with the new-found self-assertion. This is a question of self-preservation. If the Hindu society does not expand itself it will face a crisis of survival. . . .

[From *Organizer*, 7 May 1995.]

31b. Praveen Togadia confirms the admissions

The VHP virtually admitted its hand in the communal violence in Gujarat last year and also the 1992 demolition of the disputed structure at Ayodhya.

'It was we who demolished the Babri Masjid. It was we who came onto roads in Gujarat. But during this *satyagraha*, not a stone was thrown and the event remained peaceful although there was such a huge gathering of activists', VHP General Secretary Praveen Togadia said here.

The admission came as he was narrating how the organization had, despite gathering of over 1.75 lakh activists, managed a 'peaceful' week-long *satyagraha* which concluded in Delhi on Wednesday.

'We have shown that we can fight as well as be peaceful. We have demonstrated that we can manage huge gatherings peacefully,' he added.

[From *PTI*, 3 April 2003.]

32a. Advani, others instigated us: Babri accused

In a new twist to the Babri Masjid demolition case, the five accused on Saturday alleged they had pulled down the disputed structure at Ayodhya at the instigation of Deputy Prime Minister L.K. Advani and other senior BJP leaders, a charge denied by Mr Advani's lawyer: The five—Vinod Vatsa, Santosh, R.C. Khatri, Amar Nath Goyal and R.N. Das—made the charge while speaking to reporters outside the special CBI court hearing the case here.

They alleged that the accused VIPs had got their case separated by 'exerting influence' and demanded that all the accused be treated at par as far as the trial was concerned.

Denying the charge, the DPM's lawyer Satyapal Jain said in Chandigarh, 'There is no evidence against Mr Advani and the allegation seems to be tutored against him. I think there seems to be some mischief somewhere. The credentials of these people who are now saying this is yet to be established.'

He said that so far as the evidence before the Liberhan Commission of Inquiry was concerned, no leader; no witness and no CBI official had said that there was any direct evidence against Mr Advani, Murli Manohar Joshi and Uma Bharati. 'I think in the court also, so far no witness has said that they did anything at the asking of Uma Bharati or Mr Advani or Mr Joshi,' he said.

One of the accused, R.N. Das, was the priest of the sanctum sanctorum of the temple inside the then Babri Masjid. The five accused expressed resentment at 'being discriminated against those enjoying power' and on whose instigation they had demolished the disputed structure on 6 December 1992.

Meanwhile, the Congress has demanded the resignation of Mr Advani and Union Minister M.M. Joshi. Party spokesperson Anand Sharma said, 'It is a well-known fact that Mr Advani and other central ministers, all chargesheeted in the Ayodhya case, were the main conspirators of the demolition.'

'It would be a mockery of democracy if Mr Advani, prosecuted for an alleged criminal act, should continue in government,' Mr Sharma said. The CPI also demanded the resignation of Mr Advani and Mr Joshi.

[From *The Times of India*, 8 June 2003.]

32b. RSS offshoot backs claims of Babri accused

The Akhil Bharatha Ayodhya Ram Mandir Kar Sevak Sangh—an RSS splinter organization—on Monday endorsed the claims of the five accused in the Babri Masjid case saying Deputy Prime Minister, L.K. Advani had instigated the *kar sevaks* to pull down the Babri shrine.

The Ram Mandir Kar Sevak Sangh too named human resources development minister Murli Manohar Joshi as one of the key figures in the drive on 6 December 1992 to demolish the structure.

A. Venkateshwara Rao, national convener of the Kar Sevak Sangh, said his organization fully endorsed the charges levelled by the five accused two days ago.

He rubbished claims made by the Deputy Prime Minister's counsel that some forces were at work to tar Mr Advani's image by implicating him in the razing of the shrine. 'There is no pressing need for these accused to make false statements against the Deputy Prime Minister.'

The Kar Sevaks Sangh was floated in 1999 and has over 1,300 members all over the country—most of them are veterans of the 6 December Babri Masjid demolition movement. State convener of the organization T. Venkatesham, who also addressed the press conference, displayed photographs and identity cards of groups and organizations that took part in the 1992 movement to bring down the disputed shrine.

The Kar Sevak Sangh demanded that all the accused in the case be prosecuted in the same manner, 'since the crime committed by them is the same.' The sangh alleged that there was discrimination in the prosecuting of the *kar sevaks*.

Mr Venkateshwara Rao, who quit from the RSS two years after the demolition, criticized the RSS, the VHP and the BJP for trying to extract political mileage out of the issue. The BJP, which captured power on the Hindutva plank, has chosen to abandon it for its own selfish motives, Mr Rao alleged.

[From *The Times of India*, 9 June 2003.]

32c. I was betrayed: Kalyan Singh

The former Uttar Pradesh Chief Minister and Rashtriya Kranti Party leader, Kalyan Singh, today alleged that he had been betrayed by the Vishwa Hindu Parishad and the RSS leaders over the Babri Masjid demolition and was prepared to testify against them.

These leaders of the Sangh Parivar, including the Deputy Prime Minister, L.K. Advani, and the Union Minister, Murli Manohar Joshi, had kept him in the dark about their plans to demolish the mosque, he said. They had assured him that '*kar seva*' at Ayodhya would be quite peaceful and symbolic but ultimately it ended with the destruction of the Babri Masjid.

Talking to newspersons here, Mr Singh said he was given assurances in writing by Swami Chinmayananda and the late Rajmata Scindia that the '*kar seva*' would be peaceful and it was on the basis of their letter that he had given his affidavit to the Supreme Court. Even the observer sent by the Court to look at the goings-on near the disputed site, Tej Shankar, had sent a report at 11.30 am on the fateful day saying that the situation was absolutely normal. An hour later, however, the mob went berserk and the mosque came crumbling down. That was enough to gauge the mystery behind the Sangh Parivar's plans to demolish the mosque, he said. Mr Singh also came out in defence of the then Central Government led by P.V. Narasimha Rao, saying that the Central forces sent to Ayodhya were unable to move forward as the '*kar sevaks*' had erected blockades in their way. To say that the Central forces were not properly deployed was incorrect. Only the human wall created by the *kar sevaks* had prevented the forces from acting.

Security arrangements had been properly placed at the state level too but the police forces had been asked not to fire. 'All arrangements went haywire when the mob started moving menacingly towards the disputed structure,' he said.

He had owned moral responsibility for the demolition and had served a one-day prison term as he had no other way out. As Chief Minister of the State he had been forced to own up for what had happened but had expressed his displeasure to the BJP and RSS leaders who had betrayed him, Mr Singh said, 'I had protested vehemently against the betrayal of the BJP and VHP leaders.'

Mr Singh said it was ridiculous to say that the State Government was not making available the relevant records to the centre as the BJP was a part of the present coalition ruling U.P. The Central Government's claim only showed that it had to hide something, he added.

33. Jyoti Basu asks the Centre to demolish the structure erected by the VHP at the site of the demolished mosque

The West Bengal chief minister, Mr Jyoti Basu, today asked the Centre to issue orders to demolish the temporary structure erected by the VHP–BJP *kar sevaks* on the disputed site in Ayodhya and rebuild the Babri Masjid without further delay.

Speaking to newsmen at Writers' Building, Mr Basu said, 'It is an illegal construction and the government has every right to demolish it.'

On whether there would be any Hindu backlash if the *kar sevaks*' construction was demolished, Mr Basu said, 'Let there be repercussions from Hindu fundamentalists. My party will support any government willing to bring down the structure erected by demolishing the shrine.'

The chief minister dared the BJP to break a single Muslim shrine in West

Bengal. 'We are here in the government. We know how to deal with these anti-socials. My government will never allow the BJP to foment communal trouble in the state', Mr Basu said.

[From *The Telegraph*, 10 December 1992.]

34. The Union Home Secretary Madhav Godbole explains how that structure came up

The Ayodhya complex was captured by security forces at about 4 am, without firing a single shot though tear-gas shells had to be used at some places and lathi charges had also to be resorted to.

During the night of 7 December, Kumaramangalam, who was then Minister of State for Law and Parliamentary Affairs, rang me up several times asking me to make sure that the Ayodhya complex was captured by central forces during the night. He said that continued construction of a Rama temple by the *kar sevaks* was causing a lot of embarrassment; that he would have to resign and the Central Government itself might have to go if the complex was not taken over and construction of the temple stopped. 'Since the construction of the temple itself was unauthorized', Kumaramangalam asked, 'can it not be destroyed while taking over the complex?' He said he had spoken to the PM who agreed this could be done. When I pointed out that, at that late hour (it was around 1 am on 8 December), the PM must be sleeping, he said that he had woken up the PM and had spoken to him on the phone. He suggested that I should give suitable orders to the concerned police officers. I said that it would not be correct to do any such thing and that all that we could try to do was to take over the complex. The rest would have to be left to the courts to decide. I had kept the HM informed of this telephone conversation.

[From Madhav Godbole, *Unfinished Innings*, Orient Longman, 1996, pp. 389–90.]

35a. The High Court strikes down as malafide acquisition of the land in 1991 on 11 December 1992

1. Writ Petition No. 3540 (MB) of 1991
   Mohd. Hashim *versus* State of U.P. and others
2. Writ Petition No. 3541 (MB) of 1991
   Panch Ramanandi Nirmohi Akhara *versus* State of U.P. and others
3. Writ Petition No. 4183 (MB) of 1991
   Mohammad Aslam @ Bhure *versus* Union of India and others,
4. Writ Petition No. 4184 (MB) of 1991 Mohammad Aslam @ Bhure *versus* Union of India and others

5. Writ Petition No. 4185 (MB) of 1991
   Naveed Yar Khan *versus* State of U.P. and others, and
6. Writ Petition No. 4201 (MB) of 1991
   Jamaat-e-Islami Hind *versus* State of U.P. and another and others

Hon'ble S.C. Mathur, J.
Hon'ble Brijesh Kumar, J.
Hon'ble S.H.A. Raza, J.
(Delivered by Hon'ble S.C. Mathur, J.)

These six petitions are directed against acquisition of land under the provisions of Land Acquisition Act, 1894 (Act I of 1894), for short Act. The land is situate in village Kot Rama Chandra, Pargana Haveli Avadh, Tahsil Sadar, District Faizabad, and is comprised in the following plots:

	Plot No.	Area
1.	159 Part	0.3600
2.	160 part	1.0706
3.	171 Part	0.4375
4.	172 part	0.9063
		2.7744

The composite notification under Section 4 (1) and Section 17 (4) of the Act was published in the U.P. Gazette dated 7.10.1991 which was followed by notification dated 10 October 1991 under Section 6. The purpose of acquisition was disclosed in the notification as 'Development of Tourism and Providing Amenities to Pilgrims at Ayodhya in District Faizabad'. The first writ petition was filed in this Court on 16 October 1991 before a Division Bench which directed it to come up before the Special Bench. After hearing the learned counsel for the parties an interim order was passed on 25 October 1991. Between the filing of the first petition and the passing of the interim order two more petitions (3541 and 3542) had also been filed. The interim order was made applicable to these petitions also. So far as the title to the land is concerned the case of Panch Ramanandi Nirmohi Akhara, for short Akhara, is different from that of the other petitioners but there is no difference in the grounds of challenge on account of which all the petitions have been heard together and are being decided by this common judgement. Leading arguments on behalf of the petitioners were advanced in the writ petitions of Mohd. Hashim and Mohammad Aslam and the Akhara. Counsel appearing in other petitions adopted the arguments advanced in Mohd. Hashim's case. In writ petition No. 4184 of 1991 filed by Mohammad Aslam @ Bhure additional point of vires of sub-sections (1) and (4) of Section 17 of the Act has been raised.

In all the petitions except that of Akhara the petitioners claim to represent the interest of Muslims. In the writ petition of Akhara the petitioners claim to represent the interest of a sect of Hindus, namely Ramanandi Bairagis. They are worshippers of Lord Rama and claim that they had their temples etc. on the acquired land.

Topography

For a proper appreciation of the facts it will be desirable to have an idea of the topography of the place where the acquired land is situate.

At site there is an old structure which is the centre of controversy among three communities, the Hindus, the Muslims and the Ramanandi Bairagis. The Muslims claim the structure to be a mosque while the Hindus, including Ramanandi Bairagis, claim it to be a Hindu temple. They also claim it to be the birth place of Lord Rama. The difference between the orthodox Hindus and Ramanandi Bairagis is not regarding the nature of the structure but it is regarding the right of possession and management, each laying its own claim thereto. On the eastern and southern sides of the structure there is open land and on the northern and western sides there is public road and public path way. Beyond the road in the north there is again open land. Beyond the path way in the west there is a deep slope.

The aforesaid structure is divisible into three parts: (1) the main roofed structure, (2) the inner courtyard, and (3) outer courtyard. The public road is to the north of the structure. Immediately adjoining the roofed structure to the east is the inner courtyard. To the east of this courtyard is the outer courtyard.

On the outer courtyard there is a Chabutra which has been in possession of the Hindus. There are other signs on this courtyard which are objects of reverence or worship to the Hindus, like Sita Rasoi and Charan. To the east of the outer courtyard is a boundary wall having a gate. It is this gate which provides entry first to the outer courtyard, then to the inner courtyard and lastly to the roofed structure. The impugned acquisition spares the roofed structure and the inner courtyard but covers the outer courtyard, including the boundary wall and the gate.

To the east of the boundary wall and the gate is open land which the petitioners claim as a Muslim graveyard and on which, at the time of acquisition, there existed some small structures, including some temples.

The acquisition map shows a passage connecting the structure with the main road on the north. This passage runs right up to the entrance to the inner courtyard. The land covered by the acquisition does not include this passage.

History of Litigation

Another item which deserves precedence over the statement of case of the parties is the history of litigation in respect of the aforesaid property or a portion thereof. This history starts from the year 1885 when Mahant Raghubar Das filed suit no. 61/280 of 1885 in the Court of Sub-Judge, Faizabad, against the Secretary of State for India seeking permission to construct temple on the Chabutra measuring 21 feet east–west and to be struck off.

Mahant Raghubar Das took the matter in appeal to the court of the Judicial Commissioner of Avadh. Shri W. Young, the Judicial Commissioner, by his judgement dated 1 November 1886 dismissed the appeal (No. 27 of 1886) observing 'there is nothing whatsoever on the record to show that the plaintiff is in any (illegible) the proprietor of the land in question.'

I have mentioned hereinabove that the history of litigation starts from 1885. However, the judgements in the above litigation, particularly the judgement of the trial court, refers to orders passed in certain earlier proceedings. From this it would appear that prior to the above suit also there had been litigation regarding the nature of the property in question. However, the exact nature of that litigation is not clear and, therefore, I take the suit of Mahant Raghubar Das as the starting point of litigation.

The above litigation followed almost immediately the collapse of the Muslim rule in India and its replacement by the British rule. On the collapse of the British rule the next litigation starts.

On 15 August 1947 India obtained self rule with dominion status. On 23 December 1949 Pandit Ram Deo Dubey, Station In-charge, Police Station Ayodhya, district Faizabad lodged First Information Report against Abhai Ram Das, Ram Sakal Das, Sudarshan Das and 50–60 other persons under sections 147/29/449, Indian Penal Code, alleging that he came to know from Constable No. 7, Mata Prasad that the said persons had broken open the locks and entered the mosque and installed therein the idol of Sri Rama Chandraji. On the basis of the first information report and the police report, proceedings under section 145, Code of Criminal procedure, were drawn up and preliminary order was passed on 29 December 1949. The structure was attached and placed in the custody of the receiver Shri Priya Dutt Ram appointed by the Additional City Magistrate, Faizabad. The receiver was directed to submit a scheme for the management of the property in dispute during the period of its attachment. The receiver submitted the scheme on 5 January 1950 and the attached property is being managed in accordance with that scheme as modified by this Court in subsequent proceedings which will be noticed hereinafter. The worship of the idols is being ensured through a pujari appointed by the receiver. The property continues to be in possession of the receiver although the present receiver is an appointee of this Court.

The venue of litigation now shifts from the criminal court to the civil court. On 16 January 1950 against Shri Zahoor Ahmad and others including the State of Uttar Pradesh, the Deputy Commissioner, Faizabad, the Additional City Magistrate, Faizabad and the Superintendent of Police, Faizabad, claiming mainly the decree of permanent injunction to restrain the defendants from removing the idols of Shri Rama Chandraji from the place where they existed at Janmabhumi. A declaration was also sought to the effect that the plaintiff was entitled to perform Puja and Darshan by going near Bhagwan Rama Chandra Virajman Asthan Janmabhumi without any hindrance from the defendants. In this suit an application for interim injunction was made and interim injunction was granted by the Civil Judge, Faizabad. By order dated 19 January 1950 the interim order was modified at the instance of the government counsel. The modified order reads as follows:

> 'The parties are hereby restrained by means of temporary injunction to refrain from removing the idols in question from site in dispute and from interfering with puja etc. as at present carried on. . . .'

In the aforesaid suit written statement has been filed on behalf of the State of U.P. in which following averments have been made:

> '12. That the property in suit is known as Babri mosque and it has, for a long period, been in use as a mosque for the purpose of worship by the Muslims. It has not been in use as a temple of Shri Rama Chandraji.'
>
> '13. That on the night of the 22 December 1949 the idols of Shri Rama Chandraji were surreptitiously and wrongly put inside it.'
>
> '14. That as a result of the said wrongful act a situation imperiling public peace and tranquility was created and the public authorities had to intervene in order to prevent breaches of peace and tranquility.'

This written statement was verified on behalf of the State by the then deputy Commissioner, Faizabad Shri J.N. Ugra.

On 5.12.1950 suit no. 25 of 1950 was filed by Paramhans Ram Chandra Das against Zahoor Ahmad and others including State of Uttar Pradesh and the Deputy Commissioner, Faizabad. In this suit the plaintiff has sought a declaration that he is entitled to go near Bhagwan Sri Rama Chandra Virajman at Asthan Janmabhumi and to worship him and have his Darshan according to the customary rights of his religion without any check, obstruction or interference. A prohibitory injunction has also been sought to restrain the defendants from removing the idols. In this suit also written statement has been filed on behalf of the State of Uttar Pradesh and the Deputy Commissioner. In paragraphs 14, 15 and 16 of the written statement the pleas raised in paragraphs 12, 13 and 14 of the written statement filed in Suit No. 2 of 1950 have been reiterated. By order dated 1.2.1951 the Civil Judge, Faizabad consolidated the two suits.

On 17.12.1959 Nirmohi Akhara and its Mahant filed Suit No. 26 of 1959 against the receiver Shri Priya Dutt Ram and others including the State of U.P. and its officers. The suit was filed in the court of Civil Judge, Faizabad. The main relief claimed in the suit was for removal of the receiver and for delivery of the property to the plaintiffs.

On 18.12.1961 Sunni Central Board of Waqfs and others filed suit no. 12 of 1961 against Gopal Singh Visharad and others. The main relief claimed in the suit is declaration to the effect that the property indicated by letters A B C D in the sketch map attached to the plaint is public mosque commonly known as Babri Masjid and that the land adjoining the mosque and enclosed by letters EFGH is a public Muslim graveyard. In the event of plaintiffs being found to be out of possession alternative prayer for decree of possession of the mosque and graveyard by removal of the idols and other articles has also been made.

With the filing of the aforesaid suit by the Sunni Central Board of Waqf and others four suits had become pending in the court of Civil Judge, Faizabad. By order dated 6 January 1964 the learned Civil Judge consolidated all the four suits with the consent of the parties.

While the aforesaid suits were awaiting trial one Shri Umesh Chandra Pandey made application in suit no. 2 of 1950 for unlocking the gates of the structure and for allowing free entry into the building for Puja and Darshan etc. At the time the application was made, it appears the file of the case was in this Court. Accordingly the court directed that the file may be requisitioned from this Court. In the absence of file he did not pass any order on the application of Shri Umesh Chandra Pandey. The order was passed by the trial court on 28 January 1986. Against this order Shri Pandey filed appeal before the learned District Judge, Faizabad. In this appeal the petitioner Mohd. Hashim, one of the plaintiffs in Suit No. 12 of 1961, and Mohd. Farooq, son of Zahoor Ahmad, defendant no. 2 in Suit no. 2 of 1950, made application for being impleaded and heard. The learned District Judge by his order dated 1 February 1986 rejected the application of Mohd. Hashim and Mohd. Farooq and allowed the application of Shri Pandey. Against this order of the learned District Judge Writ Petition No. 746 of 1986 has been filed by petitioner Mohd. Hashim which is still pending. In this writ petition interim order was passed directing that the nature of the property in question shall not be changed till further orders of the Court.

On 12 May 1986 Sunni Central Board of Waqfs also filed writ petition to challenge the District Judge's order dated 1 February 1986.

On 16 December 1987 the State of U.P. filed application before this Court under Section. 24/1512 of the Code Civil Procedure, 1908 for withdrawal of all the four suits for trial by this Court. In this application it was also prayed that the hearing of the aforesaid writ petitions be deferred till the final disposal of the four suits. The application was allowed by order dated 10 July 1989. While withdrawing the suits to this Court a Division Bench of this Court also directed that the suits shall be heard by a Special Bench of three Judges.

While the above proceedings were going on fifth suit was filed by Shri Deoki Nandan Agarwal. This suit was also withdrawn for trial by this Court; its number is 236 of 1989. At first proceedings in the suit were stayed under Section 10 of the Code of Civil Procedure but later on the stay order was recalled and now this Suit is also being tried along with the other suits which are pending in this Court.

After all the aforesaid suits had been withdrawn to this Court the State Government made application on 7 August 1989 to restrain the parties from disturbing status quo and from organizing any activity which may lead to confrontation between Hindus and Muslims. By order dated 14 August 1989 the Special Bench directed the parties in all the five Suits to maintain status quo and to refrain from changing the nature of the property in question.

While the above Suits were pending and were almost ready for recording of oral evidence, issues having been framed earlier, the impugned Notifications were issued which led to the filing of the present six petitions. As already stated the Akhara claims to represent the interest of Ramanandi Bairagis, a sect of Hindus, while the petitioners in the other petitions claim to represent the interest of Muslims.

Pleas raised in the Writ Petitions

The acquisition is challenged on the following broad grounds—(1) Malafides, (2) Violation of Articles 25, 26, 15 and 14 of the Constitution, and (3) Non-application of mind to material facts resulting in the vulnerability of the satisfaction expressed in the impugned Notifications in respect of public purpose.

In elaboration of the plea of malafides the petitioners refer to certain political developments which took place in the State prior to the issue of the impugned Notifications. These political developments, as stated by the petitioners, may also be noticed.

On the very next day of the swearing in ceremony the Chief Minister Kalyan Singh and his Cabinet colleagues visited Ayodhya, entered the disputed structure and declared on oath their resolve to construct temple at the site of the structure. In support of the allegation, clipping from the daily newspaper *The Pioneer* dated 26 June 1991 has been filed as Annexure-5 to Mohd. Hashim's petition. The Muslim petitioners assert that this action of the Chief Minister and his Cabinet colleagues clearly shows that the present government is out to demolish and destroy the mosque and to construct temple at its site.

The petitioners point out that in furtherance of the above intention the district administration which had earlier put up barricades to protect the structure removed the same on 1st August 1991 under instructions of the Chief Minister, Shri Kalyan Singh. For this allegation also press report published in *Dainik Jagran* dated 2 August 1991 which has been filed as Annexure-6 is relied upon.

Reference is made of another statement allegedly made by Shri Kalyan Singh on 21 July 1991 at the meeting of 'Dharam Sansad' held at Ayodhya. Shri Kalyan Singh is alleged to have assured the gathering that the government will take all measures to remove hurdles in the construction of temple at the site of Babri Masjid.

On 31 July 1991 joint session of the State Legislature was held which was addressed by the State Governor. The Governor's address is also alleged to contain government's resolve to ensure construction of temple at the site of Babri Masjid. Barely two months after this statement, notification under Section 4 was issued on 7 October 1991 followed by notification under Section 6 on 10 October 1991.

In the backdrop of the above facts the petitioners assert that the notification of land for acquisition is a step in execution of the grand design hatched by the State Government, which is hand in glove with the VHP and the Bajrang Dal to destroy the mosque and the graveyard and build temple at the place. The purpose of acquisition disclosed in the notifications is alleged to be camouflaged.

The plea of camouflage is sought to be substantiated by reference to the acquisition of a nearby land in the year 1989 for construction of Rama Katha Park and its subsequent transfer by way of lease to a trust created by the VHP.

Copies of the trust deed and lease deed have been filed as Annexures 10-E and 10-F. The trust deed, Annexure-10-E, is dated 18 December 1985 and the lease deed, Annexure 10-F, is dated 20 March 1992. It is pointed out that this acquisition was also made for the purpose of development of tourism and providing amenities to pilgrims. Reference is made to the counter affidavits filed on behalf of the State in the writ petitions filed in this Court to challenge the said acquisition. Writ Petition No. 1931 of 1989 was filed by Smt Savitri Devi and Avdhesh Kumar and Writ Petition No. 436 of 1989 was filed by Tulsi Ram and others. In both the writ petitions counter affidavit was filed by a Junior Clerk in the office of the Regional Tourist Officer, Faizabad Region, Faizabad. In paragraphs 4 and 5 of the counter affidavit filed in Tulsi Ram's writ petition the following averments have been made:

> 4. That Association of Lord Rama with Ayodhya is well accepted and therefore, the government decided to create a place where tourist, pilgrims and other visitors can have special experience of being in a place which carries this special aura from Lord Rama's time.
>
> 5. That a decision was taken in the year 1986 to develop Rama Katha Park keeping in view the following objectives:
>
> (a) To create experience of cultural aspect emerging from the great epic *Ramayana*, particularly the aspects which have influenced the Indian way of life.
> (b) To create the place of unique tourists/pilgrims interest and attraction.
> (c) It should attract at least two thousand tourists everyday. The attraction will include environment, landscape, inscape components, etc. Use of traditional as well as high technology methods can be adopted for creating audio-visual and other effects depicting events from the great epic.
> (d) To generate direct and indirect employment for a fairly large number of people. The people could be employed for maintenance, management, tourism, hotel, catering etc. which is likely to result from such a place in Ayodhya.
> (e) The park should be integrated with the overall development of Ayodhya.
> (f) No built structures should be so created as to appear out of time and place context. If at all some buildings have to be made, they should not be obviously or visibly modern.
> (g) In order to have wider appeal and to uphold secular ideas, the emphasis should be on philosophic and on unique aspect of Rama's life rather than on ritualistic aspect.

The above averments have been repeated in the counter affidavit filed in Savitri Devi's writ petition. The petitioners point out that these averments show that earlier acquisition was also made for development of tourism and providing amenities to pilgrims. This land, it is alleged, instead of being utilized for the purpose stated in the counter affidavit has now been handed over by the present government to a trust controlled by VHP which is out to destroy Babri Masjid and the graveyard and to construct a temple at the site.

As another limb of the plea of malafides it is pointed out that enough vacant land is available in the vicinity of the acquired land and if the real purpose of acquisition is as disclosed in the notifications the said land could be made use of.

On the basis of the above facts the Muslim petitioners assert that the acquisition is a direct attack on their religious institutions with which are interwoven their religious practices and, therefore, the acquisition is hit by Articles 25 and 26 of the Constitution. Article 14 is invoked to press the plea of arbitrariness. According to the petitioners (1) it is arbitrary to acquire land when enough vacant land is available at the spot, (2) it is arbitrary to acquire land for the purpose of appeasing a particular religious group, (3) it is arbitrary to acquire land which is subject matter of litigation and thereby giving mileage to one party to the litigation over the other, and (4) it is arbitrary to acquire land belonging to one religious group for giving it over to another religious group.

In the counter affidavit filed on behalf of the State neither the existence of mosque is admitted nor of the graveyard. In this connection reference is made on behalf of the petitioners to several papers authored by the State Government and its officers in which existence of both is said to have been admitted. It is submitted that the mosque and the graveyard are religious institutions of the Muslims and cannot, therefore, be acquired. Alternatively it is submitted that even if they can be acquired, before proceeding to acquire, it has to be considered whether the purpose of acquisition can be achieved without touching land containing religious institutions. It is submitted that since the State Government denies the very existence of the two religious institutions of the Muslims it is obvious that the consideration mentioned herein has not been made. Therefore, the petitioners assert that the acquisition is vitiated by non-application of mind to relevant facts.

The petitioners also challenge the dispensing with of the enquiry under Section 5-A of the Act. They point out that litigation in respect of the land in question is pending for the last forty-one years and there was no such urgency as warranted dispensing with the enquiry. According to the petitioners if the enquiry under Section 5-A had not been dispensed with they would have been able to point out the vacant land available at the spot and the imprudence of acquiring the land in question which was the subject matter of litigation. It is also of the death of *kar sevaks*; 16 November 1991 and 18 November 1991 respectively were the days of Hindu festivals 'Brihad Parikrama' and 'Panch Koshi Parikrama'. On all these four days large number of pilgrims were expected to visit Ayodhya. It is stated that in the year 1990 about 98.66 lac people visited Ayodhya. In the year 1991 the influx was expected to be greater. There was not enough time left between the date of notification and the date on which these events were to take place and, therefore, the enquiry under Section 5-A was dispensed with.

It is also the case of the State that Ayodhya is a holy place and pilgrims visit the place also on the days other than the days mentioned above, of course the influx is greater on auspicious days.

Selection of site for acquisition has been justified by reference to the acquisition of adjoining land for Rama Katha park by notifications dated 20 January

1989, 23 January 1989 and 27 September 1989. It is stated that 55.6744-acres of land around and adjoining the land in question was acquired or granted for the purpose of Rama Katha Park. The land called Sri Ramjanmabhumi Asthal was at that time left out of acquisition. No plan for development of Rama Katha Park could be completed without Sri Ramjanmabhumi Asthal being included therein, as Rama Katha Park is designed to be completed around Sri Ramjanmabhumi. It is claimed that the land in question has been acquired so that an integrated plan can be prepared for development of this land and to provide amenities to pilgrims visiting Sri Ramjanmabhumi and to develop Sri Ramjanmabhumi as a tourist centre.

On aforesaid facts it is alleged that neither the acquisition nor the selection of site nor the application of urgency clause can be said to be vitiated by malafides, colourable exercise of power or ulterior motive. It is also the case of the State that the satisfaction of public purpose and selection of site are not justifiable. The State challenges also the locus standi of the petitioners to maintain the writ petitions.

Findings

(1) Acquired Land—Subject Matter of Litigation

The most important question arising for consideration is whether the acquired land or any portion thereof is subject matter of litigation between the Hindus and the Muslims.

While the case of the petitioners is that the acquired land is subject matter of litigation referred to herein above the case of the State is that no portion of the acquired land is subject matter of the said litigation.

The State does not dispute the pendency of the litigation referred to herein-above. Its plea is that the litigation is confined to the structure which is in possession of the receiver appointed in proceedings under Section 145 of the Code of Criminal Procedure. The plea of the State is entirely misconceived. Section 145 proceedings may have started with placement of idols inside the main roofed structure and the receiver may have been appointed only in respect of that portion of the structure where the idols exist but the Sunni Board's suit is not confined to that portion alone. In that suit declaration of title and possession has been sought not only in respect of the place where the idols exist but also in respect of the entire structure and the land around it which has been described as graveyard. The pendency of litigation has to be seen in respect of this property.

The acquired land is divisible into two parts—(1) the outer courtyard, and (2) the land around the structure.

Annexure A-10 is copy of the plaint in Sunni Board's suit which is the leading suit and in which steps under Order I, rule 8 of the Code of Civil Procedure, for short CPC, have been taken. It contains a sketch map of the property in suit. The property in suit is shown in the form of a rectangle and is alleged to contain a mosque and a graveyard. The mosque is delineated by letters ABCD. On all the four sides of ABCD is shown graveyard. Within the property enclosed by letters ABCD is shown 'Chabutra Masjid'. Within this Chabutra is delineated a portion of which measurements are shown as 21' x 17'. To the east of this Chabutra is shown a graveyard. The graveyard is shown to the west and south of ABCD also. Immediately to the north of ABCD is shown a graveyard and thereafter *pucca* road and again a graveyard. The entire property adjoining the mosque and the graveyard is shown enclosed by letters EFGH.

The acquisition map filed by the State is Annexure-A. The acquired land has been shown in light red colour and the property which has been left out of acquisition has been shown in yellow colour. From this map it transpires that the entire land around ABCD referred to above has been acquired except a small portion on the east which provides a passage for entry into the structure. A portion of land comprised in ABCD has also been acquired. This portion is the same which has been referred to in the topography as outer courtyard. The structure which is claimed by the Muslims as mosque and inner courtyard have been left out of acquisition. From this it would appear that only a small portion of the land which is subject matter of litigation has been left out of acquisition; this left out portion is the structure which is claimed to be mosque or temple and the inner courtyard. From this it is apparent that the acquired property is subject matter of litigation. Commissioner submitted his report against which objections were filed on behalf of the defendants. The objections were upheld and the report was rejected. On these facts all that can be said is that till date the land in suit remains unidentified. In cannot be said that it has ceased to be under litigation. The plaintiffs still have the option to chose the next step to identify the land and establish their title and possession thereto.

In view of the above, the petitioners are right in submitting that the acquired land covers substantial part of the property under litigation.

(2) Consequence of above finding

The State's consistent case has been that the acquired land is not subject matter of litigation. From this it is reasonable to infer that the State would not have proceeded with the acquisition of the land in question, if it had been informed that the acquired land was in fact subject matter of litigation. Once it is found that the acquired land is subject matter of litigation it automatically follows that the Report was lodged by an official of the State and thereafter proceedings under Section 145 of the Code of Criminal Procedure were initiated and the disputed property was attached. It is for this intervention by the State that in the suit the State of U.P. and some of its functionaries were impleaded. No relief is claimed against the State and its functionaries. The State through its application dated 23 April 1962, Annexure RA-19, in Sunni Board's case informed the Court in unmistakable terms that it has no interest in the property in dispute. In paragraph 1 it is stated—'that the government is not interested in the properties in dispute and as such the petitioners don't propose to contest the suit'. From this application it is apparent that the 'lis' in the suit is between the Hindus and the Muslims and there is no 'lis' between the State and the Hindus or State and the Muslims.

Learned counsel for the petitioners, however, points out that the State has been intervening in various ways and has been making applications even for obtaining interim orders and, therefore, it is not possible to say that there is no 'lis' with the State. . . .

There is no denial of the factum of commencement of temple. All that is stated is that the State Government have made no constructions whatsoever on the acquired land. The State Government cannot disclaim its responsibility, if any, construction is made on the acquired land during the pendency of the writ petition in view of the interim order dated 25 October 1991 passed by this Court. By that interim order the State had been allowed to take possession of the acquired land and to make arrangements for the purpose notified in the notifications. From this it is apparent that after taking possession the State could make arrangements only for the purpose notified in the impugned notifications. The further direction in the interim order is 'no structure of permanent nature shall be put up thereon although structures of temporary nature may be put up'. Construction of temple in my opinion would be putting up a structure of permanent nature. Learned counsel for the petitioners is therefore, justified in submitting that the purpose of acquiring the land in question was not the one mentioned in the impugned notifications but the one which is now revealed by the actual state of affairs, namely construction of a Hindu temple. The State was in so much hurry to get the temple constructed that it could not wait even for the disposal of the present writ petitions.

As mentioned hereinabove, in the year 1988 the State Government acquired land for construction of Rama Katha park. This land adjoins the land now acquired by the impugned notifications. In respect of this acquisition, as pointed out earlier, writ petitions numbered 436 and 1931 of 1989 have been filed in this Court. Paragraphs 4 and 5 of the counter affidavit filed in the former petition have been reproduced earlier. From the averments made in these paragraphs it is apparent that the purpose of the acquisition was also development of tourism and amenities to pilgrims. This land has now admittedly been transferred by the State through lease deed dated 20 march 1992 in favour of a private trust known as Sri Ramjanmabhumi Nyas, Annexure 10-F. The petitioner Mohd. Hashim has placed on record a copy of the trust deed creating the Nyas as Annexures 10-E which is dated 18 December 1985. A perusal of the trust deed shows that amongst the trustees are Shri Ashok Singhal, Shri Vishnu Hari Dalmia and Shri Mahant Paramhans Ram Chandra Das. The objects of the trusts are as follows. . . .

The first object of the trust is to reconstruct the temple of Sri Rama at Sri Ramjanmabhumi and the beautification of the spot all around. Rest of the objects are connected with the reconstruction of the temple and re-installation of deities. From this it would follow that the trust is a religious one. In paragraph 42-B of the writ petition it has been stated that Shri V.H. Dalmia, one of the trustees, is President of Vishwa Hindu Parishad and Shri Ashok Singhal is its General Secretary. It has also been stated that all the trustees are office bearers of the

Vishwa Hindu Parishad and the Rashtriya Swayam Sewak Sangh or the activists of these two organizations.

In paragraph 15 of the State's counter affidavit dated 15 May 1992 execution of the lease deed in favour of the aforesaid Nyas has not been disputed. The association of the trustees with the Vishwa Hindu Parishad and Rashtriya Swayam Sewak Sangh has also not been disputed.

Apart from the aforesaid documents the petitioners rely upon several newspaper clippings for substantiating the plea that ever since the Bharatiya Janata Party formed the government in the State of Uttar Pradesh it has been making all out efforts for construction of temple at the disputed place. Learned counsel for the State challenges the admissibility of these clippings. . . .

From the above averments it is apparent that the land of Rama Katha Park and the present land are to be used for one and the same purpose. The land of Rama Katha park has already been handed over to a trust whose aims and objects are religious and whose trust board is dominated by members of Vishwa Hindu Parishad. Clause (b) refers to reconstruction of the temple of Bhagwan Sri Rama Virajman. Bhagwan Sri Rama is 'virajman' within the disputed structure.

Apart from the newspaper clipping referred to hereinabove there are a large number of other such clippings. In view of the fact that the malafides are established from the aforesaid evidence, it is not necessary to refer to the other newspaper clippings.

The aforesaid evidence abundantly establishes that the purpose of acquisition shown in the impugned notifications is camouflaged.

It is also established that the impugned acquisition has been made in order to give advantage to Hindus in the litigation referred to hereinabove.

Learned counsel for the State tries to skirt the above factual position by giving a narrow interpretation to the allegations made by the petitioners of malafides, ulterior motive and colourable exercise of . . . 7 October, 1991, Annexure No. 7 is a colourable exercise of power.'. . .

XVII. Because the Notifications contained in Annexure No. 7 and No. 8 are a fraud upon the law and have been used to further political ends of the ruling party—Bharatiya Janata Party; and

'XXIV- Because there is no real purpose for the acquisition of the land in question as defined in the Act and the State Amendment and the Notifications No. 7 and 8 are totally malafide.'

Strong reliance has been placed by the learned counsel for the respondents for submitting that the only ground for alleging malafide and ulterior motive and colourable exercise of power is that the State Government intends to destroy the Babri Masjid. I am unable to agree with the submission. Apart from making the allegation relating to destruction of Babri Masjid it is also averred that the purpose of acquisition is to hand over the acquired land to Hindus for utilizing the same in construction of a temple thereon. (See paragraphs 42 and 46 above). The assurance given on behalf of the State extends only to protection of the structure and the inner courtyard. The assurance does not extend to the outer courtyard which, as held above, is also subject matter of litigation. I may now take up the assurance given by the Chief Minister and the State.

The assurance given by the Chief Minister has been reproduced hereinabove. That assurance indeed says that pending final solution the Government of U.P. will hold itself fully responsible for the protection of Ramjanmabhumi–Babri Masjid structure. This assurance has been relied upon by their lordships of the Supreme Court in their order dated 15.11.1991 passed in writ petition no. 1000 of 1991. I accept the assurance given on behalf of the State that the disputed structure shall remain protected so long as litigation is pending between the two religious groups and I proceed on the assumption that private land can be acquired for construction of temple as construction of temple is public purpose. The impugned acquisition cannot be saved in view of our findings that (1) the purpose of acquisition is to give advantage to one party to litigation over the other, and (2) to give favourable treatment to one religious group over the other. The first violates Article 14 of the Constitution as it is discriminatory as well as arbitrary, and the second violates Article 15(1) which mandates that 'the State shall not discriminate against any citizens on grounds only of religion. . . .'. Since the discrimination in the present case is based on religion, Article 15 is attracted.

Learned counsel for the State, however, submits that the action of the State cannot be said to be arbitrary as construction of temple at Ayodhya was a part of the election manifesto of the Bharatiya Janata Party. . . .

To sum up my conclusions: the purpose of acquisition mentioned in the impugned notifications is a public purpose; construction of temple is also a public purpose; a land acquired for one public purpose can be used for another public purpose, but it cannot be used for a private purpose; in the context of the religious importance of Ayodhya, construction of a Hindu temple is not beyond the connotation of the expression 'development of tourism and providing amenities to pilgrims at Ayodhya in District Faizabad'; but the present acquisition is vitiated as under the garb of the notified purpose the intention from the very beginning was to give advantage to one group of litigants over the other and to one religious group over the other, attracting violation of Articles 14 and 15; in a private dispute, the State is required to observe neutrality; neutrality is implicit in Article 14; the impugned action lacks the neutrality and is, therefore, constitutionally invalid. . . .

2. Hereinabove I have observed 'I accept the assurance given on behalf of the State that the disputed structure shall remain protected so long as litigation is pending between the two religious groups'. This observation has become irrelevant in as much as on 6 December 1992 the structure has been demolished. Of course no affidavit has been filed by either side to bring this fact to our notice but the fact has been so widely broadcast through official media that we cannot fail to take notice of it.

3. I clarify that the entire opinion is based on the position obtaining prior to the demolition of the structure on 6 December 1992.

4. The Bench has been accused of inordinately delaying pronouncement of judgement and thereby contributing to the destruction of the structure. I do not propose to offer any justification for my 'lethargy' through the present post script. I only wish to place on record a fact and the procedure of pronouncing judgement in a case which has been heard by a Bench of three Judges. First the fact which has bearing on the allegation that the delay has contributed to the destruction of the structure:

(a) The present writ petitions have nothing to do with the roofed structure which has been demolished. In the writ petitions the dispute is. . . .

(i) The arguments concluded on 4.11.1992.

(j) The leading opinion was framed by me. My brethren Brijesh Kumar and S.H.A. Raza have added their own separate opinions. Both have concurred with my final conclusion. However, brother Raza has differed on certain points.

35b. Justice S.H.A. Raza's observations

Justice S.H.A. Raza said:
The genesis of 'Ayodhya' imbroglio lay in the beliefs of crores of Indian people, that Lord Sri Rama Chandra Ji was born at 'Ayodhya'. On the scale of historicity, such a faith cannot be established for the only reason that Lord Sri Rama Chandra Ji manifested Himself in the prehistoric period. According to the scholars of Hindu scriptures, Lord Sri Rama Chandra Ji filled the world with compassion and ushered in an epoch making highest democratic order, more than five thousand years before Lord Christ.

The following words of *Bhagwad Gita* (Chapter X, *shloka* 31, translated from the Sanskrit to English by Jaya Dayal Goyandka, Gita Press, Gorakhpur) show that Lord Sri Rama Chandra Ji revealed prior to the events of *Mahabharata* which—according to the authors, who have made their expertise in Sanskrit language—dates back to about two thousand years before Lord Christ:

Pawanah pawtamasmi ramah shastra bhritamaham
Jhashanam makrashchasmi strota samismjahvi.

Meaning thereby that Lord Krishna told Arjun 'Amongst purifiers, I am wind, amongst the wielders of weapons, I am (Sri) Rama. Amongst fishes I am shark, and amongst the streams, I am Ganga.'

In 'Bal Khand Sarg-3 Adhiyatm Ramayana' (Braham Puran Uttarakhand) great saint Ved Vyasa in the following words commented that 'Ayodhya' was ruled by Raja Dasharatha:

Ath raja dasharatha shriman satyaparayanah
Ayodhyadhipatirvir sarvlokeshu vishnutah.

As per the great epic *Ramacharitamanas* composed by the greatest-amongst-the-great poet Sant Goswami Tulsidas in the verse mentioned hereinunder, stated that Dasharatha was the king of Avadhpuri:

Avadhpuri raghukulmani rado ved vidit
Tehi dasharatha nado dharamdhurandhar
Gun nidhi gyani hriday bhagati mati
Saranga pani.
(Verse 4—after Doha-187)

Meaning thereby, that the King of Avadhpuri was the jewel of Raghuvansh or Kul. He was Dasharatha, a name by which he has been known in the Vedas. He was a champion of virtue, a repository of good qualities and a man of wisdom and was a devotee of Lord Vishnu, that is wielder of the Saranga bow.

Goswami Tulsidas, dealing with the birth of great Lord, described the birth of the great Lord as mentioned below:

Mandir mahnisaburajahirbani shobhai shebihtej ki khani
Naumi tithi mahu mas puneera sukul paksh abhijit hari preeta
Bhaye pragat kripala deen dayala kaushalya hitkari
Harshit mahtari muniman hari adbhut roop vichari
Dasharatha putra janm suni kana manjhu brahamnand samana
Jakar nam sunat shubh hoi more grih aava prabhu soi
Kaikay suta sumitra do do sunder sut jahnat bhai d-do
Avadhpuri sohai khi bhanti prabhuhi milan aai janurani
(Bal Kand, earlier to Doha-195)

Meaning thereby, that the palace had shown all the Queens who were full of beauty, and virtue, of glory, and that time was an occasion of happiness. On the Sukul Pakaha Naumi of sacred Chaitramasa, the gracious Lord, who is compassionate to the lowly and poor and being benefactor of Kaushalya, revealed Himself. The thought of the marvellous face which stole the heart of sages filled the heart of mother Kaushalya with joy. Dasharatha hearing the news of the birth of a son was filled with supreme pleasure, particularly with the idea that the one whose name is such, hearing of which blessing would come to his house. Both Kaikayee and Sumitra also gave birth to beautiful sons. On this occasion the city of Avadhpuri wore a gala appearance. It looked as if night had come to meet its Lord.

Further the following words in Uttar Kand exhibits that the great Lord was born in Avadhpuri:

Ihan bhanukul kamal diwakar kapina dekhawat nagar manohar
Sunu kapis angad lankesh pawan puri ruchir yah desa
Jaddapi sab baikunth bakhana ved puran vidit jag jana
Avadhpuri sam priy nahi so-do yah prasang janai koi ko-do
Janmbhumi mam puri suhawari uttar disi bah sarjoo pawani

Neither the great Saint Ved Vyas nor Goswami Tulsidas, could have ever imagined, that their epic by the passage of time would become an article of faith for millions of men and women. As far as *Ramacharitamanas* is concerned, it is regarded as the most sacred book and is widely read over throughout the country, and in the world all over, where Indians live.

Manifestation of Lord Sri Ram Chandra Ji in Avadhpuri, which according to scholars is synonymous to 'Ayodhya' may not be established historically, but it has become an article of faith for the crores of Indian people, and it may be said that this question cannot be subjected to judicial scrutiny. . . .

In view of the aforesaid circumstances, the Special Bench while disposing of the Miscellaneous Application no. 48 of 1989 on 7.11.1989 in original suit no. 4 of 1989 in re: the Sunni Central Board of Waqfs and others *versus* Shri Gopal Singh Visharad and others had remarked: 'It is doubtful that some of the questions involved in the suit are solvable by judicial process.'

The question as to whether Lord Sri Rama Chandra Ji has ever revealed or born in Ayodhya may not be gone into by the Court, but it remains to be seen, as to whether other questions, regarding faith and belief involved in the suits can be subjected to judicial scrutiny or not.

The Judge traced the nineteenth-century litigation and said, 'The Deputy Commissioner, Faizabad in March–April, 1883 on account of objections raised by some Muslims prohibited construction of the temple, thereupon the petitioner submitted representation to the local government, but when no reply was received the plaintiff gave notice under section 414 of the C.P.C. on 18.8.1884 to the office of Secretary, local government, but no reply of that also was received, hence the cause of action of filing the suit arose on the date of prohibition at Ayodhya within the local limit of the jurisdiction of this Court.

One Mohammad Asghar, claiming him, to be the Mutwalli of the said shrine, which he claimed to be the Babri Mosque, was impleaded as the defendant. On behalf of the Secretary of the State as well as Mohammad Asghar the suit was contested. The Court appointed Shri Gopal Sahay, as a commissioner to prepare site-plan of the site and to submit his report. Shri Gopal Sahay inspected the site and prepared a site plan in the presence of Mahant Raghubar Das and Mohammad Asghar Khan and on 6.12.1885 the commissioner submitted his report along with a site plan signed by him, Mahant Raghubar Das, as well as, Mohammad Asghar. The said site plan has been filed in the present writ petition as well. The site plan shows the graves over all the four sides, facing the outer boundary of the shrine. Just after the outer wall towards the east Ganj-e-Shahidan, i.e., abode of Martyrs and 'Qabristan' finds mentioned. On the main gate of the outer wall of the said shrine towards east the word 'Allah' finds mention. In the report in the outer courtyard of the said shrine towards East and South a platform that is Chabutra '17 ft x 21 ft' finds mention. Upon the said platform a temple or idol finds place. The word 'Qabristan' that is graveyard finds mention, on all the four sides of the outer portion of the said shrine. Towards the north in the outer portion of the shrine, 'Sita Rasoi' finds mention and towards the south of the outer portion of the shrine within the outer-wall *Hauz* or Gusulkhana finds mention at least at two places.

On 24.12.1885 Pandit Hari Kishan, Sub-judge, Faizabad recorded a finding that on seeing of the spot it was evident that 'Charan' i.e. foot was embraced on 'Chabootra', which was being worshipped, and over that 'Chabootra' an idol of 'Thakur Ji' was installed. The 'Chabootra' was in possession of the plaintiff and whatever offering was made it was taken away by the plaintiff, and this fact was also admitted by Mohammad Asghar, the defendant. The witnesses of the plaintiff also proved the possession of the plaintiff. For that reason a *pakka* wall-like fence has been constructed to fix the boundaries of the land held by Hindus and Muslims. The suit was dismissed. . . .

Here it would be necessary to point out the vacillating, wavering and ever-changing stand of the State Government. In all the suits, the plaintiffs asserted their right of worship into the shrine thereby in one way or the other challenging the rights of the State and its officers who had put in an embargo into their religious rights by attaching the property. At least in two suits filed in the year 1950 the written statements as well as the objections against the grant of injunctions were filed on behalf of State and its officers. From the order sheets of the suit filed by Gopal Singh Visharad beginning from 14.10.1950 to 25.11.1961 the District Government Counsel has put in his appearance.

On 23.5.1962/28.5.1962 an application was moved by D.G.O. (Civil) in Regular Suit No. 61 filed by Sunni Board of Waqfs stating that the government was not interested in the property in suit and as such it did not propose to contest the suit. It was mentioned that in the aforesaid circumstances the State and its officers be exempted from costs. It was further averred that defendants 6 to 8 were State officers and their action in respect of the property in dispute were bonafide and in due discharge of their official duties. It was also stated in the application and that they did not want to contest the plaintiffs' application for treating the suit as a representative suit under Order 1 Rule 8 C.P.C. They prayed that the defendants be exempted from costs of the suit. This application was allowed and an order proceeding ex parte against the State and its officers was passed.

On the basis of the aforesaid averments, it was contended on behalf of the State Government that the role of the State Government was neutral. There existed no 'lis' against the State of U.P. The dispute was confined between the private parties over a private party. The interim orders or injunctions are only operative against the private parties and are not directed against the State.

The argument on the face of it appears to be misconceived. It was the State of U.P. and its officers who attached the property in question by means of a preliminary order passed under section 145 Cr.P.C. On behalf of State of U.P. as well as its officers, written statements were filed in some of the suits. Objections were filed against the application for grant of injunction. The order of injunction was modified at the behest of the District Administration that the idols kept in the Janmabhumi would not be removed, which order was upheld by the High Court.

It was the State Government which approached this court to withdraw the cases from various courts of Faizabad and try the same by itself. It was on the application of the State that interim orders were passed and later on clarified that it extends to all the plots in suit including the plot no. 586, but, suddenly after 1 June 1991 the stand of the State underwent a complete change. The government identified itself with one community against another. The counsel who was conducting the cases on behalf of one community after becoming the Advocate General identified the interest of one community with the interest of the State Government. Application for the recall of the orders passed by this court earlier, were moved and when it was rejected special leave petitions were filed in the Supreme Court. After a lapse of about 42 years from the date when the suits which were filed in 1950, the State Government preferred applications for amending its written statements and after a lapse of about 31 years from the date of filing of Regular Suit no. 12 of 1961, application for seeking permission to file written statement were filed. The contents of those applications indicate that the State Government completely identified itself with one community against the interest of another community.

In view of the aforesaid situation, it cannot be said that the State Government and its officers are only the formal party in the suits and there is no 'lis' between the State or plaintiffs in the suit. 'Lis' means, a suit, cause of action, controversy or dispute. Nobody would deny that there are about four suits, there is definitely cause of action against the State in most of the cases. A controversy or dispute exists in which the State is not only a party but a certain action of the State has been challenged. Subsequent events that led to demolition of the shrine and the masterly inaction of the State Government proved beyond any shadow of doubt, that the State Government was an accomplice of that shameful and dastardly act, which has desecrated the democratic and secular character of Indian Constitution. . . .

Regarding applicability of Art. 25 and 26 of the Constitution, the aforesaid observations were made when draft judgement prepared by brother Mathur, J. was before me. It appears that later on brother S.C. Mathur, J. revised his draft, hence it is necessary for me to say a few words about the same.

According to the petitioners, except Nirmohi Akhara the graveyard and the mosque is inseparably attached to the religious practice of the Muslims. In the *kabristan* the burial of the dead takes place according to the religious practices. Before the burial, *namaz-e-Janaza* 'burial prayer' is performed. Thereafter Muslims offer *fateha* on the graves. It has been pointed out on the basis of certain authorities on Muslim Law that burial, *fateha* and *namaz-e-Janaza* are the religious practices, which are traced from the practice of Prophet as 'Sunna'. . . . Justice Raza concurred with the other judges in striking down as invalid the State Government's notifications of 7 and 10 October 1991 acquiring the land at Ayodhya.

CHAPTER VIII

The CBI's Chargesheet on the Crime and the Sessions Judge's Charges

1. The CBI's chargesheet of October 1993

The CBI filed the chargesheet today in the court of Special Magistrate at Lucknow. 40 persons have been cited as accused in cases involving offences of criminal conspiracy, intentional destruction and defiling of a place of worship, promoting enmity between groups on grounds of religion, insulting religious feelings, criminal trespass, intimidation of public servants, etc. The case was taken over for investigation by the CBI on the request of Uttar Pradesh police immediately after the destruction of disputed structure against lakhs of *kar sevaks* in general without specifying the names of the accused persons. In one such case, chargesheet was filed in the court of Special Magistrate, Mata Tila in District Lalitpur in which the accused persons included Shri L.K. Advani, Murli Manohar Joshi, Ashok Singhal, Vishnu Hari Dalmia, Giriraj Kishore and Vinay Katiyar as also Ms Uma Bharati and Sadhvi Rithambara. At that time, the accused persons were also arrested by the U.P. Police and produced in court.

After detailed investigation, CBI has been able to collect substantial evidence establishing a case of prior planning and conspiracy and taking of steps to execute the object of conspiracy and destruction of the disputed structure at Ayodhya on 6 December 1992. The evidence has been painstakingly collected from a very large number of witnesses, transcripts of speeches collected from audio-cassettes, video-cassettes, photographs and published material as also documents recovered during searches, all of which has been carefully scrutinized and pieced together to work out the case. This entire evidence along with the statements recorded of witnesses has been analyzed and evaluated by legal experts at the top professional level.

As a result of the above efforts, a chargesheet has been filed today against the more prominent persons who participated in this conspiracy or were instrumental, directly or indirectly, in taking concrete steps in furtherance of this conspiracy which resulted in the demolition of the disputed structure. This list includes Bal Thackeray, L.K. Advani, Kalyan Singh, Ashok Singhal, Vinay Katiyar, Moreshwar Save, Pawan Kumar Pandey, Jai Bhagwan Goel, Ms Uma Bharati, Sadhvi

Rithambara, Murli Manohar Joshi, V.H. Dalmia, the former DM (Anand Srivastava), former SP (D.B. Rai), Faizabad and 26 others.

While filing the chargesheet, the CBI have not arrested or produced the accused persons in court. It is the intention to secure attendance of the accused persons through court process after obtaining the orders of court.

The investigation team of the CBI was headed by a Joint Director assisted by two Dy Inspector Generals of Police, six Superintendents of Police and a number of Dy Superintendents of Police and Inspectors. During the course of investigation, nearly 850 witnesses were examined and over 700 documents and 100 articles were seized or collected. Video-cassettes, photographs and reports made by media persons were also examined along with a number of other documents which yielded a large volume of evidence. The witnesses examined also included a number of *kar sevaks* who allegedly admitted to having taken part in the demolition on 6 December 1992 as also the media persons who were present on the spot to witness and documented the entire happenings.

The investigations further revealed that during May–June 1991, General Elections were held as a result of which BJP came to power in U.P. and other states and Shri Kalyan Singh was sworn in as the Chief Minister of U.P. on 6 June 1991 which opened avenues of a new dimension to the construction of the temple at Ayodhya. According to investigation, the BJP in its election manifesto had also emphasized the construction of the Shri Rama temple at Ayodhya and in accordance with the same, after the swearing-in-ceremony of Shri Kalyan Singh which was on 25 June 1991, that Shri Kalyan Singh along with Shri Murli Manohar Joshi and others which included the BJP members of the U.P. Cabinet and the BJP legislators visited Ayodhya and offered prayers before the idol of Rama Lalla placed under the central dome of the disputed structure as aforesaid and in the course of their visit, both Shri Kalyan Singh and Shri M.M. Joshi had taken a vow to construct temple there and in that in his tenure as Chief Minister, U.P., a temple of Shri Rama shall inevitably stand constructed and amidst other slogans Shri Kalyan Singh had assertively raised this slogan as well that '*Rama Lalla hum aye hai, Mandir yehin banayenge*'.

That in consonance with the existing scheme which ultimately projected the liberation of the temples at Ayodhya, Varanasi and also Mathura, it stands positively revealed during the investigation that accused 1 to 38 along with others entered into/were parties to criminal conspiracy during the period October 1990 to 6 December 1992 wherein while embracing in their aforesaid objective of liberating the three temples at Ayodhya, Kashi and Mathura, it was assertively decided to initiate such process with the demolition of the disputed structure, i.e. Babri Masjid–Ramjanmabhumi at Ayodhya, and to take away Mir Baqi Ka Shila Lekh, which was fixed above the main gate of the disputed structure. Such demolition was to be carried on jointly and/or severally, by deliberate acts/or omissions of all such conspirators/accused as aforesaid which in the ultimate analysis even embraced flouting/violating the specific orders of the Hon'ble Supreme Court of India and the Lucknow Bench of Allahabad High Court wherein protection of such disputed structure as aforesaid stood emphatically envisaged. That on 6.12.92 at about 12 noon some accused finally participated in the demolition of the disputed structure along with others which was committed with full knowledge that the same inevitably would not only result in causing communal disharmony between Hindus and Muslims being prejudicial to the national integration but also cause injury to the religious feelings of the Muslims by outraging/promoting enmity between Hindus and Muslims on the basis of religion with intent to incite them and also cause in wide and wild ramifications resulting in outcome of colossal loss to life and property in India and abroad by way of communal riots.

That in pursuance of the above said criminal conspiracy, Shri Moreshwar Save, MP, Shiv Sena, leader of Shiv Sena in the Parliament and Co-ordinator of North India Shiv Sena wrote a letter dated 17.7.91 to Shri Kalyan Singh, the then Chief Minister of Uttar Pradesh stating that the Hindu organizations have been running a movement for the last about five years for renovation of Shri Ramjanmabhumi temple in which accused Kalyan Singh was also connected. That after the two governments in the centre fell on the same issue, the BJP and Shiv Sena had made this an issue for the 1991 elections and hoped that they will come to power in the Centre, including Uttar Pradesh, however, on account of change of situation after the death of Shri Rajiv Gandhi, it could not be fulfilled. However, they came as formidable opposition party in the centre and the BJP formed its government in the state of Uttar Pradesh. That the public was eager to see the result of any issue immediately and that the Sri Rama temple work should be completed very early in which cause the contribution of the Uttar Pradesh Government was commendable. However, it should be necessary to expedite matters by removing some legal hurdles and the date for start of construction of the temple will have to be announced. He apprehended that the Central Government may put some obstacle in this work but he promised on behalf of the Shiv Sena that if any such situation arises, in that event the Shiv Sena will not refrain from agitating inside the Parliament and also country wide. That if there happens to be any delay in this work, then the public will not forgive them and in that situation, the Shiv Sena will not go back from starting an all India wide movement and opposing anybody. He expressed confidence in the efficiency and devotion of Shri Kalyan Singh and hoped that besides the Ramjanmabhumi Mandir, efforts will also continue to liberate other Hindu temples which symbolize Hindu faith i.e. Sri Krishna Janma temple at Mathura and Vishwanatha Dham, Kashi. It is revealed during investigation that Shri Kalyan Singh on receipt of this letter of accused Moreshwar Save while acknowledging receipt of the same vide his letter dated 31.7.91, he as well asserted that as per the contents of Shri Save's aforesaid letter necessary action was being carried on.

The investigation has revealed that in an institution run by the VHP at Sarkhej (Ahmedabad), named Yuva Shourya Prashikshan Kendra/India Welfare and Research Foundation Trust, Bajrang Dal and Durga Vahini activists were trained during 22.9.1991 to 6.10.1991 in unarmed combat, air-gun shooting, rope climbing, etc. These activists were selected by Bajrang Dal of Gujarat. On the last day of training, i.e. on 6.10.1991 the closing ceremony was attended amongst others by Shri Ashok Singhal, General Secretary of VHP, Shri Moropant Pingle, an RSS leader, Shri Giriraj Kishore, Joint General Secretary, VHP.

That in pursuance of above said criminal conspiracy, the BJP government in U.P. acquired 2.77-acres of land in October 1991 adjacent to the disputed structure under the pretext of developing the same for tourism purposes. The land was levelled and in the process of levelling a number of small temples in the complex, viz. Kaushalya Mandir, Sakshi Gopal Mandir, etc. were demolished.

That several Writ Petitions in this regard were filed in the High Court at Allahabad whereby attention was specifically drawn questioning the acquisition of land as aforesaid and the Hon'ble High Court on 25.10.91 passed order, inter-alia, while allowing the Government of U.P. to take possession of land further prohibited permanent construction on such acquired land as aforesaid.

That on 2 November 1991 at New Delhi a meeting of the National Integration Council was held which was as well attended by Shri Kalyan Singh as Chief Minister of U.P. Amongst other factors the matter in particular of serious concern to the National Integration Council was the communal tension regarding Ramjanmabhumi–Babri Masjid dispute and while expressing its concern at the happenings at Ayodhya the Council resolved for a satisfactory solution. In this regard Shri Kalyan Singh, amongst other assurances given to the Council, specifically asserted that the Government of Uttar Pradesh will hold itself fully responsible for the protection of Ramjanmabhumi–Babri Masjid structure.

That the Hon'ble Supreme Court in a pending matter before it took into account the assurances of Shri Kalyan Singh before the National Integration Council and also before the Allahabad High Court as aforesaid and vide its order dated 15.11.91 emphatically directed fool-proof compliance in respect of the same.

That according to the investigation, positive steps to achieve the objectives of the aforesaid conspiracy during the tenure of Shri Kalyan Singh as Chief Minister of the U.P. government were taken. There was a progressive and systematic reduction in the various security measures around the disputed structure thereby endangering its security.

That in furtherance of the above said 'Criminal Conspiracy', a meeting of the Kendriya Marg Darshak Mandal was held in Ujjain on 13.5.92 and was attended by Shri Ashok Singhal and others wherein two resolutions were passed for removing the obstacles in the construction of Rama *dewar* and temple and threatening the Central Government that it would be ousted out of power if it stood in the way of construction of Rama temple. In the Press Conference in presence of Shri Ashok Singhal, it was briefed that as Muslim king Babar did not give any date for demolition of the temple and the construction of the mosque, similarly the date for demolition of the Masjid and construction of temple at its place will also not be given.

That in furtherance of the above said criminal conspiracy a concrete platform was not constructed at Ramjanmabhumi complex on the 2.77-acres acquired land which was started on 9 July 1992. It was against this that contempt petitions were filed in the Supreme Court which observed on 23 July 1992 that there are already earlier orders of the Supreme Court as well as of the High Court of Allahabad which interdict any construction and those orders have been flouted and disobeyed by the respondents.

That it is further revealed from investigation that Shri Moreshwar Save wrote a letter dated 10.7.92 to accused Shri L.K. Advani congratulating him on the start of construction of Shri Ramjanmabhumi temple at Ayodhya on 9.7.92 and stated that it would be considered as an important step in the History of India towards establishment of a 'Hindu Rashtra'. He also wrote that he knew that they have to oppose the forces which are active against 'Hindu Rashtra', Hindutva and Sri Rama temple construction. He informed that the Shiv Sena would be with Shri Advani on the work of Shri Ramjanmabhumi Mandir at Ayodhya, Shri Kashi Vishveshwar and Shri Krishna Bhumi Mandir, Mathura and that they will not go back from any sacrifices. This letter was acknowledged by Shri L.K. Advani vide his letter dt. 20.7.92, wherein Shri Advani shared the feelings communicated in the letter of Shri Save.

That a meeting of the 'Dharam Sansad' was held at New Delhi from 29.10.92 to 31.10.92 and the Kendriya Marg Darshak Mandal announced starting of *kar seva* at Ramjanmabhumi–Babri Masjid Complex from 6.12.92.

That Shri Ashok Singhal on 12.11.92 addressed the students of Kanpur and at Ramjanmabhumi, Ayodhya, and asked them to take over the responsibility of Shri Ramjanmabhumi movement work. He told them that in the *kar seva* starting from 6.12.1992 they will construct Singh Dwar, Nritya Mandap, Sabha Mandap and then remove the aforesaid *Mir Baqi Ka Shila Lekh*. He told them that the hurdles which will come in the way of temple renovation will be removed by the Rama *bhakts*. He also told that the decision taken to start *kar seva* on 6.12.92, as per the directions of *Dharam Sansad*, cannot be changed.

That the course of events further revealed during investigation asserts that, on 19 November 1992, the accused Vinay Katiyar admitted that a one-lakh sacrificial squad has been formed for the *kar seva* for construction of Shri Rama Mandir at Ayodhya, all of them would reach within 25 kms of Ayodhya before 12.92 and that in total ten lakh activists will be present in that area by 6.12.92. Shri Vinay Katiyar also gave the interview to *Jan Morcha*, Faizabad on 20.11.92 that Centre may dismiss the BJP government in U.P. at any time. Therefore the *Rana-nithi* of *kar seva* is changed and the *kar sevaks* from the districts will not come on the decided dates but will come secretly and will reach 25 kms away from Ayodhya between 30 November and 6 December 1992. He said that the 25 kms area has been divided into divisions and sectors and every ten *kar sevaks* will have a Bajrang Dal sacrificial squad activist whose name will be decided a day before the *kar seva*.

It is further revealed during investigation that in pursuance of the aforesaid criminal conspiracy Shri Ashok Singhal, General Secretary, VHP along with

Shri Pramod Mahajan, MP, BJP had met Shri Bala Saheb Thackeray on 21.11.92. On 25 November 1992 Shri Bala Saheb Thackeray while addressing Shiv Sainiks at Pandharpur (Maharashtra) announced that he will participate in the *kar seva* at Ayodhya along with lakhs of Shiv Sainiks.

It further revealed from investigation that Shri Jai Bhagwan Goel, North India Shiv Sena chief, circulated letters dated 24.11.92 to different units of Shiv Sena to attend the North India Shiv Sena leaders meeting on 30.11.92 at the residence of Shri Moreshwar Save at Delhi and to decide participation of Shiv Sena in the *kar seva*.

It has also been found during investigation that Shri Satish Pradhan visited Faizabad on 28.11.92 to address the Shiv Sainiks asserting to participate in *kar seva* in Shiv Sena style. He also told, on subsequently visiting Ramjanmabhumi on the same that if Shri Bala Saheb Thackeray so decided the temple will be constructed from the *garbha griha*. He and Shri Pawan Kumar Pandey, during such visit also said that Babri Masjid disputed structure will be removed on 6.12.92.

That during the above period Bajrang Dal also trained youths in the Chambal valley as suicide squad to demolish the disputed structure. A contingent scheme along with VHP had been drawn and 50,000 *kar sevaks* from Madhya Pradesh were likely to participate in the *kar seva* at Ayodhya.

That a meeting of the North India Shiv Sena leaders was held at Flat No. 207, North Avenue, New Delhi on 30.11.92 and 1.12.92 and the same was convened by Shri Jai Bhagwan Goel. Shri Moreshwar Save presided over the meeting and Shri Satish Pradhan, Shri Jai Bhagwan Goel, Vinod Kumar Vats, Ram Chander Khatri, Sudhir Kakkar, Amarnath Goel also attended the meeting. It was decided in the meeting that lakhs of Shiv Sainiks from North India will participate in the *kar seva* with Shri Bala Saheb Thackeray and on the orders of Shri Bala Saheb Thackeray they will immediately reach Ayodhya. That Shiv Sena will not do symbolic *kar seva*, but for the construction of Shri Ramjanmabhumi temple and that temple should be built where Shri Rama was born (the portion under the Central Dome of the disputed structure where Sri Rama Lalla idol stood placed ever since December 1949), for which Shiv Sena would be ready to pay any price. In the meeting, Shri Satish Pradhan said that Ayodhya has been the ground of war and the same will be opposed/fought and as per the orders of Shri Bala Saheb Thackeray, Shiv Sena will construct Rama temple at the place of birth of Shri Rama at Ayodhya itself. Accused Moreshwar Save said in the meeting that it was a matter of joy for the Shiv Sainiks that Shri Bala Saheb Thackeray had given them a chance to struggle for the welfare/interest of Hindus by deciding to participate in the *kar seva*. It was also decided in the meeting that Babri Masjid disputed structure would be demolished on 6.12.92 and they will perform *kar seva* from *garbha griha* itself.

That accused Moreshwar Save had got allotted flat no. 207, North Avenue for two days from 30 November to 1 December 1992 from the Lok Sabha Sectt. Vide their authority slip dated 27.11.92 and Shri Jai Bhagwan Goel received/took possession of the said flat on 28.11.92 in the name of Shri Moreshwar Save.

A press conference was held on 1.12.92 by accused Moreshwar Save at his residence at 56, North Avenue, New Delhi and a press release dated 1.12.92 to the above effect was issued. In the press conference, accused Moreshwar Save, Satish Pradhan, etc. told that they do not believe in *bhajans* and *kirtans* and will do *kar seva* in Shiv Sena style (i.e. militant style) at Ayodhya and will go to Ayodhya with arms. They told the press that 1000 *kar sevaks* will be equipped with bombs and arms for the *kar seva* and they had a map of the temple and they told that they would carry building material with them for construction of the temple. The press conference was attended by Shri Arvind Kumar Singh, reporter of *Amar Ujala* and others who had published articles in the paper regarding this.

After the said meeting of North India Shiv Sena leaders at Delhi on 1.12.92, Shri Pawan Kumar Pandey was asked to make arrangements for the *kar sevaks* and the Shiv Sainiks and was told about the decision taken in the meeting and accordingly he made all the necessary arrangements and purchased implements for the demolition. That angles, *phawdas*, *belchas*, *kantas*, etc. were sold to Rama Katha Kunj office of VHP/Ramjanmabhumi Nyas by Industrial Mechanical and Electrical Stores, Faizabad during second half of November 1992 and payments were received from Shri Maheshji of that place.

That in a subsequent meeting of Shiv Sainiks at Bhiwani, Haryana on 2.12.92 it was reaffirmed to start *kar seva* at Ayodhya from the *garbha griha* itself.

That investigation has disclosed that in fact Shiv Sainiks were awaiting the clearance from Shri Bala Saheb Thackeray to proceed to Ayodhya. Shri Bala Saheb Thackeray gave clearance to Shiv Sainiks in this respect on 4.12.92 and on receipt of the said clearance Shri Moreshwar Save along with North India Shiv Sainiks proceeded to Ayodhya. Then Shri Jai Bhagwan Goel had also informed different units of Shiv Sena to proceed to Ayodhya on 4.12.92 by Ganga Jamuna Express.

That as per investigation Shri Jai Bhan Singh Paweya, Bajrang Dal, MP, had sought permission of Shri Ashok Singhal to deploy the suicide squad duly trained at Chambal Valley as aforesaid and their being put to use for the purposes of the demolition of the disputed structure at Ayodhya. In this regard a contingent scheme along with VHP was also drawn for any eventuality and that 50,000 *kar sevaks* from Madhya Pradesh were to be placed in the nearby area of Ayodhya to march in Ayodhya for the aforesaid objectives on orders as and when required.

It has further been revealed that on 5.12.92 at Ayodhya Shri Ashok Singhal had given an interview to the press wherein he stated that '*Jo bhi mandir nirman may badha ayegi usay hum dur kar denge*'. He also expressed that *kar seva* not only meant '*bhajan* and *kirtan*, but to start construction of the temple'. On 5.12.92 and 6 December 1992 morning he also arranged screening of the video films pertaining to the incidents at Ayodhya on 30 October and 2 November 1990 projecting killing of several *kar sevaks*, etc. at Karseva Puram, and this was done with the object to infuse amidst *kar sevaks* all the characteristics of violence. He also told *The Times of India* that '*Dhanche ko dahayenge, mandir vahin banayenge*'.

That the complicity of Shri Vinay Katiyar, Chief of Bajrang Dal, according to the material collected during investigation, revealed that on 12.11.92 Shri Vinay Katiyar had told the *Rashtriya Sahara*, that suicide squad will do the real *kar seva*. There was a press release issued by him on 19.11.92 from Media Centre wherein he stated that all arrangements for *kar sevaks* on 6.12.92 have been made and they will follow the policy of 'Shivaji' for *kar seva* for demolition of the disputed structure.

In accordance with the scheme of Criminal Conspiracy as aforesaid Shri Katiyar reiterating his opinion on 30 November 1992 told the *Pioneer* that there is only one definition of *kar seva* that is 'construction work and there is nothing called symbolic *kar seva*' and that what they planned to start from 6 December 1992 was the construction work of Sri Rama temple. Regarding violation of Supreme Court directives prohibiting construction activity on the disputed 2.77-acres of land Shri Vinay Katiyar said 'This country is not run by Court orders It is run by society and society will decide whether there should be construction at the site'. He said that the Court order may be applicable to individuals but it is not applicable to VHP or the Bajrang Dal and the 'judiciary has no authority to pass any orders regarding the Rama Mandir'. He also said that his organization was prepared for a confrontation on this issue. He also said '*Bigarney par hi mamla baneyga*', and '*Kuch bigarney par hi much banta hay*'. Regarding the *kar seva* he said that the *kar seva* for construction of the Rama temple would carry on till the temple was completed.

Further on 5.12.92 Shri Katiyar told the media persons that he is definitely going to start construction of Rama temple. He had also stated in unequivocal terms that the *kar seva* will not mean '*bhajan* and *kirtan*, but start of construction of Rama temple'. He had also given an interview to a correspondent of *Sunday* on 5.12.92, wherein he asserted 'This is Rama's Court, if tomorrow some Court decides that Mohammed was not born in Mecca, then will the Muslims accept it? Why should we?'

The investigation also revealed that on 5.12.92, a secret meeting was held at the residence of Shri Vinay Katiyar, which was attended by Shri L.K. Advani, Pawan Pandey, etc. wherein a final decision to demolish the disputed structure was taken. During the same period Shri Kalyan Singh when contacted by a witness told him that '*Rok* construction *per lagi hai,* destruction *par nahin*'.

That in furtherance of the above said criminal conspiracy *kar seva* mobilization journey was purposely undertaken by Shri L.K. Advani from Varanasi and Shri Murli Manohar Joshi from Mathura on 1.12.92 which finally culminated at Ayodhya on 5.12.92 and in the course of such journeys which involved public speeches between 1.12.92 and 5.12.92. Shri Advani vehemently asserted repeatedly that the *kar seva* to be held from 9.12.92 at Ayodhya would not mean only *bhajan and kirtan*. But would as well involve construction of Shri Rama temple, it would be done with bricks and shovels. He further asserted on 2.12.92 to the *Jansatta* that the BJP will break the law for the construction of Ramjanmabhumi temple at Ayodhya.

That in order to ensure every possibility for the successful achievement of the objective of the conspiracy for the demolition of the disputed structure, a well-programmed practice session of *kar sevaks* was organized in Laltila Rama Katha Kunj, Ayodhya for rehearsing the demolition of the disputed structure. It also stands revealed from the investigation that the operational control of the aforesaid practice session was in fact supervised and convened by Ramesh Pratap Singh. The said Laltila was at a distance of about 500 metres from the disputed site.

As per the investigation on account of mass mobilization of *kar sevaks* by different organizations, the *kar sevaks* started coming from various parts of the country which reached about 3 lakhs as on 6.12.92 at Ayodhya. In fact from 23.11.92 onwards the inflow of *kar sevaks* went on increasing which was a matter of grave concern. However, as per the investigation, adequate steps, under the given circumstances, by calculative deployment of the police force on the spot as well as in the surrounding vicinity of the disputed site was deliberately not undertaken by the local administration. This was all the more necessary in view of deliberate bid of some religious parties who successfully damaged mosques and Muslim graves at Ayodhya within the proceeding four to five days and of which the local administration was aware. This inflow resulted in huge accumulation of *kar sevaks* within and around the disputed site immediately after 11.45 am on 6.12.92 and it facilitated the demolition of the disputed structure. It is evident from the records that a large number of *kar sevaks* in an unmanageable form had caused concern to the Apex Court of the country and accordingly, the Supreme Court vide its order dated 28.11.92 had asked the U.P. government to maintain peace and safeguard the disputed structure. The Government of U.P. in turn assured positively to protect the disputed structure. In view of the positive assurance given by the U.P. government, the Hon'ble Supreme Court limited *kar seva* only to the extent of symbolic *kar seva* on the aforesaid acquired land and forbade any nature of construction either temporary or permanent. The Supreme Court vide its order aforesaid further placed embargo on the inflow of any nature of construction machinery/material into the acquired land. As per directions of the Supreme Court, the operative portion of the order was to be given due publicity by every possible media, pamphlets, posters and/or otherwise and accordingly it was abided.

The inflow of the *kar sevaks* at Ayodhya in huge numbers equally was a matter of concern for the Central Government whose prime anxiety was to ensure every possible protection of the disputed site. And in accordance with such concern they took every possible steps to station 195 Company of paramilitary forces to maintain peace which was dishonestly and deliberately not subjected to any use by deployment under specific instructions of U.P. Chief Minister Shri Kalyan Singh. The events of 6 December 1992 completely exposed the role and dishonest intentions of the accused in ensuring the complete demolition of the disputed structure by wholly reducing it to debris most of which were even carried away by accused/*kar sevaks* and others together with all other materials. It is further evident from the investigation that Shri Kalyan Singh in order to achieve the objectives of the criminal conspiracy as aforesaid not only failed to live up to its promises to protect the disputed structure but continued to aid and abet the criminal conspiracy to ensure its destruction. This would be apparent from the orders of the Supreme Court dated 6 December 1992 that 'A grave situation has emerged by the developments that have occurred owing to the violations of the undertaking and assurances given by the State Government to the Court. It is a great pity that a constitutionally elected government could not discharge its duties in a matter of this sensitiveness and magnitude.'

After U.P. government's assurance to the Supreme Court that the *kar seva* will be symbolic on 6 December 1992, it was expected that the senior leaders of BJP and VHP including the accused and also of Shiv Sena would tone down the mobilization of *kar sevaks* at Ayodhya and would refrain from activities tantamount to provoking the *kar sevaks* to dishonour the undertaking given as aforesaid. In reality, however, mobilization of *kar sevaks* were stepped-up by the statements of senior leaders including accused persons to the media persons and also in their public speeches on the aspect of symbolic *kar seva* became grossly provocative.

That in accordance with the material collected during the course of investigation the stage was set for 6.12.92 in accordance with the scheme of the criminal conspiracy as aforesaid for eventually demolishing the disputed structure Ramjanmabhumi–Babri Masjid. And as the investigation envisages it was on 6.12.92 that Shri L.K. Advani in a public speech in the proximity of the disputed structure shortly before the actual demolition of the disputed site amongst other facts duly projected by him had also emphasized that '*Aaj kar seva ka akhiri din hai, kar sevak aaj akhiri kar seva karenge*'. When the demolition of the disputed structure was in progress, he also said that the Central Forces were moving from Faizabad towards Ayodhya, but they were not afraid of it and instructed the public to block the National Highway straight away so that forces do not reach Ramjanmabhumi. The investigation also disclosed that as and when demolition was in progress, Shri L.K. Advani in fact advised the Chief Minister of Uttar Pradesh, Shri Kalyan Singh not to tender his resignation to the Governor of U.P. till the demolition of the disputed structure was complete.

That according to the investigation even when, the Hon'ble Supreme Court had emphasized in its order limiting the programme of *kar seva* to assemble on 6 December 1992 at Ayodhya only up to symbolic *kar seva* and forbade them to reach the site with any construction machinery and/or equipments, the local administration dishonestly and/or deliberately did not adopt any such recourse to prevent the *kar sevaks* from coming on the spot (where *kar seva* was actually to be performed) along with *belchas*, *phawras*, big hammer, big ropes, etc. It also stands revealed from the investigation that in order to aid and abet the criminal conspiracy, inadequate force was deployed at the disputed site by the local administration from 1.12.92 onwards in spite of the fact that large number of *kar sevaks* had assembled and the imminent threat to the disputed structure by the *kar sevaks* was within the knowledge of the accused officials. Non-deployment of sufficient force well in advance at all strategic points was deliberate and reveals dishonest intention on their part to aid and abet the offence. The accused public servants and Shri Kalyan Singh were well aware that the central paramilitary forces were duly equipped with riot gear and plastic and rubber bullets to avoid casualty amongst innocent civilians. Dogged refusal to deploy the said force in spite of several requests from Union Home Government to deploy the paramilitary force shows that the failure to take this steps was a part of the conspiracy and criminal design. When the actual operation of the demolition of the disputed structure was initiated by the accused persons along with others no recourse was adopted by use of such minimum force which was required under the law and which should have been adhered to so as to block the free flow of the *kar sevaks* towards the disputed structure.

That according to the investigation while the process of demolition was going on during the span of full five hours the state administration remained a mock spectator of the operation of such demolition in process and awaited its full accomplishments. This deliberate illegal omission on the part of the administration in fact encouraged the accused along with other *kar sevaks* who were well equipped with all the materials required for the demolition to take control of the entire disputed structure site uninterrupted, unhindered by any nature of resistance by the public servants Shri R.N. Srivastava, District Magistrate and Shri D.B. Roy, Senior Superintendent of Police for the protection of the disputed structure.

That further according to the investigation, the entire premises of the disputed structure was in full control of the accused/*kar sevaks* along with others for approximately 5 hours which in all certainty facilitated them to completely erase the entire structure of Ramjanmabhumi–Babri Masjid including the three domes and its surroundings and that in the process of such operation by the accused and *kar sevaks*, '*Mir Baqi ka shila lekh*', (which was fixed on the main gate of the disputed structure) in accordance with pre-determined plan of the accused/*kar sevaks* as aforesaid was removed in particular by Pawan Kumar Pandey, with the assistance of about twenty persons and a large part of which was carried away from the site to a jeep located nearby. According to the investigation the accused/*kar sevaks* who in fact were in operation for the demolition of the disputed site had in the process of such demolition as also looted the government properties from the disputed premises which amongst other included wireless sets, CCTV cameras, dragon light charger etc. In the process of such operation of demolition in addition to several accused and *kar sevaks* injuries were also caused to some of the government personnel. In accordance with the channelized programme of such operation the media persons/photographers were also attacked and injured. Their belongings such as cameras, video cameras, notebooks etc. were snatched, damaged and looted. These media persons who in fact were performing an important public duty were present there for coverage of the incident and had also photographed most of the aspects of the incident in their cameras/video recording and this looting, etc. was deliberately done with a view to cause the evidence of the commission of offences to disappear with the intention to screen the offender from legal punishment.

According to the investigation when the operation for the demolition of the disputed site pertaining to Ramjanmabhumi–Babri Masjid was in operation statements duly designed by inciting slogans on the Public Address System and/or otherwise were deliberately raised to instigate the accused/*kar sevaks* with a view to constantly encourage them in the achievement of their objective of demolishing in accordance with the criminal conspiracy as aforesaid.

That further according to the investigation it was in similar circumstances that on or about the time when operation of the demolition of disputed site was in progress as aforesaid accused Sadhvi Rithambara provoked the accused/*kar sevaks* for the demolition through speeches and she had also shouted the following slogans over the Public Address System and otherwise i.e. '*Ek dhakka aur do, Babri Masjid tod do*', '*Ram naam satya hai, Babri Masjid dhwast hai*', '*Khoon kharaba hona hai, ek baar ho jaane do*'.

Similarly Acharya Dharmendra Dev had incited/encouraged the *kar sevaks* for the demolition by raising slogans over the public address system and otherwise: that is, '*Babar bolo jai Shri Ram*', '*Ek ek eint prashad kay tor ker lay jao*'.

That similarly accused Ms Uma Bharati had shouted on 6.12.92 at Ramjanmabhumi, Ayodhya '*Ek dhakka aur do, Babri Masjid tod do*' and she had also advised the *kar sevaks* to demolish the disputed structure and shouted '*Masjid girao mandir banao, Babar ki aulado ko Pakistan bhagao*', '*Jinnah bole jai Sri Ram*', etc. On 5.12.92 she had told that *kar seva* will not mean only *bhajan* and *kirtans*, but start of construction of the temple. '*Ek ek eint prashad kay tor per lay jao*' and '*Babar bole jai Sri Ram Mecca bolo jai Sri Ram*', and that the Supreme Court had not told them not to demolish but only not to do construction work and hence they are removing the black spot from the nation's forehead. She had also said '*Ram naam satya hai, Babri Masjid dhwasth hai*'. On 10.3.93, she had said in Silchar that the demolition of the Babri Masjid was part of 'a preconceived plan, and she was the pivot of the plan and gave the signal to break the Babri Masjid'.

That accused Maharaj Swami Sakshi, BJP, MP, admitted to *The Hindustan Times* that they demolished the Babri Masjid along with the Shiv Sainiks. That accused Ram Narain Das had similarly incited and encouraged the *kar sevaks* for demolition and was found pushing the *kar sevaks* towards the disputed structure for the demolition.

That immediately after the demolition of the Babri Masjid disputed structure Jai Bhagwan Goel admitted that he and Shri Moreshwar Save were in charge and commanding the demolition and that Shri Bala Saheb Thackeray had agreed to participate and perform the Shiv Sena style *kar seva*. That all the preparation were done by them and they demolished the Babri Masjid. Shri Pawan Pandey, Vinod Kumar Vats, Ram Chander Khatri, Sudhir Kakkar, Amarnath Goel also admitted in the said video cassette that they planned and demolished the Babri Masjid disputed structure. That Shri Bala Saheb Thackeray admitted to the said video magazine that he was proud of his boys if they had demolished the Babri Masjid structure and that it was a constructive work of his people. He also said that if he would have been the Prime Minister of India, he would have demolished the disputed structure officially instead of leaving it to the Shiv Sainiks.

That accused Moreshwar Save admitted to *The Independent* newspaper that the demolition of the Babri Masjid was planned and executed in a military precision by 500 Shiv Sainiks who were trained in the Chambal valley for a fortnight.

That the materials collected during investigation reveal that Pawan Kumar Pandey, Brij Bhushan Saran Singh, Jai Bhagwan Goel, Vinod Kumar Vats, Ram Chandra Khatri, Sudhir Kakkar, Amarnath Goel, Santosh Dubey, Prakash Sharma, Jai Bhan Singh Paweya, Dharmendra Singh Gurjar, Ram Narain Das, Lallu Singh, Om Prakash Pandey, Laxmi Narain Mahatyagi, Vinay Kumar Rai, Kamlesh Tripathi, Gandhi Yadav, Hargovind Singh, Vijay Bahadur Singh and Naveen Bhai Shukla have either positively admitted their complicity in the demolition of the disputed structure which affirmatively establishes the actual participation in the demolition of the disputed structure based on their admissions and or identification in this regard. It further establishes their complicity either on their being injured on the spot or their own admissions or being identified by witnesses and/or the vital role played by them by a major contribution in the achieving of the ends of the conspiracy.

That according to the materials collected during investigation Shri Kalyan Singh has made admissions/statements to the media as well as in his public speeches made at intervals which clearly indicative of his complicity in the demolition of the disputed structure. That according to the materials collected during investigation on 15 and 16 February 1993 addressing the public meeting he said that 6 December 1992 is recorded by the BJP as a day of National Festival/Glory. On 7.5.93 he had said at Barabanki '*Goli na challaney ka adesh unke dwara he jaari kiya gaya tha aur usi vajah se prashasan ka koi adhikari doshi nahi maana jayega.*' On 28 march 1993 he had said at Lucknow, '*Vivadith danche ki suraksha na kar pane ka unhe koye afsos nahi hai, kyonki ve 464 saal purana gulami ka chinh tha*'. That on 4.5.93 at Hamirpur he said, 'I am thankful to you, you have demolished the thousand-years-old structure.' On 3.5.93 he had said at Banda, '*465 varsh purane gulami ke prateekh aur teen lakh Hinduvom ka balidan ke chinh kalankit dhanche ko giraye jane ka unhe koye pashchatap nahi hai.*' On 19.2.93 at Mainpuri he said that the structure of slavery was demolished and the structure of Rama temple has been erected. He also said in public meeting, '*Aaj sharam ke nare lagaye jaate hai, jinhe jyadah sharam aati hai, veh gehri nadi mein kood kar mare, varshon purana dhancha dhah gaya hai to unhe sharam aati hai.*' He said on 18.1.93 at New Delhi railway station, '*6 December ki ghatna ke karz mukht Bharat ke nirman ki prakriya prarambh ho gayi hai. Dhancha dwasth hona hi eshwari ghatna thi. Is par na mein sharminda hoom, na kisi ko glani mein dubane ki jarurath hai.*' On 15.2.93 he said at Muzaffar Nagar, '*Humne 6 December 1992 ko ush gulami ka dhancha dhaha diya hai jin mein Mandir ka dhancha upar ubhar kar aaya hai, abh mandir ka nirman koye nahi rok sakta.*'

That according to the investigation Shri Champat Rai had admitted that he stood decided to adopt gorilla strategy in the *kar seva* on 6.12.92. He had also procured to facilitate the demolition, the necessary implements that is, iron rods, *belchas*, *phawdas* from Khawaspura, Loha Mandi, Faizabad in a jeep.

That according to investigation Shri Murli Manohar Joshi had said at Mathura on 1.12.92 on his way to Ayodhya that no force can stop construction of Rama temple and he was encouraging the *kar sevaks* from the *manch* on 6.12.92 for the demolition of the disputed structure and was shouting provocative slogans.

That according to investigation Shri Giriraj Kishore was giving provocative slogans which excited the *kar sevaks* who demolished the disputed structure. He attended the closing ceremony of the training of Bajrang Dal–Durga Vahini activists at Sarkej, Ahmedabad on 6.10.91. He was shouting on 6.12.92 that '*Rama Lalla hum aaye hai, Mandir yehi banayenge*'. He also said on 6.12.92 that there is no need for the *kar sevaks* to be afraid because their government is in power in Uttar Pradesh.

That the investigation has further disclosed that Shri Vishnu Hari Dalmia had said that they were prepared for all eventualities. He was present on the *manch* on 6.12.92 and was shouting provocative slogans and was inciting the *kar sevaks* that their government is in power and they need not get scared.

That according to investigation, Acharya Dharmendra Dev was shouting provocative slogans like '*Babar bolo jai Sri Ram—Akbar bolo jai Sri Ram—Humayun bolo jai Sri Ram*'. On 6.12.92 he also announced from the *manch* to allow only the ambulance inside.

That the aforesaid acts of L.K. Advani, Ashok Singhal, Vinay Katiyar, Moreshwar Save, Pawan Kumar Pandey, Brij Bhushan Saran Singh, Jai Bhagwan Goel, Ms Uma Bharati, Sadhvi Rithambara, Maharaj Swami Sakshi, Murli Manohar Joshi, Giriraj Kishore, Vishnu Hari Dalmia, Vinod Kumar Vats, Ram Chander Khatri, Sudhir Kakkar, Amarnath Goel, Santosh Dubey, Prakash Sharma, Jai Bhan Singh Paweya, Dharmendra Singh Gurjar, Ram Narayan Das, Lallu Singh, Om Prakash Pandey, Lakshi Narayan Das Mahatyagi, Vinay Kumar Rai, Kamlesh Tripathi, Gandhi Yadav, Hargobind Singh, Vijay Bahadur Singh, Navin Bhai Shukla and Acharya Dharmendra Dev were present in the proximity of the disputed structure at Ayodhya on 6.12.92 amongst others and they deliberately with the object to achieve the ends of the conspiracy which emphatically envisaged the demolition of the disputed structure involved themselves by active participation and for incitement and active contribution to achieve the ends of the conspiracy in the demolition of the disputed structure which in the ultimate analysis was completely erased by the evening of 6 December, 1992.

That in pursuance of the above said criminal conspiracy, Sadhvi Rithambara, Moreshwar Save, Acharya Dharmendra Dev, Ms Uma Bharati, Vinay Katiyar, L.K. Advani, M.M. Joshi, V.H. Dalmia, Swami Sakshi, Giriraj Kishore and Ashok Singhal along with Bala Saheb Thackeray, Satish Pradhan, Champat Rai,

Ramji Gupta, Ramesh Pratap Singh, Kalyan Singh actively contributed or incited the *kar sevaks* to promote communal disharmony, prejudicial to the National Integration, incited one community against the other to injure the religious feelings of another community with the object to demolish the disputed structure.

That on 6.12.92 Shri R.N. Srivastava was functioning as District Magistrate, Faizabad, D.B. Roy was the Senior Superintendent of Police, Faizabad. All these public servants were present on or nearby the disputed structure and they had conscious knowledge of the nature of *kar seva* and order of the Hon'ble Supreme Court passed on 28.11.92 on the basis of assurances given by Shri Kalyan Singh the then Chief Minister of U.P. and they were required to prevent any nature of damage to the disputed structure. That the aforesaid public servants were also aware of the fact that lakhs of *kar sevaks* are arriving at Ayodhya and various political/religious parties have already at recurring intervals expressed their determination to destroy the disputed structure. In spite of the above, no legal embargo was fixed or any effective step was taken to prevent them from the destruction of disputed structure in accordance with the mandate of Supreme Court to ensure its protection.

That as per past experience of October 1990, they were also aware about the consequences of *kar seva* and its demolition which may result in riots and colossal loss of life and property in India and abroad by way of communal riots. That manning of the police forces near the disputed structure on 6.12.92 was considerably reduced and no sterile zone was created which facilitated the *kar sevaks* in demolishing the disputed structure. That the District Magistrate Shri R.N. Srivastava had also sent back three battalions of paramilitary forces at 1.45 pm on 6.12.92 and even during the entire span of about 5 hours when the demolition was in progress. Shri R.N. Srivastava and Shri D.B. Roy took no step to protect the structure as well as the attack on the media persons which was being carried on as aforesaid.

The deliberate acts and or illegal omissions as aforesaid on the part of public servants Shri Kalyan Singh, the ex-Chief Minister, U.P., Shri R.N. Srivastava, the then DM, Faizabad and also Shri D.B. Roy, the then SSP, Faizabad is not only totally inexplicable in view of the assurances given to the Hon'ble Supreme Court as aforesaid but was a worse example of gross irresponsibility and abdication of duty by them who had taken oath to defend the Constitution and uphold the rule of law in the country.

The aforesaid acts of Shri Bala Saheb Thackeray, Chief of Shiv Sena, Bombay; Shri L.K. Advani, MP, BJP, presently BJP President; Shri Kalyan Singh, ex-Chief Minister of Uttar Pradesh; Shri Ashok Singhal, General Secretary, VHP; Shri Vinay Katiyar, MP, Bajrang Dal; Shri Moreshwar Save, MP, Shiv Sena; Shri Pawan Kumar Pandey, ex-MLA, Shiv Sena; Shri Brij Bhushan Saran Singh, MP, BJP; Shri Jai Bhagwan Goel, north India Chief, Shiv Sena; Ms Uma Bharati and Gajra Singh, MP, BJP; Sadhvi Rithambara, VHP leader; Maharaj Swami Sakshi, MP, BJP; Shri Satish Pradhan, MP, Shiv Sena; Shri Murli Manohar Joshi, ex-President, BJP; Shri Giriraj Kishore, Joint General Secretary, VHP; Shri Vishnu

Hari Dalmia, President, VHP; Shri Vinod Kumar Vats, President of Shiv Sena, Haryana; Shri Sudhir Kakkar, Organizing Secretary, Shiv Sena, Punjab; Shri Amarnath Goel, Shiv Sena activist; Shri Santosh Dubey, leader of Shiv Sena, Ayodhya; Shri Prakash Sharma, Joint Secretary, Bajrang Dal; Shri Jai Bhan Singh Paweya, All India General Secretary, Bajrang Dal; Shri Dharmendra Singh Gurjar, Convenor, Bajrang Dal, Gwalior; Shri Ram Narayan Dass, ex-*pujari* of Ram-janmabhumi; Shri Ramji Gupta, Supervisor Ramjanmabhumi Nyas; Shri Lallu Singh, ex-MLA, BJP; Shri Champat Rai, Joint Zonal Organizing Secretary, VHP; Shri Om Prakash Pandey, Hindu activist; Shri Lakshmi Narayan Das, *Mahatyagi*, Activist, BJP; Shri Vinay Kumar Rai, Hindu activist; Shri Kamlesh Tripathi; Sait Dubey, Bajrang Dal activist; Shri Gandhi Yadav, BJP activist; Shri Hargovind Singh, Hindu activist; Shri Vijay Bahadur Singh, Chief Security Officer, Shri Krishna temple, Mathura, U.P.; Shri Navin Bhai Shukla, Hindu activist; Shri Ramesh Pratap Singh, BJP activist and Acharya Dharmendra Dev, leader, Bajrang Dal constitute offences u/s 120-B IPC r/w 153-A, 153-B, 295, 295-A and 505 IPC and substantive offences u/s 153-A, 153-B, 295, 295-A and 505 IPC.

That the aforesaid acts of Shri L.K. Advani, MP, BJP, presently BJP President; Shri Ashok Singhal, General Secretary, VHP; Shri Vinay Katiyar, MP, Bajrang Dal; Shri Moreshwar Save, MP, Shiv Sena; Shri Pawan Kumar Pandey, ex-MLA, Shiv Sena; Shri Brij Bhushan Saran Singh, MP, BJP; Shri Jai Bhagwan Goel, north India Chief, Shiv Sena; Ms Uma Bharati and Gajra Singh, MP, BJP; Sadhvi Rithambara, VHP leader; Maharaj Swami Sakshi, MP, BJP; Shri Murli Manohar Joshi, ex-President, BJP; Shri Giriraj Kishore, Joint General Secretary, VHP; Shri Vishnu Hari Dalmia, President, VHP; Shri Vinod Kumar Vats; Ram Chandra Khatri, Vice President of Shiv Sena, Haryana; Shri Sudhir Kakkar, Organizing Secretary, Shiv Sena, Punjab; Shri Amarnath Goel, Shiv Sena Activist; Shri Santosh Dubey, leader of Shiv Sena, Ayodhya; Shri Prakash Sharma, Joint Secretary, Bajrang Dal; Shri Jai Bhan Singh Paweya, All India General Secretary, Bajrang Dal; Shri Dharmendra Singh Gurjar, Convenor, Bajrang Dal, Gwalior; Shri Ram Narayan Dass, ex-*pujari* of Ramjanmabhumi; Shri Lallu Singh, ex-MLA, BJP; Shri Om Prakash Pandey, activist; Hindu activist Shri Lakshmi Narayan Das Mahatyagi, activist, BJP; Shri Vinay Kumar Rai, activist, Hindutva; Shri Kamlesh Tripathi and Sait Dubey, activist, Bajrang Dal; Shri Gandhi yadav, activist, BJP; Shri Hargobind Singh, Hindu activist, Hindutva; Shri Vijay Bahadur Singh, Chief Security Officer, Shri Krishna temple, Mathura, U.P.; Shri Navin Bhai Shukla, Hindu activist and Shri Acharya Dharmendra Dev, leader, Bajrang Dal and others constitute offences u/s 147 IPC and also u/s 153-A, 153-B, 295, 295-A, 505 r/w Section 149 IPC.

The aforesaid acts of accused Shri Pawan Kumar Pandey, Brij Bhushan Saran Singh, Jai Bhagwan Goel, Vinod Kumar Vats, Ram Chandra Khatri, Sudhir Kakkar, Amarnath Goel, Santosh Dubey, Prakash Sharma, Jai Bhan Singh Paweya, Dharmendra Singh Gurjar, Ram Narain Dass, Lallu Singh, Om Prakash Pandey, Laxmi Narain Dass Mahatyagi, Vinay Kumar Rai, Kamlesh Tripathi, Gandhi Yadav, Hargovind Singh, Vijay Bahadur Singh, Navin Bhai Shukla, and others constitute offences u/s 332, 338, 201 IPC r/w Section 149 of the IPC and Section 395 IPC.

That the acts of Shri R.N. Srivastava the then District Magistrate and D.B. Roy, the then SSP, Faizabad constitute offences u/s 153-A, 295, 295-A, 505, 201 r/w Section 114 IPC.

That the Central Government has issued sanction u/s 196 of the code of Criminal Procedure 1973 for prosecution of aforesaid accused A1 to A40 for commission of offences u/s 153-A, 153-B, 295-A, 505 IPC r/w 120-B IPC and for substantive offences which is enclosed in original.

That the Governor of Uttar Pradesh has issued sanction u/s 197 of the code of Criminal Procedure 1973 for prosecution of Shri Kalyan Singh, ex-Chief Minister of Uttar Pradesh for commission of aforesaid offences which is enclosed herewith in original.

That A-2, A-4, A-5, A-10, A-11, A-14, A-15, A-16 were arrested during the investigation of Crime No. 198/92 by the CB:CID, U.P. and are on bail.

That A-6, A-8, A-9, A-12, A-17 to A-19, A-22, A-26, A-36, A-37 were arrested by the CBI during the course of investigation of this case and all of them are on bail. That A-29 to A-30 were arrested by the U.P. police during the course of investigation of Crime No. 197/92 and are on bail. That the other accused have not been arrested.

From the above mentioned facts and circumstances a *prima facie* case is made out against accused No. 1–40 in respect of the offences which were committed in the course of the same transaction as detailed above.

It is, therefore, prayed that cognizance of offences may kindly be taken against all such accused persons as aforesaid and they may be summoned to stand their trial according to law.

(*Note*: On 27 August 1994, Special Judicial Magistrate, Mahipal Sodhi found that a *prima facie* case did exist against the accused and committed the case to the sessions court for a full trial.)

2. The Sessions Judge frames charges on 9 September 1997 against Advani, Joshi, Bal Thackeray and others

Court of Additional Sessions Judge (Ayodhya Episode) Lucknow
Sessions Case No 344/94

State *versus* Bala Saheb Thackeray and thirty-nine others u/s 153-A/153-B/295/295-A/505/395/120-B Indian Penal Code, Police Station Ramjanmabhumi, Ayodhya, District Faizabad and

Session Case No 749/96
State *versus* Mahant Avaidyanath and eight others u/s 153-B/295-A/505/120-B/149 IPC Police Station Ramjanmabhumi, Ayodhya, District Faizabad.

Order
9.9.97

1. Present Sessions Case No. 344/94 is registered vide FIR No. 197/92 on the report of Shri Priyambada Nath Shukla SHO Ramjanmabhumi Dist Faizabad u/s 395/397/332/337/338/295/297/153-A IPC and section 7 of Criminal Law Amendment Act against accused persons Bala Saheb Thackeray and thirty-nine others and Sessions Case No. 749/96 is registered vide FIR No. 198/92 u/s 153-A/153-B/505/IPC against Mahant Avaidyanath and eight others on the report lodged by Shri J.P. Tiwari Sub-Inspector, Police Station Ramjanmabhumi, Chowki Faizabad.

2. Since both cases mentioned above are inter-connected they are taken together for consideration.

3. CBI filed chargesheet against Bala Saheb Thackeray, Lal Krishna Advani, Kalyan Singh, Ashok Singhal, Vinay Katiyar, Moreshwar Save, Pawan Kumar Pandey, Brij Bhushan Saran Singh, Jai Bhagwan Goel, Ms Uma Bharati, Sadhvi Rithambara, Maharaj Sumai Sakshi, Satish Pradhan, Murli Manohar Joshi, Giriraj Kishore, Vishnu Hari Dalmia, Vinod Kumar Vats, Ram Chander Khatri, Amarnath Goel, Santosh Dubey, Prakash Sharma, Jai Bhagwan Paweya, Dharmendra Singh Gurjar, Ram Narani Dass, Ramji Gupta, Lallu Singh, Champat Rai, Om Prakash Pandey, Laxmi Narain Dass, Vinay Kumar Rai, Kamlesh Tripathi, Gandhi Yadav, Har Govind Singh, Vijay Bahadur Singh, Narim Bhai Shukla, Ramesh Pratap Singh and Acharya Dharmendra Dev u/s120-B IPC with 153-A/153-B/295/295-A and 505 IPC. Accused Shri Lal Krishna Advani, Ashok Singhal, Vinay Katiyar, Moreshwar Save, Pawan Kumar Pandey, Brij Bhushan Saran Singh, Jai Bhagwan Goel, Ms Uma Bharati, Sadhvi Rithambara, Maharaj Swami Sakshi, Murli Manohar Joshi, Giriraj Kishore, Vishnu Hari Dalmia, Vinod Kumar Vats, Ram Chander Khatri, Sudhir Kakkar, Amarnath Goel, Santosh Dubey, Prakash Sharma, Jai Bhan Singh Paweya, Dharmendra Singh Gurjar, Ram Narain Dass, Lallu Singh, Om Prakash Pandey, Laxmi Narain Dass, Vinay Kumar Rai, Kamlesh Tripathi, Gandhi Yadav, Har Govind Singh, Vijay Bahadur Singh, Naveen Bhai Shukla, Acharya Dharmendra Dev have been sent for trial u/s 147/153-A/153-B/295/295-A/505 read with Section 149 of Indian Penal Code. Accused persons Shri Pawan Kumar Pandey, Brij Bhushan Saran Singh, Jai Bhagwan Goel, Vinod Kumar Vats, Ram Chander Khatri, Sudhir Kakkar, Amarnath Goel, Santosh Dubey, Prakash Sharma, Jai Bhan Singh Paweya, Dharmendra Singh Gurjar, Ram Narain Dass, Lallu Singh, Om Prakash Pandey, Laxmi Narain Dass Mahatyagi, Vinay Kumar Rai, Kamlesh Tripathi, Gandhi Yadav, Har Govind Singh, Vijay Bahadur Singh, Naveen Bhai Shukla are sent for trial u/s 332/338/201 read with Section 149 and 295 of Indian Penal Code and Accused persons S/Shri R.N. Srivastava, D.B. Rai are challenged u/s 153-A/295/295-A/505/201 read with section 114 of Indian Penal Code. Central Government has sanctioned the prosecution of Shri Bala Saheb Thackeray to Shri D.B. Rai (Accused 1 to 40) u/s 196 of code of criminal procedure u/s/153-A/153-B/295/295-A/505 IPC read with Section 120 IPC and the U.P. State Government has granted sanction for prosecution of Sant Shri Kalyan Singh, R.N. Srivastava and D.B. Rai.

4. Accused persons Shri Mahant Avaidyanath, Ram Vilas Vedanti, Dharam Dass, Mahant Nritya Gopal Dass, Mahamandaleshwar Jagdish Muni Maharaj, Baikunth Nath Lal Sharma Prem, Paramhansa Ram Chander Dass, Smt Vijaya Raje Scindia and Dr Satish Kumar Nagar have been sent for trial ups 153-A/153-B/505/147 and 148 of Indian Penal Code.

5. Prosecution submitted that a dispute about Ayodhya structure at Babri Masjid–Ramjanmabhumi has been pending before High Court and Supreme Court for a long time. Dispute about Ramjanmabhumi–Babri Masjid has been pending and it has also been stated in the chargesheet that from December 1948 to 6.12.92 the disputed structure was never used in the name of Masjid. Hindus alleged that Babri Masjid was built by Mir Baqi on Ramjanmabhumi, Vishwa Hindu Parishad campaigned for liberation of Mandir at Ayodhya, Kashi and Mathura and in that campaign Lal Krishna Advani took *rath yatra* from Somnath to Ayodhya in the course of which he was welcomed by Bala Saheb Thackeray at Dadar, central Bombay on 1.10.90, same day Lal Krishna Advani declared in his public meeting at Panchavati that BJP, Vishwa Hindu Parishad, Shiv Sena and other Hindu organizations have firm determination to construct Rama temple at Ayodhya and he said that Babri Masjid has never been a Masjid. Bala Saheb Thackeray welcomed the speech of Shri Advani and Thackeray said that only by constructing Shri Rama temple Hindus will find their identity in the country, his Party would follow BJP 'in this work'. On 30.10.90 the U.P. government imposed a ban on entry of *kar sevaks* in Ayodhya, in spite of this *kar sevaks*, entered Ayodhya on 30 October 1990, tried to damage the disputed structure for which local Administration issued orders of shoot at sight due to which many people got injured. Thereafter a receiver was appointed. In 1991 BJP come to power in U.P. Immediately after taking the oath, Chief Minister Shri Kalyan Singh, Shri Murli Manohar Joshi and other ministers and BJP legislators took oath at Ayodhya on 25.8.91 that Shri Rama Mandir would be constructed at the same site. Shri Kalyan Singh categorically stated that '*Rama Lalla hum aye hein Mandir yehin banayenge*', and shouted slogans to this effect.

6. Accused No. 1–30 committed criminal conspiracy between October 1990 to 6 December 1992 to get the Ayodhya, Varanasi and Mathura mandirs fully liberated. In this it was decided to raze the Babri Masjid to the ground and to remove the citation stone fixed at the main *gali* of the structure by Mir Baqi and this work was to be accomplished by all in a concerted action. On 6.12.92 at 12 noon some accused persons demolished the disputed structure. They had the knowledge that their act could create tension between Hindus and Muslims which is dangerous for integrity of the nation and would create tension between religions sentiments of Hindus and Muslims as a result of which life and property of people all over the world and within the country would be lost.

7. In the backdrop of above mentioned criminal conspiracy Shri Moreshwar Save wrote a letter dated 17.7.91 to the then Chief Minister Shri Kalyan Singh for construction of Ramjanmabhumi Mandir. This letter was replied by Shri Kalyan Singh on 31.7.91 in which Shri Save was informed about appropriate

action in that direction. BJP, Bajrang Dal, Vishwa Hindu Parishad and Shiv Sena entered into a criminal conspiracy for construction of Ramjanmabhumi Mandir and made plans to demolish the disputed structure of Babri Masjid; under the criminal conspiracy 2.77-acres of land was acquired on 9.7.92 and a *pucca* platform was constructed near Ramjanmabhumi. On 10.7.92 Shri Moreshwar Save congratulated Shri Lal Krishna Advani for commencing the construction of Ramjanmabhumi Mandir and he said that this step of theirs was necessary for establishment of Hindu *rashtra*. He said Shiv Sena would be with them in the construction of mandirs at Ayodhya, Mathura and Kashi. Shri Lal Krishna Advani replied on 20.7.92.

8. Thereafter Shiv Sena and other Hindu organizations participated in *Dharam Sansad* and Bajrang Dal trained the *kar sevaks* for bringing down the structure. On 28.11.92 Shri Satish Pradhan asked Shiv Sainiks to work like Shiv Sena and said that Shri Bala Saheb Thackeray had decided that the Mandir would be constructed at *garbha griha*. Shri Satish Pradhan and Shri Pawan Kumar Pandey expressed their opinion to demolish Babri Masjid disputed structure on 6.12.92. On 4.12.92 Shri Bala Saheb Thackeray ordered Shiv Sainiks to go to Ayodhya and Shri Jai Bhan Singh Paweya asked Shri Ashok Singhal to deploy a suicide squad of Bajrang Dal which was trained in Chambal Ghati. On 5.12.92 Shri Ashok Singhal said in his press conference at Ayodhya that 'whatever obstacle come in the way of construction of Mandir would be removed.' And that *kar sevaks* are not for *bhajan kirtan* but are there to start the construction of Mandir.

9. Accused No. 1–38 expressed similar views at different times and different places about construction of Ramjanmabhumi Mandir at the place of disputed structure. On 5.12.92 a secret meeting was held at the house of Shri Vinay Katiyar which was attended by Shri Lal Krishna Advani, Pawan Kumar Pandey and a final decision to demolish disputed structure was taken. Their argument was that there was a ban on construction not on demolition and accused no 1–38 assembled near Ramjanmabhumi–Babri Masjid on 6.12.92 and Shri Lal Krishna Advani categorically said in his public speech, before the demolition of disputed structure that 'Today is the last day of *kar seva*. *Kar sevaks* would perform last *kar seva*.' When he came to know that central force was proceeding from Faizabad to Ayodhya then he asked the public to block National Highway so that central forces do not reach Ramjanmabhumi. Prosecution has also contended that when disputed structure was being pulled down Shri Advani asked Kalyan Singh not to tender his resignation till the disputed structure is completely pulled down.

10. The demolition of disputed structure continued for 5 hours but the local Administration did not take any legal action against *kar sevaks* for demolishing the disputed structure and the local administration remained a silent spectator till the entire structure was pulled down. In this manner accused no 39 and 40 Shri R.N. Srivasatava the then District Magistrate and Shri D.B. Rai the then Senior Superintendent of Police Faizabad committed illegal omission in discharge of their duty. Accused persons and *kar sevaks* laid a seize of disputed structure for five hours and in the process of pulling it down citation of Mir Baqi fixed at the

main gate was taken out by accused Pawan Pandey and his twenty accomplices and was taken away from the disputed spot in a jeep. In pulling down the disputed structure, government property, wireless set CCTV camera, dragon light, charger were damaged and government servants were injured. Newspersons and photographers were attacked and they were injured. Cameras of the photographers, video camera, notebooks were snatched and were damaged. Property(s) was looted. Ms Uma Bharati instigated *kar sevaks*, '*Ek dhakka aur do Babri Masjid toor do*' '*Ram naam satya hein Babri Masjid dhwast hein*' '*Khoon kharaba hona hein ek bar ho jane do*' and like instigating slogans were raised and instigating speeches about demolition of disputed structure were made.

11. After demolition of disputed structure accused Jai Bhagwan Goel, Moreshwar Save, Bala Saheb Thackeray admitted that demolition of disputed structure was pre planned. Shri Kalyan Singh too admitted in his different speeches and statements after 6.12.92 that he had ordered not to fire and for that reason no officer of the Administration would be held guilty. He has no remorse for not protecting disputed structure because it was mark of 464-years-old slavery. In advance interview Shri Kalyan Singh had said 'A process of development of free India has begun with the incident of 6 December. Demolition of disputed structure was an act of God. On this I am not shamed nor is there any need to feel'. All the accused worked under a criminal conspiracy to demolish the disputed structure according to their capability as result of which national integrity and communal harmony was disturbed. The then District Magistrate and Senior Superintendent of Police abdicated their official duty. According to the prosecution *prima facie* case is made out under above mentioned sectors against accused no 1–40 in sessions case No. 344/94.

12. Sessions case No. 749/96 filed against accused persons Avaidyanath and eight other is crime case no. 198/92 is also connected with the events leading to the incidents of 6.12.1992 in which nine accused named in crime no 198/92 also delivered instigating speeches about demolition of disputed structure. As per prosecution officers 153-A/153-B/505/147/148 of IPC is *prima facie* made out against the accused persons.

13. Ld. Counsel of Bala Saheb Thackeray and others contended that the prosecution charges are false. Shri Bala Saheb Thackeray, etc. had not entered into criminal conspiracy to demolish disputed structure of Babri Masjid–Ramjanmabhumi. Chargesheet filed by the prosecution is illegal as the entire chargesheet is based on newspaper reports which cannot be relied upon. The incident of removing inscription plate of Mir Baqi is not true. Bala Saheb Thackeray and Satish Pradhan were not present on the spot of incidents. Charge levelled against Moreshwar Save is without any basis on behalf of accused Mahant Avaidyanath, Dharam Dass, Mahant Nritya Dass Gopal Dass, Jagdish Muni, Dr Ram Vilas Vedanti, B.L. Prem Sharma, Ram Chander and Smt Vijaya Raje Scindia, Narain Dass, Brij Bhushan Saran Singh, Champath Ram, Shri L.B. Singh Advocate submitted that photographs of newspapers, video-cassettes do not show the presence of accused on the place of incident. There is no legal provision to consolidate

First Information Reports nor is there any provision to join the chargesheets. There is no legal importance of the statement to the press by leaders. Reference to the white paper D-256 by prosecution about criminal conspiracy is illegal. There is no evidence against accused Champat Rai. There is no recovery of *shilalekh* of Mir Baqi. Nothing anti-national in the leaders' saying that '*Bharat mein rehna hoga, Vande Mataram kahna hoga*'. *Namaz* was never held in Babri Masjid. Several disputes about the disputed structure are pending in the court. Shri Tej Shaukar was appointed as observer by the Supreme Court in respect of Ramjanmabhumi–Babri Masjid. Situation was described as normal in his report at 11.45 am on 6.12.92, Shri Lal Bahadur Singh Advocate has submitted that *prima facie* no offence, as alleged in the chargesheet, is made out.

On Behalf of accused Shri Kalyan Singh, Swami Sakshi Maharaj, Kamlesh Tripathi, council Shri B.B. Saxena, Advocate, argued that the officers are triable by the Magistrate. No person saw them pulling down Babri Masjid–Ramjanmabhumi. Shri Kalyan Singh was not present at the place of incident Shri Kalyan Singh did not make any statement. Joint chargesheet is illegal. There cannot be joint trial. Charge for the offence u/s 395 against Shri Kalyan Singh cannot be framed. He is entitled to be acquitted of the charges. There is no evidence of criminal conspiracy against accused Swami Sakshi Maharaj. Charge u/s 395 IPC cannot be framed and the order of transfer of the trial from Rae Bareli to Lucknow is wrong.

14. Once cognizance of offence was taken by Chief Judicial Magistrate Lalitpur then how can cognizance be taken again by Chief Judicial Magistrate Lucknow. Therefore there is no criminal offence against Shri Kalyan Singh, Swami Sakshi Maharaj and Kamlesh Tripathi. They are entitled to be acquitted of the charges.

15. Shri B.L. Gupta Advocate submitted on behalf Shri Moreshwar Save that filing of joint chargesheet is illegal. Charges are false and baseless. *Prima facie* no offence is made out against Moreshwar Save.

16. On behalf of accused Ram Narain Dass, Laxmi Narain Dass, Gandhi Yadav, B.L. Sharma, Narain Bhai Shukla, Shri S.K. Saxena, Advocate, argued that joint chargesheet in the present case in wrongly filed. Incident does not fall under sec. 120-B of IPC. *Prima facie* no offence is made out against the accused persons.

17. On behalf of Ms Uma Bharati, Sadhvi Rithambara, Shri Jai Bhan Singh Paweya, Vinay Katiyar, Champat Rai, Dr Ram Vilas Vedanti, Shri S.P. Singh Advocate argued that no camera was snatched from any correspondents. FIR is false. None of the accused made instigating speech. Most of the witnesses have said that they have not seen disputed structure falling. Ms Uma Bharati made no instigating speech to put down the structure. Instead she asked the *kar sevaks* to climb down. And she had also said that if they wish they could distribute the Masjid and distribute the same like *prasad*, amongst Ram *bhakts* but she never wanted it. There is no definite evidence against Ram Vilas Vedanti. In the same way accused Vinay Kumar Rai and Ramesh Pratap contributed in the rehearsal

of *kar seva* in which sand was to be laid first and their water had to be dropped.

18. On behalf of accused Vishnu Hari Dalmia, Acharya Jugal Kishore, Ashok Singhal, Har Govind Singh Shri S.K.G. Bhargava argued that no conclusion can be drawn only on the basis of FIR that accused persons demolished disputed structure. There is no evidence of criminal conspiracy against these accused persons. Mir Baqi's *shilalekh* does not describe that it was our Masjid. Only symbolic *kar seva* was held. Everything was normal on the day of incident. Shri Ashok Singhal asked the *kar sevaks* to be disciplined. Nothing is mentioned about the people sitting on the dais in the white paper D-256 nor is it mentioned in the FIR.

19. Shri T.K. Upreti, Advocate argued on behalf of the accused Dr Satish Kumar Nagar that Dr Nagar did not make a public speech nor is there any evidences against him about the demolition of disputed structure.

20. Shri K.K. Sood and Shri Mahipal, Advocate argued on behalf of Shri Lal Krishna Advani and Shri Murli Manohar Joshi that the present case in not a fit case to be tried by the court of sessions. No criminal conspiracy was hatched by their clients. No Masjid existed on the spot, as no *namaz* was ever held there. Disputed structure was a Mandir for centuries. The court had restrained from constructing Mandir. There was no injunction on the demolition of Mandir. Alleged offence is not made out against the accused Shri Advani and Shri Murli Manohar Joshi. They had not made any instigating speeches. Chargesheet has been filed against their clients only on the basis of News paper report. Only symbolic *kar seva* was organized on 6.12.92. Report of the observer Shri Tej Shaukar is silent about the accused persons Shri L.K. Advani and Shri Murli Manohar Joshi.

21. On behalf of accused Shri R.N. Srivastava and D.B. Rai council Shri I.P. Singh Advocate argued that a charge cannot be joined together for joint trial in the present case. Whatever offence is committed it is committed by *kar sevaks*. FIR in crime No. 197/92 Shri R.N. Srivastava and Shri D.B. Rai are not named accused and in second FIR crime No. 198/92 both their clients are cited as witness. Only offence alleged against them is that of illegal omission. Cognizance in the present case is wrong and joint chargesheets is illegal. District Magistrate and Senior Superintendent of police were not correctly apprised of the events. Hon'ble Supreme Court had allowed *kar seva*. On 6.12.92 on the platform for which the chief minister had given undertaking. District Magistrate and Senior Superintendent of police are under State Government. District Magistrate of Faizabad and Senior Superintendent of Police were not invited in any meeting. State Government had to decide in sensitive matter. There is no report against the then District Magistrate and Senior Superintendent of Police by Shri Shanker observer. Prosecution has nowhere alleged that the then District Magistrate and Senior Superintendent of Police did not perform their duties lawfully. Whereas District Magistrate and Senior Superintendent of Police kept on informing the State Government about the happenings at the spot through radiogram, wireless and telex.

22. On behalf of Mahant Avaidyanath, Dharam Dass, Nritya Gopal Dass, Mahamandaleshwar Jagdish Muni, Acharya Ram Vilas Vedanti, B.L. Sharma, Ram Chander Paramhansa and Smt Vijaya Raje Scindia, Smt Shoraj Singh Advo-

cate argued that in the present case false allegations are made. Joint trial cannot take place. There is no evidence against the accused persons. Allegations are based on the basis of speeches recorded in the newspapers. No offence is made out against the accused persons. The above named accused persons are entitled to be discharged.

23. Learned counsels of the accused persons were heard at length. Main issue in the present case for consideration is whether any offence is made out against the accused persons on the allegations made in the chargesheet or the accused be discharged.

24. Prosecution advanced the argument that at the stage of framing of charge intricacies of laws should not be gone into. Instead accused should be charged if *prima facie* an offence is made out on the basis of chargesheet. The question whether prosecution has been able to establish the offence against the accused persons or not can only be decided after the parties have heard their respective evidences. It will not be just to discharge the accused at the stage of charge without parties producing their evidence. Section 277 of CPC provides for discharge of the accused and Section 228 of CPC provides for framing of the charges. It will be just for the court to frame the charge. Keeping in view of the facts and circumstances and gravity of offence, u/s 227 and 228 of CRPC it is not necessary to examine the entire evidence nor it is necessary to minutely examine the evidence. The court is not required to pass its order on each and every aspect of the case at the stage of framing of charge. The court has to see whether there is any evidence available on record of the chargesheet and whether there is just basis for framing of charge. Prosecution produced the following cases in support of its contentions:

1. Richard Bin Harkesh *versus* State of West Bengal—1975 Cr. L J. page 1256.
2. State of Bihar *versus* Ramesh Singh—1977 Cr. L J page 1606
3. Superintendent and Remembrances of legal affairs *versus* Anil Kumar—Bhunja—1979 SCC (Criminal) 1038
4. R.S. Nayak *versus* A.R. Antulay AIR—1986 Sec page 2045
5. Crime against women Parishad *versus* Dilip Nathu Malkode—1989 Sec (criminal) page 285
6. Radhey Shyam *versus* King Bihare—1990 Cr L J page 668
7. State of Maharashtra *versus* Priya Saran Maharaja Judgement

25. In the above cited cases the hon'ble Supreme Court and High Courts have laid down legal proposition that at the stage of framing of charges the court has to peruse the available evidences on record and if the court comes to the conclusion that *prima facie* accused has committed the alleged offences then its justified to frame the charges. Therefore the prosecution has contended that on the basis of evidence available on the *challan*, the charges should be framed against the accused persons.

26. On behalf of the accused it is contended that since it is a political dispute and in the present case in which most of the accused are political leaders,

they have been involved by the ruling party government in the Centre through CBI by trumped up evidence in this chargesheet. It will not be proper and justified to peruse only the available evidence. In the first chargesheet submitted by the prosecution the learned Advocate representing accused persons submitted the following authorities:

1. Shri Satish Mehra *versus* Delhi Administration—1996 SCC page 704.
2. Babau Lal *versus* Tilak Kumar—1989 Crimes page 456.
3. Shri Niranjan Singh Karam Singh Punjabi *versus* Jitender Bhim Raj Vigia—1990 Cr. L.J. page 1969.

27. According to the above referred authorities the court has a right to take into consideration any evidence which the accused may produce at the time of framing of chargesheet.

28. On a careful perusal of evidence produced by the prosecution in the present case, I have come to conclusion that the *prima facie* evidence is alleged against the accused persons is made out when section mentioned in the chargesheet will be detailed as the section of the offence then it would be clear as to against which of the accused of the offence is made out *prima facie*.

29. First of all on the question whether in fact there was a conspiracy plan by the accused person for demolition of Ramjanmabhumi–Babri Masjid in Ayodhya. According to the prosecution it is undisputed fact that on the spot of incident for the construction of Rama Mandir on the disputed land and for demonstrating the emotions of Hindus; the accused no. 2 Shri Lal Krishna Advani began a *rath yatra* from Somnath to Ayodhya in September, 1990. In the same chain of events Shri Advani reached Bombay on 1.10.90 where accused no. 1 Shiv Sena Chief Shri Bala Saheb Thackeray welcomed Shri Advani and the workers of Bharatiya Janata Party accorded reception to Shri Advani on behalf of the public. He publicly declared in Panchavati that Bharatiya Janata Party, Vishwa Hindu Parishad and Shiv Sena or other Hindu organizations are one in their resolve that Rama Mandir should be constructed in Ayodhya. Shri Advani also said the emotions of the public would be aroused in a peaceful manner through *rath yatra*. In Ramjanmabhumi Nandi would be constructed in all situation. The above speech was reported in the *Indian Express* in its edition of 2.10.90. The document no. D-34 and PW-604 Ram Krishna and PW-717 Vijay Raghavan Chari PW 179 Shri Joshi; PTI Nasik had released the same. Shri Advani also issued a warning that if any one tries to stop *rath yatra* or the construction of Rama Mandir at Ayodhya it would entail disaster. Shri Advani said in Vannsara in his speech that none can stop *rath yatra*. On 21.10.90 Shri Advani said in Nagda, Bihar that construction of Rama Mandir at Ayodhya would be started on 30 October. Babri Masjid cannot be described as Masjid as the same is not situated on the spot. The government should acquire the disputed land and hand it over to Vishwa Hindu Parishad. Again he warned that if any one interfered in the construction of Mandir or *kar seva* it would be disastrous. The speeches made by Shri Advani created communal tension and he was arrested in Bihar against which there was a nationwide bandh.

30. Accused no. 1 Shri Bala Saheb Thackeray said, while addressing his press conference on 23.10.90 that the object of his party was to keep the identity of Hindu in the Nation and construction of Rama Mandir was first step in that direction. Shiv Sena are performing national duty in the construction of Rama Mandir. He further said that prior to Masjid it was a Hindu Mandir is connection of which D-115, D-137, PW-601, PW-599, PW-875 and PW 191 are fourteen evidences. PW-191 said that on banning of *kar seva* some of the *kar sevaks* damaged disputed structure in which some of them died and some of them were injured.

31. BJP came to power in the State at the General Elections, Kalyan Singh became Chief Minister. After taking oath he along with his Cabinet Colleagues and Shri Murli Manohar Joshi and other members of BJP took pledge on 25.6.91 at disputed site of Ramjanmabhumi for construction of Rama Mandir and declared that '*Rama Lalla hume aye hein Mandir yenhi banayage*'. Accused Moreshwar Save in a letter to Kalyan Singh asked to take the next step for the construction of Ramjanmabhumi Mandir because Bharatiya Janata Party and Shiv Sena had issued Election Manifestos for the construction of Ramjanmabhumi Mandir. Moreshwar Save asked for to begin construction of Ramjanmabhumi Mandir and for that he demanded declaration of date to begin construction of Mandir.

He further said that the Central Government will put obstacles in this work. But he assured that construction of Rama mandir can be completed with the help of Shiv Sena without any problem. Beside this Kalyan Singh must try to get the Hindu mandirs at Mathura and Kashi liberated. Shri Kalyan Singh replied to the letter of Shri Moreshwar Save on 31.7.91 that necessary action was being taken. In this background, BJP government acquired 2.77-acres of land adjoining disputed construction for the purpose of Tourism and immediately the land was levelled by demolishing smaller *mandirs* like Kaushalya Mandir, Sakshi Gopal Mandir. After acquisition of above land, security measures were withdrawn and the public was allowed to go up to disputed site. In this connection the prosecution produced D-436, D-256, PW-699, PW-191, PW-299 and PW-706.

32. *Santh Sammelan* was held at Ujjain on 13.5.92 in which accused Paramhansa Ram Chander Dass, Mahant Avaidyanath, Smt Vijaya Raje Scindia and Ashok Singhal participated, as Central Advisory Board, which adopted a resolution that the obstacle in construction of Mandir be removed. Central Government be removed if it creates any hindrance. It was declared by Shri Ashok Singhal in his press conference. Accused Paramhansa Ram Chander Dass had said, in the press conference, that 'there is no Masjid at the birth place of Rama'. It is only a religious propaganda that there was a Masjid. Babar had constructed only a structure in his time. Babar had not given any date for its construction so we will also not tell the date of its destruction. Ashok Singhal, Mahant Avaidyanath, Paramhansa, etc. were present in press conferences. Mahant Avaidyanath had said in the *sammelan* that they would not wait for the decision of the court or of the government and would begin the construction of Rama Mandir immediately at the same time. Vishwa Hindu Parishad, Bajrang Dal, Bharatiya Janata Party constructed a platform through *kar seva* on acquired land of 2.77-acres on 9.2.92.

Accused no. 6 Shri Moreshwar Save congratulated on 9.7.92 for starting the construction of Sri Rama Mandir through a letter in which he said that he will work against those forces who will oppose. Hindu *rashtra*, Hindutva and construction of Rama Mandir at Ayodhya. He committed his help for the liberation of Rama Mandir at Ayodhya, and mandirs at Mathura and Kashi. Shri Lal Krishna Advani in his letter dated 20.7.92 acknowledged the letter of Shri Moreshwar Save and said, 'I am grateful for your congratulations and well wishes for the start of the construction of Ramjanmabhumi.'

33. *Kar seva* was postponed till July 1992 with the intervention of the Central Government. Dharam Sansad and Central Advisory Board met in Delhi from 29.10.92 to 31.10.92 in which it was decided to begin *kar seva* at Ramjanmabhumi, Ayodhya on 6.12.92 as PW-236, PW-237, PW-191 say. Ashok Singhal General Secretary of Vishwa Hindu Parishad said at Ayodhya on 2.11.92 that *kar seva* will be done on 6.12.92 and inscription plate of Mir Baqi will be removed from its place. Except this inscription plate everything belongs to Hindus as mentioned in D-86, PW-510, PW-360, PW-875. On 14.11.92 Shri Vinay Katiyar, Bajrang Dal, Member of Parliament, said in Ayodhya that suicide squad (Bajrang Dal) is ready to do *kar seva* and that on 6.12.92 suicide squad will use tactics of Shivaji while doing *kar seva* and construction of Rama Mandir shall begin in this condition. In this connection there are documents and witness in D-81, D-87, PW-129, PW-206, PW-706.

34. On 20.11.92 Shri Ashok Singhal (VHP) and Member of Parliament Shri Pramod Mahajan (BJP) met Shri Bala Saheb Thackeray and invited him to participate in *kar seva*. On 24.11.92 accused Jai Bhan Paweya said that suicide squad from amongst the youth of Chambal ravine was trained to demolish disputed structure and that the permission to take the said suicide squad to Ayodhya was sought from Shri Ashok Singhal as is recorded in D-91, D-100, PW-109, PW-157, PW-108. On 23.11.92 Smt Vijaya Raje Scindia said in the meeting that on the disputed *site* there was no sign of Masjid. No power can stop the construction of Rama Mandir. Lord Rama was born on the same place therefore construction of Rama Mandir has become necessary. For how many more years, Hindu sentiments would be hurt. No one can stop the *kar seva*. Shri Champat Rai said on 24.11.92 that *kar seva* will be done in the form of *baner sena* which is recorded in D-26, PW-258.

On 25.11.92, Shri Bala Saheb Thackeray, said at Pandharpur, that they along with the Shiv Sainiks will take part in the *kar seva* at Ayodhya, as mentioned in D-22, D-211, PW-146, PW-161. On 24.11.92, Jai Bhagwan Goel wrote a letter to Shiv Sena urging them to participate in the *kar seva*. Sainiks led by Bala Saheb Thackeray would begin the construction of the Sri Rama Mandir from *garbha griha*. The temple would be built only from the *garbha griha*, and on the same day, Shri Satish Pradhan, Shri Pawan Kumar Pandey inspected the Ramjanmabhumi, and said that the disputed structure will be demolished on 6.12.92. On 28.11.92, Acharya Giriraj Kishore, said that if the government tried to create hurdles in the construction of Rama Mandir, it would be given a fitting reply.

35. According to the documents D-217, D-233, PW-616, PW-309, Vishwa Hindu Parishad bought *belchas*, *favras,* etc. at the end of November 1992 and stored the same at Rama Katha Kunj which is near to the disputed structure. On 1.12.1992 Shri Moreshwar Save and Satish Pradhan said that Shiv Sainiks would start the construction of Ramjanmabhumi Mandir under the leadership of Bala Saheb Thackeray from the place where Rama was born. In this connection Shiv Sena had its meeting at different place.

36. In this background Shri Lal Krishna Advani and Shri Murli Manohar Joshi started for Ayodhya from New Delhi on 1.11.92 via Varanasi and Mathura. On 1.12.92 Shri Advani said in Kanpur that *kar seva* does not mean *bhajan* and *kirtan* but it is meant for starting construction of Rama Mandir. Dr Joshi asked the Central Government to withdraw the central forces and he further said that his party would face any hindrance whatsoever comes in the way of construction of Rama Mandir. On 2.12.92 Shri Advani said in Varanasi that the State Government would not use force of any kind on *kar sevaks*. During the same time, Sadhvi Rithambara said at Nagpur, Balarasha and Wardha that the Babri Masjid is a Mandir. Mandir shall be constructed there with struggle. She asked *kar sevaks* to reach Ayodhya for construction of a Mandir which is supported by PW-357, PW-358. . . .

37. *Kar sevaks* who have come to become martyrs be allowed to do so. Mahamandaleshwar Jagdish Muni declared that *kar sevaks* should demolish the disputed structure for which they enjoy the full support of Kalyan Singh's government. Shri Advani said, 'Today is the last day of *kar seva* and today *kar sevaks* will do the last *kar seva*.' Shri Dharam Dass asked the photographers not to take the photographs. Dr S.K. Nagar said that his brother Amit Kumar Nagar had died in 1990 while doing *kar seva,* in his memory he will sacrifice for the construction of the Mandir. The *kar sevaks* assaulted newsmen while the structure was being pulled down on the asking of Shri Vinay Katiyar, Ashok Singhal and Dharam Dass from the dais. When the correspondents complained about it to the leaders on the podium, Smt Vijaya Raje Scindia said 'You deserve it'. When the tomb was being pulled down, she embraced Ms Uma Bharati and said, 'I can die in peace now'. Leaders on the podium were distributing sweets on the wrecking of the Tomb. At 2.30 pm, Ashok Singhal and Advani asked the *kar sevaks* to block the main road so that the central forces are not allowed to reach the spot. Paramhansa Ram Chander Dass asked the *kar sevaks* to take advantage of the opportunity and asked them to demolish the wall of disputed structure so that Tomb comes down on its own. While the structure was being pulled down, Shri Kalyan Singh talked to Advani on telephone at Ramjanmabhumi Ayodhya and Shri Advani asked Shri Kalyan Singh to delay his resignation. In support of the above version PW-69, PW-217, PW-441, PW-135, PW-533, P-W-536 and D-121, 442, D-339, D-328 and D-128 are on record. Therefore, as per prosecution an offence of criminal conspiracy to demolish the disputed structure of Ramjanmabhumi–Babri Masjid is *prima facie* made out against accused No. 1 to 38 and Nos 41 to 49.

38. Prosecution produced the following case law in support of its argument on criminal conspiracy.

1. Mohd. Hussain Umar Kochhra *versus* K.S. Dilip Singh, AIR-1970, SC, p. 45.
2. Yashpal Mittal *versus* State of Punjab AIR 1970, SC, p. 2433.
3. Mohd Reaz *versus* State of U.P.-1980, Cr. L J, p. 369.
4. Shiv Narain Laxmi Narain Joshi *versus* State of Maharashtra 1980 Cr LS, p. 388.
5. Mohd Usman Mohd. Hussain Maniya *versus* State of Maharashtra—1981 Cr Ls. p. 588.
6. Kehar Singh *versus* State 1988 SCC (Criminal), p. 711.
7. Ajay Aggarwal *versus* Union of India-1993 SCC (Criminal), p. 961.
8. Ek Chander Sainau *versus* State of Kerala-1995, SCC, p. 329.
9. P.K. Narayanan *versus* State of Kerala-1995, SCC, p. 142.

39. In the above decided case Hon'ble Judge clearly opined that no direct evidence are available to establish conspiracy, for criminal conspiracy it is not necessary that every person must be in know of it. Each conspirator comes to know about it when it is complete. It is necessary for the criminal conspiracy that in which sequence it is planned, the events before the incident, in the sequence of incident, events during the incident and of the incident will be taken into consideration so that role of all the persons involved can be examined on behalf of accused Shri L.K. Advani, emphasis was given on Kehar Singh *versus* State AIR 1988, SC page 833 on the aspect of conspiracy. On behalf of accused Narain Dass, the counsel produced the case law on criminal conspiracy as laid down on the aspect of conspiracy. On behalf of accused Narain Das, the counsel produced the case law on criminal conspiracy as laid down by Hon'ble Supreme Court in KTMS Mohd etc. *versus* Union of India and Amanullah Qurase *versus* Union of India, Supreme Court cases (criminal) page 572, according to which conspiracy can be established only through direct evidence and public evidence. Counsel for L.K. Advani submitted that no statement was attributed to his client which may establish that there was any talk between his client and other people about the demolition of disputed Ramjanmabhumi. Ld counsel contended the act must *prima facie* be conspiracy u/s 10 of Indian evidence act in order to bring the Act of conspiracy u/s 120 IPC. Second part of sec 10 of Indian evidence Act says that in order to constitute a conspiracy something must be said, written or must for a common object among same people.

In the present case nothing is attributed to Shri Lal Krishna Advani, which may be against him, Ld. Counsel for Shri Advani submitted Kanpur Security Karamchari Union *versus* R.N. Sharma AIR 1988, SCC, page no 1965, according to which if a criminal conspiracy is planned by two or more persons, then statement against another will be read in evidence. Present case is entirely different. In the present case it is clearly established that the accused person acted in the demolition of disputed structure of Ramjanmabhumi–Babri Masjid and in this backdrop, Shri Lal Krishna Advani, took out a *rath yatra* for Ayodhya from Somnath. He contacted the leaders different political parties of Hindus, in which the main issue was of the demolition of disputed structure of Ramjanmabhumi–Babri Masjid. In the present case all accused persons except accused No. 39–40 had hatched a criminal conspiracy.

40. On Bharatiya Janata Party coming into power in Uttar Pradesh in 1991 what importance was given to this dispute and in this connection leaders of Bharatiya Janata Party, Vishwa Hindu Parishad and Shiv Sena and people connected with the religious organizations under as criminal conspiracy to demolish Babri Masjid–Ramjanmabhumi, the 'disputed construction' and to fulfil this objective they made speeches at different times in different places and acquired 2.77-acres of land near the disputed structure for the purpose of tourism and ultimately under that design on 6.12.1992 when the main leaders were sitting on the dais, the *kar sevaks* demolished the disputed structure of Ramjanmabhumi–Babri Masjid in their presence.

41. The Chief Minister did not allow 190 companies of Central Reserve Police posted at Faizabad about 10 km away from the disputed spot. Thereafter Shri Kalyan Singh resigned as Chief Minister after demolition of disputed structure and thereafter leaders of Bharatiya Janata Party, Vishwa Hindu Parishad, Shiv Sena and religious organizations expressed their happiness over the demolition of disputed structure of Babri Masjid–Ramjanmabhumi. On 8.12.92 the inscription plate of Mir Baqi on the main gate of the Babri Masjid was taken away in the jeep by the accused Pawan Kumar Pandey and Shiv Sena and others. In this way it is crystal clear that Shiv Sena, Bharatiya Janata Party, Bajrang Dal hatched a criminal conspiracy due to which the disputed structure was pulled down. On the basis of the evidence available on the challan except accused No. 39 and 40, a *prima facie* evidence under section 120-B of IPC is established.

42. The accused persons contended that *namaz* was never held in the disputed Masjid, therefore, it does not fulfil within the definition of Masjid. The accused relied upon Shahid Ganj *versus* Shiromani Gurudwara Prabandhak Committee AIR 1938 Lahore, page 369 in which Hon'ble Judge had laid down that if *namaz* is to held in Masjid and it is in averse possession of non-Muslims then it cannot be recognized as Masjid. However, it is not an issue involved in the present case and the case cited is not applicable to the facts of the present case.

43. The prosecution as submitted in respect of accused persons no. 39 and 40 in criminal case no. 197/92 that Shri R.N. Srivastava and Shri D.B. Rai were District Magistrate Faizabad and Senior Superintendent of Police, Faizabad respectively on the day of incident that is on 6.12.1992. Both the public servants were present near the disputed structure site and they were fully aware about the *kar seva*. They were also in know of Supreme Court's orders dated 28.11.1992 in which the then Chief Minister, Shri Kalyan Singh had assured that no damage would be caused to the disputed structure. On the other hand it would be protected. Accused no. 39 and 40 were also in know of the fact that lakhs of *kar sevaks* were coming to Ayodhya and different political parties had declined to demolish the disputed structure at different times even on this the then District

Magistrate and SSP did not take any step to protect the disputed structure. While in October 1990 *kar sevaks* made unsuccessful attempt to demolish the disputed structure as a result of which communal riots took place all over the country and as a result of which life and property were destroyed. In such situations it was not justified to deploy less police force near the disputed structure on 6.12.92. The District Magistrate Shri R.N. Srivastava sent back three battalions of para-military force at 1.45 pm on 6.12.92.

44. The demolition of the entire structure took 5 hours. Shri Srivastava and Shri D.B. Rai who did not do anything to protect the disputed structure and for the protection of newspaper reporters. The omission of these persons would be taken as intentional and illegal omission on the part of public servants, Shri R.N. Srivastava, Shri D.B. Rai and the then Chief Minister, Shri Kalyan Singh, did not act on the undertaking given to the Hon'ble Supreme Court. Although he had taken oath of the constitution and allegiance to the law of the country. In this connection PW-42, PW-82, PW-81, PW-83, PW-84, PW-132 and PW-617 are there. PW-694, S.C. Chobey, I.G., C.R.P.F., PW-697, C.K. Malik, I.G. Security and PW-700, Shri Hari Das Rao, Additional D.G. are important witnesses, according to whom the District Authorities who were entrusted with the responsibility to maintain law and order did not perform their duty. The correspondence with them also goes to prove that they did not discharge their duty lawfully. On the other hand, they acted illegally. A meeting of Additional D.G. Intelligence, I.G. Lucknow, I.G. Security, S.S.P. Faizabad, D.I.G. Faizabad, D.I.G. Faizabad, I.G. Lucknow Zone, S.S.P. Basti, Gonda, Barabanki was held in which the Director General of Police reviewed the situation created by *kar sevak* reaching Ayodhya and it was also decided as to how much force was required by S.S.P. Faizabad. The Director General of Police had also ordered that *kar sevaks* should not be allowed to support of *kar seva* in groups. The suggestions given by the Police Director General were placed before the Chief Minister on 1.12.92. They were discussed which was informed by the Home Secretary Shri Prabhat Kumar to the Police Director General by his semi administrative letter dated 2.12.92. Shri P.K. Malik, PW-692 produced to Shri Hari Das, Additional D.G. and Director General I.G. in which it was informed that there was no barricade in reaching the disputed 2.77-acres of land and disputed structure and then the *kar sevaks* can reach near the disputed structure on 6.12.92 without any hindrance. In this connection, the definite orders were issued to the S.S.P. Faizabad that police force in sufficient numbers and security arrangement be so that the law and order be maintained and disputed structure be protected.

45. In the same manner CRPF Commander Shri J.S. Bisht also informed on 2.12.1992 about the possible demolition of disputed structure. On 3.12.92 Shri Hari Dass Rao, Additional Police I.G. sent a letter to Shri D.B. Rai, Senior Superintendent Police Faizabad in which he was informed about the orders issued by Home Secretary Shri Prabhat Kumar. It was also informed that *kar sevaks* were armed with dynamite and explosives, for this the disputed structure is required to be fully protected. Shri A.K. Saran, I.G. Lucknow also issued orders to Shri

D.B. Rai for complete security. In document D-435 the Home Secretary New Delhi also informed the U.P. government that some people may attempt to demolish the disputed structure and for this proper action should be taken. The Home Minister of India also wrote letter dated 1.12.92 to the Chief Minister of U.P. for the security of disputed structure. The Special Secretary Home (Centre)—vide base dated 4.12.92 asked the Chief Minister of U.P. to take appropriate steps to ensure the protection of disputed structure. On 4.12.92, I.G. of Police Shri S.B.M. Tripathi ordered the Senior Superintendent of Police and D.I.G. Faizabad to procure the services of Central Police Force to provide protection to the disputed structure. On 5.12.92 Shri Shekhar Aggarwal PW-796 sent a radiogram document no. D-436 to the district authority on behalf of Chief Home Secretary in which the security arrangement at Ayodhya were detailed. Shri Kalyan Singh assured the Central Home Minister that proper action will be taken to protect the disputed structure of Babri Masjid–Ramjanmabhumi but he protested against the Central Forces which were sent to Faizabad. On 5.12.92 Shri Prabhat Kumar Chief Home Secretary placed his notings D-436 before the Chief Minister in which it was requested to have the services of Central Forces for maintaining satisfactory order and security of disputed structure on 5.12.92, the Chief Minister and I.G. of Police said that the situation was normal and there was no cause of concern. At about 1.15 pm on 6.12.92 fax with information about the instigating speeches of Shri L.K. Advani and other leaders at about 12.17 was sent to Home Department and Police Inspector General in which *kar sevaks* were instigated as a result of which *kar sevaks* had started throwing stones at this disputed structure. *Lathi* charge of PAC and CRPF and lodging of tear gas shells had no effect. No effect on demolition of disputed structure in the last moment, the action taken by the District Administrative Officer had no effect because the disputed structure had been demolished.

46. From this it is clear that the accused persons Shri R.N. Srivastava and D.B. Rai are guilty of offence u/s 120-B/153-A/295-A/505/201 Indian Penal Code read with Section 114 of IPC. On behalf of Shri R.N. Srivastava and Shri D.B. Rai it is argued that since they had no power to take any decision in the serious matters like that of Ayodhya, they cannot be held guilty. Counsel for accused person produced case law Gopal Chander Sarkar *versus* Phoolmani Devi decided by Calcutta High Court reported in Volume 8, *Indian Law Reports*, p. 728. The ratio of the case cited is different from the present case because in the cited case it was a chowkidar of a village where as accused Shri R.N. Srivastava was District Magistrate and Shri D.B. Rai was Senior Superintendent of Police Faizabad, who had to perform their duty according to their conscience. It is worth mentioning that accused Shri R.N. Srivastava and Shri D.B. Rai were present near the spot when the disputed structure was being demolished on 6.12.92. *Prima facie* both the accused are liable to charged. It is also apparent from these facts that accused Shri R.N. Srivastava and Shri D.B. Rai acted illegally and the disputed structure was pulled down under conspiracy and both above named officer acted illegally in collusion with Shri Kalyan Singh. It is also found from this that accused persons

Shri R.N. Srivastava and Shri D.B. Rai and Kalyan Singh were not only parties to the conspiracy but they are guilty of criminal conspiracy in the conspiracy hatched by Shri Bala Saheb Thackeray and others.

47. Learned Advocate for Shri R.N. Srivastava and Shri D.B. Rai argued that in all forty-seven first information reports (FIR) were lodged in the police station. Main FIR is crime No. 197/92 and the second one is 198/92. None of the accused is named in any of the FIR. Only above named two public servants are made accused whereas there is no evidence against them. After the incident of 6.12.92 Shri R.N. Srivastava District Magistrate and Shri D.B. Rai Senior Superintendent of Police were suspended on 7.12.92. On 6.12.92, Shri R.N. Srivastava and Shri D.B. Rai were present on report and a chargesheet u/s 153-A/295-A/505/201 read with Section 114 IPC was submitted against them. No offence is made out against them in the above said chargesheet. Accused persons have been impli-cated for political reasons. *Kar seva* was allowed by Hon'ble Supreme Court construction work was prohibited. No information was given by any intelligence Agency to the effect that disputed structure will be demolished by *kar sevaks*. Other senior officers have not been made accused whereas all the decisions about Ayodhya were taken by the State Government. District and Police Administration were not concerned. Newspaper reports cannot be read as evidence.

48. From the evidence against Shri R.N. Srivastava and Shri D.B. Rai on record it is *prima facie* established that being public servant they did not perform their duty properly and allowed the demolition of disputed structure of Ramjanmabhumi–Babri Masjid by their illegal omission while sufficient police force was waiting for their orders.

49. In the present case FIR in crime No. 197/92, u/s 395/397/332/337/338/295/297/153 IPC and Section 7 of criminal law Amendment Act was registered at Police Station Ramjanmabhumi, Ayodhya on 6.12.92 at 17.15 hrs by police inspector Shri P.N. Shukla investigation of which was entrusted by the Central Government to CBI at the request of State Government. Thereafter again the FIR in crime no. 198/92 was lodged by Shri Ganga Prasad Tiwari police inspector Ramjanmabhumi police post against eight persons u/s 153-A/153-B/505 IPC investigation of which was conducted by CBI DC&P and CBI filed chargesheet u/s 153-A/505/147/149 IPC before Special Judicial Magistrate, Lalitpur who took cognizance against Shri Lal Krishna Advani and six others that was also entrusted to CBI by the Central Government at the request of the State Government. Central Government also asked CBI to investigate forty-seven other incidents on 6.12.92 in which newspersons were involved and reported in various police station. Thereafter seeking permission for further investigation submitted chargesheet against nine other accused u/s 395/397/332/338/295/297/153-A IPC. All these offences were investigated along with main offence of demolition of Ramjanmabhumi–Babri Masjid on 6.12.92, on 10.9.93 an application was moved in the court of Special Magistrate, Rae Bareli by CBI for further investigation in crime No. 198/92 in which concerned Magistrate wide order dt 10.9.93 allowed filing of additional *challan*. Thereafter on 15.9.93 Shri Vijay Verma Special Magistrate

CBI was appointed to examine the *challan* in respect of demolition of Ramjanmabhumi–Babri Masjid. A total of forty-seven cases relating to the assault on newspersons and snatching of video camera were entrusted to CBI on 26.8.93 out of which permission to investigate one case u/s 323/427 NCR No. 157/92 was obtained from the Special Magistrate. After investigation a common chargesheet in forty-eight cases, was filed before Special Magistrate, Ayodhya Episode Lucknow. Later on case relating to crime no. 198/92 in connection of demolition of disputed structure at Ayodhya on 6.12.92 was also made over to Shri Vijay Verma. In this manner Shri Vijay Verma took cognizance of forty-nine cases including crime no. 198/92 on 11.10.93 for which he was fully competent. All these cases arose in one sequence. On behalf of accused persons it was contended that when a challan has already been filed in the court of Special Magistrate, Lalitpur and thereafter chargesheet was filed in the court of Special Magistrate, Rae Bareli and cognizance was taken by that court then cognizance by the Special Magistrate, Lucknow Shri Vijay Verma again is illegal. In this connection since Shri Vijay Verma was invested with the power to dispose the case, by appointing him Special Magistrate in my opinion cognizance in crime No. 198/92 by Shri Vijay Verma is legal, and since all the offence are chain in the same sequence therefore chargesheet filed in the present case is as per rule. Earlier the accused raised dispute that separate chargesheet should have been filed for separate offences a revision petition was filed against the orders of Special Magistrate Shri Verma in which the then Addt. District and Special Judge rejected the contention of accused in Revision No. 344/94 and order acquired finality. Therefore the accused persons cannot regulate the same. Filing one *challan* by the prosecution is legal and it seems proper to examine one case on the basis of chargesheet as is held by Bombay High Court in State of Maharashtra *versus* Anjana Bai and Anjana Mohan Govind 1997 cr. L.S. page 2309.

50. *Prima facie* offence under Section 147/135-A/135-B/295/295-A/505 read with Section 149 IPC is made out against accused persons Shri Lal Krishna Advani, Ashok Singhal, Vinay Katiyar, Moreshwar Save. Pawan Kumar Pandey, Brij Bhushan Saran Singh, Jai Bhagwan Goel, Ms Uma Bharati, Ms Sadhvi Rithambara, Maharaj Swami Sakshi, Murli Manohar Joshi, Giri Raj Kishore, Vishnu Hari Dalmia. Offence u/s 332/338/201 read with sec 149 IPC is *prima facie* made out against accused persons Pawan Kumar Pandey, Brijbhushan Saran Singh, Jai Bhagwan Goel, Vinod Kumar Vats, Ram Chander Khatri, Sudhir Kakkar, Amarnath Goel, Santosh Dubey, Prakash Sharma, Jai Bhan Singh Paweya, Dharmendra Singh Gurjar, Ram Narain Dass, Lallu Singh, Om Prakash Pandey, Laxmi Narain Dass Mahatyagi, Vinay Kumar Rai, Kamlesh Tripathi, Gandhi Yadav, Har Govind Singh, Vijay Bahadur Singh, Narain Bhai Shukla. On the basis of evidence produced by the prosecution a *prima facie* offence u/s 120-B of IPC read with 153-A/153-B/295/295-A/505 IPC is made out against Shri Bala Saheb Thackeray, Lal Krishna Advani, Kalyan Singh, Ashok Singhal, Vinay Katiyar, Moreshwar Save, Pawan Kumar Pandey, Brij Bhushan Saran Singh, Jai Bhagwan Goel, Maharaji Swami Sakshi, Satish Pradhan, Murli Manohar Joshi,

Acharya Giri Raj Kishore, Vishnu Hari Dalmia, Vinod Kumar Vats, Ram Chander Khatri, Sudhir Kakkar, Amarnath Goel, Santosh Dubey, Prakash Sharma, Jai Bhan Singh Paweya, Dharmendra Singh Gurjar, Ram Narain Dass, Ramji Gupta, Lallu Singh, Champat Rai Bhansal, Om Prakash Pandey, Laxmi Narain Mahatyagi, Vinay Kumar Rai, Kamlesh Tripathi, Gandhi Yadav, Har Govind Singh, Vijay Bahadur Singh, Narain Bhai Shukla, Ramesh Pratap Singh, Acharya Dharmendra Dev, Ms Uma Bharati, Ms Sadhvi Rithambara.

51. As far as conspiracy u/s 120-B IPC is concerned no proved evidence is required for that because conspiracy is planned secretly and the other accused persons come to know about it in the course of level and this information came through the speeches and acts done by them. In respect to criminal conspiracy Hon'ble Supreme Court in Kehar Singh *versus* State of Delhi 1988, Supreme Court cases (Criminal), page 711 has held that under conspiracy every one does the work assigned to him, one is not aware about the work assigned to others till the same is accomplished. In the same way those connected with conspiracy are held guilty for the illegal work done in the conspiracy because every one is expected to perform one part. This is held in the following decided case.

1. Ajay Aggarwal *versus* Union of India-1993 Supreme Court Cases (Criminal), page 961.
2. P.K. Narayanan *versus* State of Kerala 1995 Supreme Court Cases, page 1421.
3. State of Maharashtra *versus* Somnath Thapan 1996 Crl. L.S. page 2448.

52. According to above mentioned cases decided by Hon'ble Supreme Court although Shri Kalyan Singh, accused Shri R.N. Srivastava and Shri D.B. Rai were not present on spot yet they are held *prima facie* guilty of offence u/s 120-B of Indian Penal Code. Because they are civil servants. *Prima facie* it will be taken as their criminal act. Shri Kalyan Singh had assured National Integration Council that disputed structure will not be allowed to be demolished and the Hon'ble Supreme Court had allowed only symbolic *kar seva*. Shri Kalyan Singh had also said that he will fully protect the structure of Ramjanmabhumi–Babri Masjid and that will not be demolished. But he acted contrary to his assurance. Shri Kalyan Singh did not order for the use of central force. From all this *prima facie* it seems that he was a party to the criminal conspiracy.

53. Accused person Pawan Kumar Pandey, Brij Bhushan Saran Singh, Jai Bhagwan Goel, Vinod Kumar Vats, Ram Chander Khatri, Sudhir Kakkar, Amarnath Goel, Santosh Dubey, Shri Prakash Sharma, Jai Bhan Singh Pawaya, Dharmendra Singh Gurjar, Ram Narain Dass, Laxmi Narain Dass Mahatyagi, Lallu Singh, Om Prakash Pandey, Vinay Kumar Rai, Kamlesh Tripathi, Gandhi Yadav, Har Govind Singh, Vijay Bahadur Singh, Navin Bhai Shukla named in chargesheet are guilty u/s of offence u/s 395 GPC because they took away inscription plate of Mir Baqi, video camera and other valuables fixed for the safety of disputed structure on 6.12.92. Prior to 6.12.92 Shri Ashok Singhal had said on 12.11.92 that in the *kar seva* to be held on 6.12.92 inscription plate of Mir Baqi will be removed, except that everything in the compound belongs to Hindus.

54. On 6.12.92 suicide squad of selected trained workers broke the security cordons and vandalized the structure, damaged the police implements, wireless set detector, telephone, dragon light and took away inscription plate of Mir Baqi with them. Part of inscription plate of Mir Baqi was forcibly taken away by Shri Pawan Kumar Pandey and his twenty accomplices. Which is proved by witness PW-52 and photograph D-9. Therefore the offence of dacoity is *prima facie* made out against the above named accused because they took away inscription plate of Mir Baqi and other articles by injuring police force on the spot and by terracing them as is proved by PW-8 Khem Singh Kharak, Magistrate on duty, and other witnesses. Prosecution has also argued that aforesaid dacoity is in the chain of same sequences which is apart of conspiracy of demolition of disputed structure and the other offences committed, apart from demolition of disputed structure are also acts of the same sequence. In such a situation a joint trial of offences committed in the chain of the same sequence, as mentioned in chargesheet is legal and justified.

55. It is mentioned in the chargesheet that *kar sevaks* are in control of the disputed structure and is surrounding for five hours and as a sequel to the demolition of this structure inscription plate of Mir Baqi, wireless set, CCTV camera and dragon light charger, video-cassettes and cameras, etc., were looted and the *kar sevaks* and accused persons caused injuries to the public servants who were on duty and assaulted the photographers and newspersons, snatched their camera, video-camera and notebook. They were robbed. This act was done intentionally to cause destruction of evidence. On the basis of the available evidence *prima facie* it is clear that the offence of dacoity was committed by more than five persons jointly with common intention. Prosecution in support of its contention that offences of dacoity is made out against the accused persons, produced following cases.

1. Ram Chander *versus* Emperor AIR 1993 Allahabad, page 114.
2. Arodaram Naidu *versus* State of Andhra Pradesh, 1980 Supreme Court cases (Criminal), page 322.
3. Kishore Kumar *versus* State of U.P.—1985 Allahabad criminal cases, page 391
4. Kalika Tripathi *versus* State of Bihar—1977 Supreme Court Cases (Criminal) p. 600.

As per above case law dacoity is committed by more than accused person jointly as is defined in Section 391 of Indian Penal Code.

56. On behalf of the accused persons it was argued that, in the present case, a joint trial cannot be launched legally because all the accused persons are not involved in one offence. Therefore, the present trial is not legal. The prosecution relied on Section 223 Code of Criminal Procedure which provides for joint trial of more than one persons in more than one offence. On the other hand, Section 223 sub-section (a)–(d) laid down that if the accused are involved in the offence committed in the same sequence then, in order to avoid multiplicity of the prosecution, it is necessary to have a common trial against different accused for all the

offences committed in the same sequence. The prosecution, in support of its contention, produced the following cases:

1. State of Andhra Pradesh *versus* Ganeshwar Rai AR 1963 SC, page 1850.
2. Kadri Kunah Ahmed *versus* State of Madras AIR 1960 SC, page 101.
3. Banwar *versus* State of U.P. AIR 1962 SC, page 1198.
4. Kamleshwar *versus* State 1958 Cr. L.J., page 583
5. Gorelal *versus* State 1994 Allahabad Criminal Cases, page 420.
6. Directorate of Enforcement *versus* Deepak Mahajan 1994 SC Cases (Criminal), page 785.
7. Suresh Chander Habri *versus* State of Bihar 1995 SC cases (Criminal), page 60.

57. In the above referred cases, Hon'ble judges have laid down that if different offences are committed by different persons as part of same sequence, then their joint trial would be proper.

In the present case keeping in view the criminal conspiracy which was in respect of demolition of structure of Ramjanmabhumi–Babri Masjid anything done in that respect would be considered in the same sequence. Section 395 of Indian Penal Code is also concerned with the conspiracy to demolish Babri Masjid. This act was a act in the same sequence under section 395 and in this respect PW-37 Sanjay Khera, PW-112 Mohan Sahai, PW-16, Om Mehta, PW-42, Praveen Jain, have said so and the newspapers reporting that is, PW-384. Ram Chander Pradhan said that at about 1.30 pm when the *kar sevaks* failed to pull down the Tomb from the above then *kar sevaks* started demolishing the walls of the Tomb and Shri Vinay Katiyar, Shri Lal Krishna Advani, Shri Murli Manohar Joshi and Shri Ashok Singhal declared a number of times for the *kar sevaks* to climb down from the tomb because the tomb was to come down at any time. Therefore, all the people should raise barricade on the main roads so as to prevent CRPF from coming near the spot. Smt Vijaya Raje Scindia also asked *kar sevaks* to climb down the Tomb and when the Tomb was being pull down sweets were being distributed at the podium.

58. From our description it is concluded that in the present case a criminal conspiracy to demolish the disputed structure of Ramjanmabhumi–Babri Masjid was hatched by the accused persons in the beginning of 1990 and was completed on 6.12.92. Shri Lal Krishna Advani and others hatched criminal conspiracies to demolish the disputed premises on different times at different places. Therefore, I find a *prima facie* case to charge Shri Bala Saheb Thackeray, Shri Lal Krishna Advani, Shri Kalyan Singh, Shri Vinay Katiyar, Shri Moreshwar Save, Shri Pawan Kumar Pandey, Shri Brij Bhushan Saran Singh, Shri Jai Bhagwan Goel, Ms Uma Bharati, Ms Sadhvi Rithambara, Maharaj Swami Sakshi, Shri Murli Manohar Joshi, Giriraj Kishore, Vishnu Hari Dalmia, Champat Rai Bansal, Om Prakash Pandey, Satish Pradhan, Mahant Avaidyanath, Dharam Dass, Mahant Nritya Gopal Dass, Mahamandaleshwar Jagdish Muni, Dr Ram Vilas Vedanti, Baikunth Nath Lal Sharma alias Prem, Param Hans Ram Chander Dass, Smt Vijaya Raje Scindia, Dr Satish Kumar Nagar under section 147/153-A/153-B/295/295-A/505/

Indian Penal Code read with section 120-B of Indian Penal Code and they are charged under the aforesaid offences.

60. On the basis of evidence on record, I find a *prima facie* case to charge the accused persons Pawan Pandey, Brij Bhushan Saran Singh, Jai Bhagwan Goel, Vinod Kumar Vats, Ram Chander Khatri, Sudhir Kakkar, Amarnath Goel, Satish Dubey, Prakash Sharma, Jai Bhagwan Singh Paweya, Dharmendra Singh Gurjar, Ram Narain Dass, Vinay Kumar Rai, Lallu Singh, Ramji Gupta, Om Prakash Pandey, Kamlesh Tripathi, Gandhi Yadav, Har Gobind Singh, Vijay Bahadur Singh, Naveen Bhai Shukla, Ramesh Pratap Singh, Acharya Dharmendra Dev under section 332/338/201 read with section 149/395 and section 120-B of Indian Penal Code and I charge them under the aforesaid offences.

61. Accused persons Shri Ravinder Nath Srivastava, Devender Bahadur Rai are charged under section 120-B, section 153-A/295/295-A/505/201 read with section 114 of Indian Penal Code on the basis of *prima facie* offence against them. Therefore, both the said accused persons are charged under the aforesaid sections.

All the accused persons are directed to be presented in the Court on 17.10.1997 for framing of the charges.

[From Jagdish Prasad Srivastava, Additional Sessions Judge (Ayodhya Episode), Lucknow.]

CHAPTER IX
Criminal Proceedings, 1993–2003

1. Explanatory note on state of the criminal cases

. . . A criminal case is initiated by lodging a First Information Report (FIR) with the police which, after investigations, files a chargesheet in the Magistrate's Court. On a perusal of the document charges are framed by that court. If the offence is grave and warrants a sentence greater than he can award, the magistrate 'commits' the case to the Sessions Court.

The Babri Masjid was demolished on 6 December 1992 when a Bharatiya Janata Party Ministry headed by Kalyan Singh was in power in Uttar Pradesh and the Congress(I) government of P.V. Narasimha Rao was in power at the centre. Kalyan Singh resigned immediately after the deed was done and President's Rule was imposed. Two FIRs were filed that day, FIR in Crime No. 197 was lodged by the Station House Officer of Police Station Ramjanmabhumi at 17.15 hours.

The nomenclature is itself significant. The time of the offence was given as 12.15 pm. However, it did not name as accused anyone in particular but 'lakhs of unknown *kar sevaks*'. Only ten minutes later, another officer, who was in charge of the outpost of the same police station, lodged an FIR in Crime No. 198 citing 10 am as the time of occurrence and naming eight politicians as accused—Ashok Singhal, Giriraj Kishore, L.K. Advani, Murli Manohar Joshi, V.H. Dalmia, Vinay Katiyar, Uma Bharati and Sadhvi Rithambara.

The two FIRs differed in the matter of the offences they alleged. The first, No. 197, alleged the wider case against 'unknown' *kar sevaks* under the Indian Penal Code—Section 395 (dacoity); 397 (robbery or dacoity with attempt to cause death or grievous hurt); 332 (causing hurt to deter public servants); 337 (hurt by endangering life or personal safety of others); 338 (grievous hurt); 295 (injuring or defiling place of worship with intent to insult the religion of any class); 297 (trespass in any place of worship) and 153A (promoting enmity between different groups on grounds *inter alia* of religion), read with Section 7 of Criminal Law Amendment Act.

The eight politicians were charged in Crime No. 198 only under Section

153A, Section 153B (imputations prejudicial to national integration) and 505 (statements conducing to public mischief). These are the ones the police cite when rabidly communal speeches are delivered. This FIR was in respect of their speeches on the morning of 6 December, just prior to the process of demolition.

Once an FIR is lodged and it is obvious both were recorded in a chaotic situation—the police are not limited in their investigation either by the offences alleged or the persons named. If the investigations disclose other offences or offenders, besides the ones listed in the FIR, the police can and ought to mention that fact in the chargesheet.

Eventually, 49 FIRs were filed against 49 persons. (Additionally 47 other FIRs were filed in respect of the offences the *kar sevak* goons committed against mediapersons and expensive cameras they carried. This note does not deal with those cases.)

There were, thus, two distinct but related cases initiated at one and the same police station in respect of offences committed the same day, 6 December 1992. No. 197 concerned the demolition while No. 198 concerned provocative speeches preceding it. *Seeds of confusion were sown shortly thereafter when they were assigned to different courts and a slip occurred when the second case (No. 198) was assigned to the court trying the first (No. 197).* On 10 December, investigation in case No. 198 was assigned to CB CID, Uttar Pradesh; the State police. Three days later, investigation in the graver demolition case (No. 197) was assigned to the CBI. The State was under President's Rule.

On 16 December, the State Government set up, after consulting the High Court, a Special Court of Judicial Magistrate at Lalitpur to try the No. 198 case. Section 11 of the Criminal Procedure Code empowers it to do that in respect of 'any particular case or particular cases' but only 'after consultation with the High Court'. Its presiding officer is appointed by the High Court, not the State Government. The State police submitted to the Special Court a chargesheet against the eight politicians, on 27 February 1993, and the court took cognizance of the case on 1 March. The venue was shifted to Rae Bareli again, after consulting the High Court.

The State now requested the Centre to entrust to the CBI this case (No. 198) as well as 47 other related cases. The Centre did so on 26 August 1993 (Case 48/93). On 8 September, the State Government established a Special Court of Additional Chief Judicial Magistrate, a higher rank, for trial in Lucknow of the demolition cases. The next day, on 9 September, it issued a formal notification under Section 11 of the Cr.P.C. setting up this Special Court 'after consultation with the High Court'. The offences it was to try or inquire into for committal to the Sessions Court were the ones investigated by the CBI. The Schedule listed 48 cases specifically. *They included No. 197 and 47 other cases, but No. 198 was not included though it had also been entrusted to the CBI on 26 August.* This case was pending before the Special Judicial Magistrate Rae Bareli.

Meanwhile, the High Court appointed Vijay Verma to preside over the Special Court in Lucknow trying Case No. 197 and 47 others. It was before him that on 5 October 1993 that the CBI filed the consolidated chargesheet against the eight politicos, in Crime No. 198, as well as 32 others in Crime No. 197 and 47 other related cases. The eight were also involved in Case No. 197. Since then Case No. 198 was pending before the Rae Bareli Court, the notification of 9 September had to be amended to join this case with the rest. That was done by an amending notification on 8 October, but, this one time, *without* consultation with the High Court. It was a careless slip. On 11 February 2001, Justice Jagdish Bhalla of the Allahabad High Court rightly struck down this amendment since it did not comply with the essential safeguard of consultation with the High Court. Having enforced the law, he repeatedly stressed that the defect was 'curable'. Another notification can be issued by the Uttar Pradesh government after consultation with the High Court. . . .

CBI's Counsel P.K. Chaubey pointed out to Special Judge Srikant Shukla on 23 February, even if FIR No. 198 is kept in abeyance, the Special Court should frame charges against all the accused named by the chargesheet. *This is because the subject matter of FIR No. 198 is anyway covered by FIR No. 197.*

No. 198 relates only to the provocative speeches delivered by eight leaders (including the three who are now Ministers) from Rama Katha Kunj Manch, a makeshift dais in the vicinity of the Babri Masjid, on the fateful day.

On the other hand, FIR No. 197 has 'a wider canvas' as it covers the demolition and the criminal conspiracy that led to it. *The CBI's chargesheet accuses the three Ministers of having been part of the criminal conspiracy to demolish the mosque. . . .*

There is no bar to the Special Court which is trying Case No. 197 from receiving evidence in respect of the speeches on 6 December 1992 since they form part of the same transaction. It would be evidence in support of the charges of conspiracy it is already seized of. L.K. Advani, M.M. Joshi, Uma Bharati and others are already arraigned before the Special Judge in Case No. 197.

It is important to note that every single argument against the order of 9 September 1997, for framing charges, was rejected by Justice Bhalla—save the one regarding the careless amendment of 8 October 1993 adding Case No. 198 to the rest before the Lucknow Court. This case was transferred from the Rae Bareli court to the Lucknow court, which had no jurisdiction to try it. As Justice Bhalla pointed out, it was not necessary 'to annex any schedule' and list 48 cases. But once that was done, the 49th cannot be added without consulting the High Court. For the rest, Justice Bhalla upheld the validity of: (a) Vijay Verma's appointment as Special Judge and his cognizance of all cases (save No. 198); (b) the constitution of the Special Court in Lucknow; (c) the CBI's investigations and (d) the consolidated chargesheet of 5 October 1993.

Justice Bhalla upheld the order of 9 September 1997, framing the charges. Even if the one concerning the speeches of 6 December 1992 is dropped, the conspiracy case survives. The charges are validly framed.

'This Court while keeping in mind the above considerations has earnestly considered and examined the impugned order dated 9 September 1997 passed by the trial court for framing charges against the accused revisionists *and does not find any infirmity* with respect to the cases referred to in the Schedule of Notification No. 4421/VII-Nyaya-2-793/87 dated 9 September 1995. Further, the courts below committed jurisdictional error as far as case Crime No. 198 of 1992 is concerned, *which is curable*. In the light of the above no interference is warranted in the impugned order of the trial court as far as the cases referred to in the schedule of Notification No. 4421/VII-Nyaya-2-739/87 dated 9 September 1993 are concerned'. A trial can no longer be averted. . . .

The judgement which Justice Jagdish Bhalla of the Lucknow Bench of the Allahabad High Court delivered on 12 February 2001, in the criminal cases against Union Home Minister L.K. Advani and other Sangh Parivar leaders arising out of the demolition of the Babri Masjid on 6 December 1992, not only paved the way for speedy prosecution but censures the prosecution and, *sotto voce*, the accused, for the delays.

Justice Bhalla pointedly concluded what is, with respect, an able and manifestly impartial judgement with these stinging remarks:

'According to the prosecution the accused persons are either rich, influential or politically strong. In the process I recall the observations of the Hon'ble apex Court in the case of *Ganesh Narain Hegde versus S. Bangarappa and others*, 1995, SCC (Cri) 634, which are as follows: "The slow motion becomes much slower motion when *politically powerful* or rich and influential persons figure as accused. FIRs are quashed. Charges are quashed. Interlocutory orders are interfered with. At every step, there will be revisions and applications for quashing and writ petitions. In short, no progress is ever allowed to be made. And if ever the case reached the stage of trial after all the interruptions, the time would have taken its own toll: the witnesses are won over; evidence disappears; the prosecution loses interest—the result is an all too familiar one".'

'The concept of the joint chargesheet and joint trial has been adopted by the prosecution and accepted by the courts below. I am afraid this may not add to the slow motion becoming slower which is evident from the fact that for the last eight years the case is moving at a snail's pace. I pondered over the matter and it occurred to my mind that the above circumstances can further delay the completion of the trial. In the light of the above I am of the considered opinion that the trial court should ensure speedy trial and in the process take necessary steps' (emphasis added throughout). This is not exactly an exoneration of Advani and Co.

On 9 September 1997, Judge Jagdish Prasad Srivastava, Additional Sessions Judge (Ayodhya Case), Lucknow, said in Para 59 of his order: 'It is concluded that in the present case a criminal conspiracy to demolish the disputed structure of Ramjanmabhumi–Babri Masjid was hatched by the accused persons in the beginning of 1990 and was completed on 6.12.92. *Shri Lal Krishna Advani and others hatched criminal conspiracies to demolish the disputed premises on different times at different places. Therefore, I find a prima facie case to charge Shri Bala Saheb Thackeray, Shri Lal Krishna Advani, Shri Kalyan Singh, Shri Vinay Katiyar, Shri Moreshwar Save, Ms Uma Bharati, Ms Sadhvi Rithambara, Maharaj Swami*

Sakshi, Shri Murli Manohar Joshi, Giriraj Kishore, Vishnu Hari Dalmia and several others 'under sections 147/153A/153B/295/295-A/505 Indian Penal Code read with Section 120-B of Indian Penal Code and they are charged under the aforesaid offences'.

R.N. Srivastava and D.B. Rai, who were at the time of demolition, District Magistrate and Senior Superintendent of Police respectively, of Faizabad district in which Ayodhya is situated, were also charged with conspiracy 'under Section 120-B, Section 153-A/295/295-A/505/201 read with section 114 of Indian Penal Code on the basis of *prima facie* offence against them. Therefore, both the said accused persons are charged under the aforesaid sections. All the accused persons are directed to be presented in the Court on 17.10.1997 for framing of the charges.'

The Judge insisted on their presence because the law required it so that 'the charge shall be read and explained to the accused, and the accused shall be asked whether he pleads guilty of the offence charged or claims to be tried' (Section 228 (2) of the Criminal Procedure Code). The accused must himself be *present* to hear the charges and personally enter his plea of guilt or otherwise. His lawyer's presence will not suffice.

But the accused did not appear on that appointed date, 17 October 1997. They successfully averted the opening of the trial for over three years by filing revision applications in the High Court—precisely the tactic to which the Supreme Court alluded in the case of former Chief Minister of Karnataka S. Bangarappa.

Immediately after quoting the Supreme Court's remarks in that case, Justice Bhalla proceeded to uphold the order of the Sessions Judge in the main conspiracy case (No. 197) but set it aside in respect of one episode (covered in case No. 198) which was limited to a meeting on the morning of the demolition at which Advani and others were present. This was because while issuing a notification assigning this limited case to the court dealing with the wider conspiracy, the State government did not consult the High Court as the law required it should. That can be done even now. Indeed, it *ought* to be done.

This is how Justice Bhalla's judgement concludes: 'In the premise the impugned order dated 9 September 1997 passed by the Special/Sessions Judge (Ayodhya Prakaran), Lucknow, for framing of charges is *upheld* as 48 cases referred to in the Schedule of Notification No. 4421/VII-Nyaya-2-739/87 dated 9 September 1993 are concerned and the impugned order is set aside with respect to case Crime No. 198 of 1992 mentioned in Notification No. 5175/VII-Nyaya-2-739/87 dated 8 October 1993 which being invalid does not confer any jurisdiction upon the courts below to take cognizance, commit and try the case relating to Crime No. 198 of 1992 under Section 153-A, 153-B and 505 of the Indian Penal Code, Police Station Ramjanmabhumi, Ayodhya, District Faizabad. However, the mistake in issuing the said notification dated 8 October 1993 is *curable* and it is open for the State Government to cure the legal infirmity.'. . .

The Sessions Judge's order, which the High Court has upheld, found explicitly that such a prima facie *case exist*. 'On a careful perusal of evidence produced by the prosecution in the present case, *I have come to conclusion that the* prima facie *evidence as alleged against the accused persons is made out* when section mentioned in the chargesheet will be detailed as the section of the offence then it would be clear as to against which of the accused of the offence is made out *prima facie*.'

The Sessions Judge's order of 9 September 1997 is a most revealing document. This order was the culmination of a long-drawn investigative process. On 5 October 1993, the Central Bureau of Investigation (CBI) filed a chargesheet in the Magistrate's court after a thorough probe. On 27 August 1994, Special Judicial Magistrate Mahipal Sirohi found that a *prima facie* case existed which warranted full trial by the Sessions Court which alone, he felt, could pass an appropriate sentence. Thus, a judicial authority put the imprimatur on the CBI's work as did a higher authority, the Sessions Judge, later. Justice Bhalla of the High Court rejected challenges to the validity of the committal order and upheld it—except in regard to Case No. 198 relating to the meeting of 6 December 1992. . . .

Even if the speech of 6 December (which is covered by Case No. 198) is omitted the wider case of conspiracy for demolition (No. 197) still stands.

Justice Bhalla has explicitly upheld the committal to trial before the Sessions Judge of the main case based on the consolidated chargesheet of 5 October 1993. 'I am of the opinion that no illegality has been committed by the courts below while taking cognizance of a joint/consolidated chargesheet on the ground that all the offences were committed in the course of the same transaction and to accomplish the conspiracy; *that the evidence for all the offences is almost the same and therefore these offences cannot be separated from each other irrespective of the fact that 49 different FIRs were lodged on the basis of which 49 criminal cases were registered by the police*. Although there is no provision in the Cr.P.C. with regard to joinder of chargesheets by the prosecution agency but on the other hand there is no prohibition also for the same. Learned courts below by permitting the filing of joint/consolidated chargesheet has accepted in principle the permissibility of the joint/consolidated chargesheet. As regards the offences regarding criminal conspiracy and common object of unlawful assembly they *prima facie* made out against the accused revisionists and *since these offences are alleged to have been committed in the course of same transaction therefore the Special Court of ACJM (Additional Chief Judicial Magistrate) rightly took cognizance of the same and also rightly committed the same to the court of sessions*.'

Shortly thereafter on 5 May 2001, as a direct result of the High Court's ruling, the Sessions Judge Srikant Shukla at Ayodhya dropped further proceedings against 20 accused persons including L.K. Advani, Bal Thackeray, Murli Manohar Joshi, Uma Bharati and others, in short, the leading figures. 28 other accused were ordered to stand trial. The Judge specifically referred to Justice Bhalla's ruling and observed: 'Although this defect in the notification is *curable* and the State Government has opportunity to rectify the same, despite the above order, *the State Government has not rectified the said mistake in the said notification*'. The neglect was deliberate.

Advani, Joshi and others were not slow to take advantage of the technical defect confident that it would not be cured by the State Government, headed by Rajnath Singh of the BJP. They filed an application (No. 719B) that further proceedings against them in respect of FIR No. 198 'be dropped'. The Judge permittedly noted 'No written objection has been filed by the prosecution' to this application. The prosecution opposed them 'orally'.

Justice Bhalla upheld the joint chargesheet. He found that 'evidence for all the offences is almost the same and therefore these offences cannot be separated from each other'. This exposes the lapse in splitting cases between Rae Bareli and Lucknow. He also said 'all the offences were committed in the course of the same transaction *and to accomplish the conspiracy*'—the speeches in FIR 198 also formed part of the conspiracy in FIR 197. Lastly, he held that 'as regards the offences regarding criminal conspiracy and common object of unlawful assembly they (are) *prima facie* made out against the accused'. The High Court thus confirmed the findings of the Sessions Judges as well as the Magistrate that a *prima facie* case of conspiracy is disclosed by the chargesheet.

But the High Court's ruling was set at naught by the Sessions Judge at Lucknow, Srikant Shukla, on 4 May 2001. He had no right to do so. Justice Bhalla had merely struck down the transfer of the speeches case (198) from Rae Bareli to Lucknow. Judge Shukla went beyond it and *dropped even the conspiracy charge* in Case 197 before him.

Shukla pointedly noted 'No written objection has been filed by the prosecution' to the applications. His reasoning is tortuous. He confines FIR 197 (demolition) to the *kar sevaks* alone, ignores the conspiracy charge and exonerates the leaders. They are accountable only in FIR 198 (speeches) which he could not try. He writes 'Two distinct cases were registered which are different. In the first FIR were *kar sevaks* who pulled down the structure . . . and in the other FIR are conspirators/abettors who instigated the *kar sevaks*. This way, the State has considered both the case different and separate and has treated them so.' This is in flat contradiction to the High Court's judgement delivered by Justice Bhalla.

What Shukla did was to transpose the conspiracy charge, which properly belongs to the demolition case (197) he was trying, to the speeches case (198) *in Rae Bareli* which he could not try. Having done so, he dropped proceedings not only against the 8 in the speeches case but 13 others who were not; including Bal Thackeray. Thrown at the Rae Bareli court like a shuttle cock, the conspiracy charge was buried there by the CBI two years later, on 19 July 2003. No Sessions Judge can thus flout a High Court Judge's ruling. Interestingly the CBI had moved the High Court on 19 June 2001 against Shukla's order. On 6 August 2003. Justice N.K. Mehrotra ordered stay of proceedings in the Lucknow Court till September 24.

On 16 June 2001 the CBI requested the U.P. government to issue a fresh notification to cure the defect after consulting the High Court. The government neither issued the notification nor appealed against the High Court's judgement. Eventually, special leave petitions were filed in the Supreme Court by Mohammad Aslam Bhure, Society for Justice and a few concerned citizens, including this writer. On 28 September 2002, shortly before the petitions came up for hearing, the High Court of Allahabad issued a notification appointing Vinod Kumar Singh, Civil Judge, Junior Division as Judicial Magistrate First Class, Rae Bareli and simultaneously appointing him as presiding officer of the special court of judicial magistrate first class at Rae Bareli 'for trying cases relating to offences committed in Ayodhya (Faizabad) in Crime No. 198/92 .'. . . This was not a cure for the defect. It was its aggravation. To split the two cases (Nos. 197 and 198) between two courts in Lucknow and Rae Bareli was to inflict hardship on prosecution no less than the accused. The two cases were interconnected. The arose the same day at the same place. The speeches (Case No. 198) proceed the demolition (Case No. 197) The Supreme Court, in a brief, rather perfunctory, order on 29 November 2002, overlooked this aspect when it observed; 'No person much less the petitioners in public interest can claim any special court at any particular place for trial of any criminal case'. The petitioners did not 'claim' any particular venue for themselves or in their own interest. They did so in the 'public interest', in the interests of expeditious justice. A review petition was filed in the Supreme Court against his order in March 2003.

On 30 May 2003, the CBI filed a supplementary chargesheet in the Rae Bareli Court against Advani and others, including Murli Manohar Joshi, Uma Bharati, Vinay Katiyar and Ashok Singhal in Case No. 198. But it dropped the charge of conspiracy under S. 120B of the Penal Code) against the accused. The charge had been levelled in explicit terms in the consolidated chargesheet of 5 October 1993, for Cases Nos. 197 and 198. A Sessions Judge found that a *prima facie* case did exist and framed charges on 9 September 1997. The High Court judgement delivered by Justice Bhalla on 12 February 2001 observed as explicitly. 'I am of the opinion that no illegality has been committed by the courts below while taking cognizance of a joint/consolidated chargesheet on the ground that all the offences were committed in the course of the same transaction and to accomplish the conspiracy; that the evidence for all the offences is almost the same and therefore these offences cannot be separated from each other irrespective of the fact that 49 different FIRs were lodged on the basis of which 49 criminal cases were registered by the police. Although there is no provision in the Cr.P.C. with regard to joinder of chargesheets by the prosecution agency but on the other hand there is no prohibition also for the same. Learned courts below by permitting the filing of joint/consolidated chargesheet has accepted in principle the permissibility of the joint/consolidated chargesheet. As regards the offences regarding criminal conspiracy and common object of unlawful assembly, they are *prima facie* made out against the accused revisionists and since these offences are alleged to have been committed in the course of same transaction therefore the special Court of A.C.J.M. (Additional Chief Judicial Magistrate) rightly took cognizance of the same and also rightly committed the same to the court of sessions.'

The chargesheet of 1993 very much included the grave and crucial charge of conspiracy. A decade later, the same investigation and prosecution agency, the CBI, excluded it in 2003. Nothing had changed to warrant that except that the some prominent ones among the accused were now at the apex of power. L.K. Advani was now not only Union Home Minister but also Deputy Prime Minister.

Incidentally, Justice Bhalla took full note of the fact that the Uttar Pradesh police, the CB CID, had filed a chargesheet in Case No. 198 on 27 February 1993 in which it accused Advani and others of offences under Section 147 ('rioting' defined as use of force by an unlawful assembly or by any of its members 'in prosecution of the common object of such assembly' (S. 146) and S. 149 of the Penal Code which renders every member of the assembly guilty of offence committed 'in prosecution of the common object of that assembly'.

The charge of conspiracy (S. 120 B) implies prior agreement to do 'an illegal act'. It can be proved by circumstantial evidence. Concert can be established by necessary implication. Additionally the accused persons were charged under Ss. 153-A, 153-B and 505 (promotion of disharmony between different communities; imputations of disloyalty; and statements conducing to public mischief). They were, however, not charged with conspiracy.

On 25 August 1993, a Central Agency, the CBI had taken over from the State agency, the CB CID. The State Government authorized the CBI to conduct investigations into FIR 198. The Rae Bareli court accorded its permission to conduct this investigation, on 10 September 1993. The CBI accordingly filed a consolidated chargesheet on 5 October 1993 in which it charged the accused with conspiracy to demolish the mosque.

Justice Bhalla upheld the legality of the charges as well as the Magistrate's order committing the accused to the Sessions Court on 9 September 1997 to face trial *inter alia* on the charge of conspiracy. He found fault only with the venue of the trial because of a technical, but easily curable, error. He did not find any legal defect in the consolidated chargesheet or in the charge of conspiracy. Neither was quashed. Both were upheld the altered chargesheet, filed a decade later omitting the conspiracy charge, betrays its bias. There is no suggestion whatever that further evidence required deletion of the charge.

The Union Law Minister Arun Jaitley's assertion in *India Today* (4 August 2003) that 'Against Advani the (High Court) set aside the charging order in relation to Crime No. 198, the only case in which he was charge' is manifestly untrue. Justice Bhalla did no such thing. On the contrary, he strongly deplored the failure of the legal process to bring the powerful to look, citing the Supreme Court's strictures in 1995 in the case of the former Chief Minister of Karnataka S. Bangarappa.

It is absurd to suggest that once a chargesheet is presented to a court it cannot be revised even if further investigation warrants inclusion of a graver charge. Section 173 (8) of the Criminal Procedure Code, 1973 permits that. Nor it is tenable to suggest that a chargesheet presented to one court cannot be presented to another even if the case is transferred to it. Jaitley's reliance on a noting on the file, dated 9 September 1993, by one P.N. Behl, Advisor to the Governor of Motilal Vohra is misplaced since the noting was clearly misconceived 'Can a chargesheet filed before a Court be presented to another? And, should an additional chargesheet be filed, which court would evaporate it?' (*India Today*, 4 August 2003). Given the fact that the State Government itself had, on 25 August 1993, consented to the CBI investigating into FIR 198 and had set up a special Court for Ayodhya cases on 8 September, the Adviser's noting on 9 September casts it in a very poor light, indeed.

The fact remains that the CBI, authorized by the Central and State governments as well as the Rae Bareli Court, investigated into the case and presented its chargesheet on 5 October 1993—charging Advani and others with conspiracy. The recital of notifications in Justice Bhalla's judgement is suggestive of oversight, not a conscious decision to exclude Case No. 198 from Lucknow.

When proceedings in this case were resumed the CBI's advocate, S.S. Gandhi, opened arguments before special Judge V.K. Singh, on 5 July 2003. He read out statements of eye-witnesses before a special court in Rae Bareli stating that Union Ministers L.K. Advani and Murli Manohar Joshi and others, including Ms Uma Bharati, Sadhvi Rithambara and Mr Ashok Singhal, had delivered inflammatory speeches and instigated the *kar sevaks* to demolish the Babri Masjid. He said the witnesses had averred that the accused, including Mr Advani, Mr Joshi, Ms Bharati, Sadhvi Rithambara and Mr Singhal, had given inflammatory speeches on the morning of 6 December 1992. They had also instigated the *kar sevaks* to demolish the Babri Masjid, Gandhi amplified quoting the witnesses' statements. He said that he would produce before the Court audio and *video cassettes* and paper-cutting as evidence in the case. (*The Asian Age*, 6 July 2003) Quoting witnesses, he added that the accused had raised provocative slogans like '*Rama Lalla hum aye hain, mandir yahin banayenge*' (Lord Rama, we have come, will build the temple here) on the fateful day.

There was a furore over the dropping of the conspiracy charge when Parliament met for its monsoon session on 21 July 2003. The Law Minister Arun Jaitley's contention that the chargesheet before the Rae Bareli Court on 27 February 1993, did not include the charge of criminal conspiracy was true only in the literal, which is misleading, sense. It implied that the CBI's chargesheet of 5 October 1993 before the Lucknow Court, which included this charge is of no relevance. He was, therefore, wrong is asserting in Parliament on July 21 that 'there is absolutely no dropping of any charge by the CBI'. The denial is palpably untrue.

A report in *The Times of India's* of 26 July 2003 exposed these pretexts completely. It revealed that the Union Home Ministry had given sanction the CBI a consolidated chargesheet by a 10-page letter dated 1 October 1993, four days before the CBI filled it in the Lucknow court. This reduced the officials

But far worse followed. On 30 July, the CBI screened video films before the Court that did not show any of the eight accused, Advani included, delivering inflammatory speeches at Ayodhya in the morning of the mosque's destruction. 'The video cassettes did not show them giving any speech'. The prosecutor S.S. Gandhi told the press (*The Telegraph*, 30 July 2003), contradicting his own presentation on 5 July. Once again, there was an uproar in both houses of Parliament on 31 July. S. Jaipal Reddy, M.P., the Congress' chief spokesman, accused Advani and others of 'misutilizing CBI unscrupulously to get out of the case'. He contended that according to his information, the CBI was in possession of cassettes that contained speeches by these leaders. 'All proceedings on 6 December 1992, (at Ayodhya) were recorded and videographed. Where have they vanished' (*The Hindu*, 1 August 2003).

Justice Raza Khan's observations will ever continue these proceedings. On 7 August 2003, Mohammed Aslam Bhure moved the Supreme Court for a stay of proceedings in the Rae Bareli Court and alleged that the CBI had filed an 'incorrect and truncated chargesheet' with the intention of saving Advani and seven others.

On 1 September 2003 the Supreme Court issued notices to Advani and seven others on petitions challenging the CBI's chargesheet of 30 May 2003 which dropped the charge of conspiracy. The Court also has before it a petition for review of its judgement in November 2002 upholding the Rae Bareli Court's trial of case No. 197 (demolition). The Rae Bareli Court was due to frame charges against Advani and the others accused on 3 September 2003 but adjourned the case to 12 September. Barring the speech of Rithambara, none of the cassettes exhibited in the Court contained speeches by Advani and other leaders, the CBI now claimed.

Having regard to the CBI's behaviour and the prosecution stand, no one was surprised when on 19 September 2003 the Special Court of Judge V.K. Singh at Rae Bareli framed charges—under sections 147 and 149 (rioting) and 153A and 153B (spreading communal disaffection) and 505 of the Penal Code—against all the accused, including Murli Manohar Joshi. However, L.K. Advani was discharged, much to the dismay of his friends.

Amidst all this, one important fact has been overlooked. Case No. 197 before the Lucknow Court covers the charge of demolition of the Babri Masjid. Case No. 198 covered only the provocative speeches before that. Justice Bhalla upheld assignment of Case No. 197 to the Lucknow Special Court. Why the CBI is not proceeding with this case expeditiously is hard to understand. The evidence which the prosecutor, S.S. Gandhi, read out it to the Rae Bareli Court on 5 July in Case No. 198 (the 'Speeches Case') can very well be produced before the Lucknow Court in Case No. 19), the 'Demolition Case'. And Advani and associates can be added to the list of the accused. The law permits it (S. 319 of the Criminal Procedure Code) as it does alteration of the charge (S. 216) any time before judgement is pronounced.

FIR No. 197, filed at 17.15 hrs on 6 December 1992, understandably charged 'lakhs of unknown *kar sevaks*' with the demolition. FIR No. 198, filed only ten minutes later at the same police station, charged the eight politicians with delivering provocative speeches. If later investigations yield the identity of the leaders of the 'unknown' ones, the police is surely not precluded from including them in its chargesheet. This is what the CBI did on 5 October 1993. Advani and others can be tried in the Lucknow Court also. They were cited as accused in the Sessions Judge's Order framing the charges on 9 September 1997.

2. Judgement of Justice Jagdish Bhalla on 12 February 2001

Criminal Revision No. 199 of 1997.
Jagdish Bhalla, J.
All the above revisions are directed against the same order dated 9 September 1997 passed by the Special Additional Sessions Judge (Ayodhya Prakaran), Lucknow for framing charges against the revisionists, therefore, they were heard together and are being disposed of by a common judgement.

In Criminal Revision No. 199 of 1997 (*Moreshwar Savey versus State of U.P. and another*) the revisionists is to be charged with offences punishable under Sections 147, 153-A, 153-B, 295, 295-A, 505 read with Section 120-B of the Indian Penal Code (hereinafter referred to as the IPC)

In Criminal Revision No. 201 of 1997 (*Ms Uma Bharati alias Gajra Singh and others Versus State of UP and another*) revisionists nos 1, 3 to 10 are to be charged with offences punishable under Sections 147, 153-A, 153-B, 295, 295-A, 505 read with Section 120-B IPC.

In Criminal Revision No. 211 of 1997 (*Ravindra Nath Srivastava and another Versus State of U.P.*) the revisionists are to be charged with offences punishable under Sections 120-B, 153-A, 295, 295-A, 505, 201 read with Section 114 IPC.

In Criminal Revision No. 255 of 1997 (*Ashok Singhal and others Versus State of U.P. and another*) revisionists 1 to 3 and 5 to 8 are to be charged with offences punishable under Sections 147, 153-A, 153-B, 295, 295-A, 505 I.P.C. read with Section 120-B IPC, whereas revisionists 4, 5 and 9 to 19 are to be charged with offences punishable under Sections 332, 338, 201, read with Sections 149/395 and 120-B IPC. It has come to the notice of this Court through print and electronic media that one of the revisionists, Rajmata Vijaya Raje Scindia, has passed away and is no more. I expected the learned counsel for the revisionists to move application before this Court informing about the sad demise of Rajmata Vijaya Raje Scindia and praying for deletion of her name but no such application was moved. My conscience does not permit me to carry on with the name of late Rajmata Vijaya Raje Scindia as revisionist therefore I take judicial notice of her death. Accordingly I delete the name of late Rajmata Vijaya Raje Scindia from the army of the revisionists in Criminal Revision No. 255 of 1997.

For deciding these revisions it is necessary to have a glance on the facts of the case which, in brief, are that on 6 December 1992 the disputed structure, popularly known as Ramjanmabhumi–Babri Masjid at Ayodhya was demolished. In respect of this incident firstly two First Information Reports (hereinafter referred to as FIRs) were lodged on the same day that is, 6 December 1992. The details of these FIRs are given below:

(i) Crime No. 197/92 under Sections 395, 397, 332, 337, 338, 295, 297, 153-A IPC and Section 7 Criminal Law Amendment Act, Police Station Ramjanmabhumi, district Faizabad. This FIR was lodged by Shri Priyambada Nath Shukla, Station Officer of Police Station Ramjanmabhumi against lakhs of unknown *kar sevaks* at 17.15 hours on 6.12.1992. The time of incident was stated to be 12.14 pm on 6 December 1992.

(ii) Crime No. 198/92 under Sections 153-A, 153-B, 505 IPC, Police Station Ramjanmabhumi, district Faizabad. This FIR was lodged by Shri Ganga Prasad Tewari, Incharge Outpost Ramjanmabhumi, Police Station Ramjanmabhumi on 6 December 1992 at 17.25 hours alleging the time of occurrence to be 10.00 am on 6 December 1992 and the following accused persons were named therein:

(1) Ashok Singhal, Revisionist in Crl. Revision No. 255 of 1997,
(2) Giriraj Kishore, Revisionist in Crl. Revision No. 255 of 1997,
(3) Lal Krishna Advani,
(4) Murli Manohar Joshi,
(5) Vishnu Hari Dalmia, Revisionist in Crl. Revision No. 201 of 1997,
(6) Vinay Katiyar, Revisionist in Crl. Revision No. 255 of 1997,
(7) Uma Bharati, Revisionist in Crl. Rev. No. 201 of 1997, and
(8) Sadhvi Rithambara, Revisionist in Crl. Revision No. 201 of 1997

Besides the above mentioned two FIRs regarding demolition of disputed structure, forty-six other FIRs with respect to cognizable offences and one FIR relating to non-cognizable offences, (all relating to offences committed against media persons who were recording the occurrence of demolition of the disputed structure and whose video cameras, etc. were snatched away or broken/stolen/robbed of, etc.) were also lodged at Police Station Ramjanmabhumi on 6 December 1992 and thereafter, on the basis of which the following case crime numbers were registered:

(1) Crime No. 203 of 1992 under Section 394 IPC.
(2) Crime No. 204 of 1992 under Section 394 IPC.
(3) Crime No. 205 of 1992 under Section 394 IPC.
(4) Crime No. 206 of 1992 under Section 392 IPC.
(5) Crime No. 207 of 1992 under Section 392 IPC.
(6) Crime No. 208 of 1992 under Section 392 IPC.
(7) Crime No. 209 of 1992 under Sections 147, 323, 427 IPC.
(8) Crime No. 210 of 1992 under Section 395 IPC.
(9) Crime No. 211 of 1992 under Section 394 IPC.
(10) Crime No. 213 of 1992 under Section 392 IPC.
(11) Crime No. 215 of 1992 under Section 392 IPC.
(12) Crime No. 225 of 1992 under Sections 398, 336 IPC.
(13) Crime No. 226 of 1992 under Sections 395, 114 IPC.
(14) Crime No. 227 of 1992 under Section 394 IPC.
(15) Crime No. 228 of 1992 under Sections 394/427 IPC.
(16) Crime No. 229 of 1992 under Section 394 IPC.
(17) Crime No. 230 of 1992 under Section 394 IPC.
(18) Crime No. 231 of 1992 under Section 394 IPC.
(19) Crime No. 232 of 1992 under Section 394 IPC.
(20) Crime No. 233 of 1992 under Section 394 IPC.

(21) Crime No. 234 of 1992 under Section 392 IPC.
(22) Crime No. 235 of 1992 under Section 394 IPC.
(23) Crime No. 236 of 1992 under Section 394 IPC.
(24) Crime No. 237 of 1992 under Section 394 IPC.
(25) Crime No. 238 of 1992 under Section 394/406 IPC.
(26) Crime No. 239 of 1992 under Section 392 IPC.
(27) Crime No. 247 of 1992 under Sections 147, 323, 427 IPC.
(28) Crime No. 267 of 1992 under Section 394/427 IPC.
(29) Crime No. 268 of 1992 under Sections 394, 427. 506 IPC.
(30) Crime No. 285 of 1992 under Section 395 IPC.
(31) Crime No. 318 of 1992 under Section 394 IPC.
(32) Crime No. 319 of 1992 under Sections 394/427 IPC.
(33) Crime No. 320 of 1992 under Sections 395, 427 IPC.
(34) Crime No. 321 of 1992 under Section 147, 352, 427 IPC.
(35) Crime No. 322 of 1992 under Section 392 IPC.
(36) Crime No. 481 of 1992 under Section 147, 336, 323, 506 IPC.
(37) Crime No. 482 of 1992 under Section 395 IPC.
(38) Crime No. 1 of 1993 under Sections 395, 397 IPC.
(39) Crime No. 2 of 1993 under Section 395, 397 IPC.
(40) Crime No. 16 of 1993 under Section 395 IPC.
(41) Crime No. 27 of 1993 under Section 395 IPC.
(42) Crime No. 31 of 1993 under Sections 394, 342 IPC.
(43) Crime No. 32 of 1993 under Section 394 IPC.
(44) Crime No. 33 of 1993 under Section 395 IPC.
(45) Crime No. 61 of 1993 under Section 395 IPC.
(46) Crime No. 70 of 1993 under Section 394 IPC.
(47) NCR No. 57 of 1992 relating to non-cognizable offences under Sections 323, 427 IPC.

On 10 December 1992 the investigation regarding Case Crime No. 198 of 1992 was entrusted to CB CID, UP while investigation with respect to case Crime No. 197 of 1992 was entrusted to Central Bureau of Investigation (hereinafter referred to as the CBI) on 13 December 1992 upon which the CBI registered the case Crime No. 197 of 1992 with it as R.C.No. 8(S)/92-SIU.V-New Delhi. The other case i.e. Crime No. 198 of 1992 remained with the CB CID.

The State Government of Uttar Pradesh, after consultation with the High Court, issued Notification No. 6517(1)/VII-Nyaya-2-92-539-G, dated 16 December, 1992, under Section 11 of the Code of Criminal Procedure (hereinafter referred to as Cr.P.C.) which was published in the U.P. Gazette, Extra Part IV, Section *kha*, dated 16 December 1992, establishing a Special Court of Judicial Magistrate with its place of sitting at Lalitpur to try the case relating to Crime No. 198 of 1992. The said notification is reproduced below:

> Notification No. 6517 (1)/VII Nyaya 2-92-539-G dated 16 December 1992.
>
> In exercise of the powers under proviso to subsection (I) of Section 11 of the

> Code of Criminal Procedure, 1973 (Act II of 1974), the Governor, after consultation with the High Court of Judicature at Allahabad, is pleased to establish with effect from the date of the publication of this notification in the Gazette, a Special Court of Judicial Magistrate of the first class for the local area comprising the whole of the State of Uttar Pradesh with its place of sitting at Lalitpur to try the case specified in the Schedule below:
>
> Schedule
> 1. Case relating to Crime No. 198/92 under Sections 153-A, 153-B and 505 of the Indian Penal Code, 1860, P.S. Ramjanmabhumi, Ayodhya, district Faizabad, State Versus Shri Ashok Singhal and others.

Before the Court of Special Judicial Magistrate at Lalitpur constituted by the above notification the CB CID submitted a chargesheet in case Crime No. 198 of 1992 against all the eight accused persons named in the FIR, as mentioned above, under Sections 153-A, 153-B, 505, 147, 149 IPC on 27 February 1993 whereupon the Special Judicial Magistrate sitting at Lalitpur took cognizance of the case Crime No. 198 of 1992 on 1 March 1993. Thereafter the State Government, after consultation with the High Court, shifted the place of sitting of the Court of Special Judicial Magistrate from Lalitpur to Rae Bareli by Notification No. 3123/VII-Nyaya-2-539-G-92-T.C. dated 8 July 1993. The said notification is as under:

> Notification No. 3123/VII-Nyaya-2-539-G-92-T.C. dated 8 July 1993.
>
> In exercise of the powers under proviso to sub-section (1) of Section 11 of the Code of Criminal Procedure, 1972 (Act II of 1974) read with Section 21 of the General Clauses Act, 1897 (Act No. X of 1897), the Governor, after consultation with the High Court of Judicature at Allahabad, is pleased to modify the Notification No. 6517 (1)/VII-Nyaya-2-92-539-G, dated Lucknow, 16 December 1992 regarding the establishment of a Special Court of Judicial Magistrate of the 1 Class to the extent that now the place of sitting of that Special Court of Judicial Magistrate 1 Class shall be at Rae Bareli instead of Lalitpur.

On 25 August 1993 the State Government made a request to the Central Government to entrust the investigation of case Crime No. 198 of 1992 as well as forty-seven other related cases, including one NCR case mentioned above o the CBI upon which the Central Government entrusted the investigation of the above cases to the CBI by Notification No. 228/28/93-AVD-II dated 26 August 1993. Thereafter the CBI registered the case Crime No. 198 of 1992 with it as R.C. No. 1/93 and forty-seven other related cases as R.C. Nos. 2/93 to 48/93.

On 8 September 1993 the State Government of Uttar Pradesh, after consultation with the High Court, vide Notification No. 4420/VII-Nyaya-2-739/87 created and established a Special Court of Additional Chief Judicial Magistrate/ Judicial Magistrate first class at Lucknow for disposal of cases arising out of demolition of disputed structure at Ayodhya in district Faizabad investigated by the Central Bureau of Investigation.

On 9 September 1993 the State Government of Uttar Pradesh, after consultation with the High Court, issued Notification No. 4421/VII-Nyaya-2-739/87 under Section II Cr.P.C. establishing a Special Court of Judicial Magistrate sitting at Lucknow to try or inquire into and commit to the court of Sessions the cases arising out of Crime No. 197 of 1992 and forty-seven other cases. The said notification is reproduced below:

> Notification No. 4421/VII-Nyaya-2-739/87 dated 9 September 1993.
>
> In exercise of the powers under proviso to sub-section (I) of Section II of the Code of Criminal Procedure, 1973 (Act No. 2 of 1974), the Governor after the consultation with High Court of Judicature at Allahabad, is pleased to establish, with effect from the date of the publication of the notification in the Gazette, a Special Court of Judicial Magistrate of the first class for the local area comprising the whole of the State of Uttar Pradesh with its place of sitting at Lucknow, to try or inquire into and commit to the Court of Sessions all cases specified in the Schedule below in which investigations are made or chargesheet filed by the Special Police Establishment constituted under the Delhi Special Police Establishment Act, 1946 (Act No. XXV of 1946).

Sr.No.	*Crime Number*	*Police Station*	*Sections*
1.	*197/92*	Ramjanmabhumi	395, 397,332, 337, 338, 295, 297 and 153-A IPC and Sec. 7 of Criminal Law Amendment Act.
2.	203/92	-do-	394 IPC
3.	204/92	-do-	394 IPC
4.	205/92	-do-	394 IPC
5.	206/92	-do-	392 IPC
6.	207/92	-do-	392 IPC
7.	208/92	-do-	392 IPC
8.	209/92	-do-	147, 323, 427 IPC
9.	210/92	-do-	395 IPC
10.	211/92	-do-	394 IPC
11.	213/92	-do-	392 IPC
12.	215/92	-do-	392 IPC
13.	225/92	-do-	398, 336 IPC
14.	226/92	-do-	395, 114 IPC
15.	227/92	-do-	394 IPC
16.	228/92	-do-	394/427 IPC
17.	229/92	-do-	394 IPC
18.	230/92	-do-	394 IPC
19.	231/92	-do-	394 IPC
20.	232/92	-do-	394 IPC
21.	233/92	-do-	394 IPC
22.	234/92	-do-	392 IPC

Contd/-

Sr.No.	Crime Number	Police Station	Sections
23.	235/92	-do-	394 IPC
24.	236/92	-do-	394 IPC
25.	237/92	-do-	394 IPC
26.	238/92	-do-	394/406 IPC
27.	239/92	-do-	392 IPC
28.	247/92	-do-	147, 323, 427 IPC
29.	267/92	-do-	394/427 IPC
30.	268/92	-do-	394, 427, 506 IPC
31.	285/92	-do-	395 IPC
32.	318/92	-do-	394 IPC
33.	319/92	-do-	394/427 IPC
34.	320/92	-do-	395, 427 IPC
35.	321/92	-do-	147, 352, 427 IPC
36.	322/92	-do-	392 IPC
37.	481/92	-do-	147, 336, 323, 506 IPC
38.	482/92	-do-	395 IPC
39.	NCR No. 57 of 1992	-do-	323, 427 IPC
40.	1/93	-do-	395, 397 IPC
41.	2/93	-do-	395, 397 IPC
42.	1693	-do-	395 IPC
43.	27/93	-do-	395 IPC
44.	31/93	-do-	394, 342 IPC
45.	32/93	-do-	394 IPC
46.	33/93	-do-	395 IPC
47.	61/93	-do-	395 IPC
48.	70/93	-do-	394 IPC

After the investigation of case Crime No. 198 of 1992 having been entrusted to the CBI by the Central Government vide Notification No. 228/28/93-AVD-II dated 26 August 1993 the CBI on 9.9.1993 moved an application before the Special Judicial Magistrate, Rae Bareli, who was trying the said case at that point of time, to grant permission for further investigation in case Crime No. 198 of 1992 and on 10 September 1993 the learned Magistrate granted permission to the CBI for further investigation in the above case.

Thereafter one Shri Vijay Verma, the then III Additional Chief Judicial Magistrate (hereinafter referred to as ACJM), Lucknow was appointed by the High Court as Additional Chief Judicial Magistrate Special Court, the newly established Court, vide Notification dated 8 September 1993. The said notification is reproduced below:

'*High Court of Judicature at Allahabad.*
Notification
Dated: Allahabad: 15 September 1993.
No. 1371/JR(S)/93.
Shri Vijay Verma, III Addl. Chief Judicial Magistrate, Lucknow to be Additional Chief Judicial Magistrate, Lucknow (Special Court) created vide G.O. No. 4420/

VII-Nyaya-2-739/87 dated September 8, 1993, for trial and disposal of cases investigated by CBI pertaining to demolition of the disputed structure at Ayodhya, District Faizabad.
By order of the Court
(K.S. Rakhara)
Addl. Registrar.'

On 5 October 1993 the CBI filed a consolidated chargesheet against all the eight accused persons in case Crime No. 198 of 1992 as well as thirty-two other accused persons in case Crime No. 197 of 1992 and forty-seven other related, above mentioned, cases. This chargesheet was filed in the Special Court of ACJM presided over by Shri Vijay Verma.

On 8 October 1993 the Special Court at Lucknow was given jurisdiction with respect to case Crime No. 198 of 1992. Thereafter on 11 October 1993, the Presiding Officer of the Special Court at Lucknow, Shri Vijay Verma, who was appointed vide Notification dated 15 September 1993, took cognizance of all the cases including case Crime No. 198 of 1992.

On 18 October 1993 the Special Judicial Magistrate sitting at Rae Bareli, in whose court the case relating to Crime No. 198 of 1992 was pending, who still had jurisdiction to try the same and who had given permission to the CBI for further investigation, directed the CBI to file progress report regarding investigation in case Crime No. 198 of 1992.

On 18 October 1993, the Special Judicial Magistrate sitting at Rae Bareli, in whose court the case relating to Crime No. 198 of 1992 was pending, who still had jurisdiction to try the same and who had given permission to the CBI for further investigation, directed the CBI to file progress report regarding investigation in case Crime No. 198 of 1992. On 6 December 1993 the CBI submitted its report before the Special Judicial Magistrate at Rae Bareli informing about the progress, subsequent developments, and also about filing of the consolidated chargesheet before the Special Court of ACJM at Lucknow presided by Shri Vijay Verma as also indicating inclusion of the case Crime No. 198 of 1992 in the consolidated chargesheet and also about the consequent cognizance taken by the Special Court of ACJM at Lucknow on 11 October 1993. Thereafter on 24 January 1994 the judicial record of Criminal Case No. 1/93 relating to Crime No. 198 of 1992 was transferred by Shri Amitabh Sahay, Special Magistrate, Rae Bareli through District Judge, Rae Bareli and further through District Judge, Lucknow to the Special Court of ACJM at Lucknow presided by Shri Vijay Verma which was received in the Special Court of ACJM Lucknow on 25 January 1994. On 31 January 1994 the CBI moved an application before the Special Court at Lucknow praying to fix an early date so as the judicial record received from Rae Bareli be ordered to be taken as part of the case that is, State *versus* Bala Saheb Thackeray and others, arising out of Crime No. 197 of 192. The prayer of the CBI regarding clubbing of the records was objected to by some of the accused persons that is, Shri Kalyan Singh, Swami Sakshi Maharaj, R.N. Srivastava and D.B. Roy even though they nowhere figured as accused before the Special Court at Rae Bareli. The said Special Court of ACJM at Lucknow after hearing both the parties decided the application of the CBI as well as the objections of the above accused persons by order dated 23 March 1994. By the said order dated 23 March 1994 the prayer of the CBI for taking the judicial record received from Rae Bareli as part of the case was allowed and the objections of accused persons to the effect that the Special Court of ACJM at Lucknow had no jurisdiction with regard to the case Crime No. 198 of 1992 were dismissed.

Against the said order dated 23 March 1994 passed by the Special Court of ACJM at Lucknow taking the judicial record of case Crime No. 198 of 1992 as part of case Crime No. 197 of 1992 and other forty-seven FIRs one of the accused persons, namely, Vinay Katiyar (revisionist No. 4 of present Criminal Revision No. 255 of 1997) filed Criminal Revision No. 6 of 1995 on 18 June 1994 challenging the aforesaid order. This revision was dismissed by the Additional Sessions Judge (Ayodhya Prakaran), Lucknow, Shri Vimal Kishore, by order dated 20 February 1995.

All the cases referred to above were committed by the Special Court of ACJM at Lucknow to the Court of Sessions on 27.8.1994.

Thereafter on 1 September 1994 the CBI moved an application before the Special Court of ACJM at Lucknow praying for further investigation in the above referred cases. This application was rejected by the Special Court of ACJM Lucknow on 7 October 1994. Against this order the CBI filed Criminal Revision No. 143 of 1994 in the Court of Special Judge (Ayodhya Prakaran). This revision was allowed by the Special Judge (Ayodhya Prakaran) on 19 November 1994.

The CBI after collecting further evidence in the case filed a supplementary chargesheet on 11.1.1996 against nine more accused persons, that is, (i) Mahant Avaidyanath, (ii) Nritya Gopal Das, (iii) Dharmendra Das, (iv) Dr Ram Vilas Vedanti, (v) Paramhansa Ram Chandra Das, (vi) Mahamandaleshwar, the revisionists of Criminal Revision No. 201 of 1997, (vii) Rajmata Vijaya Raje Scindia (since dead) and (viii) Baikunth Lal Sharma 'Prem', the revisionists of Criminal Revision No. 255 of 1997 and (ix) Dr Satish Kumar Nagar. On 10.4.1996 the Special Court of ACJM also committed the aforesaid nine accused persons to the Court of Sessions.

On 9 September 1997 the Additional Sessions Judge (Ayodhya Prakaran) (J.P. Srivastava) passed the impugned order for framing charges against the revisionists and others as mentioned above.

Heard the learned counsel for the parties at considerable length. On behalf of the revisionists Shri Kr. Mridul Rakesh and Shri I.B. Singh mainly addressed the Court. The other counsel appearing for the revisionists adopted the arguments made by Shri Kr. Mridul Rakesh and Shri I.B. Singh and nothing was added by them. On behalf of opposite parties Shri P.K. Chaubey appearing for the CBI argued the matter and Additional Government Advocate for the State of U.P. produced the relevant records with regard to consultation with the High Court for constituting the special courts.

Learned counsel for the revisionists have assailed the impugned order dated 9.9.97 for framing charges against the revisionists, on the following issues:

1. Whether the Special Court of Additional Chief Judicial Magistrate, Lucknow (Ayodhya Prakaran) had jurisdiction and was legally competent to try, inquire into and commit the case relating to Crime No. 198 of 1992.
2. Whether Notification No. 5175/VII-Nyaya-2-793/87 dated 9.9.1993 amending Notification No. 4421/VII-Nyaya-2-739/87 dated 8.10.1993 by adding case Crime No. 198 of 1992 is a valid notification?
3. Whether Shri Vijay Verma was competent to preside over the Court of Special ACJM created and established vide Notification No. 4421/VII-Nyaya-2-739/87 dated 9.9.1993 and whether the orders passed by him (including the orders of taking cognizance) are bad in law and are not protected under Section 460 (e) Cr.P.C.?
4. Whether the Special Judge (Ayodhya Prakaran) could not take cognizance of the cases under Section 193 Cr.P.C. on the ground that the same were committed by a court having no jurisdiction to commit those cases?
5. Whether the offences are triable by the Magistrate and not by the Court of Sessions?
6. Whether the CBI intended to make fresh investigation in the garb of further investigation under Section 173 (8) Cr.P.C.?
7. Whether joint/consolidated chargesheet in the matter filed by the CBI is permissible or not?
8. Whether the offences of Conspiracy, dacoity (Section 395 IPC), common object of unlawful assembly committed in the course of same transaction and abatement etc. are *prima facie* made out against the revisionists?
9. Whether the disputed structure was a sacred place of worship for Muslims and whether an already defiled structure can be defiled again?
10. Whether it was a dispute of civil nature and has wrongly been shown as a criminal offence?
11. Whether actual culprits who had received injuries while demolishing the disputed structure and who were arrested by the police and later released on bail, as well as the accused persons of forty-seven FIRs lodged by media persons, have not been chargesheeted? If so, its effect?
12. Whether the impugned order dated 9.9.1997 for framing charges against the accused revisionists is sustainable or not?

He (counsel for the petitioners) has further submitted that the Special Court created and established on 9 September 1993 vide Notification No. 4421/VII-Nyaya-2-739/87 had no jurisdiction to try or inquire into and commit to the court of sessions the case arising out of Crime No. 198 of 1992 because in the schedule appurtenant to the said notification a list of those cases was given for which the Special Court was created and established by the said notification after due consultation with High Court and in its schedule case Crime No. 198 of 1992 does not figure.

Subsequently vide Notification No. 5175/VII-Nyaya-2-739/87 dated

Lucknow: 8 October 1993 His Excellency, the Governor of Uttar Pradesh, was pleased to make amendment in Notification No. 4421/VII-Nyaya-2-739/87 dated 9 September 1993 inserting the case Crime No. 198 of 1992, Police Station Ramjanmabhumi, under Sections 153-A, 153-B, 505 IPC. The said Notification is reproduced below:

> Notification NO. 5175/VII-Nyaya-2-739/87 dated Lucknow: 8 October 1993.
>
> In exercise of the powers under proviso to sub-section (I) of Section II of the Code of Criminal Procedure, 1973 (Act No. 2 of 1974) read with Section 21 of the General Clauses Act, 1897 (Act No. 10 of 1897), the Governor is pleased to make the following amendment in the Notification No. 4421/VII-Nyaya-2-739/87, dated Lucknow: 9 September 1993.
>
> Amendment.
>
> In the Schedule to the aforesaid notification after item 48, the following item columnwise shall be inserted, namely:

S.No.	*Crime No.*	*Police Station*	*Sections*
49.	198/92	Ramjanmabhumi	153-A, 153-B, 505 IPC

By order,
A.K. Srivastava,
Sachiv.

Shri Kr. Mridul Rakesh (for the petitioners) has further submitted that the notification referred to above is of no legal sanctity because while making the aforesaid amendment in the principal/parent notification dated 9 September 1993 no consultation with the High Court ever took place . . . therefore the said notification dated 8 October 1993 . . . cannot confer any power upon the Special Court of Additional Chief Judicial Magistrate at Lucknow to try, inquire into and commit the case relating to Crime No. 198 of 1992.

. . . Shri I.B. Singh has submitted that the Special Magistrate at Lucknow was not competent to take cognizance of the matter as cognizance of the same offence had already been taken by the Special Magistrate at Lalitpur on 1.3.1993 regarding case Crime No. 198 of 1992 on the chargesheet filed by the CB CID on 27.2.1993. Thereafter on 8.7.1993 the Court of Special Magistrate was shifted from Lalitpur to Rae Bareli. On 26.8.1993 the investigation of the above case was handed over to CBI and the CBI on 10.9.1993 sought permission from the court of Special Judge sitting at Rae Bareli for further investigation in case Crime No. 198 of 1992 in which chargesheet had already been filed by the CB CID. It means that after 8.10.1993 two courts of Special Judicial Magistrate were simultaneously working for one case i.e., case Crime No. 198 of 1992. I am of the considered opinion that it shows that the State Government, the Central Government and the CBI were in a dilemma and were unable to find a harmonious solution and to decide the correct method to be applied. Ultimately a consolidated chargesheet was submitted in the Court of Special Judicial Magistrate, Lucknow on 5.10.1993. Since a chargesheet relating to case Crime No. 198 of 1992 had already been filed in the Court of Special Judicial Magistrate Lalitpur who had also taken cognizance thereof on 1.3.1993, hence cognizance of the same offence cannot be taken by another Special Judicial Magistrate sitting at Lucknow.

Shri P.K. Chaubey, learned counsel appearing on behalf of the CBI while replying to the above submissions made on behalf of the revisionists, has submitted that by 26.8.1993 all the forty-nine cases correlated with forty-nine different FIRs (inclusive of Crime No. 197/92 and Crime No. 198/92 as also forty-seven other such FIRs lodged at the behest of media persons) stood legally transferred for the purpose of investigation to the CBI since all of them had cognate relationship with the demolition of the disputed structure at Ayodhya. In accordance with the basic requirement under proviso to Section 11(1) of the Cr.P.C. whereby in respect of any particular case or particular class of cases it was in consultation with the High Court that the State Government could establish Special Court of Judicial Magistrate (First Class) for any local area fixing its place of sitting and thus vesting it with the jurisdiction to try any case of such class of cases, the process for such consultation stood initiated inter-se between the High Court and the State Government after 26 August 1993. . . .

I have given my anxious consideration to the submissions made by the learned counsel for the revisionists as well as learned counsel for the CBI. It is admitted case of parties that in the schedule annexed with Notification No. 4421/VII-Nyaya-2-739/87 dated 9 September 1993 case Crime No. 198 of 1992 was not included. It is also admitted that the said notification was issued after consultation with the High Court. Three reasons have been given by the learned counsel for the CBI for not including the case Crime No. 198 of 1992 in the said notification i.e. (a) it might be due to casual slip, (b) the CBI by then might not have arrived at the conclusion that all the forty-nine cases had arisen out of the same transaction; and (c) a court of competent jurisdiction was already functioning at Rae Bareli which had already taken cognizance of case Crime No. 198/92. These reasons may or may not be true but the fact remains that case Crime No. 198 of 1992 was not included in the said notification. Now the question arises as to whether the subsequent notification No. 5175/VII-Nyaya-2-739/87 dated 8 October 1993 amending the earlier notification dated 9 September 1993 is a valid notification or not? It is an admitted case of the CBI that for issuing the said notification there was no consultation between the State Government and the High Court. According to Shri Chaubey learned Counsel for the CBI, since all the correspondence between the State Government and the High Court for establishing a Special Court of Judicial Magistrate (First Class) took place in general that is, for trial and disposal of cases arising out of demolition of disputed structure at Ayodhya, there was consultation in general for all the cases arising out of demolition of the disputed structure at Ayodhya and since the case Crime No. 198 of 1992 also arises out of demolition of the disputed structure therefore it would be deemed that consultation with the High Court regarding case Crime No. 198 of 1992 had also taken place and therefore there was no necessity to further consult the High Court before issuing the subsequent Notification No. 5175/VII-Nyaya-2-739/87 dated 8 October 1993 and therefore the said notification is a valid document. This contention of the learned counsel for the CBI is not acceptable rather it is believed by the own conduct of the State Government while issuing earlier notifications in the matter. Firstly by Notification No. 6517(1)/VII-Nyaya-2-92-539-G dated 16 December 1992 the State Government after consultation with the High Court established a Special Court of Judicial Magistrate First Class with its place of sitting at Lalitpur to try case Crime No. 198 of 1992. Thereafter when the place of sitting of the above court shifted by Notification No. 3123/VII-Nyaya-2-539-G-92-T.C. dated 8 July 1993 the High Court was again consulted before issuing the said notification. If the logic of Shri Chaubey that since consultation in general already took place at the time of issuing the earlier notification, there was no need to consult the High Court again before issuing the subsequent notification; is accepted then there was no need again to consult the High Court before issuing the said notification No. 2123/VII-Nyaya-2-539-G-92-T.C. dated 8 July 1993.

Since it is admitted case of the parties that no consultation took place between the State Government and the High Court for issuing notification dated 8 October 1993 it is not necessary for this Court to delve on the meaning and definition of the word 'consultation'.

Shri Chaubey has further submitted that the words 'any particular case or particular class of cases' as used in Section 11(1)Cr.P.C. cover the case Crime No. 198 of 1992 because this case cannot be excluded from the particular class of cases i.e. the cases arising out of demolition of disputed structure and therefore the consultation with the High Court for the said particular class of cases would also be deemed to be consultation for case Crime No. 198 of 1992. In this context he has also given reference of Notification No. 4420/VII-Nyaya-2-739/87 dated 8 September 1993 issued by the State Government creating a Special Court of ACJM at Lucknow and Notification No. 1371/JR(S)/93 dated 15 September 1993 issued by the High Court appointing Shri Vijay Verma in the said Special Court wherein the words 'for trial and disposal of cases investigated by CBI pertaining to demolition of the disputed structure at Ayodhya, District Faizabad' have been used. No doubt, case Crime No. 198 of 1992 belongs to the same class of cases i.e. the cases arising out of demolition of disputed structure at Ayodhya but knowingly it was discriminated by the State Government itself by not including this case in the schedule of cases annexed with Notification No. 4421/VII-Nyaya-2-739/87 dated 9 September 1993 issued by the State Government after consultation with the High Court. Actually there was no need to annex any schedule with the said notification dated 9 September 1993 and adhering to the 'generality' and 'particular class of cases' it was expedient to use the words 'for trial and disposal of cases pertaining to demolition of the disputed structure at Ayodhya, District Faizabad' in the said notification. In not doing so and in not mentioning the case

Crime No. 198 of 1992 in the schedule annexed with the notification dated 9 September 1993 the State Government itself excluded this case from the 'particular class of cases'. For this reason also it was necessary to consult the High Court for issuing notification dated 8 October 1993.

There is another aspect of the matter. Once consultation takes place between the State Government and the High Court for creation and establishment of a Special Court under Section ii(1) Cr.P.C. and in consequence thereof a notification is issued by the State Government, the 'consultation' stands exhausted and cannot be re-used for issuing subsequent notification. . . . In the instant case at a particular juncture the Executive has ignored the statutory consultation with High Court and issued Notification No. 5175/VII-Nyaya-2-739/87 dated 8 October, 1993 which ultimately has culminated into jurisdictional error of the two courts below.

In view of the above discussion it is held that Notification No. 5175/VII-Nyaya-2-739/87 dated 8 October 1993, amending the earlier notification dated 9 September 1993, is illegal, without jurisdiction and violative of the provisions of Section 11(I) Cr.P.C. as well as Section 21 of the General Clauses Act. This notification being illegal and without jurisdiction is invalid. Therefore it could not confer jurisdiction upon the Special Court of ACJM Lucknow to try or inquire into and commit to the Court of Sessions case Crime No. 198 of 1992. Therefore the said Special Court of ACJM at Lucknow had no jurisdiction to try, inquire into and commit case Crime No. 198 of 1992. Since committal of accused persons relating to case Crime No. 198 of 1992 by order dated 27.8.1994 passed by the Special Court of ACJM at Lucknow was illegal, subsequent proceedings in the Court of Special Judge (Ayodhya Prakaran) including the impugned order dated 9 September 1997 for framing of charges as far as the accused persons of case Crime No. 198 of 1992 are concerned are illegal, without jurisdiction and are liable to be set aside. However the mistake committed by the State Government in issuing the Notification No. 5175/VII-Nyaya-2-739/87 dated 8 October 1998 is curable and it is open to the State Government, if they so desire, to rectify its mistake/illegality by issuing fresh notification after consultation with the High Court in accordance with law.

I am of the considered opinion that Shri Vijay Verma was very well empowered and competent to take cognizance, try and/or commit the cases as mentioned in the schedule of Notification No. 4421/VII-Nyaya-2-739/87 dated 9 September, 1993 (except the case arising out of Crime No. 198 of 1992 as held under issues nos. 1 and 2) and all the orders passed by him are protected by Section 190 and 460 (e) Cr.P.C. and the notification regarding Vijay Verma's appointment the argument of the learned counsel for the revisionists that Shri Vijay Verma was not empowered to take cognizance and commit the said cases to the court of sessions, fails and has no legs to stand except the case arising out of Crime No. 198 of 1992 as held under issues nos 1 and 2. . . .

While considering issue No. 3 above it has already been held Shri Vijay Verma was competent to deal with these matters and all the orders passed by him are legal except that he had no jurisdiction with regard to case arising out of

Crime No. 198 of 1992, as decided in issue nos 1 and 2. Consequently the cognizance of the cases taken by the Special Judge (Ayodhya Prakaran) is also legal and does not suffer from any infirmity. Therefore the above argument of Shri Kr. Mridul Rakesh has no legs to stand.

Shri I.B. Singh has submitted that the learned Special Judge had not jurisdiction to frame the charges as the creation of the court of Special Judge itself is illegal because there is no provision in the Cr.P.C. for creation of a Special Court for trial of an offence which took place in a different district.

It is true that the Code of Criminal Procedure, 1973 (Act No. 2 of 1974) is silent on this point. But silence does not mean denial. There is also no provision in the Code to the contrary. It is not for the first time that the Court of Special Judge has been established but it has happened time and again in the past not only in Uttar Pradesh but in other states also and the validity of such courts has also been recognized by the apex Court. Keeping in view the cardinal principle of law that every law is designed to further the ends of justice but not to frustrate on the mere technicalities I hold that the establishment of the Court of Special Judge is not against the purpose, intendment and the spirit of the Code of Criminal Procedure, 1973. Therefore, it is held that the Special/Sessions Judge (Ayodhya Prakaran) sitting at Lucknow was competent to take cognizance of these cases and he has jurisdiction to try these cases except the case arising out of Crime No. 198 of 1992 as held under issues nos 1 and 2. . . .

It is well settled that the investigation agency has the power under subsection (8) of section 173 Cr.P.C. to further investigate every fresh fact that comes to their notice irrespective of the fact that the chargesheet in the same matter has already been submitted under Section 173(2) Cr.P.C. and the case is pending before the court during further investigation. To investigate fresh fact does not amount investigation of the entire case afresh but it is in continuation of the earlier investigation. In the present case the CBI while moving applications seeking permission of the Court for further investigation has enumerated a number of facts which had come to their knowledge and upon which further investigation was necessary. In the above circumstances I am of the opinion that the CBI did not intend to re-investigate or carry fresh investigation in the garb of further investigation and courts below have not committed any illegality much less irregularity in granting permission for further investigation. The CBI was legally entitled and empowered to further investigate the matter under Section 173(8) Cr.P.C. and on completion of the further investigation file its report/reports under Section 173(2) Cr.P.C. which the CBI has done in accordance with law. The argument of the learned counsel for the revisionists that actually the CBI wanted to re-investigate the matter or making the investigation afresh in the garb of further investigation, fails. . . .

In view of the above discussions I am of the opinion that no illegality has been committed by the courts below while taking cognizance of a joint/consolidated chargesheet on the ground that all the offences were committed in the course of the same transaction and to accomplish the conspiracy; that the evidence for all the offences is almost the same and therefore these offences cannot be separated from each other irrespective of the fact that forty-nine different FIRs were lodged on the basis of which forty-nine criminal cases were registered by the police. Although there is no provision in the Cr.P.C. with regard to joinder of chargesheets by the prosecution agency but on the other hand there is no prohibition also for the same. Learned courts below by permitting the filing of joint/consolidated chargesheet has accepted in principle the permissibility of the joint/consolidated chargesheet. As regards the offences regarding criminal conspiracy and common object of unlawful assembly they are *prima facie* made out against the accused, revisionists and since these offences are alleged to have been committed in the course of same transaction therefore the Special Court of ACJM (Additional Chief Judicial Magistrate) rightly took cognizance of the same and also rightly committed the same to the court of sessions. . . .

. . . .This court while keeping in mind the above considerations has earnestly considered and examined the impugned order dated 9 September 1997 passed by the trial court for framing charges against the accused revisionists and does not find any infirmity with respect to the cases referred to in the Schedule of Notification No. 4421/VII-Nyaya-2-793/87 dated 9 September 1993. Further the courts below committed jurisdictional error as far as case Crime No. 198 of 1992 is concerned, which is curable. In the light of the above no interference is warranted in the impugned order of the trial court as far as the cases referred to in the scheduled of Notification No. 4421/VUU-Nyaya-2-739/87 dated 9 September 1993 are concerned.

It is indeed a matter of great concern that though the unfortunate incident took place eight years ago, but the stage of the case is at framing of charge. No chargesheet has been filed against 423 accused persons who were injured on the spot, taken into custody and later released on bail and whose identity is known to the prosecution. Under the scheme of criminal jurisprudence it is specifically provided that immediately after the investigation is over the prosecution has to take decision for filing chargesheet under Section 173 Cr.P.C. on the basis of the material/evidence available, and in the alternative if no offence is made out then submit a final report under Section 169 Cr.P.C. I am of the view that the prosecution has no right to linger on with the matter because such omission unnecessarily creates doubt in the mind of the public at large if connected matter are delayed. Nothing has come on either side as to whether final report in the cases relating to forty-seven FIRs of media persons has been submitted or not. According to the prosecution the accused persons are either rich, influential or politically strong. In the process I recall the observations of the Hon'ble apex Court in the case of *Ganesh Narain Hegde versus S. Bangarappa and others, 1995 SCC (Cri) 634* which are as follows: 'The slow motion becomes much slower motion when politically powerful or rich and influential persons figure as accused. FIRs are quashed. Charges are quashed. Interlocutory orders are interfered with. At every step, there will be revisions and applications for quashing and writ petitions. In short, no progress is ever allowed to be made. And if ever the case reaches the stage of trial after all the interruptions, the time would have taken its own toll: the witnesses are won over; evidence disappears; the prosecution loses interest—the result is an all too familiar one.'

The concept of the joint chargesheet and joint trial has been adopted by the prosecution and accepted by the courts below. I am afraid this may not add to the slow motion becoming slower which is evident from the fact that from the last eight years the case is moving at a snail's pace. I pondered over the matter and it occurred to my mind that the above circumstances can further delay the completion of the trial. In the light of the above I am of the considered opinion that the trial Court should ensure speedy trial and in the process take necessary steps.

In the premise the impugned order dated 9 September 1997 passed by the Special/Sessions Judge (Ayodhya Prakaran), Lucknow for framing of charges is upheld as far as forty-eight cases referred to in the Schedule of Notification No. 4421/VII-Nyaya-2-739/87 dated 9 September 1993 are concerned and the impugned order is set aside with respect to case Crime No. 198 of 1992 mentioned in Notification No. 5175/VII-Nyaya-2-739.87 dated 8 October 1993 which being invalid does not confer any jurisdiction upon the courts below to take cognizance, commit and try the case relating to Crime No. 198 of 1992 under Sections 153-A, 153-B and 505 of the Indian Penal Code, Police Station Ramjanmabhumi, Ayodhya, district Faizabad. However, the mistake in issuing the said notification dated 8 October 1993 is curable and it is open for the State Government to cure the legal infirmity.

In the light of the above all the four revisions are decided.

12 February 2001 — Sd/- Jagdish Bhalla
Shakir — 12.2.2001

3. Judgement by the Sessions Judge (Ayodhya Episode), Lucknow, on 4 May 2001

(Translation)
In the Court of the Sessions Judge,
(Ayodhya Episode), Lucknow
Sessions Trial No. 344/94
State *versus* Bala Saheb Thackeray and thirty-nine others
And
Sessions Trial No. 749/96
State *versus* Mahant Avaidyanath and eight others

4.5.2001

Order

My predecessor had passed an order on 9.9.1997 for framing of charges U/Ss

147/153-A/153-B/295/295-A/505 IPC against the following persons:

1. Bala Saheb Thackeray
2. Lal Krishna Advani
3. Kalyan Singh
4. Ashok Singhal
5. Vinay Katiyar
6. Moreshwar Save
7. Pawan Kumar Pandey
8. Brij Bhushan Saran Singh
9. Jai Bhagwan Goel
10. Uma Bharati
11. Sadhvi Rithambara
12. Maharaj Swami Sakshi
13. Murli Manohar Joshi
14. Giri Raj Kishore
15. Vishnu Hari Dalmia
16. Champak Rai Bansal
17. Om Prakash Pandey
18. Satish Pradhan
19. Mahant Avaidhnath
20. Dharam Das
21. Mahant Nritya Gopal Das
22. Mahamandaleshwar Jagdish Muni
23. Dr Ram Vilas Vedanti
24. Baikunth Lal Sharma Prem
25. Paramhansa Ramchandra Das
26. Vijaya Raje Scindia (since dead)
27. Dr Satish Kumar Nagar

In the same order, my predecessor ordered for framing of charges U/Ss 323/338/201 IPC r/w Section 149/395/120-B IPC against the following accused.

1. Pawan Kumar Pandey
2. Brij Bhushan Saran Singh
3. Jai Bhagwan Goel
4. Vinod Kumar Vats
5. Ram Chandar Khatri
6. Sudhir Kakkar
7. Amar Nath Goel
8. Santosh Dubey
9. Prakash Sharma
10. Jai Bhan Singh Pawaiya
11. Dharmendra Singh Gurjar
12. Ram Narain Das
13. Vinay Kumar Rai

14. Lallu Singh
15. Ramji Gupta
16. Om Prakash Pandey
17. Kamlesh Tripathi
18. Gandhi Yadav
19. Hargovind Singh
20. Vinay Bahadur Singh
21. Naveen Bhai Shukla
22. Ramesh Pratap Singh
23. Acharya Dharmendra Dev

The predecessor had also ordered on 9.9.1997 that a *prima facie* case is made out and hence ordered for framing of charges U/Ss 120-B/153-A/295/295-A/505/201 r/w Sections 114 IPC against the accused R.N. Srivastava and D.B. Rai.

In the order dated 9.9.97, accused Narain Das Mahatyagi was also found *prima facie* guilty but his name was not there in the concluding part of the order and this accused has obtained stay from the Hon'ble High Court.

Accused Vijaya Raje Scindia is dead and hence the case has abated against her.

Being aggrieved by the order dated 9.9.97, accused R.N. Srivastava and D.B. Rai preferred Criminal Revision No. 211/1997, Moreshwar Save filed Criminal Revision No. 199/92 Uma Bharati and others filed Criminal Revision No. 201/1997 and Ashok Singhal and others need Criminal Revision No. 255/1997 in the Hon'ble High Court.

The Hon'ble High Court disposed of all the above said Revisions by a common judgement dated 12.2.2001. The Hon'ble High Court upheld the order dated 9.9.97 in respect of 48 FIRs which find a mention in the Notification No. 4421/VII/Jud.2.739/87 dated 9.9.93 but the High Court partly sets aside the order dated 9.9.1997 in respect of case FIR No. 198/97 which finds a mention in the Notification No. 5175/VII--Jud.2-739/87 dated 8.10.1993 and since the said notification is illegal, therefore, it does not confer any jurisdiction on the lower court to take cognizance and commit the case to Session U/Ss 153-A/153-B/505 IPC, Police Station Ramjanmabhumi, Ayodhya, Faizabad. Although, this defect in the notification is curable and the State Government has opportunity to rectify the same.

Despite the above order, the State Government has not rectified the said mistake in the said notification.

After the above judgement passed by the High Court, Shri R.N. Srivastava and Shri D.B. Rai have filed application No. 715-B to the effect that proceeding against them be dropped as they were charged in the case FIR No. 198/1992, Police Station Ramjanmabhumi, District Faizabad.

Application No. 718-B was filed by Acharya Dharmendra Dev, Mahant Avaidyanath, Dr Ram Vilas Vedanti, Dharam Das, Mahant Nritya Gopal Das,

Mahamandaleshwar Jagdish Muni, Paramhansa Ramchandra Das, Champak Rai Bansal, Lallu Singh, Brij Bhushan Saran Singh, Maharaj Swami Sakshi, Baikunth Lal Sharma Prem, Naveen Bhai Shukla, Prakash Sharma, Vijay Bahadur Singh, Hargovind Singh, Jai Bhan Singh Paweya, Dharmendra Singh Gurjar, Ram Narain Das, Kamlesh Tripathi, Sait Dubey, Vinay Kumar Rai, Gandhi Yadav and Ramesh Pratap Singh praying therein to drop further proceeding against them in respect of the case FIR No. 198/92, Police Station Ramjanmabhumi, District Faizabad.

Application No. 719-B was filed by L.K. Advani, Dr Murli Manohar Joshi, Ashok Singhal, Uma Bharati, Sadhvi Rithambara, Vinay Katiyar, Vishnu Hari Dalmia and Acharya Giriraj Kishore to the effect that further proceeding against them be dropped in respect of the case FIR No. 198/92.

No written objection has been filed by the prosecution to the above three applications.

The learned Counsels for the prosecution have orally opposed the above three applications.

I have heard the learned counsels of both the parties and the High Court Judgement.

All the three applications are disposed of together as in all the three applicants, the accused persons have prayed that since their committal to the sessions court has been held illegal in respect of case FIR No. 198/97, this court cannot further prosecute the accused persons in the said criminal case.

It is noteworthy that the Special Additional CJM, CBI, Ayodhya Episode, Shri Mahipal Sirohi committed the accused persons in case No. 1/93 State *versus* Bala Saheb Thackeray and others (40) to the Court of Sessions on 27.8.94 and the same was received in Sessions Court, Lucknow on 6.9.1994 upon which Sessions Trial No. 344/94 U/Ss 153-A/153-B/295-A/505/147/323/338/201/395/ 120 IPC was registered.

On page 55 of its judgement, the Hon'ble High Court has held that the Special Additional CJM, Lucknow had no power to enquire into and commit the case FIR No. 198/92. Accordingly, the committal of the accused of the case FIR No. 198/92 to the Court of Sessions is illegal and hence all the proceedings including the order dated 9.9.1997 passed by the Special Court, Ayodhya Episode are illegal being beyond its jurisdiction.

The Special CBI Magistrate, Shri Mahipal Sirohi had committed forty accused to the Court of Sessions in case Crime No. 197/92, including Case Crime No. 198/92, 225/92 to 239/97, 247/92, 267/92, 268/92, 285/92, 318/922, to 322/ 92, 481/92, 482/92, 1/93, 2/193, 16/93, 27/93, 31/93, 32/93 to 33/93, 61/93, 70/ 93 and NCR 57/92.

Case Crime No. 197/92 U/Ss 395/397/332/337/338/295/297/153-A IPC and u/s 7 Criminal Amendment Act, Police Station Ramjanmabhumi, District Faizabad was registered by the CBI as R.C. 8(S)/92 dated 13.12.1992.

In the said FIR, there was no accused named. It was registered by the officer in charge, P.N. Shukla, against lakhs of *kar sevaks*. The FIR was registered in the Police Station Ramjanmabhumi on 6.12.1992 at 5.15 pm. In which the time of occurrence was 12 noon–12.15 pm on 6.12.1992. The report is as follows:

> Today, 6.12.1992, I Priyambada Nath Shukla, Officer-in-Charge, Police Station Ramjanmabhumi, was on duty for law and order in the premises of the Ramjanmabhumi where *kar seva* was organized by the VHP at about 12 noon–12.15 pm from the side of the fixing gate No. 1, thousands of *kar sevaks* were reaching the Chabutra/platform and *sants* and *mahants* in large numbers sat for *kar seva*. The *kar sevaks* had in their hands *phawra*, *belcha*, rods, pipes and other implements, who, in place of sants, became busy in *kar seva* and demolition. They were stopped but they became more agitated and the number of demolishers was increasing and by jumping and breaking the barricade, climbed on the upper portion of the disputed structure and started breaking it. The police present there resorted to the lathi-charge upon which the *kar sevaks* in lakhs shouted 'Jai Sri Ram' and other inflammatory speeches, attacked the disputed structure from all sides and started demolishing and damaging the disputed structure. Seeing no effect of the lathi charge on the indisciplined *kar sevaks*, order was given to lob tear gas shells available on the spot. On this order, many tear gas firings were done but the *kar sevaks* had coating of different things on their faces and this too had no effect on them. Rather, they started throwing stones on the police. The mob of lakhs of *kar sevaks* started breaking the disputed structure. In the lathi charge and other actions, many *kar sevaks* were injured. In this action, the *kar sevaks* pulled down the disputed structure and broke and took away the government property like, wireless set, CCTV, camera, dragon light, charger, torch, iron windows, barricading wires, pipe angles, chairs, tables and benches etc.

From reading the FIR, following things emerge:

1. The FIR is against lakhs of *kar sevaks* whose names and addresses are unknown.
2. The time of occurrence was 12.15 pm on 6.12.1992.
3. *Kar sevaks* were armed with *phawra*, *sambal*, *gaiti*, *belcha*, pipe etc.,
4. The *kar sevaks* broke the barricade and demolished the disputed structure.
5. The *kar sevaks* shouted inflammatory speeches.
6. The *kar sevaks* threw stones on the police.
7. The *kar sevaks* looted the government property.

In the said report, there is nothing to the effect that the *kar sevaks* shouted slogans to spread hatred between different communities so that people of one community hate the persons of the other community.

The second report is case crime No. 198/92 registered at 5.25 pm on 6.12.1992 by Ganga Prasad Tiwari in which the following information was given:

To
The SHO,
P.S. Ramjanmabhumi
Ayodhya, District Faizabad

Sir, I, Ganga Prasad Tiwari, incharge Police Post Ramjanmabhumi, Police Station Ramjanmabhumi, was on duty today 6.12.1992 to maintain peace at the *kar seva* organized by the VHP. Inspecting the disputed spot, Rama *Chabutra*, Shesha Avtar temple, reached the meeting spot in the Rama Katha Kunj, around 10 am, where, on the dais, were sitting Ashok Singhal, General Secretary VHP, Shri Giriraj Kishore, Joint General Secretary VHP, Lal Krishna Advani, Murli Manohar Joshi, Vishnu Hari Dalmia, BJP MP and Bajrang Dal Chief Vinay Katiyar, MP Uma Bharati and Sadhvi Rithambara, etc. The above said speakers were instigating the *kar sevaks* by delivering inflammatory speeches. Their slogan was 'Give one push more and demolish the Babri Masjid. Demolish this Mughal period structure which is a sign of slavery'. So agitated were the *kar sevaks* by their inflammatory speeches that during the speeches of the leaders, they shouted slogans, like, '*Jab katooye kate jaenga, baap baap chillaenge, Rama Lalla ham ayenge, mandir yahin banaegen*' (When the circumcised will be cut, they will shout father, father, Rama Lalla, we have come to construct the temple here'). During the speeches of these leaders, repeated indications were given to demolish the mosque. As a result, lakhs of *kar sevaks* attacked and pulled down the disputed structure which caused damage to the national integration. Police and administrative officers on duty, public servants, listeners and media persons, etc., have heard and seen the occurrence on the spot. Hence, kindly register a case and do the needful.'

The above case was registered at Police Station Ramjanmabhumi U/Ss 153-A/153-B/505 IPC. This report was against eight named persons.

Here, the case crime No. 198/92 is important. It is this case in respect of which the High Court has held that the committal of this crime to the Sessions and the order dated 9.9.97 are illegal. This second case Crime was registered by the CBI on 28.8.1993 vide R.C.-2(S)/93 SIC-4. Apart from the above two case crime Nos, the following case crimes were also registered. . . .

The predecessor found sufficient material for framing charge against twenty-three accused whose particulars have been given on earlier page u/s 323/338/201 IPC r/w Sections 149/395/120-B IPC. From the perusal of case crime No. 197/92, it is clear that these twenty-three accused persons are—[*sic*] from case No. 197/92 because there is clear charge against them u/s 323/338/201 r/w Sections 149 and 120-B IPC.

The predecessor found accused R.N. Srivastava and D.B. Rai chargeable u/s 120-B/153-A/295/295-A/505/201 114 IPC. According to the chargesheet, R.N. Srivastava, in the capacity of DM and D.B. Rai in the capacity of SSP were on duty where the occurrence took place. Both the public servants were near the disputed structure and they had the knowledge about the actual *kar seva* and knew about the undertaking given in the Supreme Court by Kalyan Singh, the then Chief Minister and it was their duty to not let the disputed structure be demolished. Both of them knew about the coming of lakhs of *kar sevaks* and about the determination of religious and political organizations to demolish the disputed structure. Despite this, the accused did not take effective steps to stop them. They also know about the consequences of the demolition of the disputed structure. Despite this they intentionally lessened the number of police near the disputed structure which made the task of demolition easier. Shri R.N. Srivastava sent back three battalion of paramilitary forces at 1.45 pm and for five hours during the course of investigation, these accused took no steps to protect, though it was their duty, nor they took any steps to prevent attack on the media persons. Therefore, this charge is not in case crime No. 197/92 and other FIRs got registered by the media persons.

A total of twenty-five out of forty-nine accused persons, whose particulars have been given above, are concerned with case crime No. 197/92. Smt Vijaya Raje Scindia is dead. Hence, the case has abated against her. One accused Lakshmi Maha Narain Tyagi has obtained stay from the Hon'ble High Court. Thus, the number of the remaining accused is twenty-two.

Accused Ashok Singhal, Giriraj Kishore, L.K. Advani, Murli Manohar Joshi, Vishnu Hari Dalmia, Vinay Katiyar, Uma Bharati and Sadhvi Rithambara, total eight, are accused in case crime No. 198/92. Before the charge of the CBI, the CB CID had filed the chargesheet in which the said accused persons had also been challaned. In respect of those not named, it was written, 'therefore, after completion of the investigation, charge is being filed against the above accused persons. It is prayed to summon the accused and witnesses and try them'. Investigation is on in respect of other accused named in the FIRs, whose names have not been given. On page 4 of this charge, it has been stated that the accused, apart from those who promoted the temple construction movement and its participants were to use violence and force against the Muslim community and will create sense of fear and insecurity amongst the Muslims. Their common intention was to promote enmity and ill-feeling. Thus, the accused hatched conspiracy to create communal disharmony in U.P. and India and created atmosphere against the Constitution of India. Therefore, this charge of criminal conspiracy is proved.

It has also been stated in the written report of the case crime No. 198/92 as follows, 'I, SI Ganga Prasad Tiwari, reached near the dais at 10 am where VHP General Secretary Ashok Singhal, Joint Secretary Giriraj Kishore, L.K. Advani, M.M. Joshi, Vishnu Hari Dalmia, BJP MP and Bajrang Dal President Vinay Katiyar, MP Uma Bharati, Sadhvi Rithambara, etc., were sitting on the dais. They were delivering inflammatory speeches. . . .

Register a case and take action.'

It is clear from this that apart from named accused in the case crime No. 198/92, there were other accused also. Not only this, the CBI filed application for further investigation in case Crime No. 198/92 and the supplementary chargesheet contained the names of (1) Mahant Avaidyanath (2) Dr Ram Vilas Vedanti, (3) Dharam Das (4) Mahant Nritya Gopal Das, (5) Mahamandaleshwar Jagdish

Muni, (6) Baikunth Lal Sharma, Prem (7) Paramhansa Ramchandra Das (8) Smt Vijaya Raje Scindia and (9) Dr Satish Kumar Nagar.

As stated above, Smt. Scindia is dead and the case has abated against her. Therefore, eight named accused and eight accused of the supplementary chargesheet (total sixteen) have been challaned U/Ss 147/153-A/153-B/295/295-A/505 IPC r/w Section 120-B IPC. Apart from them, are (1) Bala Saheb Thackeray, (2) Moreshwar Save, (3) Maharaj Swami Sakshi, (4) Champat Rai, (5) Satish Pradhan, (6) Kalyan Singh.

It is clear from the perusal of the chargesheet, that on the dais in Rama Katha Kunj were also sitting, (1) Mahant Nritya Gopal Das, (2) Paramhansa Ramchandra Das (3) Dr Ram Vilas Vedanti, (4) Vijaya Raje Scindia and Dr Ram Vilas Vedanti introduced (5) Mahamandaleshwar Jagdish Muni Maharaj (6) Mahant Avaidyanath, (7) Dharam Das, (8) Baikunth Lal Sharma Prem.

It has also been stated in the chargesheet that accused Champat Rai instigated the *kar sevaks*.

Case crime No. 198/92 was instigating *kar sevaks* for demolition of the disputed structure by the *kar sevaks* u/s 295 r/w Section 214/295/153A/153B/505 IPC. In the chargesheet filed by the CBI, conspiracy for demolition has been mentioned. From the *challan* filed by the CBI, it is clear that Bala Saheb Thackeray and Moreshwar Save were also conspirators. In the said circumstances, apart from named accused in case Crime No. 198/92, there are accused of the supplementary chargesheet also like Bala Saheb Thackeray, Moreshwar Save, Champat Rai and Satish Pradhan. Thus, twenty-one accused come in the purview of case Crime No. 98/92.

Mr Kalyan Singh was the Chief Minister of U.P. on the date of occurrence. It was his duty to protect the disputed structure as per his undertaking given in the Hon'ble Supreme Court. It has been stated in the chargesheet that he ordered the local administration to cut down the number of Security police near the disputed structure and also helped in the conspiracy to pull down the disputed structure. He has also been charged U/Ss 147/153A/153B/295/295A/505 IPC r/w Section 120-B IPC.

It is worthy to note here that the case Crime No. 197/92 is about the *kar sevaks*, who, agitated, broke the barricade and climbed the roof of the disputed structure and started demolishing it. The police restored to the lathi charge but the *kar sevaks* in lakhs got agitated and shouting slogan like *Jai Sri Ram* surrounded the disputed structure and started damaging and breaking it. The lathi charge and tear gas had no effect and they in turn pelted stones on the police. People in large numbers were injured in the lathi charge. The *kar sevaks* demolished the disputed structure and looted and damaged the government property inside it. On its perusal offences, U/Ss 147//153-A/332/338/295/297/395/397 IPC are made out. This case was against the *kar sevaks* who formed unlawful assembling to demolish the disputed structure. This is the reason that this FIR was registered, but when the State Government found that there were people on the dais who were instigating and abetting the *kar sevaks*, another case Crime No. 98/92 against them was registered U/Ss 153-A/153-B/505 IPC. This way, two distinct cases were registered which are different. In the first FIR were *kar sevaks* who pulled down the structure, looted government property and in the other FIR are conspirators/abettors who instigated the *kar sevaks*. This way, the State has considered both the cases different a separate and has treated them so.

Keeping in view the above circumstances, Kalyan Singh is proved to be the accused of case crime No. 98/92 and thus there are twenty-one accused in case Crime No. 98/92, whereas Sakshi Maharaj is the accused at first registered case Crime No. 197/92. The number of accused in case crime No. 197/92 and cases got registered by the mediamen comes to twenty-six.

In the light of the High Court Judgement, the order dated 9.9.97 passed by my predecessor is illegal, though the Hon'ble High Court has held that the defect in the notification is curable and has given opportunity to the State Government to rectify the same. Since, the mistake has not been removed, hence further proceeding cannot proceed against the accused of case Crime No. 198/92.

The order dated 9.9.1997 passed by the predecessor in respect of remaining accused has been upheld by the Hon'ble High Court.

In these circumstances, this court has two options:

The whole case be kept pending till the defect pointed out by the Hon'ble High Court is cured.

Or

Stop proceeding/trial of the accused of case Crime No. 198/92 and start the trial of the remaining accused.

It is worthy to note here that the Hon'ble High Court has directed the trial court to take necessary steps for a speedy trial. Operative portion of the judgement is as follows:

> The concept of the joint chargesheet and joint trial has been adopted by the prosecution and accepted by the courts below. I am afraid this may not add to the slow motion becoming slower which is evident from the fact that from the last eight years the case is moving at a snail's pace. I pondered over the matter and it occurred to my mind that the above circumstances can further delay the completion of the trial. In the light of the above I am of the considered opinion that the trial court should ensure speedy trial and in the process take necessary steps.

In view of the Hon'ble High Courts observation, the second option be adopted and trial be started in respect of the accused against whom trial can be started and trial of others be stopped. It is proper to order that the trial of the accused of the case crime No. 198/92 be dropped till the rectification of the said defect and the remaining accused be present in the court on 8.6.2001 for proceeding u/s 228(2) Cr.P.C.

Order

Further proceeding is dropped against (1) Bala Saheb Thackeray (2) L.K. Advani (3) Kalyan Singh (4) Ashok Singhal (5) Vinay Katiyar (6) Moreshwar Save (7)

Uma Bharati (8) Sadhvi Rithambara (9) M.M. Joshi (10) Giriraj Kishore (10) Vishnu Hari Dalmia (12) Champat Rai Bansal (13) Satish Pradhan (14) Mahant Avaidyanath (15) Dharam Das (16) Mahant Nritya Gopal Das (17) Mahamandaleshwar Jagdish Gupta (18) Ram Vilas Vedanti (19) Baikunthlal Sharma Prem (20) Mahant Ram Chandra Das (21), Dr Satish Kumar Nagar.

Accused (1) Pawan Kumar Pandey (2) Braj Bhushan Saran Singh (3) Jai Bhagwan Goel (4) Vinod Kumar Vats (5) Ram Chandra Khatri (6) Sudhir Kakkar (7) Amar Nath Goel (8) Santosh Dubey (9) Prakash Sharma (10) Jai Bhan Singh Paweya (11) Dharmendra Singh Gurjar (12) Ram Narain Das (13) Vinay Kumar Rai, (14) Lalloo Singh (15) Ramji Gupta (16) Om Prakash Pandey (17) Kamlesh Tripathi (18) Gandhi Yadav (19) Hargovind Singh (20) Vijay Bahadur Singh (21) Naveen Bhai Shukla (22) Ramesh Pratap Singh (23) Acharya Dharmendra Deo (24) R.N. Srivastava (25) D.B. Rai and (26) Maharaj Swami Sakshi be present in the Court on 8.6.2001 for proceeding u/s 228(2) Cr.P.C. On that date, the charge shall be read over and explained to them and they will be asked whether they plead guilty or stand trial. Accordingly, applications 215-B, 718-B are disposed.

Srikant Shukla
Sessions Judge (Ayodhya Episode)
Lucknow
4.5.2001

4. High Court of Judicature at Allahabad Notification

No. 1269 DH (S)/2002
Shri Vinod Kumar Singh, Civil Judge, Junior Division, Purwa (Unnao) is appointed u/s 11(2) of the Code of Criminal Procedure 1973 (Act No. 2 of 1974) as Judicial Magistrate Fist Class Rae Bareli

In suppression of all previous orders he is also appointed under Section 11(2) of the Code of Criminal Procedure 1973 (Act No. 2 of 1974) as Presiding Officer of the Special Court of Judicial Magistrate First Class at Rae Bareli for trying cases relating to offences committed in Ayodhya (Faizabad) in Crime No. 198/92 against the Special Court established under Government Notification No. 6617 A/D-N-2-839-G-92 dated 16 December 1992 read with Government Notification No. 3123/VII-Nyaya-2-539-G-92 TC dated 8th July, 1993.

By order of the Court
K.S. Rakhra
Registrar General

5. Upon hearing counsel the court made the following order

Permission granted to file S.L.Ps.
Heard the learned counsel for the parties.
The grievance of the petitioners in this bunch of cases is that there is no notification appointing a special Judge to try the offences committed in Ayodhya (Faizabad) in Crime No. 198/1992 after the Allahabad High Court struck down the pending proceeding in the special court at Lalitpur on the ground that there had been no consultation with the High Court. The state of U.P. has filed an affidavit stating there in that there exists a special court at Rae Bareli where the offences in relation to crime No. 198/92 can be tried. Mr O.P. Sharma, appearing for the petitioners, however, submitted with vehemence that there does not exist any such court at Rae Bareli. This statement of Mr Sharma is belied by the notification issued by the High Court of judicature at Allahabad dated 28 September 2002 which unequivocally indicates that the presiding officer of the special Court of Judicial Magistrate at Rae Bareli would try cases relating to offences committed in Ayodhya (Faizabad) in Crime No. 198/92. Mr Sharma, however, contended that the special court should be at Lucknow and there is no reason the special court at Rae Bareli would be asked to try the offences in question. This is a matter in which the government in consultation with the High Court has constituted a Special Court and the High Court in its discretion has constituted the Special Court at Rae Bareli for trying the cases in relation to crime No. 198/92. No person much less the petitioners in public interest can claim any Special Court at any particular place for trial of any criminal case.

In the aforesaid premises, we see no justification for any grievance of the petitioners and these petitions accordingly stand dismissed.

J.S. Rawat
Court Master

Suneet Bala Sharma
Assistant Registrar

6. NDA government may have amended decision concerning Advani

The Vajpayee government appears to have amended the then Narasimha Rao government's 1 October 1993 decision while allowing the CBI to drop the criminal conspiracy charges against Deputy Prime Minister L.K. Advani, Murli Manohar Joshi and six others in the Babri Masjid demolition case.

The Union Home Ministry in its ten-page letter, signed by R.K. Mishra (Director) had given sanction to the CBI for the prosecution of persons accused in the Babri demolition case. It was after this permission the investigating agency had filed a joint/consolidated chargesheet (dated 4 October 1993) at the ACJM, Lucknow on 5 October 1993. The Court had taken cognizance of all cases on 11 October 1993.

The Union Home Ministry's sanction dated 1 October 1993 categorically states that 'the Central Government after fully and carefully examining all the relevant material and circumstances of the case is satisfied that acts of the accused, including Mr Advani, Mr Joshi and others, constitute offences u/s 120-Br/w with 153-A, 153-B, 295, 295-A and 505 of the IPC'.

The Union Home Ministry's secret document blows to smithereens the CBI and the Centre's claim that they did not dilute the supplementary chargesheet against Mr Advani and others filed at the Special CBI court, Rae Bareli, on 30 May by dropping Section 120-B.

Significantly, the Home Ministry's letter, which dwelt at length on criminal charges, has landed the CBI in a piquant situation. While the CBI has made BJP General Secretary Pramod Mahajan as one of its forty-nine witnesses in case no 198/92 against Mr Advani and others, the Home Ministry's letter had dragged the former minister in the list of conspirators.

'In pursuance of the Criminal Conspiracy Act, Ashok Singhal and Pramod Mahajan had met Shiv Sena Chief Bal Thackeray in Bombay on 21 November 1992. Pursuant to this, on 25 November 1992, Mr Thackeray made a public announcement at Pandharpur of his participating in *kar seva* alongwith lakhs of *kar sevaks*', the letter said.

It was after carefully going through the CBI draft chargesheet and material evidence, the Union Home Ministry had given permission for prosecuting all forty-nine (now forty-seven) accused in the Babri demolition case.

[From *The Times of India,* 26 July 2003.]

CHAPTER X

The BJP's Ayodhya Campaign 1985–2003: Misusing the name of Rama as symbol of Hindutva

1. The BJP's Election Manifestos

1a. The BJP's 1991 Election Manifesto

Sri Rama Mandir at Janmasthan

BJP firmly believes that construction of Sri Rama Mandir at Janmasthan is a symbol of the vindication of our cultural heritage and national self respect. For BJP it is purely a national issue and it will not allow any vested interests to give it a sectarian and communal colour. Hence party is committed to build Sri Rama Mandir at Janmasthan by relocating super-imposed Babri structure with due respect.

[From *BJP Election Manifesto*, 1991, p. 5.]

1b. The BJP's 1996 Election Manifesto

Sri Rama Mandir at Ayodhya

The BJP is committed to the concept of one nation, one people, one culture—our nationalist vision is not merely bound by the geographical or political identity of India, but defined by our ancient cultural heritage. From this belief flows our faith in '*Cultural Nationalism*' which is the core of *Hindutva*. That, we believe, is the identity of our ancient nation—*Bharatvarsha.*

Hindutva is a unifying principle which alone can preserve the unity and integrity of our nation. It is a collective endeavor to protect and re-energize the soul of India, to take us into the next millennium as a strong and prosperous nation. *Hindutva* is also the antidote to the shameful efforts of any section to benefit at the expense of others.

We hold that only by recognizing the limitless strength of cultural nationalism, can the nation be moulded. When the BJP joined the movement for the construction of the Sri Rama Mandir at Ayodhya, it was to strengthen just these foundations.

On coming to power, the BJP government will facilitate the construction of a magnificent Sri Rama Mandir at Janmasthan in Ayodhya which will be a tribute to *Bharat Mata*. This dream moves millions of people in our land; the concept of Rama lies at the core of their consciousness.

[From *BJP Election Manifesto,* 1996, p. 15.]

1c. The BJP's 1998 Election Manifesto

Our National Identity: *Cultural Nationalism*

The BJP is committed to the concept of 'One Nation, One People and One Culture'. The unique cultural and social diversity in India is woven into a larger civilizational fabric by thousands of years of common living and common and shared values, beliefs, customs, struggles, joy and sorrow, as well as symbols of high degree of unity without uniformity. Our nationalist vision is not merely bound by the geographical or political identity of *Bharat* but it is referred by our timeless cultural heritage. This cultural heritage which is central to all regions, religions and languages, is a civilizational identity and constitutes the cultural nationalism of India which is the core of Hindutva. This we believe is the identity of our ancient nation '*Bharatvarsha*'.

Every effort to characterize Hindutva as a sectarian or exclusive idea has failed as the people of India have repeatedly rejected such a view and the Supreme Court, too, finally endorsed the true meaning and content of Hindutva as being consistent with the true meaning and definition of secularism. In fact, Hindutva accepts as sacred all forms of belief and worship. The evolution of Hindutva in politics is the antidote to the creation of vote banks and appeasement of sectional interests. Hindutva means justice for all.

The BJP is convinced that Hindutva has immense potentiality to re-energize this nation and strengthen and discipline it to undertake the arduous task of nation-building. This can and does trigger a higher level of patriotism that can transform the country to greater levels of efficiency and performance. It is with such integrative ideas in mind, the BJP joined the Ramjanmabhumi movement for the construction of Sri Rama Mandir at Ayodhya. This greatest mass movement in post-independence history reoriented the polity in India and strengthened the foundation of cultural nationalism.

The BJP is committed to facilitate the construction of a magnificent Sri Rama Mandir at Ramjanmasthan in Ayodhya where a makeshift temple already exists. Sri Rama lies at the core of Indian consciousness. The BJP will explore all consensual, legal and constitutional means to facilitate the construction of Sri Rama Mandir at Ayodhya.

[From *BJP Election Manifesto*, 1998, p. 4.]

2. Vajpayee asks Muslims to drop their claims on the Masjid, 15 February 1987

Drop Masjid claim, says Vajpayee

Bharatiya Janata Party leader Atal Behari Vajpayee urged Muslims to give up their claim to the Babri Masjid and hand over the entire place to the Hindus as a gesture of goodwill towards and with respect for their sentiments.

Addressing a large gathering at the Shivaji Park in Bombay at a function to felicitate him on his 61st birthday, he said the Hindus should reciprocate by allowing the present structure of the Masjid to stand as it is while constructing a temple adjoining it befitting the Ramjanmabhumi, to offer prayers.

Clarifying that it was his personal view, Mr Vajpayee said if this suggestion was acceptable, further details could be worked out in consultation with all parties concerned.

[From *Indian Express*, 16 February 1987.]

3. Vajpayee demands handover of the mosque, 6 April 1989

'Hand over the site to Hindus for that only is the solution for the Ramjanmabhumi–Babri Masjid dispute in Ayodhya', demanded, Mr Atal Behari Vajpayee amidst rapturous applause at the '*Viraat Hindu Sammelan*' (mammoth Hindu congregation) here this evening.

Calling the controversy unfortunate, Mr Vajpayee, who spoke as '*swayamsevak*' of the RSS, said the generations to come would never accept it as a national monument for the sake of political expediency. Neither could the court settle it. 'If the court declared the site as Ramjanmabhumi, would it be acceptable to the government?' asked Mr Vajpayee. 'Rama was born centuries before Babar and Rama and Krishna were Hindu gods, therefore Hindus were the rightful claimant of the site', he asserted.

He said a Court had already ruled the site in Ayodhya as the Ramjanmabhumi. The lock was opened by the Court. 'But even the force of the people could have done it', he asserted. He wondered why the Muslims were not respecting the Hindu sentiments, when Indonesia, an Islamic state, recognizes Ayodhya as Rama's birthplace.

[From *Indian Express*, 7 April 1989.]

4. Vajpayee's speech at the National Integration Council, 16 May 1989

Mr Atal Behari Vajpayee, leader of the BJP Parliamentary Party, today expressed unhappiness over the official briefing on the proceedings at the Home Minister's meeting with leaders of opposition parties in Parliament yesterday, particularly in regard to his views on the Ramjanmabhumi–Babri Masjid issue.

The two-day meeting which concluded yesterday was held to discuss the communal situation in the country prior to the convening of the National Integration Council.

What Mr Vajpayee had said in his thirty-minute speech at the meeting on the Ramjanmabhumi issue regarding handing over of the present site to the Hindus but building of a temple and a mosque at two other places, was a suggestion he had made two years ago in his 'personal capacity', but which was rejected then, the BJP leader told *The Hindustan Times* this evening. This was not the suggestion he had made only yesterday.

He had also stated that it was not possible to resolve the issue through judicial process because it was not possible to pinpoint the exact spot where Lord Rama was born thousands of years ago. He considered that Lord Rama was a historical figure and Ayodhya was a historical city where Rama was born and where a temple dedicated to him had been in existence since the time of Emperor Vikramaditya. This temple was built and rebuilt over the ages.

[From *The Hindustan Times*, 18 May 1989.]

5. Resolution of BJP's National Executive, Palampur, 11 June 1989, demanding that 'Ramjanmasthan be handed over to the Hindus'

The National Executive of the Bharatiya Janata Party regards the current debate on the Ramjanmabhumi issue as one which has dramatically highlighted the callous unconcern which the Congress Party in particular, and the other political parties in general, betray towards the sentiments of the overwhelming majority in this country—the Hindus.

According to all available records, the Mughal Emperor Babar visited Ayodhya in 1528, destroyed the temple situated at the site believed to be Ramjanmasthan, and constructed a mosque in its place. Ever since, Hindus have been longing to see the resuscitation of the temple at the site which they hold as extremely sacred. During the 1857 war of independence, the Muslims responding to the sentiments of the Hindus had accepted their claim over the Ramjanmasthan, but the vile Britishers in pursuance of their policy of divide and rule scuttled the settlement. Though efforts have been continuing to persuade Muslims to respect the feelings of the Hindus and abandon their claims to the site, this site has also been subject matter of prolonged litigation.

Lately the Congress government has unleashed a virulent campaign against the BJP and the Vishwa Hindu Parishad, which has been representing the Hindu point of view in the negotiations with government, alleging that while other sections of opinion have accepted reference of the dispute to the Allahabad High Court, the BJP and the VHP are unwilling to abide by a judicial verdict in this case. This propaganda is slanderous, and is based on a total misrepresentation of facts.

The BJP holds that the nature of this controversy is such that it just cannot be sorted out by a Court of law. A Court of law can settle issues of title, trespass, possessions etc. But it cannot adjudicate as to whether Babar did actually invade Ayodhya, destroy a temple and build a mosque in its place. Even where a Court does pronounce on such facts, it cannot suggest remedies to undo the vandalism of history. As far back as in 1885, a British Judge Col. F.E.A. Chamier, disposing off a civil appeal relating to the site, observed in a helpless vein: 'It is most unfortunate that a Masjid should have been built on land specially held sacred by the Hindus, but as that occurred 356 years ago, it is too late to remedy the grievance.' (dated 18 March 1886 Civil Appeal No. 27 of 1885 District Court, Faizabad).

In this context, it should not be forgotten that the present turmoil itself stems from two court decisions, one of 1951 and the second of 1986.

On 3 March 1951, in Gopal Singh Visharad *versus* Zahur Ahmad and others, the Civil Judge, Faizabad observed, inter alia: 'at least from 1936 onwards the Muslims have neither used the site as a mosque nor offered prayers there, and that the Hindus have been performing their *puja* etc. on the disputed site'.

Then on 1 February 1986, District Judge, Faizabad referred to this 1951 order and directed that as 'for the last thirty-five years Hindus have (had) an unrestricted right of worship' at the place, the locks put on two gates in 1951 on grounds of law and order should be removed (Civil Appeal No. 6/1986).

The 1951 order had provoked little reaction. Till then, secularism had not yet become a euphemism for Hindu baiting, as it has become today. It is noteworthy that around this very time the Government of India, under the leadership of Pandit Nehru and Sardar Patel, and with the blessings of Gandhiji, had itself decided to undo a similar act of vandalism, and to restore the great Somnath temple at Prabhas Patan (Gujarat).

When the Archaeological Department suggested that the site be declared a protected monument (these days a similar suggestion is being canvassed in respect of Ramjanmabhumi also), Home Minister Sardar Patel put it on record in the official files:

> The Hindu sentiment in regard to this temple is both strong and widespread. In the present conditions it is unlikely that the sentiment will be satisfied by mere restoration of the temple, or by prolonging its life. The restoration of the idol would be a point of honour and sentiment with the Hindu public.

When the *jyotirling* was formally installed at Somnath, the country's Rashtrapati, Dr Rajendra Prasad participated in the ceremony.

However, by the time the second court order of 1986 came, secularism had come to be equated with an allergy to Hinduism, and a synonym for minority appeasement. The Muslim League lobby in the country had acquired a new militancy and aggressiveness. The campaign launched by this lobby against the Supreme Court's judgement in the Shah Bano Case in 1985 had brought it rich dividends. A panic-stricken government had amended the criminal law; the Supreme Court judgement was legislatively annulled. Having thus tasted blood, this lobby set up the Babri Masjid Action Committee, and mounted a vicious assault on the decisions of the Faizabad Court, and went to the length of boycotting Republic Day celebrations in protest against these orders. A rally organized by this lobby in front of Parliament House actually held out threats of violence unless these orders were reversed. It is significant that most of the members of the Babri Action Committee belonged to the Congress (I).

Against the above background, the reference made to the High Court is just an expedient device to sweep issues beneath the carpet. The move satisfied the Muslim League lobby, and so is electorally convenient. It certainly does not reveal any earnest desire on the part of government to solve the problem.

The BJP believes that theocracy is alien to our history and tradition. It is, therefore, that in 1947 even though India was partitioned on religious grounds, and even though Pakistan declared itself an Islamic State, India opted for the present Constitution, and guaranteed equality to all citizens irrespective of their religion.

Secularism, according to our Constitution-makers, meant *sarva dharma sama bhava*. It did not connote an irreligious state. It certainly did not mean rejection of our history and cultural heritage.

The National Executive records its appreciation of the attempts made by some Shia leaders to persuade the community that it was contrary to the tenets of Islam to have a mosque built upon a place of worship of another religion, and that, therefore, the site in dispute should be handed over to the Hindus and a mosque built at some other suitable place.

The BJP calls upon the Rajiv Gandhi government to adopt the same positive approach in respect of Ayodhya that the Nehru government did with regard to Somnath. The sentiments of the people must be respected, and Ramjanmasthan handed over to the Hindus—if possible through a negotiated settlement, or else, by legislation. Litigation certainly is no answer.

[From *The RSS and the BJP*, by A.G. Noorani, Leftword Books, 2000, pp. 7–8.]

6. Advani is confident the Rama movement will translate into votes

Immediately on the passing of the Palampur resolution on Ayodhya on 11 June 1989, Advani said, 'I am sure it will translate into votes'. On 3 December 1989, after the general elections, he expressed satisfaction that the issue had contributed to the BJP's success. On 24 February 1991, as India teetered towards another election, he was confident that the issue would 'influence the electoral verdict in favour of the BJP'. On 18 June 1991 he made this pathetic confession: 'Had I not played the Rama factor effectively, I would have definitely lost from the New Delhi constituency'. Shortly after the demolition of the Babri Mosque on 6 December 1992, and another wave of carnage that came in its train, Advani wrote that if the Muslims were to identify themselves with the concept of Hindutva there would not be any reason for riots to take place (*The Times of India*, 30 January 1993). In July 1992, he argued in the Lok Sabha Speaker's chamber: 'You must recognize the fact that from two seats in Parliament in 1985 we have come to 117 seats in 1991. This has happened primarily because we took up this issue [Ayodhya].' Behind the BJP's religio-cultural rhetoric, however, there has always been cold political calculation. BJP leader Sushma Swaraj ripped apart this pretence in Bhopal on 14 April 2000, when she admitted that the Ramjanmabhumi movement was 'purely political in nature and had nothing to do with religion' (*The Telegraph*, 16 April 2000).

[From *The RSS and the BJP*, by A.G. Noorani, Leftword Books, 2000, pp. 7–8.]

7. Advani offers to drop the move for construction of temples in Mathura and Kashi if Muslims allow the Rama temple to be built in Ayodhya, 13 August 1990

The BJP president, Mr L.K. Advani, today offered to intercede with the Vishwa Hindu Parishad and also his party to drop their plans for construction of temples in Mathura and Kashi if the Muslim leaders allowed the Ramjanmabhumi temple to come up at Ayodhya.

'I appeal to the leaders of Muslim public opinion in the country of recognize the strong feelings of Hindus with regard to Ramjanmabhumi and to cooperate with the VHP leaders to ensure that the remains of the Babri Masjid are respectfully shifted to some other site close by, a proper mosque built there and a befitting Sri Rama temple built at the site believed to be the sacred birthplace of Rama', Mr Advani told the audience.

In his speech, Mr Advani said 'if Hindu sentiment is not going to be respected in India where else in the world can it command respect? If a Rama Mandir cannot be constructed in Ayodhya would it have to be constructed in London or in New York.'

The BJP president said his party was of the view that this controversy was such that it could not be sorted out by a court of law. A Court of law could settle issues of title, trespass or possession but it could not adjudicate as to whether Babar did actually invade Ayodhya or destroyed a temple and built a mosque in its place.

'Even where a Court does pronounce on such facts, it cannot suggest remedies to undo the vandalism of history. A problem of this kind can be sorted out either by negotiation between contending parties or by government decision or legislation and not by litigation', Mr Advani said.

[From *Indian Express*, 14 August 1990.]

8. The BJP opposes settlement by law

8a. The BJP says the temple issue cannot be resolved through litigation, 19 September 1990

The BJP today reiterated that the Ramjanmabhumi temple issue cannot be resolved through litigation.

BJP president L.K. Advani, in a statement here, said that official briefing of yesterday's meeting of the National Integration Council's sub-committee on communal harmony had conveyed 'a totally misleading' impression about BJP's stand on Ramjanmabhumi.

[*The Hindustan Times*, 20 September 1990.]

8b. The BJP declares that no court can give a verdict on the Ramjanmabhumi–Babri Masjid issue

The Bharatiya Janata Party (BJP) today accused the National Front government of fooling the nation by declaring that it will stand by a court verdict on the Ramjanmabhumi–Babri Masjid issue.

'No court can give a clear verdict on the issue and even if a verdict was forthcoming no government can implement it', the BJP leader, Mr A.B. Vajpayee, declared at a function to bid farewell to the party president, Mr L.K. Advani, on the eve of his *rath yatra* from Somnath to Ayodhya on 25 September 1990.

Mr Vajpayee alleged that the government's reiteration that it would stand by the verdict was nothing but a 'vote-catching gimmick'.

Mr Advani, who replied to the felicitations, made it clear that the BJP respected the judiciary. But it was of the view that on the Ramjanmabhumi issue, no court could give a clear verdict.

Justifying BJP's boycott of the National Integration Council (NIC) meeting at Madras, Mr Vajpayee said the party had kept away as it was of the view that the deliberations would only be a repeat of the Communal Harmony Committee meeting at Delhi.

Mr Vajpayee made it clear that the Rama temple would come up at the disputed place in Ayodhya at any cost and the BJP was committed to make the temple plan a success.

[From *The Times of India*, 24 September 1990.]

9. The Gujarat phase of the *yatra* marked by clear signals of growing militancy

To what distance the 10,000 km-long Somnath–Ayodhya Rama *rath yatra* of Bharatiya Janata Party president L.K. Advani will take the party to its political destination—Delhi *simhasana*—is too early to say. But the response to the *yatra* which started on Tuesday was just overwhelming, fanatical at times.

During the first four days of the Gujarat lap, covering about 800 km from Somnath to Surat, the *rath* attracted thousands. It had a variety of welcome. People danced with swords and bows and arrows while maidens played *ras-garba* balancing auspicious *kumbh* and coconut on their heads.

It was a virtual *tandava* the followers of Mr Advani performed on the route as he set off on the *dharam yuddha yatra* from the seaside town after a *Rama yagna* in the historic Shiva temple. Just opposite the temple members of the Vishwa Hindu Parishad (VHP) and the Bajrang Dal danced with naked swords, bows and arrows and it continued all the way.

A youth in saffron stabbed his left arm and put a *tilak* with his blood on Mr Advani's forehead at his public meeting in Ahmedabad. This public show of violent passion was not a solitary event. On the first day of the *yatra*, Mr Advani was presented a *kumbh* of blood when he reached Jaipur near Rajkot. The blood was donated by 101 young members of the newly-formed Bajrang Dal, the suicide squad of the BJP.

The *yatra* emanated clear signals of growing militancy in the party as well as the Hindu society. With this the final nail has been driven into the coffin of the party's moderate leader Atal Behari Vajpayee's dream of Gandhian socialism which was scoffed at during the famous Palampur convention of the party. . . .

At the very outset, Mr Advani, in one of the rare but a highly calculated move, acknowledged the existence of the VHP as a frontal organization of the party and commended its role at the press conference before leaving for Somnath from Ahmedabad.

It is for the first time that the BJP has come out in the open with a religious movement without hiding its intentions. A cause it had always let the VHP lead from the front. To some extent, in this new role, it resembles the old Jana Sangh after a decade of hobnobbing with moderate ideas.

The reason behind the hardening of the party's stand is obvious. It firmly believes that its electoral success during the last Lok Sabha and Assembly elections had much to do with the nation-wide *shila pujan* campaigns. The aim is obvious—to tap the growing Hindu militancy.

In this regard the party does not seem to be quite off the mark. The response to the *yatra* is a case in point. In his public speeches and press conferences in Gujarat, Mr Advani himself admitted that the response was not to his presence, his appeals or the BJP. People flocked in the name of Rama, he said.

In such a situation it is apparent that this time the party wants to directly cash in on Hindu sentiment instead of routing it through the VHP as it did in the past. In any case the *yatra* has made the lotus a familiar symbol and when it comes to electioneering in the future the party will have to make little efforts to make people recognize, it says a senior leader.

People are for Rama and the party's main task is to identify itself with the hero of the *Ramayana* to the extent that both become synonymous, a political bonanza powerful enough to fulfil its dream of turning the country into a Hindu *rashtra* by the turn of the century, many of them feel.

Obviously to retain the gains of the *yatra*, the party has launched a country-wide *Rama jyot* campaign along with the *yatra*. Every Hindu should have a *jyot* for Rama on Diwali is the appeal, party workers are making.

But, to convert the religious response into a political achievement may still be a difficult task. This is evident from the fact that though huge crowds witnessed the *rath*, the attendance at the public meetings of its occupant, Mr Advani, was thin, the least the party had expected.

The image of the *maryada Purushottam Rama* the party is trying to portray is to attract votes.

The cadre-based party with the support of its wings like the VHP, the Bajrang Dal and the Rashtriya Swayamsevak Sangh (RSS) probably can do it. But not without Rama, the ideal man playing Krishna, a shrewd manipulator.

[From *Indian Express*, 30 September 1990.]

10. The BJP's ultimatum to the government

Following is the text of the resolution adopted by the National Executive of the BJP at its emergent meeting.

'The *Rama rath yatra* has been a tremendous success. From Somnath to Delhi so far, literally millions of people belonging to all castes and communities have given it tremendous ovation. Here was a great act of national integration. Any government interested in national unity should have welcomed it, but, the government has responded by carrying on a ceaseless slanderous campaign against the *yatra*, and in U.P. embarking on a repressive course by arresting thousands including BJP leader in the U.P. assembly, Shri Kalyan Singh, barrister Narendrajit Singh Ji, respected *sanghachalak* of U.P. Justice Devki Nandan Agarwal (retd.).

We are sorry to say that we are not exactly surprised. The performance of this government has been a total disappointment.

The country has welcomed, and the BJP had backed, the Janata Dal government, with great expectations. But all these expectations have been belied.

The Punjab and Kashmir issue bungled by the Rajiv government, have been worsened by the V.P. Singh government. And on top of that, terrorism in Assam and Andhra Pradesh has been allowed to assume menacing proportions.

Thanks to the wrong economic and fiscal policies, prices have sky-rocketed, making life miserable for more and more millions.

The BJP has been in favour of reservations to socially and educationally backward classes. However, the manner in which the government announced its decision about the Mandal Commission report without any consultation with supporting parties, and without qualifying it with any economic criteria, was utterly wrong. The decision was prompted not by any concern for the backward classes, but by considerations of political expediency. The government's decision can only lead to dividing and subdividing society. The result has been not only serious disturbance of peace and enormous loss of life and property, but the immolation of some of the flower of our youth.

'The issue of Ramjanmabhumi Mandir–Babri Masjid has been hanging fire for long. The people want the Ayodhya sites restored to close the old unhappy chapter of Mandir desecrated, and converted into mosque. This is not a communal issue. It is a matter of national honour, calculated to promote national reconciliation. But instead of seeing the matter in this positive light, the government has communalized the issue. Some leaders of the ruling party have been whipping up communal passions, leading to serious rioting.

'The BJP holds that Hindu sentiment can be satisfied only if a temple is constructed at the Ramjanmasthan. The mosque built by Babar was abandoned in 1936. Since 54 years, thus, no *namaz* has been offered at this place, and since at least 1949, *puja* and *parikramas* have been regularly going on. The dispute in fact is between a Mandir and a non-Masjid. Even so, in deference to Muslim sentiment, the VHP has offered to relocate the Masjid structure elsewhere.

'The BJP's National Executive calls upon the government to honour the sentiment of the people and allow a temple to be built at the Janmasthan. The executive warns the government that if it fails to do so, or, if it disrupts the *rath yatra* which has come to symbolize this sentiment, the BJP would be constrained to withdraw support to this government.'

[From *Indian Express*, 18 October 1990.]

11a. Advani declares that Ramjanmabhumi issue will decide the next election

Bharatiya Janata Party president L.K. Advani attempted to set the agenda for the next elections—whenever they may be—saying that it would be the issue of the Ramjanmabhumi that the electorate would have to decide on.

Addressing a massive gathering on the banks of the Saryu river in this temple town, Advani declared: 'Henceforth only those who fight for Hindu interests would rule India.'. . .

Speaking at the fag end of the meeting, Advani described the Ramjanmabhumi movement as the turning point in the history of the country. 'Henceforth, the Hindu community will not let anybody trifle with its sentiments' he said.

The BJP president maintained that it was the BJP alone that stood for Hindu rights whereas all the other parties pandered to the minorities. Describing himself as a politician with a firm belief in the Hindu religion, Advani said his aim was to integrate the various communities by spreading nationalism but for every other political party, nationalism had been replaced by minorityism.

Appealing to the gathering not to consider the fight for the Ramjanmabhumi movement as a fight against the Muslims, Advani reminded them that the Hindu tradition and ethos was such that it bound people together. He appealed to the minorities to respect the sentiments of the Hindus and to come to an agreement with the majority community.

He said the 'structure (in Ayodhya) ceased to be a mosque long back and, as a gesture of goodwill towards Muslim sentiments, the Hindus could be persuaded to agree to the shifting of structure', because, for the Hindus, the question of Lord Rama's birthplace was a matter of faith which was not justiciable. . . .

[From *Independent*, 20 November 1990.]

11b. Advani kicks off BJP's election campaign in Ayodhya, 19 November 1990

The BJP president, Mr L.K. Advani, who arrived here today to a massive reception, set the tone for his party's election campaign.

'Jo Rama hit ki baat karega, wahi Hindustan par raj karega' (He who talks in Rama's favour will rule over India), Mr Advani told a massive gathering on the banks of the Saryu, underlining the point that no government can last ignoring the majority community's interests.

Mr Advani, who has been shaping the BJP as a party espousing distinctly the interests of the majority community, said, 'No government can survive without supporting Rama'. He said the developments of 30 October and 2 November had shown everybody that no one could any longer afford to play with the identity of the nation which, according to his definition, is safeguarding the interests of the majority community. . . .

Mr Singhal said he had asked the Prime Minister, Mr Chandrashekhar, to hand over the possession of the *shilanyas* site and the sanctum sanctorum of the disputed shrine at Ayodhya.

Mr Singhal said during his discussions with Mr Chandrashekhar, soon after he took oath of office, the Prime Minister had suggested converting the disputed shrine into a national monument.

[From *The Telegraph*, 20 November 1990.]

12. Advani admits that the *rath yatra* had a political purpose, 20 November 1990

. . . *Would you agree that Ayodhya issue was never high on your party agenda during the time of S.P. Mukherjee or any of your predecessors?*

It was never high in the Indian political debate until 1986.

So why now?

It all began with the Congress government's capitulation on the Shah Bano issue and its readiness to overturn the Supreme Court judgement in 1985. Everyone said the judgement was sound yet the Rajiv Gandhi government capitulated before a campaign. It was because of this that the Babri Action Committee was formed. Having tasted blood, they felt that since they have undone a Supreme Court judgement, what is this Faizabad district court judgement? They revived the Babri Masjid dispute and held a huge demonstration in front of Parliament and threatened to boycott Republic Day celebrations. Now this has been the course of events when in 1989, my party decided to pass a resolution on the issue. . . .

Your recent actions indicate that you and the BJP now believe that religion and politics are inseparable.

(Pause). Not inseparable. People who criticize me for putting a BJP symbol on the *rath* don't see the contradiction. If I put a Rama idol or a *moorti* or *agarbattis* there, then your charge would be correct that I am using religion. I am projecting myself as a political leader, saying in a simple and straightforward manner that this is a BJP *rath* . . . this is my symbol, this is my lotus.

You are not defensive about it.

Not at all. I on the other hand hold that my objective is not merely the temple. Side by side I regard the temple and the attitude of all political parties and the government to the temple issue as a characteristic example of pseudo-secularism.

So the rath yatra did have a political purpose?

Yes, it did have (pause). It did have. I passed a resolution in Palampur, it was a political resolution.

So it does seem that your party used god . . .

I am not a ritualistic person myself. But at the same time I do believe that all those who fought for India's freedom were not apologetic about the cultural heritage of the country and the fact that they were Hindu. . . .

13. 'The Hindu mind is made up. The Rama temple shall be built at the Janmabhumi and nowhere else.'

Mr Advani said. 'The Hindus' mind is made up. The Rama temple shall be built at the Janmabhumi and nowhere else. If the Rama temple cannot be built in

Ayodhya, should it be built in London or New York?' He said the BJP was not for the demolition of the mosque and if the young members of the party advocated this, they would only weaken the Ayodhya movement. 'Many mosques have been constructed in this country after demolishing temples, but no temples have been built by demolishing mosques. That is why the Babri Masjid cannot be demolished', Mr Advani said.

Babri Masjid

The BJP leader said that since 1936 no *namaaz* (prayers) had been offered at the Babri Masjid. The site was a defected temple where there was a Rama idol and *pujas* were being offered daily following the verdict of a court. 'The dispute is not a temple–mosque dispute. It is a dispute between a temple and a non-mosque' Mr Advani felt.

Muslims should not be inspired by the pseudo-secularism of political parties which were only interested in minority votes. There was no need for Muslims in the country to feel insecure.

[From *The Telegraph*, 23 November 1990.]

14. Temple not the main election issue, says Vajpayee

The Bharatiya Janata Party leader, Mr A.B. Vajpayee, today said the Ramjanmabhumi issue was 'one of the issue' but 'not the main issue' in the coming Lok Sabha election.

Talking to reporters, Mr Vajpayee said if the BJP was voted to power, Parliament would amend the constitution for the reconstruction of the Rama Mandir at Ayodhya. The sentiments and overwhelming support in favour of the temple could not be overlooked. The other political parties making this an issue for retaining their vote bank would definitely help the BJP, he said.

Mr Vajpayee said his party was projecting Mr L.K. Advani as the future Prime Minister. . . .

Asked about the party fielding reformed dacoits in the election, Mr Vajpayee said there was nothing wrong in fielding them as they were 'past dacoits' and not 'present dacoits' as seen in some political parties' list. Asked to name the political parties, he said the Congress and the Janata Dal have fielded several 'present dacoits' in Uttar Pradesh and Bihar.

[From *The Times of India*, 1 May 1991.]

15. Advani on the VHP

What about your allies, the VHP and the Bajrang Dal?

. . . Have any of you taken note of the fact that here is a political party, the

BJP, which has benefited enormously from the campaign organized by the VHP. And the VHP does not want to exact any price. It does not want to say that we want to see your manifesto, we want to see your list of candidates, you must accommodate so and so, otherwise we cannot support you.

But you do have VHP candidates on your list . . .

I have accommodated ten or fifteen in the whole country, whom I wanted to accommodate, who I thought would be useful. The VHP told its own members, we are not in favour of you contesting. People like Ashok Singhal, who would win hands down from anywhere, refused repeated requests to stand. No one takes notice of these facts.

And here is the Shahi Imam, dictating to the Janata Dal, the Muslim League dictating to the Congress and the manifestos actually drafted as they want them to be. And yet, it is we who are in the dock for being communal. Everyone asks, why aren't you fielding Sadhvi Rithambara? But they have said that they will not contest.

Aren't you embarrassed by what Sadhvi Rithambara says?

You have any mass movement, even Gandhiji's movement, which preached non-violence, the sort of things people said then. . . . What about the Janata Dal, what sort of people have become members of Parliament from that party and the things they say? And no one thinks it necessary that VHP should feel embarrassed.

Yes, but are you embarrassed?

Certainly, I won't encourage it . . . even if my own colleagues say something, I try to tell them that not a word of yours should seem anti any other community or religion. . . .

[From *Sunday*, 12–18 May 1991.]

16. Advani ascribes his win in the New Delhi constituency to the Rama factor, 18 June 1991

'Had I not played the Rama factor effectively, I would have definitely lost from New Delhi constituency', said a relaxed Mr L.K. Advani after he edged past his Congress rival, Rajesh Khanna, by over 1,500 votes last morning.

He attributes his rival's scintillating performance to the Mandal factor, which went against the BJP. According to him, the Rama factor clouded the Mandal issue which ultimately paved the way for his victory. This constituency had witnessed some of the most violent incidents during the anti-Mandal agitation.

Rajesh Khanna, on the other hand, was very angry after the result was announced. 'I will go to the Court', a desperate Khanna shouted when his application for a recount was rejected. There is no justice here. The court will give me justice, he said to his supporters, while sitting on an impromptu dharna on the lawns of the counting centre, protesting against the rejection of his plea for a recount.

[From *The Times of India*, New Delhi, 19 June 1991.]

17. Advani firm on *kar seva* in Ayodhya, 1 December 1992

The leader of opposition in Parliament, Mr L.K. Advani, today declared that *kar seva* would be performed at all costs on the 2.77-acre plot in Ayodhya from 6 December.

Mr Advani, who is on a temple campaign trail to whip up euphoria for the proposed *kar seva*, was addressing an impromptu meeting at the Kanpur central station. He said '*kar seva* does not mean *bhajans* and *kirtans*. We will perform *kar seva* with shovels and bricks on the 2.77-acre land acquired by the Uttar Pradesh government'.

Mr Advani said an 'unfavourable decision' of the High Court over the stay on the 2.77-acre plot would not be as 'binding on us as the construction of the Rama temple in Ayodhya is a resolve of the Rama bhakts of the country.'

The leader of the opposition who arrived here by the Northeast Express, said the Rama temple in Ayodhya was not an issue of any political party, but the resolve of the nation and hence no power on earth could stop the building of the temple.

The senior BJP leader blamed the centre for putting obstacles to block the construction of the temple and warned the Congress government of serious repercussions if it did not change its stand on the issue.

Mr Advani alleged that the Centre was deliberately trying to embroil the temple issue in legal labyrinths. 'We have given enough time to the Rao government to find the solution of the issue, but he misutilized the time only to create confusion among the masses in this regard', he pointed out.

The BJP leader reiterated that the saints and seers have decided not to give more time to the Congress government and go ahead with the construction of the Rama temple in Ayodhya. 'We have no faith in the Central Government now', he added.

Amidst deafening slogans of *Jai Sri Rama*, Mr Advani said the *kar seva* this time would not stop till the construction of the temple. In his brief speech which was punctuated with slogans of '*Advaniji tum sangarsh karo, hum tumhare saath hai*', he appealed to the people to reach Ayodhya in great strength for the *kar seva*.

Earlier Advani was given an enthusiastic send-off in New Delhi this morning. He was given a traditional send-off by women who applied *tilak*, on his forehead. Many people garlanded him and showered flower petals.

The BJP president, Dr Murli Manohar Joshi also left for Ayodhya via Mathura.

The leaders will carry out processions from the respective places and converge at Ayodhya by 6 December.

The BJP has demanded immediate withdrawal of paramilitary forces from Ayodhya as they 'are behaving as an army of occupation' and were stationed there without and permission of the Uttar Pradesh government.

Dr Joshi said the Centre was attempting to create a situation similar to the one prevalent at the time of the Mulayam Singh government in Uttar Pradesh in 1990.

Dr Joshi cautioned the Centre against creating an atmosphere whereby the very credibility of the Supreme Court would be questioned and people would lose faith in the judiciary.

He charged the Centre of misusing the electronic media to portray that everyone was opposed to the construction of the Rama temple.

[From *The Times of India*, 2 December 1992.]

18. 'BJP wave will turn into votes', says Advani, 21 February 1993

The leader of the Opposition in the Lok Sabha, Mr L.K. Advani, said the BJP's organizational machinery has the capacity of converting the 'pro-BJP wave' in the country into votes.

[From *The Telegraph*, 22 January 1993.]

19. BJP's White Paper on Ayodhya and the Rama Temple Movement, April 1993 (Extracts)

Foreword by L.K. Advani

Sri Rama is the unique symbol, the unequalled symbol of our oneness, of our integration, as well as of our aspiration to live the higher values. As *maryada purushottam* Sri Rama has represented for thousands of years the ideal of conduct just as Rama Rajya has always represented the ideal of governance. . . .

It is natural therefore that the place of His birth has been an object of the deepest devotion for Hindus through the millennia—the inscription which has been found at the site and which speaks of a magnificent temple with a pinnacle of gold, dedicated to Lord Vishnu Hari who had humbled King Bali and defeated the wicked Dashanana, that is, Ravana; the record of the unremitting struggle of the Hindus to regain the site; the pathetic history of their worshipping the spot from a distance when they were denied access to it, of their circumambulating it—all these bear testimony to their deep and abiding, and indeed stirring, devotion to Sri Rama.

On the other hand, the structure which Mir Baqi put up on the orders of Babar never had any special significance from a religious point of view. . . . It was for the country the symbol of its subjugation.

The Hindus had been trying for centuries to reacquire access to the spot and to reconstruct the magnificent temple. That was one stream of the Ayodhya movement—a stream that has been unbroken through centuries, one that predates by centuries all the persons and organizations which are today associated with the Ramjanmabhumi movement. The *sadhus* and *sants* who set up the Ramjanmabhumi Nyas in 1986—when no political party or organization was seized of the matter—represent that continuous stream in our times.

But another powerful current arose among the people, and the confluence of the two has given the power to the Sri Ramjanmabhumi movement which we see today. . . . The double standards which came more and more to mar public discourse in India to the point that the word 'Hindu' became something to be ashamed about, to the point that nationalism became a dirty word—these ignited a great revulsion among the people. As all this was being done in the name of 'secularism'. . . . Reconstructing the temple for Sri Rama became the symbol of this rising consciousness—ridding the country of the perversities to which it was being subjected in the name of secularism, forging a strong and united country. The object of the movement thus became not just to construct yet another temple, the object became to put our country back on its feet, to purify our public life, our public discourse. . . .

I regret to say that the Courts heeded our people no more. The governments remained lost in calculations; our leaders continued to be obstructive, and to put their trust in being clever, our Courts allowed themselves to remain entangled in legalisms. The *kar sevaks* pulled down the structure. For millions in the country, the construction of the temple had begun. But the *kar sevaks* did more. They did not just erase a symbol of our subjugation. They did not just begin building a symbol of resurgence. They showed us as if in a flash how far we have to travel. For the country reacted in two diametrically opposite ways, as virtually two different peoples. For a handful—those in government, in political parties, and in large sections of the English Press, for instance, what had happened was 'a national shame', it was 'madness', it was 'barbaric'. For the rest of the country it was a liberation—a sweeping away of cobwebs. The depth of devotion to Sri Rama, the depth of anger at the recent politics, had surprised me, as I said; the depth of the chasm between these two nations—the microscopic minority at the top and the people—did not.

But as the organs of communication—Parliament, the English Press, Doordarshan—were in the hands of very persons whose politics and double-talk the *kar sevaks* were tearing down, calumny was rained down upon the *kar sevaks*, on the Ramjanmabhumi movement, on the BJP in particular. . . .

The Ayodhya movement, in particular the erasure of Mir Baqi's insignia of conquest and the commencement of the temple of Sri Rama, has already occasioned deep reflection and rethinking in our country—on what a truly secular polity should be, on how a country can even survive if the deepest sentiments of 85 per cent of its people are spurned, on how we should find better ways to attend to such issues so that the people are not driven to force solutions on all. In no selection is this rethinking deeper and more evident than the Muslims.

The Background: Chapter I
Introduction
. . . The Ayodhya issue was always a potentially political issue and eventually graduated into one; how the Indian leaders ignored history and wanted the people too to ignore it; how the provocative ocular effect of the invaders' monuments was underplayed rather than understood as to its political effect; how false unity was promoted instead of an understanding rooted in facts and resulting in assimilation; how the consequence was distorted secularism; how Rama and Rama Rajya are our national heritage whose potentiality is being realized only now; how the evolution from Somnath was suspended after the death of Sardar Patel and how Ayodhya is the recommencement from the point where the spirit of Somnath stood suspended.

What does Ayodhya symbolize?
The Bharatiya Janata Party (BJP) had always affirmed that the Ayodhya movement was not just a plea for a temple for Sri Rama, that instead it reflected a far deeper quest for recapturing our national identity. The movement is firmly rooted in the inclusive and assimilative cultural heritage of India. It represents the soul of the nationalist thrust of our freedom movement. The post-independence political creed of the Congress and of most other political parties had come to regard everything that inspired this nation in the past as less than secular—in fact, communal, and even anti-national. The movement for restoration of the temple at the birthplace of Sri Rama evolved as a corrective to this distortion. . . .

Despite the mandate, time and again, the BJP and also the organizers of the Ramjanmabhumi movement, had maintained that, although the disputed structure at Ayodhya was not a mosque at all, the structure would be shifted with all reverence to another place, respecting the sentiments of the Muslims who believed —rather, who had been led to believe—it to be a '*mosque*'. . . .

This historical background of the Mohammedan invasion and the provocative ocular reminders of that violent and barbaric invasion were completely ignored even after the partition of India. This neglect resulted in the failure to evolve a sound basis for Indian nationalism and durable relationships between Hindus and Muslims. The effort was to suppress the historical facts from history books, and explain away irrefutable facts by falsehoods—such as claiming that Babar was secular and tolerant. If, instead, there had been an honest admission that the invaders were foreigners and that the India Muslim, 90 per cent of whom were converts from Hindus, were not their descendants but of the forefathers of their Hindu brethren, that would have prepared the ground for cultural and social assimilation and unity. . . . While normally one would not object to what Pandit Nehru had said namely, that Indian culture was a composite one, it was not intended to nor did it convey the meaning that our *culture* was one continuous flow into which several streams had *merged*. Instead the concept of composite culture was cited to support and sustain *distinct cultural and even political identities outside the mainstream*. The more appropriate view nearer to truth is *that*

Indian culture is one with continuity and change over 500 years and if it has a name it is only Hindu. . . .

The Integrative effect of Rama, Rama Rajya and Ayodhya

No one—not even those who oppose the Ayodhya movement—can deny the fact that Sri Rama is not just an idol of worship, but provides cultural and spiritual, and even physical linkage throughout India and the psychological glue that animates and integrates the Indian mind cutting across the barriers of language, caste, religion and region. The Kutchi Memon Muslims have, in their only book *Dasavatar,* accepted and revered Rama as an avatar. Rama thus provided the finest illustration of national integration. . . .

The nation in India always remained Hindu, whether the State was controlled by Turks, Afghans, Mughals, Portuguese, French, English or Nehruvian Secularists. The Ayodhya movement became relevant and inevitable when the post-independence digression in the national mind seriously undermined the ethos and traditions of the nation in India, and as a result, the state and the nation again got virtually divorced by the rupture of national identity and the mindless adoption of the western as the modern. The Ayodhya movement is intended to recapture the lost identity and restore the national pride. . . .

What happened on 6 December 1992 is the culmination of a battle that commenced not in 1989 when the BJP decided to join the Ayodhya movement or in 1984 when the VHP launched the mass struggle to liberate the Janmabhumi; it is the fruition of 400 years of Hindu struggle to regain their holy place. . . .

The Relentless Hindu Struggle for Ramjanmabhumi

The Struggle in Three Phases

The Hindus have been waging unremitting struggle for centuries to repossess the birthplace of Sri Rama.

First, by military expedition and war diplomacy, when barbaric aliens were ruling the country and there was no Rule of Law;

Secondly, by legal means, when the British established their model of Rule of Law (from 1885);

And thirdly, by mass movement from 1984, (along with legal steps) when Rule of Law became insensitive to their legitimate plea even under indigenous dispensation. . . .

In 1934, serious Hindu–Muslim armed encounter occurred in and around the Babri mosque, occasioned by a cow-slaughter incident. Many people were killed and the structure seriously damaged. The damaged structure was repaired by the British government which recovered the cost of the repair by a punitive fine on the Hindus ('Sri Ramjanmabhumi Historical and Legal Perspective', Justice Deoki Nandan Agarwala, cited in *Ramjanmabhumi–Babri Masjid: Historical Documents, legal opinions and judgement*, The Bar Council of India Trust, pp. 5–6). . . .

On 25 May 1885 Mahant Raghubardas appealed to the Faizabad District

Judge that an order be given for the construction of temple on the Ramjanmabhumi.

First, an unknown advocate (Umesh Chand Pande) filed an application on 21 January 1986, within two days after the Sants' ultimatum in the Munsif Court at Faizabad;

Second, on 28 January 1986, the Munsif refused to pass any orders;

Third, an appeal was filed forthwith, in the Court of District Judge, Faizabad,

Fourth, on 1 February 1986, that is, within three days of the Munsif Court order, the District Court passed an order directing the Government of Uttar Pradesh to open the locks and further directed that they shall not impose any restriction or hurdle in the *darshan* or *puja* of the Hindu community;

On 19 January 1986, in a conference of Sants held at Lucknow, it was decided to commence the struggle on 8 March 1986 (Sivaratri Day) and break open the locks, if the locks were not opened by that time.

It was thereafter that the government gave in and the judiciary too, responded with lightning speed—an application to open the locks was filed within two days, that is, on 21.1.1986; it was rejected on 28.1.1986; an appeal was filed and an order in appeal for unlocking the doors of the structure was made within three days, i.e. on 1.2.1986; the order was implemented within hours with full-scale publicity by Doordarshan. Would anyone believe that it was the very Courts, and the very government, that were handling the issue since at least 1949—were acting in 1986?

By 26 November 1992, the Central Government had sent 135 companies of Central Security Forces to Ayodhya and Faizabad, in spite of the Uttar Pradesh government's protests.

On 27 November 1992, the Supreme Court ordered the Uttar Pradesh government to give an undertaking regarding *kar seva* in compliance with court orders.

On 28 November 1992, the Supreme Court gave permission for symbolic *kar seva*, on the assurance given by the Uttar Pradesh government, and letter sent by Rajmata Vijaya Raje Scindia and Swami Chinmayananda stating that the *kar seva* would be symbolic. A judicial observer was also appointed by the Supreme Court in Ayodhya.

On 29 November 1992, Shri L.K. Advani and Dr Murali Manohar Joshi declared that they would respectively proceed from Varanasi and Mathura to Ayodhya, to mobilize *kar sevaks* and participate in the *kar seva*.

By 3 December 1992, over 25,000 armed policemen were stationed in Ayodhya and over 1,25,000 *kar sevaks* had assembled.

On 4 December 1992, the Rama Temple Restoration Programme Committee of the Ayodhya movement consented to whatever decision is taken on the nature of *kar seva* by the *Dharma Sansad*.

On 5 December 1992, the Margadarshak Mandal of the VHP expressed its consent to *kar seva*, as decided by the *Dharma Sansad*. The *Dharma Sansad* decided to have symbolic *kar seva* from 6–10 December, and possibly to commence construction from 11 December, after the High Court judgement was delivered.

On 6 December 1992, in a sudden development the disputed structure was demolished by the *kar sevaks*, and Rama Lalla was re-installed in the very place where it had been originally installed. . . .

The Evidence and Dialogue on Ramjanmabhumi

Besides the position of the Ayodhya movement that the Rama temple at Ayodhya is a matter of faith, the case of the temple is strengthened by massive and documented evidence of a pre-existing Hindu structure which was disposed of, and again provenly, a mosque was constructed. . . .

The demolition has settled once and for all the basic issue whether an existing temple was brought down to erect the mosque. The truth that has tumbled out of the demolition is that, as in the case of Varanasi and Mathura where positive and unimpeachable proof of demolition of Hindu structures and raising of the present mosques exists, the Ayodhya mosque was also raised on the debris of a temple that was brought down by Babar. . . .

Demolition, not in spite of Court orders or the actions of Shri P.V. Narasimha Rao, but precisely because of them.

The demolition took place not despite the Court orders or the efforts of Shri P.V. Narasimha Rao, but precisely because of them. To put it in brief, the *kar sevaks* were impelled to demolish the structure by the provocative actions of the Central Government, by its taking refuge under an aloof judiciary which in turn was dealing with the question as if it was an ordinary property dispute which could be handled by the usual adversary procedures of bilateral litigation. . . .

The highly provocative structure on the one hand, government's calculated strategy to use courts to thwart *kar seva* and the provocative speeches of the pseudo-secular leaders in Parliament, set the stage for an emotive outburst.

The result was demolition—an unexpected act. The government's efforts to prevent the construction succeeded, but only at the cost of failure to prevent demolition. The structure was demolished, not in spite of the Court orders, but because of the Court orders, and despite the efforts of the organizers. The role of the organizers is now a matter of public knowledge. They certainly wanted the structure to go, though not the way it went. The observer appointed by the Supreme Court reported to the court on 6 December 1992 that 'no construction took place' on that day. It is precisely because no construction took place that the destruction happened. . . .

The aftermath of Ayodhya revealed, as never before, the depth and strength of the Ayodhya movement. The culturally Anglicized elite of India alone came to regard the demolition as 'a betrayal of the nation' and as 'a national shame', but the ordinary people of India appear to have owned the demolition and welcomed it. All political parties in India which had functioned in a certain environment after Independence could not correctly gauge the popular sentiments that the Ayodhya movement commanded. Even the leadership of the Ayodhya movement and the BJP which whole-heartedly supported the movement could not entirely judge the intensity of the common man's sentiment on Ayodhya. The real strength of the Ayodhya movement became manifest only after 6 December 1992. Every political party save few, all intellectuals excepting a handful, and every English language newspaper invariably, not to speak of the government controlled Doordarshan or the foreign media which had no love for any nationalist assertion, were all aligned on one side and the people of India on the other. . . .

The shrill reaction against the demolition orchestrated by the government, and articulated by the Anglicized Indian intellectuals which singled out Ayodhya to discredit the Hindus, brought forth even greater indignation from the masses. The debate soon turned on what we mean by secularism, communalism and nationalism. . . .

The Chief Minister (of U.P., Shri Kalyan Singh) had clearly instructed, in his own hand, at 12.45 pm (which was made known forthwith at 1.00 pm by the Chief Minister to Home Minister Shri S.B. Chavan) and again at 2.20 pm (p. 7) that under no circumstances firing should be resorted to. So the Central Government knew, and Shri Narasimha Rao also knew (as from 9.30 am to 7.30 pm on 6 December 1992 the Home Minister was continuously in touch with the Prime Minister) that Shri Kalyan Singh had decided not to order firing upon the *kar sevaks* and that without firing, the Central Forces could not even enter Ayodhya. Why then did Shri Narasimha Rao not dismiss the Kalyan Singh government and order firing, which Shri Kalyan Singh had defiantly refused to do? The White Paper says everything except that at 5.30 pm Kalyan Singh resigned as Chief Minister. It was thereafter that the reinstallation of the idols (6.45 pm) and the *kar seva* for the temporary temple (7.30 pm) commenced. Why did the Central Government, that is Shri Narasimha Rao, not act—dismiss Kalyan Singh, impose President's Rule, and fire upon the *kar sevaks*? In fact, the constitutional duty of the Prime Minister to the act—dismiss Shri Kalyan Singh and order firing—became imminent and inevitable the minute Shri Kalyan Singh refused to order firing. That a Court order operated on Shri Kalyan Singh and not on Shri Narasimha Rao, did not make any difference to Shri Rao's constitutional obligations, the Court order on Shri Kalyan Singh does not reduce the constitutional obligations of the Prime Minister. In fact, once Shri Kalyan Singh failed, and failed to the knowledge of the Prime Minister, the latter's responsibility became double. . . .

The first legal case for repossession of Ramjanmabhumi was filed by Mahant Raghubardas in 1885 and the judgement of the Faizabad District Court was delivered in March, 1886. An English Judge Col. F.E.A. Chamier acknowledged;

> It is most unfortunate that a Masjid should have been built on land specially held sacred by the Hindus, but, as that event occurred 356 years ago, it is too late now to remedy the grievance. All that can be done is to maintain the party in *status quo*. In such a case as the present one any innovation may cause more harm and derangement of order than any benefit.

Thus the Hindus won the case, but could not get the Janmasthan. Purely in legal terms, this judgement was correct. Even now, what this English judge said is the intellectual justification offered by the Leftist and Anglicized section in India, namely, that it happened over 400 years ago. But can that answer the faith and sensibilities of the Hindus? If it cannot, should the law change or the faith? Could this law, or judgement have been applied to Somnath? Purely in the legal sense, could the Somnath temple have been built? But it was built. How? Because the responsible national leaders decided that was the correct way.

Judicial proceedings restart in 1950 after the Hindus physically take possession of the structure

So the law could not help the Hindus for more than 60 years, from 1885 to 1949. But when they physically occupied the structure after the idols of Sri Rama appeared on 22–23 December, 1949, the same law okayed it, and the same law enforcing courts—the District Court in 1950 and later in 1955 the High Court—granted to the Hindus the right to worship and injuncted against removing the idols. Two suits were filed by Shri Gopal Singh Visharad and Paramhansa Ramachandra Das (who is today heading the temple construction committee)—one for a permanent injunction against removing the idols, and the other for performance of *puja*. The court granted both. . . .

How did the Faizabad District court allow the appeal ordering the opening of locks in a matter of two days when the Hindus had been pleading for nearly thirty-seven years? How did the Doordarshan cameras click the opening of the locks within an hour of the court orders? All these questions have only one answer—when the government is not against, such things can, and do, happen. Even the courts respond. . . .

In the final analysis, it would appear that a bipartite legal system and principles meant for determination of private property rights cannot decide far-reaching historical issues that are related to faith and politics.

20. 'Ayodhya is a question of our national identity', says Vajpayee, 20 May 1993

Bharatiya Janata Party leader Atal Behari Vajpayee stated today that the Ayodhya issue was bound to be raised during the next elections in the country if it was not resolved by then.

Addressing a 'Meet the Press' function organized by the U.P. Press Club here, Mr Vajpayee asserted that Ayodhya was not a religious issue. 'It is a question of our national identity', he said while urging the Centre to resolve this politico-religious issue expeditiously.

Mr Vajpayee, however, denied that the BJP would take up or support the temple issue of Varanasi and Mathura. He parried a question on the proposed Central legislation banning use of religion during elections. In this context, he emphasized that Ayodhya was no more a question of a Rama temple or Hindu religion, 'but it is a question of our national identity as it touches the heart of Hindu masses', he remarked.

Mr Vajpayee expressed the hope that this volatile issue would be solved before the next elections. However, if this question remained unresolved, Ayodhya is bound to be on the national agenda of the BJP. He also admitted that this issue had given an unexpected mass support to his party which had raised the strength of the BJP members in the Lok Sabha from a mere two in 1984 to 118 in the last elections. . . .

On the question of Israel, Mr Vajpayee said that Israel would have to vacate the Arab territory annexed by it with the help of arms and urged the Arab countries to tell Pakistan that it should also vacate Indian territory annexed by it in Kashmir in 1948.

Mr Vajpayee did not favour the idea of the Army being given command of anti-terrorist operation in Kashmir. But he suggested that Army should be deployed to help the civilian authority to flush out terrorists as was done in Punjab. Besides, the Centre should put up barbed wire fencing to check infiltration from across the border.

On the question of Dunkel proposals, Mr Vajpayee said no meaningful dialogue had been held in the country so far while extreme positions taken by the parties had blurred the main issue. He commended the Indian patent law and urged the Centre to reject American suggestion for changes in this law. 'Dunkel cannot be accepted in its present form', he said.

[From *The Hindustan Times*, 21 May 1993.]

21. Vajpayee criticizes VHP movement to 'liberate' the Gyanvapi mosque in Kashi, 27 February 1995

Senior Bharatiya Janata Party leader Atal Behari Vajpayee has condemned the Vishwa Hindu Parishad for launching a movement to 'liberate' the Gyanvapi mosque in Kashi. 'You cannot go on undoing history. Unlike Ayodhya, the Gyanvapi is an active mosque. Thousands of Muslims offer *namaz* there. You cannot do this to a place of worship', he said.

As thousands of VHP and Bajrang Dal activists streamed into the holy city of Varanasi for *jalabhishek* on Mahashivratri, the leader of the Opposition in Lok Sabha told *The Asian Age,* 'The VHP is violating the Religious Sites Act of the Government of India which, except for Ayodhya, clearly states that no individual or organization can revert the religious status of any shrine.'

The VHP has 3,000 shrines on their list which were forcibly converted into mosques by Muslim rulers, said Mr Vajpayee. 'Can they launch an agitation for all of them? How long can you go on correcting historical wrongs? This has to stop somewhere', he said.

Completely distancing the BJP from the activities of the VHP, Mr Vajpayee said if the banned organization flouted laws, they would have to 'face consequences themselves'.

However, not all in the BJP are toeing a similar line. Briefing reporters on Monday, party spokesman K.L. Sharma said though the BJP was not involved with the VHP's movement the party had not taken a stand on the Gyanvapi mosque so far.

But as far as the leader of the BJP Parliamentary party is concerned, there is no question of dithering. 'We will not get involved in this. First, let them solve the Ayodhya issue', said Mr Vajpayee. Ayodhya, from the BJP's point of view, he said, is a different issue. 'The Babri mosque was defunct, there were statues of Lord Rama in the shrine and there was proof that it was the birthplace of Lord Rama. This is not the case in Kashi. *Bhagwan* Shiva is not a person. He was not born, he did not die. He is a mythical figure, a concept. From that perspective, Mathura is more similar to Ayodhya, but never Kashi'. Terming the VHP movement as 'lot of bravado', Mr Vajpayee said he did not foresee any law and order trouble. 'Nothing much has happened. In my view, the VHP probably announced their programme because they wanted to protest against the unjustified ban', he said. As a consequence, what has happened now is a hastily chalked out programme. 'There has not even been any dialogue with the Muslim parties'. The only condition the BJP would get involved with the Kashi issue, was if there was mutual consent and the Muslims themselves came forward and offered it to the Hindus. 'And that is not as unlikely a scenario as many people think', he said.

[From *The Asian Age*, 28 February 1995.]

22. Vajpayee vows to build a Rama temple at the disputed site in Ayodhya, 15 May 1996

Prime Minister designate Atal Behari Vajpayee vowed on Wednesday to construct the Rama temple at the disputed site in Ayodhya and threatened to build a nuclear bomb.

He told a crowded news conference a day before he is to be sworn in as the country's tenth Prime Minister that the Bharatiya Janata Party was committed to building a temple in Ayodhya.

He said the BJP election manifesto had promised a grand temple in Ayodhya.

'We went to the people with the manifesto. And they have elected us', Mr Vajpayee said. 'We want that the temple construction should begin after talks with everyone. We will start work at the site'. Mr Vajpayee said India believed in universal nuclear disarmament, but it could go for nuclear weapons if necessary. 'No country should have nuclear weapons. Those with nuclear weapons should listen to us', said Mr Vajpayee a former foreign minister. 'We want to make India strong, to make India's border secure', he said. Mr Vajpayee also reiterated

India's right over Pakistan-occupied Kashmir but hastened to add that his government would be for friendly relations with Islamabad. 'Pakistan occupied Kashmir really and rightfully belongs to India', he said. He said he would form a coalition ministry on Thursday and said he was confident that he would prove his majority on the floor of the Lok Sabha well before the 31 May deadline.

Mr Vajpayee ducked questions on the future of economic reforms. He also refused to say who would be his finance minister. Asked if he would invite Dr Manmohan Singh to join his government, he quipped: 'All suggestions are welcome.' *(AFP)*

[From *The Telegraph*, 16 May 1996.]

23. Prime Minister Vajpayee pledges loyalty to the RSS, 20 May 1996

Prime Minister Atal Behari Vajpayee has said there will be no compromise on the construction of a Rama temple at Ayodhya.

'There will be no softening in our stance. Our goals are the same. The path that we adopt to achieve these objectives is part of our strategy', Mr Vajpayee said in an interview in the coming (26 May) issue of Hindu weekly *Panchajanya*.

'But it is sad that we haven't got a majority otherwise things would have been different. I hope the people realize our difficulties. If we had run away from the field, they would not have liked it. So now, within the given limitations we will make all the efforts to achieve our goals', the Prime Minister added in reply to a question whether the BJP and its coalition partners will take a soft stance on issues like Ayodhya, Kashmir, infiltration and appeasement.

On Babri Masjid demolition, Mr Vajpayee said, 'What happened at Ayodhya on 6 December 1992 was not part of a pre-planned conspiracy. If speedy solutions are not found to problems related to religious places, this is what happens. Those who dilly–dallied on resolving the issue are responsible for what happened. These things can only be solved through talks or through the courts. We will make all efforts in this direction.'

Commenting on secularism, the Prime Minister said the word was not part of the Constitution when it was framed. 'Secularism was included in the Constitution only during the Emergency and since then it has been used to appease the Muslims. This is nothing but politics of vote-banks and it has done immense harm to the country. . . . Today, the issue is being raked to insult us which is a slap on the face of the people's verdict.'

Mr Vajpayee urged the minority communities to enter the national mainstream. 'They are always thinking of a separate identity . . . they refuse to be part of the mainstream which makes them pawns in political games', he said and urged them to 'stop thinking in the language of minorityism'.

'If they think in the language of minorityism, then the majority community will start thinking in the language of majorityism. . . . If we remain in power for a few years, we will try to change their mindset', Mr Vajpayee said.

When reminded of his days as a *pracharak* (propagator) of the Rashtriya Swayamsevak Sangh, Mr Vajpayee pledged that he will do nothing to undermine the 'glory' of the RSS.

'Nothing will be done by these hands of mine that will cast a slur on the shining glory of the RSS', Mr Vajpayee said. 'Attempts are being routinely made to weaken our national efforts, bans are imposed on the RSS and discrimination is practised against us all the time.' He said he will have no regret if he loses the vote of confidence in Parliament.

[From *The Telegraph*, 21 May 1996.]

24. Prime Minister Vajpayee declares BJP's willingness to 'freeze' its stand on construction of the temple, 28 May 1996

The Prime Minister Mr Atal Behari Vajpayee today declared that the Bharatiya Janata Party (BJP) was ready to 'freeze' its controversial stand on construction of the Rama temple, abrogation of Article 370 and the implementation of a uniform civil code in the interest of evolving a consensus in the country.

Replying to the two-day debate in the Lok Sabha on the confidence motion moved by him yesterday, Mr Vajpayee said that was why there was no mention of these issues in the President's Address to a joint sitting of both Houses of Parliament. 'We understand that when a consensus has to be evolved everyone has to make some compromise or the other and the BJP is prepared for it', the Prime Minister said.

Mr Vajpayee categorically acknowledged that the BJP had not been returned with a majority and that was precisely why the government had refrained from mentioning any controversial issues in the President's address.

Taking the Congress and the United Front to task for criticizing the BJP for keeping these three issues in abeyance, Mr Vajpayee said: 'We realize that we do not have a majority and we want that things should get on the basis of a consensus for a common minimum programme'. 'We deliberately did not raise anything which was controversial', he asserted.

Accusing the United Front partners of being in a hurry to come to power, Mr Vajpayee asked: 'Is it my fault if the voters have not given a clear majority to any party.'

[From *The Hindu*, 29 May 1996.]

25. Vajpayee promises legislation to solve the Ayodhya issue, 28 January 1998

Atal Behari Vajpayee today said that if the BJP was voted to power, it would introduce a legislation to solve the Ayodhya issue only if all efforts for a negotiated settlement fail.

Addressing a meet-the-press programme here, Vajpayee said if 'all efforts fail, only then BJP will bring a legislation to solve the Ayodhya issue', he said.

Asked if the BJP had abandoned the idea of introducing a Bill in Parliament to facilitate construction of the Ayodhya temple, Vajpayee said the Bill would be brought only if the talks failed to resolve the issue.

[From *Indian Express*, 29 January 1998.]

26. Bal Thackeray's proposal to resolve the Ayodhya issue, 10 January 1998

What I am suggesting is an ideal via-media to resolve the prolonged Ayodhya dispute—construct a national monument at the disputed site, allot separate sites for construction of Rama Mandir and mosque and stop the damned dispute.

There could not be any better solution than this to avoid a communal riot and to ensure harmony between Hindus and Muslims in the country.

The via-media is essential when we do not have a strong government at the Centre and we cannot afford to let the issue linger this long through litigations. The courts have taken unnecessarily long to decide on the dispute, despite the corroborating evidences produced before them by both the communities.

I would not budge from my current stand on the Ayodhya issue, even in the event of the BJP and its allies coming to power at the Centre after the Lok Sabha polls. Muslims in the country want peace. As long as they believe in national tricolour, why should we fight them? Hindutva does not mean that we should always be fighting Muslims.

[From *The Pioneer*, 10 January 1998.]

27. Workshops busy preparing material for temple at Ayodhya

Despite the many legal and political obstacles in the way of re-construction of Shri Rama temple at Ayodhya, three workshops in Ayodhya and Rajasthan are working regularly preparing material which will be used in the re-construction. According to an activist of the Sri Ramjanmabhumi Trust, material for 32 ft height of the temple (total height 132 ft) is almost ready. The on-going cutting, carving and sculpturing of stones for the temple shows the Trust's self-confidence and its commitment to the re-construction of the temple at Ayodhya.

In fact, the stone work, as per the proposed model of the temple was started in 1991 at the Nyas Karyashala in the Ramghat area of Ayodhya. Since then, hundreds of skilled artisans and technicians from Rajasthan, Gujarat and Uttar Pradesh are busy cutting, carving and sculpturing the stones. In order to accelerate the work, the Trust had last year installed several latest machines. Several new workshops at Ajari and Pindwara villages of Rajasthan (district Sirohi) were also set up in 1998. The stones after being carved at these workshops are sent to the main workshop at Ayodhya.

Talking about preparations for re-construction of the temple, the joint secretary of Vishwa Hindu Parishad (VHP), Shri Champat Rai, said that cutting, carving and sculpturing of stones was an essential part of the process of re-construction of the temple. If the stones are ready we can start the re-construction work beginning from the sanctum sanctorum as soon as circumstances favour us. He pointed out that about 2.5 lakh sq ft of stone including two lakh red sandstone as well as granite and marble are to be used in the proposed two-storey grand temple. Sculpturing of stones for the floor and the stairs is almost complete and the work on forty-nine whole and twenty-four part pillars out of a total of 144 whole and 68 part pillars, is on in these workshops. Right now only stones for the sanctum sanctorum are being cut.

[From *Organizer*, 5 April 1998.]

28. Sonia Gandhi's letter to Vajpayee and his Reply

28a. Sonia Gandhi's letter

June 06, 1998

Sonia Gandhi
President

Dear Prime Minister
I am constrained to write this letter to you because of the repeated mention in the media about preparations being made to construct a temple to Lord Rama at the site where the Babri Masjid structure stood before it was demolished. I do hope you are also aware of the very specific statements made by the leaders of the VHP that they are ready to go ahead with the building of the temple within a specified time frame. Recent media reports in various newspapers and magazines go on to suggest that a pre-fabricated structure will be raised and all preparations in this regard are going on in full swing in some parts of the country.

The tragic trail of events leading to the shocking incident on 6 December 1992 and its bloody aftermath are still fresh in the memory of the nation. I am sure you will agree that every right thinking citizen in our country would never like a repetition of these unfortunate events.

My party has been raising questions in this regard at various points to elicit information from the government about the precise situation with regard to the reports in the media relating to this matter. This issue was also raised in Parliament. But no satisfactory answer came from the government. Keeping in mind the recent developments in our country, it is imperative not to allow such divisive issues to come to the fore to the detriment of the larger national interests. In this background I would request you to enlighten the country in categorical terms about the following points so that all apprehensions and suspicions are laid to rest.

The first point is whether the whole issue relating to the Ayodhya dispute has to be resolved through the judicial process which is already underway and is continuing with the endorsement of the Supreme Court or it is open to any party to take recourse to actions which have no judicial sanction.

The second point is whether your government is aware that the VHP or some other organizations controlled by the 'Sangh Parivar' are engaged in activities with the objective of constructing the Rama temple at Ayodhya even before the judicial processes which have been set in motion are concluded, if so, what steps are being contemplated to stop these activities.

The country would like to be reassured that your government is prepared to uphold the sanctity of the judicial processes and deal firmly with anyone who may choose to violate the basic tenets that govern the judicial determination of any issue before a Court of Law.

I do hope that you will take cognizance of this matter which deals with an extremely serious and sensitive issue having a direct bearing on the well-being of our country. I shall be grateful for an early reply.

Yours sincerely,
Sd/-
(Sonia Gandhi)

Shri Atal Behari Vajpayee
Prime Minister of India
7, Race Course Road
New Delhi

28b. Vajpayee's Reply

June 7, 1998

Dear Shrimati Gandhi,
I am in receipt of your letter dated 6 June 1998 and have studied its contents carefully.

It seems to me that certain political parties, yours included, have started raising the issue of Ayodhya based on reports in a section of the media. It is ironical that, whereas my government has scrupulously kept this contentious issue out of its National Agenda for Governance, today the Opposition should be exerting to bring it to the centre-stage of national politics.

Let me state in categorical and unambiguous terms my government's position on the specific points raised by you.

1. As far as my government is concerned, the Constitution and the Rule of Law are supreme. The judiciary will be unfettered in discharging its duty in the Ayodhya matter. If the Supreme Court paves the way for the construction of the Rama Mandir at Ayodhya, the verdict will be given effect to accordingly. If, on the other hand, the apex court gives a contrary ruling, my government will perform its constitutional duty of ensuring that nobody will act against that verdict.

2. I cannot comment on your second point as it is based on media reports and your own interpretation thereof. All I will say—and I will say it with all the strength at my command—is that my government will not allow any organization to violate the sanctity of the judicial process.

When the National Agenda for Governance was drafted and adopted as the policy blueprint for my government, my Party and its allies unanimously and consciously decided to keep the Ayodhya issue out. We did so because of our paramount commitment to national security, communal harmony and socio-economic development. We did so also out of a profound faith in the wisdom of the Indian people to sort out all contentious issues amicably in conditions of stable peace and all-round development.

I have time and again stated that considerations of competitive politics should not make any political party to lose sight of these national imperatives. I do hope to receive your party's cooperation in furthering these goals in conditions of political stability which our country so badly needs today.

Yours sincerely,
Sd/-
(A.B. Vajpayee)

Smt Sonia Gandhi
President
All India Congress Committee
10, Janpath
New Delhi

29. Statement issued by MPs of Left Parties after visiting Ayodhya on 13 June 1998

(A team of members of Parliament belonging to the Left parties visited Ayodhya on 13 June and issue the following statement the next day. The team comprised

Basudeb Acharya, Dipankar Mukherjee, Gurudas Dasgupta, Amar Roy Prahdhan, Abani Roy, Ajay Chakraborty and Joachim Baxla.)

We have visited Ayodhya on 13 June 1998, representing the parliamentary wings of the CPI(M), CPI, RSP and Forward Bloc. Our intention was to be acquainted with the construction work of Rama Mandir at Ayodhya and the security arrangements for the protection of the disputed area. The district administration helped us to visit the area. The local leaders of the CPI(M) and the CPI were with us.

Our estimate on proper scrutiny is that the construction work of the Mandir was being carried on in a workshop, which is at a distance of 1.5 km from the disputed spot.

The model of 128 ft high Rama Mandir is on display in the workshop. The work is being done with precision, according to the model. Nearly 50/60 workers along with the supervisors and managers are at work. The workshop has recently installed a large stone cutting machine to expedite the work. The workshop has its own generator to maintain uninterrupted supply of power. The work at the place is constantly supervised and monitored by the Vishwa Hindu Parishad and RSS.

The structure of the Mandir above the ground level is being constructed in pieces, by parts, and the predetermined strategy is to enable the organizers to assem-ble the parts and set up the Mandir, with breakneck speed, as and when the opportunity arises. The only work that is left out is the digging of the foundation of Rama Mandir.

We also came to know that similar construction work is going on with pink stones in three other places at Pindori in Rajasthan. Therefore, it is clear that the construction of the 'structure' of the Mandir, as it is taking place in four different places, is in a well advanced stage, and that is going on in the states where the BJP is in power.

When we asked the people at work where the Mandir will be built, we had the unambiguous answer that it will be in the Ramjanmabhumi area.

Therefore, the point is that, when the court is seized with the issue of construction of Rama Mandir at the disputed site called the Ramjanmabhumi, and the judicial verdict is yet to be pronounced, why such work of a vigorous nature is being undertaken. While the judicial pronouncement cannot be pre-judged, Vishwa Hindu Parishad, RSS and Bajrang Dal who had taken upon themselves the responsibility of carrying on the construction of the Rama Mandir in parts in anticipation of a favourable court order, must have been guided by the political consideration of keeping the issue alive, whipping up passions among its hardcore support base, thus putting constant pressure on the judiciary. The construction of Mandir at an undisputed spot is anybody's choice. But to indulge in the build-up of a Mandir in parts so near to the disputed site gives clearly the signal of an attempt to set up the Mandir at any cost, only at the disputed site and nowhere else. Therefore, the developments is a matter of grave concern, and is too dangerous to be over-looked by the country and by the government.

The assurance of the Prime Minister on the floor of the Parliament, that the construction of Rama Mandir at the disputed site can be done only with judicial approval, is of little significance in view of the construction being done so close to the disputed area, with the avowed declaration of the VHP and RSS that the Mandir will be built only where the disputed site is. It is for the government to take appropriate steps to ensure that judicial process is not again subverted on the soil of Ayodhya.

[From *People's Democracy*, 21 June 1998.]

30. Vajpayee shares the dais with VHP leaders and *sadhus* at a friends of BJP Overseas meeting in New York, 10 September 2000

Mr Atal Behari Vajpayee shared a dais with VHP leaders and sadhus here last night, where he said his party would build the 'India of our dreams' if ever it came to power on its own.

The VHP president, Mr Ashok Singhal, was present at the meeting organized by Friends of BJP Overseas along with 108 sadhus who are in New York to attend a summit of religious leaders.

One of them, Swami Satyamitranand, wanted to know when a Rama temple would be built in Ayodhya. The Prime Minister, skirting a direct answer, said amid thunderous applause: 'If the electorate gives us a clear two-thirds majority we will build the India of our dreams. There is not doubt about that.'

'I will not always remain the Prime Minister, there are plenty of people for the job in Delhi. But my right to remain a *swayamsevak* cannot be taken away', he told the meeting. It wasn't clear whether he was referring to his identity as an RSS member.

The Prime Minister, who received a traditional Indian welcome on arrival, delivered his twenty-minute extempore address sitting in his chair in view of his knee problem.

He also released a compact disc on Hindu heritage and activated a website which promotes Indian education.

[From *The Statesman*, 11 September 2000.]

31a. Prime Minister Vajpayee revives the Ayodhya issue, 6 December 2000

The Prime Minister, Mr Atal Behari Vajpayee, today strongly defended the Ayodhya agitation for the construction of a Rama temple terming it an 'expression of nationalist feelings' and said the 'task has remained unfinished'.

Mr Vajpayee was talking to reporters informally after both the Houses of Parliament had been adjourned for the third consecutive day with the Opposition vociferously demanding resignations of Mr L.K. Advani, Dr Murli Manohar Joshi and Ms Uma Bharati, all Cabinet Ministers chargesheeted in the Babri Masjid demolition case.

Speaking in Hindi he said: '*Ayodhya mein Rama mandir ka nirman ek rashtriya bhavna ka prakatikaran ka kaam tha, weh abhi poora nahin hua*'. (In Ayodhya the Rama temple construction project was the expression of nationalist feelings, the work has not yet been completed.)

The Prime Minister's remarks immediately came under attack from the Opposition and even his allies, including the Telugu Desam, felt he should have avoided making such comments.

Mr Vajpayee's remarks come even as the Vishwa Hindu Parishad is preparing to announce at the '*kumbh mela*' next month a firm date to start construction of the temple. Significantly, the Prime Minister's statement—almost his first major defence of the Ayodhya agitation—follows a crucial dinner meeting with top RSS leaders at his residence last week where partymen feel the issue would have been discussed at length. The Home Minister, Mr Advani, was also present. Also, at yesterday's parliamentary party meeting, BJP MPs were told to go on the offensive on the Ayodhya issue.

The Vajpayee cue was picked up immediately by the party general secretary, Mr Pyarelal Khandelwal, who said: 'If this is what the Prime Minister has said, I welcome it'. And separately, Swami Chinmayanand and Swami Aditya Nath, both BJP MPs from Uttar Pradesh, demanded that the completion of the unfinished agenda through legislation to enable the building of a grand Rama temple at the disputed site without waiting for the Court verdict. The party spokesperson, Mr Vijay Kumar Malhotra, did not want to comment on the Prime Minister's remarks, but described the Opposition's stalling tactics today as a 'black day for democracy'.

Separately, in a statement from Jaipur, the party president, Mr Bangaru Laxman, warned political parties not to politicize the Ayodhya issue or use it to brandish their 'secular credentials'. The BJP did not make any mistake and would not tender any apology on the issue, he added.

The Prime Minister also strongly defended his Ministers and said there was no basis for demanding their resignations. 'This case was different from others. The whole background of the Ayodhya agitation would have to be looked at'. His view was that 'they were present at the site on 6 December 1992, when the structure was demolished, but to associate them with pulling down the disputed structure was against established facts'.

Giving the ministers a certificate of innocence (although the trial is yet to take place and the matter is in the courts), Mr Vajpayee said that 'they were trying to control the crowd. The were telling them they had gathered at the place to protest, not to pull down the structure.'

The coming Uttar Pradesh Assembly election, the fact that the party's base has been half eroded even in urban centres where it was strong (as evident from the recent municipal elections), and the restiveness among BJP–RSS cadres are being seen as factors that could lead the BJP to go strong on the Ayodhya issue once again despite its 1999 commitment to the NDA to abandon Ayodhya and other 'contentious issues' for five years.

Vajpayee clarifies

New Delhi, 6 December: Hours after the political furore caused by his remarks on Ayodhya this morning, the Prime Minister, Mr A.B. Vajpayee, tried to somewhat temper what he had said and insisted that he had not supported the demolition of the Babri Masjid.

At the same time he reiterated what he said in the morning, that 'the demand for the building of a Rama temple was the expression of nationalist feelings. *(Mandir ka nirman rashtriya bhawna ka prakatikaran hai).*' 'What is of significance is how the temple should be constructed', he added. ('*Mandir kis tarah banaya jaye yeh mahatvapoorna hai*'.)

The brief clarification was also made informally, while talking to reporters at a function at Rashtrapati Bhavan this evening.

[From *The Hindu*, 7 December 2000.]

31b. 'The entire country wants a Rama temple at Ayodhya', Vajpayee says, 7 December 2000

The entire country wants a Rama temple at Ayodhya—the question is how to make it and where, the Prime Minister said here today.

But he asserted that his government, formed on a National Agenda for Governance agreed among ruling NDA partners, has no 'hidden agenda on the Ayodhya issue'.

'The entire country wants the temple. The Muslims do not oppose it. The issue is how to make it and where', Mr A.B. Vajpayee told reporters at an *iftar* party hosted by the Minister of State for Human Resources Development, Syed Shahnawaz Hussain.

The Prime Minister continued to walk a tightrope as he suggested that there are two ways to resolve the controversy. One, through the judicial process with everyone accepting the Court verdict. Two, through negotiations between Hindus and Muslims, especially on where to make the temple.

The first option goes against the BJP's stand that courts cannot decide matters of faith; but his stress on temple construction and the suggestion that it can be done through negotiation contained more than a whiff of his party's original agenda.

Mr Vajpayee, whose party doesn't have a majority in either House of Parliament, however ruled out the VHP demand for legislation to settle the dispute.

He tried to clarify his statement on Wednesday that the Ayodhya movement was an expression of national sentiment and that the task was unfinished.

'By "unifinished" I meant the dispute was not yet resolved', he said and stressed that it should be resolved.

'The rumour that the BJP's allies were not satisfied about what I said on Ayodhya is not true. Ms Mamata Banerjee and Mr Yerran Naidu (TDP) met me (this morning). I apprised them of the situation. They returned satisfied.

'I told them what I had said was not to influence the Court (as the Opposition has alleged) or the CBI. The Court is independent and takes decisions without fear. The CBI is under me, but I have not interfered with it on Ayodhya or any other matter.'

After the meeting, during which both allies urged the Prime Minister to issue a clarification, Ms Banerjee said she wouldn't judge Mr Vajpayee on the basis of one statement.

At another *iftar* party, hosted by Mr G.M.C. Balayogi, Mr Vajpayee made a dig at the media. 'Media *hum logon ke beech me bhram paida karne ki koshish na kare* (the media shouldn't try to create a misunderstanding between the BJP and its partners).'

Another agenda?

The BJP today said it is committed to building a Rama temple at Ayodhya—the matter has been shelved because of the NAG, effective for five years.

'What will happen after five years we cannot say', the BJP parliamentary party spokesman, Mr V.K. Malhotra, told reporters. 'There may be another agenda, who knows?'

[From *The Statesman*, 8 December 2000.]

32. Atal Behari Vajpayee's Kumarakom Musings, January 2001 (Extracts)

. . . The Ayodhya issue is another problem from the past that we should not allow to remain unresolved too far into the future. It is a challenge to the collective wisdom of our society that we find a peaceful and amicable solution to this problem, sooner rather than later. I had consciously not commented on this issue for the past three years. However, I am sad to note that, when I was constrained to speak on the subject after the Opposition stalled the proceedings of Parliament for three days in a row, my comments were twisted and turned for no other reason but to gain political advantage.

Overnight I was transformed by a section of the media and the political class from a 'moderate' to a 'hardliner'. 'Vajpayee unmasked', they said, conveniently masking the fact that my long stint in public life is an open book. Worse still, a campaign was launched to create misgivings about me in the minds of our minority brethren.

I had hoped—and I am sure that most of our countrymen too had hoped—that my comprehensive replies to the debate, first in the Lok Sabha and then in Rajya Sabha, would put an end to the controversy. Alas, that has not been the case. I must confess that I am pained by some of the comments, observations and speculations in the aftermath of the recent developments in Parliament. My political adversaries are entitled to disagree with me, but they will not be able to see any inconsistency in my views on the Ayodhya issue, all of which are well recorded.

I have always held that there are only two ways to resolve this contentious issue; the judicial route or the route of negotiations leading to a mutually acceptable solution. I have stated that the government will accept, and is constitutionally bound to implement, the judiciary's verdict, whatever it might be. But this does not foreclose the need for negotiations in a non-governmental and non-political framework. The judicial route and the option of talks do not exclude, but are rather complementary to one another.

Irrespective of what the judicial verdict might be, its smooth implementation would require a conducive social atmosphere. Resumption of talks between representatives of the two communities, conducted in an atmosphere of trust, goodwill and flexibility, has the potential to create such an atmosphere. The ongoing controversy over implementing the Supreme Court's verdict in the case of relocation of polluting industries out of Delhi has strikingly highlighted the need for a supportive social environment involving all the parties to a dispute.

Few can deny that Rama occupies an exalted place in India's culture. He is one of the most respected symbols of our national ethos. Respect for him transcends sectarian barriers. Many Indians revered him as an *avataar* of God and some regard him as *maryada purushottam*. Non-Hindus, too, see in him an ideal king and an embodiment of great human qualities. Had it not been so, poet Allama Iqbal would not have penned the following eulogy to Rama.

> The cup of India has always overflowed
> With the heady wine of truth.
> Even the philosophers from the West
> Are her ardent devotees.
> There is something so sublime in her mysticism
> That her star soars high above constellations.
> There have been thousands of rulers in this land.
> But none can compare with Rama,
> The discerning ones proclaim him
> The spiritual leader of India
> His lamp gave the light of wisdom
> Which outshone the radiance
> Of the whole of humankind.
> Rama was valiant, Rama was bold,
> Rama yielded deftly his word,

He cared for the poorest of poor,
He was unmatched in love and compassion.

No wonder, then, that the movement for construction of a Rama temple at Ayodhya struck a supportive chord in more than one political party. Had it not been so, the government of late Rajiv Gandhi would not have taken the kind of specific steps it did to facilitate the construction of a Rama temple at Ayodhya. Rajivji even inaugurated the Congress Party's 1989 election campaign from the vicinity of Ayodhya with a promise to usher in Rama Rajya, which was also Mahatma Gandhi's dream. There was nothing communal about either Gandhiji's vision or Rajiv Gandhi's initiatives at Ayodhya.

This shows that there was no dispute over a Rama temple at Ayodhya being an expression of the national sentiment, in the same way that reconstruction of a temple at Somnath too was recognized by the then government as an expression of the national sentiment. (The government of Pandit Jawaharlal Nehru had set up a committee for the reconstruction of Somnath temple under the chairmanship of K.M. Munshi. Babu Rajendra Prasad, the then President himself participated in the temple's inaugural function, calling Somnath a 'symbol' of India's national culture.)

The only dispute at Ayodhya was over where and how. On the contentious matter, too, my views have been clear and consistent. I never stated that the temple should be built at the disputed site without either a judicial verdict or an amicable agreement between the two communities. This is how it should be in a law-governed country. I wish to make it absolutely clear that the law will take its course, should any organization attempt to disturb the status quo. The government will not remain a silent spectator and adopt delaying tactics, as unfortunately happened eight years ago.

In my reply to the debate in the Lok Sabha, I had stated that, in addition to Rama, many other personalities and places symbolize our national culture.

Be it the Dargah of Ajmer Sharif or the shrine of Nizamuddin Aulia in Delhi, the Golden Temple at Amritsar or the Church of St Francis at Goa—these are all proud symbols of our syncretic national culture.

My statement that the movement for construction of a Rama temple in Ayodhya was an expression of the national sentiment has been misrepresented in many ways. What is overlooked is the past tense that I had consciously used in my statement. In my reply to the debate in the Rajya Sabha, I had clearly stated that although the movement for the construction of a Rama temple at Ayodhya was an expression of our national sentiment, this sentiment became narrow, and its inclusive character became restrictive, because of the unfortunate demolition of the disputed mosque structure on 6 December 1992. A flagrant violation of the law, it certainly was. But it was also totally at variance with the Hindu ethos. The wrongs of a medieval past cannot be righted by a similar wrong in modern times.

The status quo at Kashi, Mathura and other disputed places of worship must remain undisturbed. Far from indicating the Hindu society's weakness, this will show the strength of our national ethos of tolerance and religious harmony.

Deeply saddening though that December Sunday was, we cannot forever remain shackled to the debate on demolitions, either of the distant or the recent past. India must move on. . . .

[From *The Hindustan Times*, 3 January 2001.]

33a. The Kanchi Sankaracharya's proposal to resolve the Ayodhya issue

Sri Chandramouleeswaraya Namaha
Sri Sankara Bhaghavadpadacharya Paramparagatha Moolanmaya Sarvagnacouia
Sri Kanchi Kamakoti Peetadhipathi
Jagadguru Sri Sankaracharya Swamigal
Srimatam Samathanam
1, Salai Street, Kancheepuram - 634 502

Date: 8 March 2002

Maulana Mujahidul Islam Qasmi
President
All India Muslim Personal Law Board
New Delhi
11 March 2002

Respected Maulanaji
His Holiness Sri Jayendra Saraswathi Swamigal visited Delhi on 5th instant. Some of the prominent devotees of His Holiness brought members of the Muslim Personal Law Board for a discussion with His Holiness. Unfortunately you could not take part in the discussions because of your indisposition. His Holiness is happy to learn that you have since returned to your home and wish you a speedy recovery.

The General Secretary of your Law Board Maulana Nizamuddin, brought a good delegation for an exchange of views on resolving the Ayodhya issue. The specific proposals presented by His Holiness at the meeting are restated hereunder for your records. The delegation was kind enough to inform His Holiness that a special meeting of the Law Board would soon be convened to discuss the said proposals.

1. Both Hindus and Muslims will abide by the Court's verdict in case of the disputed site. Ramjanmabhumi Nyas has confirmed its commitment to this effect in writing.

2. The Central Government will take the necessary steps for speedy disposal of the suit in respect of the disputed site.
3. Status quo will be maintained by both sides on the disputed site until the court pronounces its final verdict.
4. His Holiness appealed to the Law Board Members and through them to the Muslim community to accord their consent for the start of the construction of Rama Mandir by Ramjanmabhumi Nyas on the undisputed acquired land (the purpose for which the land was acquired) of which the Nyas is the original owner and a permanent lessee.
5. A separation wall may be built between the adjacent land near the disputed site and the remaining portion of the undisputed acquired land.

His Holiness, as planned, went to Gujarat on 7th instant and visited the riot-affected areas of Ahmedabad. His Holiness also visited the civil hospital where the affected persons are undergoing treatment. Apart from consoling them, His Holiness also blessed them for speedy recovery and return to their homes. His holiness also issued an appeal to the government and people of Gujarat to make an all-out effort to restore peace and normalcy immediately and to provide quick and quality relief and rehabilitation to the affected families without any discrimination—particularly to the Muslims.

This letter is being communicated to you on the instruction of His Holiness and we await a positive response from you and your organization, which we are sure will go a long way in finding a just and acceptable solution to this problem.

Sri Karyam and Agent

33b. Resolution of the Executive Committee of the All India Muslim Personal Law Board in response to the Sankaracharya's proposal

(Following is the text of the resolution unanimously passed by the Executive Committee of All India Muslim Personal Law Board on 10 March 2002 at New Delhi.)

After the assassination of Mahatma Gandhi by the fascist forces a brake was put on the communal frenzy in the country. However the fascist forces failing in their designs came up with a fresh nefarious mode to flare communal tension by installing the idols in a 425-years-old mosque in Ayodhya for the political purposes. This culminated in the barbaric demolition of Babri Masjid on 6.12.92, which was not only the demolition of a place of worship but an attack on the secular democratic fabric of the country. This not only deeply hurt the religious sentiments of the Muslim community but also caused national shame. To add insult to the injury the Acquisition of Certain Area at Ayodhya Act 1993 was passed which gravely violated the principle of secularism and equality, the basic features of our constitution. However, the Board is duty-bound to accept the verdict of the Supreme Court of October 1994.

After the judgement of the Supreme Court, the Hindutvawadi forces continued their defiant attitude and threatened the nation to proceed with the proposed temple construction during pendency of the litigations. Instead of checking this illegal and defiant attitude they were then backed, encouraged and appeased by the government of the day. Egged on by appeasement the VHP launched countrywide movement of mobilizing *kar sevaks* for the construction of Rama temple at Ayodhya and thereby alter the status quo and defy the verdict of the Supreme Court given in the Ismail Farooqi case. Such movements aroused communal frenzy.

The AIMPLB has all along been reiterating that as law-abiding citizens of this country the Muslim community stands by the rule of law under all circumstances. It is an open secret that whereas the AIMPLB has always affirmed its commitment to abide by the final verdict of the court it is the Sangh Parivar, including VHP, which have no faith in the judicial process. In the normal circumstances these forces should have been brought to book for their criminal actions but unfortunately they have all along been left scot-free.

The most condemnable incident of Godhra occurred, manipulating the same, there have been systematic pogroms of ethnic cleansing of the Muslims amounting to genocide in Gujarat. In such an atmosphere surcharged with communal tension on 4 March 2002, the Board's office was informed by Mr Kulkarni, the SDO of Prime Minister's Office, of the initiative launched by or at the instance of His Holiness Sankaracharya Shri Jayendra Saraswati of Kanchi Kamakoti Peeth for the issuance of a joint appeal for peace and tranquility in Gujarat. The General Secretary of the Board positively responded to the same and led a delegation, which met the Sankaracharya on 5 March 2002. In the meeting the joint appeal for peace and amity in Gujarat was issued by the Sankaracharya and the Members of the Board. In the meeting the Sankaracharya also conveyed to the delegation proposals for allowing construction of Rama Mandir on the so-called undisputed site by Ramjanmabhumi Nyas. On further clarification by members of the delegation, the Sankaracharya stated:

1. That he has the unflinching consent from all the parties concerned with the Ramjanmabhumi movement to negotiate with the Muslims on their behalf.
2. That all the concerned parties will abide by the Court verdict on the disputed site.
3. That the proposed construction of Rama temple will be on 42-acres of the acquired land excluding the land on which the Babri Masjid structure stood and a wall will be constructed to demarcate such 42-acres of land and status quo will be maintained till the final verdict of the court on the Babri Masjid site.
4. That Muslims would be allowed to reconstruct the Masjid at the same spot where it existed before demolition if they win the title suit in the court of law.

5. That the settlement would be legally binding on all the concerned including the government.

The delegation keeping in mind the exalted moral and spiritual status of the Sankaracharya as held by the Hindu brethren and as a matter of respect to him agreed to convey his proposals to the Board's executive committee and requested for more particulars of the proposal. The delegation requested the Sankarạcharya to provide:

1. Formal proposal in writing.
2. Copy of the building construction plan.
3. Copy of the site plan in colour.
4. Copy of the undertaking given by the Ramjanmabhumi Nyas Trust to the Hon'ble Prime Minister.
5. Any other document, which will facilitate in settling the issue.

In spite of several reminders all the above were not supplied to the Board. The letter dated 8 March 2002 (received to the Board at 2 pm on 9 March 2002) also falls short of the commitments. In the meantime there are conflicting reports of dangerous moves on the part of the government as well as the Sangh Parivar regarding their intentions.

The Board takes note of the efforts of the Sankaracharya in holding negotiations on the Babri Masjid issue and the Board sincerely hopes that the Sankaracharya will also appreciate the Board's difficulties in reacting to the proposals, which are inchoate and incomplete as:

- Without the construction plans it is difficult to understand the purported written undertaking given by Ramjanmabhumi Nyas.
- It is also not clear as to how Ramjanmabhumi Nyas is entitled to undertake such constructions and further that the linkage between the Nyas on the one hand and VHP and other organizations of Sangh Parivar on the other has not been clarified.
- Besides, the proposals contain no assurance that VHP would abide by the Court's verdict, which has been spearheading the movement since 1980s. Such glaring omission leaves VHP free to carry on mobilization and agitation. Several organizations compendiously known as the 'Sangh Parivar' are known to act in concert and collusion with each other but they have cleverly disguised their interconnections to escape the dragnet of law. The proposals do not provide any scheme to rope in all the organizations of Sangh Parivar.
- The proposal do not contain any assurance to the Muslims that if they win the title suit, the construction plan of the proposed temple will be suitably amended to shift *garbha griha* elsewhere and there will be no obstruction in the way of construction of the mosque on the site. With freedom to VHP to carry on mobilization and agitation, there is no guarantee even about the dividing wall.
- The proposal ensures the commencement of construction of the Rama temple with immediate effect while the Muslims are merely asked to wait for the

final judicial verdict. At best the proposals are 'workable arrangement' and do not offer solution of the problem in its entirety.

The Board, therefore, resolves to convey to His Holiness Sankaracharya Shri Jayendra Saraswati Swamigal its inability to accept his proposals as contained in the letter dated 8 March 2002 as being incomplete and inchoate.

The Board welcomes the proposal for expeditious hearing of the pending title suits and has already given its consent in the court proceedings and the court has already passed the order for day to day hearing on 12 July 2001.

The Board calls upon the Government of India to fulfil its duty to maintain status quo in the entire area acquired under the Acquisition of Certain Areas at Ayodhya Act and take adequate and effective steps for that purpose and prohibit any symbolic *kar seva* or *puja* etc. on the acquired land and enforce orders/ judgement of the Supreme Court.

The Board while appreciating the efforts of His Holiness Sankaracharya to maintain peace and tranquility among all the communities in the country wish to reiterate that the settlement of the dispute is not possible in piecemeal manner. It has to be resolved in the holistic manner in such a way that construction of the mosque is also not delayed.

Issued by
(MI) Syed Nizamuddin
General Secretary

34. Prime Minister Vajpayee's Goa Musings, January 2003 (Extracts)

. . . Hinduism's acceptance of the diversity of faiths is the central feature of secularism in India. As Maharshi Aurobindo points out, Indian religion has always felt that since the minds, the temperaments and the intellectual affinities of men are unlimited in their variety, a perfect liberty of thought and of worship must be allowed to the individual in his approach to the Infinite.

On the other hand, Hindutva, which presents a *viraat darshan* (broad, all-encompassing view) of human life, is being projected by some people in a narrow, rigid and extremist manner in an unfortunate and unacceptable interpretation that runs totally contrary to its true spirit. Hindutva is an integral understanding of the entire creation, showing the way both to the here and hereafter. It emphasizes the inseparable relationship between the individual and society, as well as between man's material and spiritual needs. Hindutva is liberal, liberating and brooks no ill-will, hatred or violence among different communities on any ground.

We need to affirm and promote that true understanding of Hindutva which is forward-looking, not one that seeks to take us back; that which makes us capable of meeting the challenges of the modern world, not one that is stuck in the grooves of the past; that which is reform-minded, and not one that protects obscurantism and injustice, against which all the reformers of the past have fought. If understood and practised in this enlightened sense, which is how Swami Vivekananda and other great patriots propounded it, the current controversy over Hindutva will be seen as wholly unnecessary.

There is no difference between such Hindutva and Bharateeyata, since both are expressions of the same *chintan* (thought). Both affirm that India belongs to all, and all belong to India. It means that all Indians have equal responsibilities. It entails recognition of our common national culture, which is enriched by all the diverse religious and non-religious traditions in India. For centuries, both have synonymously pointed to our national identity. Even the Supreme Court has held that Hindutva is neither a religious nor a political concept, but connotes a noble and elevating way of life.

This Indianness is what we should all elaborate and further strengthen. . . .

35. Exchange between Sri Kanchi Kamakoti Charitable Trust and All India Muslim Personal Law Board

35a. Sri Kanchi Kamakoti Charitable Trust's letter to All India Muslim Personal Law Board

Administrative Office:
No., Salal Street,
Kancheepuram - 631 502

16 June 2003

Maulana Syed Mohammad Rabey Nadwi
President
All India Muslim Personal Board
Lucknow
Uttar Pradesh

Dear Nadwi Saheb

Having come to know that your good-self is not keeping well, His Holiness decided to make a private visit to Nadwa to see you and pray for your well-being. Accordingly, on the 7th June, He took a private trip from Delhi to Lucknow and visited you in the afternoon and was indeed happy to be with you in the pious ambience. I am indeed thankful to you as the President of the All India Muslim Personal Law Board for the hospitality and courtesy extended to his Holiness and His followers.

In the course of discussion we indeed reviewed the present situation arising out of the Ayodhya dispute which have been unfortunately exploited by some vested interests. This is the main reason as to why His Holiness has been insisting that the issue should be amicably settled between the concerned religious top leaders keeping aside as far as possible the political approach to the problem, to avoid creation of feelings of apprehension, hatred and fear amongst the various communities. By doing so, we, the religious heads of the two communities can find a solution which would be conducive to communal harmony and national integration.

Since the matter of Mandir and Masjid is currently under the judicial reference, we may have to wait (how long, I do not know). Therefore we should try to work out a formula of compromise. To initiate this compromise formula, His Holiness would request you to discuss in your Board the following:

1. Your Board, on our request, may consider giving a 'no objection' statement regarding construction of Mandir upon the undisputed/acquired area.
2. Disputed area also can be discussed after some time and an amicable settlement may be given to the court and verdict can be given by the Court based on the settlement.
3. In order to protect the disputed area, a wall may be constructed separating it from undisputed/acquired area.
4. If we reach a final negotiated settlement on the undisputed area, we shall both ensure support for the same from the various religious groups/subgroups on each side to ensure that no further demands would be raised on the undisputed area.
5. Once we arrive at a cordial understanding, we may together approach the Government of India for its effective and time bound implementation.

His Holiness is sure under your benign leadership, the above suggestions would be supported and reciprocated. I am sure this will lead the communities towards a peaceful coexistence and prosperity.

His Holiness further prays to Almighty for your health, peace and prosperity for our nation.

Regards,

Yours sincerely
N. Sundaresan
Trustee

35b. All India Muslim Personal Law Board's Reply

To
Shree N. Sundaresan, Trustee — 23 June 2003
Sri Kanchi Kamakoti Peetam Charitable trust
No. 1 Salai Street
Kancheepuram - 631502

Dear Shri N. Sundaresan,

Maulana Syed Mohammed Rabey Nadwi, the President, All India Muslim

Personal Law Board has directed me to acknowledge the receipt of your letter dated 16 June 2003 which was delivered on 20 June 2003.

Maulana appreciated the personal courtesy extended to him by His Holiness Jagadguru Sankaracharya by his touching gesture of having taken the trouble of travelling from Delhi to Lucknow to enquire after his health. By the Grace of Allah Maulana's health has improved considerably.

Love for motherland is the article of faith for every Muslim. Our beloved country is passing through delicate times. To achieve prosperity and strength it is absolutely necessary that all the segments of India citizenry should march together and are bound in the bonds of affection and good will. Hindu–Muslim unity, which was the corner stone of our struggle for freedom, still remains the bedrock of our nations progress, towards prosperity with justice to all. His Holiness has made sincere efforts in this direction and your letter under reference is looked upon as endeavor in this area.

Maulana as the President of All India Personal Law Board has convened a meeting of its executive committee on 6 July 2003. But before Maulana puts the letter before executive committee, certain clarification are needed as detailed below to enable the executive committee to come to some final conclusions.

First, may I request you to turn to the letter dated 8 March 2003 written on behalf of His Holiness by Sri Kanchi Kamakoti Peethadipati Jagadguru Sri Sankaracharya Swamijee (Srimatam Sansthanam) addressed to the late Maulana Mujahid-ul-Islam Qasmi, the then President of the Board, containing similar proposals which contained categorical assurance, 'I both Hindus and Muslim will abide by the court verdict'. The present proposal however is silent on this assurance. The Maulana desires to know whether such assurance is still valid and binding and if it is so, what practical/legal measures are conceived to implement such assurances.

Secondly, as you are well aware, the Executive Committee of the Board has passed the resolution dated 10 March 2002, expressing its inability to consider the proposals contained in the letter dated 8 March 2002 with detailed reasons. Please see our resolution dated 10 March 2002. The Maulana desires to know whether His Holiness will be able to furnish the details as desired by the Board. You will kindly appreciate that above clarification amongst others are extremely crucial and important and Maulana humbly requests His Holiness to respond to these positively well before the 6 July 2003. Such response will go a long way in establishing congeniality and confidence between our two great communities.

Yours Sincerely
(Mohammed Hamza Hasani)
Personal Secretary to the President

35c. Sri Kanchi Kamakoti Peetam Charitable Trust (Regd)

Administrative office
No. 1 Salai Street
Kancheepuram 631 502
Date: 1.7.2003
To
Maulana Syed Mohammad Rabey Nadwi
President
All India Muslim Personal Law board
Nadwa
Lucknow

Dear Nadwi Saheb,
Your fax letter dated June 2003 seeking certain clarifications was received and placed before His Holiness. His Holiness is happy that you are improving in your health.

1. It was pointed out that if a no-objection-certificate could be given for the undisputed area it will facilitate the vacation of Court stay in this regard

2. A suggestion was made that a compound wall be erected in between the disputed and undisputed areas to physically separate them

3. The judgement of the Court regarding the disputed area is likely to be delayed if we can settle the matter out of Court by discussions, we may go before the Court with that settlement/agreement and pray for a consent judgement. As a whole this was considered keeping in view the necessity of maintaining the communal harmony.

4. Supreme Court has ruled that the stay will not be vacated and ordered that the verdict of the Supreme Court would be pronounced only after the Lucknow high Court gives its judgement on the disputed area case. Status quo will have to be maintained till then. Therefore even if a No Objection Certificate is forthcoming and given it may not serve the desired purpose.

Under these circumstances we offer the following explanation to our suggestion that the matter could be settle by mutual discussion.

a. The disputed area in Ayodhya is a place which is highly revered by the Hindus. It is a historical fact that Babar, the Great, constructed a building at that place in commemoration of his victory. At present, due to some unavoidable reasons, there is no building in that place. The status quo position is that Rama is sitting over there it is almost certain that the Court judgement will not come early and when it comes it will not be satisfying to any community. In the present circumstances if the judgement goes in favour of one community or even in favour of both the communities we cannot expect communal harmony. Both the sides are charged so much. Even though the disputed area may belong to the

Waqf Board and is a place of faith to Muslims as well, since the place is of great faith and reverence to the Hindus, the Muslim community and Waqf Board may mentally think that they have donated the said area to the Hindus.

b. Generally, if daily prayers are being offered in any mosque, asking for that place is not justifiable. In view of the fact that at present the area is without any building (empty) and an idol of Rama is placed there, it will not be right or possible to remove Rama from that place and construct a mosque over there in the interest of communal harmony. Local Muslims are already offering prayers in their mosques, that the idol of Rama is being worshipped, that the area is a disputed one and keeping in view the larger interests of the nation and the communal harmony in particular, the Muslim community and Waqf board can decide to donate that area which is a place of matter of faith and belief to the Hindus of the country. By doing so and presenting it before the court we may be able to obtain a court judgement faster and earlier.

His Holiness Sankaracharya appeals that the disputed area be donated to the Hindus and acceding this request by the Muslim community will itself enhance the prestige of the Indian Muslims in the world. History will record that the Indian Muslims stood for communal harmony by this generous act of theirs and their name and fame will get a permanent place in the history. Giving a no-objection-certificate to the undisputed area or raising a wall between the disputed and undisputed area are only positive steps in the direction. Even though we have been discussing the disputed and undisputed areas separately, it is essential that both the issues are discussed together comprehensively to ensure a lasting peaceful and early solution. Donation of the disputed area will only be the permanent solution.

All the above explanations/clarifications have been given as an amplification of our proposal that the issue should be settled amicably by mutual discussion.

A point was made that Kashi, Mathura and Ayodhya—all the three—belong to the Hindus and keeping in mind the larger interest of the country and communal harmony, if not today but at some time or other, these places have to be given to the Hindus. The Muslims have to mentally prepare themselves for this.

Even if this proposal is not accepted by all sections of the Muslim society or is opposed by the Muslims with political connection, history will record that the religious leaders the Hindus and Muslim have decided on such a bold step. His Holiness also opines that in the present circumstances this will only bring amity between the two communities.

His Holiness will be at Kanchipuram between 5 July and 4 October and will not move out of Kanchipuram during this period.

Yours sincerely
N. Sundaresan, Managing Trustee
Sri Kanchi Kamakoti Peetam Charitable Trust

35d. Resolution of the Executive Committee of All India Muslim Personal Law Board (AIMPLB), 6 July 2003

In the background of the meeting the President of All India Muslim Personal Law Board had with the Sankaracharyaji on the 7 June 2003 and the correspondence that ensued thereafter the Executive Committee of AIMPLB met on 6 July 2003. The President acquainted the Executive Committee with facts and the correspondence that ensued, were deliberated upon by the Committee and has passed the necessary resolution. The salient features of the background are as follows.

- The meeting of 7 June was at the instance of the Sankaracharya and the President conveyed to him that he would not discuss any other issue.
- However in the meeting of 7 June the Sankaracharya conveyed his desire to discuss the Babri Masjid and he was requested to communicate his proposals in writing which would be placed before the Executive Committee.
- Thereafter on behalf of the Sankaracharya the letter dated 16 June was delivered to the President which contains the following formula:

1. Your board on our request may consider giving a 'no objection' statement regarding construction of Mandir upon the undisputed/acquired area.
2. Disputed area can also be discussed after sometime and an amicable settlement may be given to the court and the court based on the settlement can give verdict.
3. In order to protect the disputed area a wall may be constructed separating it from undisputed/acquired area.
4. If we reach a final negotiated settlement on the undisputed area, we shall both ensure the support for the same from the various religious groups/subgroups on each side to ensure that no further demands would be raised on the undisputed area.
5. Once we arrive at a cordial understanding we may together approach the Government of India for its effective and time bound implementation.

The formula contained in the letter dated 16 June was lacking in material particulars and was silent on many major issues, namely, whether the Hindus will abide by the verdict of the Court. This was all the more necessary because the Sankaracharya earlier in the meeting with the delegation of the Board held on 5 March 2002 at New Delhi had categorically and fairly assured the Board that both Hindus and Muslims will abide by the court verdict in case of the disputed site and further that the Muslims would be allowed to reconstruct the Masjid at the same spot where it existed before the demolition, if they win the title suit in the court of law.

Such clarifications were sought before 6 July and on behalf of Sankaracharya a letter dated 1 July 2003 far from sticking to the assurances held out by Sankaracharya in March 2002, totally resiled from the proposal/formula that he had conveyed in his letter dated 16 June 2002. On the contrary the letter dated 1 July

2003 contains an appeal to the Indian Muslim to donate the Babri Masjid site in Ayodhya and also contains veiled threats to the Indian Muslims to prepare themselves for giving up the mosques at Kashi and Mathura.

The Committee came to the conclusion that the stand taken by Sankaracharya in his letter dated 1 July 2003, has left no scope for any further discussion.

Considering the above the Committee reiterates its oft-repeated stand that under the shariat, the site of Babri Masjid is the property of Allah and cannot be alienated by sale, gift or otherwise.

The Committee is of the view that the proposed gift will not promote communal harmony or national integration because such gift is under duress and not based on the principles of fair play, justice and constitutionalism. The proposals for the settlement must be within the parameters of the basic values of the Constitution namely rule of law, secularism, equality of treatment to all without discrimination on the ground of race or religion and religious sentiments of the Muslims pertaining to their places of worship. Consistent with these values the Board has always kept and still keeps its doors open for negotiation.

Adverting to the suggestions in the letter dated 1.7.2003 the Board feels distressed that the convoluted vision of history is used for the divisive purpose and a *fait accompli* achieved by the trespass into the religious place belonging to other denomination and undermining the basic values of Constitution is sought to be hallowed with religious sentiments depicted as if the same is of the entire Hindu community; the Board puts on record with due respect to the Sankaracharya that it looks upon the proposals contained in the letter dated 1.7.2003 as thinly veiled threats to the Muslims to submit and surrender themselves unconditionally to all the unreasonable demands made by the Sangh Parivar. The Board, therefore, resolves that such proposals are not just and reasonable and are totally inconsistent with the honour, dignity and self respect of the Indian Muslims and the same cannot therefore be accepted.

The Committee takes this opportunity to appeal to the people of the country to rise to the occasion to uphold the rule of law and fundamental and human rights enshrined in the Constitution and raise the stature and dignity of our country internationally by joining the hands with secular forces of the country.

The Committee authorizes the President of the Board to deal with any proposal on the issue of Babri Masjid consistently with the previous resolution of the Board dated 3 December 1990, 9 January 1993 and 10 March 2002.

[President's Office: P.O. Box 93, Nadwa-Lucknow 226007 (U.P.) Phone: 323864-2788442, Fax: 2788376–2787310; Head Office: 76-A/1, Okhla Main Market, Jamia Nagar, New Delhi - 110025, Phone and Fax: 011-26322991.]

CHAPTER XI

The Law's Course: Civil Suits, 1950–2003

1. Chart showing the civil suits in the dispute

Chart chowing the array of parties and the reliefs claimed in the five suits pertaining to the dispute

(1) Suit No. 2 of 1950 of the Court of the Civil Judge, Faizabad, now registered as Other Original Suit No. 1 of 1989 in the High Court: Plaint dated 16.1. 950.

Array of Parties
Shri Gopal Singh Visharad, since deceased, after his son Shri Rajendra Singh
. . . Plaintiff
(. . . No. 6)
Versus

1. Zahoor Ahmad (Dead) Name struck off
2. Faji Fekoo (Dead) Name struck off
3. Mohammad Faiq (Dead) Name struck off
4. Mohammad Shami (Dead) Name struck off
5. Mohammad Acchan Mian (Dead) Name struck off
6. Uttar Pradesh State through Chief Secretary (Respondent No. 9)
7. Deputy Commissioner, Faizabad (Respondent No. 10)
8. Additional City Magistrate, Faizabad (Respondent No. 11)
9. Superintendent of Police, Faizabad (Respondent No. 12)
10. Sunni Central Waqf Board, Uttar Pradesh, Lucknow, through Secretary (Added vide Court's order dated 7.1.1987). (Respondent No. 1)

Reliefs claimed:
(*Ka*) It may be declared that the Plaintiff is entitled to go near Bhagwan Sri Ramachandra, etc., *Virajman* at Asthan Janmabhumi, whose description is given below, and to worship them and have their *darshan* according to the customary rites of his religion, without any check or obstruction or interference; and that the defendants Nos. 1 to 6 and 7 to 9 and defendant No. 10 or their legal representatives have no right to interfere in the said right of the Plaintiff.

(*Kha*) A permanent and perpetual prohibitory order may be issued against the Defendants that the Defendants Nos 1 to 6 and 7 to 9 and Defendant No. 10 their legal representatives should never remove the idols of Bhagwan Ramachandra, installed at Asthan Janmabhumi whose description is given below from the place where they are and should not close its entrance door or other ways of ingress and egress and should not in any way obstruct or interfere in the *puja* and *darshan*.
(*Ga*) Costs
(*Gha)* Any other relief.

Description of Disputed Place
East—*bhandar* (Store) and *chabutra* (platform) of Janmabhumi
West—*parti* (i.e., vacant land)
North—*Sita Rasoi*
South—*parti* (i.e., vacant land)

(2) Suit No. 25 of 1950 of the Court of Civil Judge, Faizabad, now registered as other Original Suit No. 2 of 1989 in the High Court Plaint dated 5.12.1950.

Array of Parties:
Sri Paramhansa Ramchandra Das, Chela Mahant Ram Das . . . Plaintiff (Respondent No. 7)

Versus

1. Zahoor Ahmad (Dead) Name struck off
2. Haji Fekoo (Dead) Name struck off
3. Mohammad Faiq (Dead) Name struck off
4. Mohammad Shami (Dead) Name struck off
5. Mohammad Achhan Mian (Dead) Name struck off
6. Uttar Pradesh State through Chief Secretary (Respondent No. 9)
7. Deputy Commissioner, Faizabad, (Respondent No. 10)
8. Sunni Central Waqf Board (Respondent No. 1)
9. Sunni Central Waqf Board (Defendants)
   (Added vide Court's order dated 28.1.1989)

Reliefs claimed:
(*Ka*) It may be declared that the Plaintiff is entitled to go near Bhagwan Sri Ramachandra, etc., *Virajman* at Asthan Janmabhumi, whose description is given below, and to worship that and have their *darshan* according to the customary rites of his religion, without any check, obstruction or interference, and that the Defendants Nos 1 to 5 and 6 and 7 and 8 or their legal representatives have no right to interfere in the said right of the Plaintiff.

(*Kha*) A permanent prohibitory order may be issued against the Defendants that the Defendants Nos 1 to 5 and 6 and 7 and their legal representatives, etc., should never remove the idols of Bhagwan Ramachandra, etcetera, installed at Asthan Janmabhumi, whose description is given below, from the place where they are and should not close its entrance door or other ways of ingress and egress and should not in any way obstruct or interfere in the *puja, paath* and *darshan.*

Description of Disputed Place
East—*bhandar* (store) and *chabutra* (platform) of Janmabhumi
West—parti (vacant land)
North—*Sita rasoi*
South—*parti* (vacant land)

(3) Suit No. 26 of 1959 of the Court of Civil Judge, Faizabad, now registered as Other Original Suit No. 3 of 1989 in the High Court: Plaint dated 17.12.1959.
Array of Parties:

1. Nirmohi Akhara through its Mahant (Respondent No. 8)
2. Mahant Raghunath Das (Dead) Name struck off (Plaintiffs)

Versus

1. Babu Priya Dutt Ram (Dead)
2. State of Uttar Pradesh
3. Deputy Commissioner, Faizabad (Respondent No. 9)
4. City Magistrate, Faizabad (Respondent No. 10)
5. Superintendent of Police, Faizabad (Respondent No. 11)
6. Haji Fekoo (Dead)
7. Mohammad Faiq (Dead)
8. Mohammad Achhan Mian (Dead)

Reliefs claimed:

(a) A decree be passed in favour of the Plaintiffs against the defendants for removal of the defendant No. 1 from the management and charge of the said temple of Janmabhumi and for delivering the case to the Plaintiffs No. 2 on behalf of the Plaintiff No. 1.
(b) Any other relief.
(c) Costs.

(4) Suit No. 12 of 1961 of the Court of Civil Judge, Faizabad now registered as other Original Suit No. 4 of 1989 in the High Court: Plaint dated 18.12.1961.
Array of Parties:

(1) The Sunni Central Board of Waqfs, U.P., through Secretary (Respondent No. 1)
(2) Molvi Mohammad Qasim (Dead)
(3) Haji Mohd. Ehtran (Dead) Name struck off
(4) Molvi Mohammad Faiq (Dead)
(5) Molvi Mohammad Naseer (Respondent No. 2)
(6) Shahabuddin (Dead)
(7) Mohammad Hashim (Respondent No. 3)
(8) Vakiluddin (Respondent No. 4)

(9) Mahmood Ahmad (Respondent No. 5)
(10) Zahoor Ahmad (Dead)

Versus

1. Gopal Singh Visharad (Dead)
2. Paramhansa Ramchandra Das (Respondent No. 7)
3. Nirmohi Akhara through Mahant (Respondent No. 8)
4. Mahant Raghunath Das, after him Mahant Pran Das (Dead) Names struck off
5. The State of Uttar Pradesh—through Chief Secretary (Respondent No. 9)
6. The Collector, Faizabad (Respondent No. 10)
7. The City Magistrate, Faizabad (Respondent No. 11)
8. The Superintendent of Police, Faizabad (Respondent No. 12)
9. Priya Dutt Ram (Dead)
10. President—All India Hindu Mahasabha (Respondent No. 13)
11. President—All India Arya Samaj (Respondent No. 14)
12. President, All India Sanatan Dharma Sabha (Respondent No. 15)
13. Abhiram Das (since deceased) after him Dharam Das (Petitioner)
14. Pundarik Mishra (Respondent No. 16)
15. Ram Lakhan Saran (since deceased) after him Ram Dayal Saran (Respondent No. 17)
16. Sant Narain Das (Dead)
17. Ramesh Chandra Tripathi (Respondent No. 18)
18. Mahant Ganga Das (Dead)
19. Swami Govindacharya (Dead)
20. Shri Madan Mohan Gupta, Convenor, Akhil Bharatiya Sri Ramjanmabhumi Punaruddhar Samiti
    Added by order of High Court, dated 23.10. 1989 (Respondent No. 19)

Reliefs claimed:

(a) A declaration to the effect that the property indicated by letters A B C D in the sketch map attached to the plaint is a public mosque commonly known as 'Babri Masjid' and that the land adjoining the mosque shown in the sketch map by letters E F G H, is a public Muslim graveyard as specified in Para 2 of the plaint, may be decreed.
(b) That in case in the opinion of the Court delivery of possession is deemed to be the proper remedy, a decree for delivery of possession of the mosque and graveyard in suit by removal of the Idols and other articles which the Hindus may have placed in the mosque as objects of their worship be passed in the plaintiff's favour against the defendants.
(c) Costs.
(d) Any other relief.

(5) Original Suit No. 236 of 1989 of the Court of the Civil Judge, Faizabad, now registered as other/Original Suit No. 5 of 1989 in the High Court: Plaint dated 1 July 1989.

Array of Parties:

1. Bhagwan Sri Rama *Virajman* at Sri Ramjanmabhumi, Ayodhya, also called Bhagwan Sri Rama Lalla *Virajman*
2. Asthan Sri Ramjanmabhumi, Ayodhya
3. Sri Deoki Nandan Agarwala, Senior Advocate and Retired Judge, High Court, Allahabad

Versus

1. Shri Rajendra Singh, Gonda
2. Paramhansa Ramchandra Das, Mahant, Digambar Akhara, Ayodhya
3. Nirmohi Akhara, Ayodhya
4. Sunni Central Board of Waqfs, U.P., Lucknow
5. Shri Mohammad Hashim, Ayodhya
6. Shri Mohammad Ahmad, Faizabad
7. State of Uttar Pradesh, through Home Secretary, Lucknow
8. The Collector and District Magistrate, Faizabad
9. The City Magistrate, Faizabad
10. The Senior Superintendent of Police, Faizabad
11. The President, All India Hindu Mahasabha, New Delhi
12. The President, All India Arya Samaj, Delhi
13. The President, All India Sanatan Dharma Sabha, Delhi
14. Shri Dharam Das, Adult, Chela Baba Abhiram Das, resident of Hanuman Garhi, Ayodhya
15. Shri Pundarik Mishra, Faizabad
16. Shri Ram Dayal Saran, Ayodhya
17. Shri Ramesh Chandra Tripathi, District Faizabad
18. (Deleted vide order dated 20.9.1989)
19. (Deleted vide order dated 20.9.1989)
20. Shri Umesh Chandra Pandey, Ayodhya
21. Sri Ramjanmabhumi Nyas, through Shri Ashok Singhal, Delhi
22. Shia Central Board of Waqfs, U.P., Lucknow
23. Shri Javvad Hussain, District Faizabad
24. Prince Anjum Quder, Lucknow
25. All India Shia Conference

Reliefs claimed:

(a) A declaration that the entire premises of Sri Ramjanmabhumi at Ayodhya, as described and delineated in Annexures I, II and III, belong to the plaintiff deities.

(b) A perpetual injunction against the Defendants prohibiting them from interfering with, or raising any objection to, or placing any obstruction in the construction of the new temple building at Sri Ramjanmabhumi, Ayodhya, after demolishing and removing the existing buildings and structures, etc., situate threat, in so far as it may be necessary or expedient to do so for the said purpose.

(c) Costs.

(d) Any other relief.

2. Plaint in suit filed by the Sunni Central Board of Waqfs

Amended Plaint: In the Court of Civil Judge, Faizabad
(Reg. Suit No. 12 of 1961)

1. The Sunni Central Board of Waqfs, U.P., Lucknow, Moti Lal Bose Road, Police Station Kaiserbagh, City Lucknow through Shah Ghyas Alam, Secretary.
Deleted vide order dated 9.12.91 Sd/- 9.12.91

2. Molvi Mohammad Qasim, aged about 53 years, son of Sheikh Abdul Razzaq, General Secretary, Jamaitul Islami Hind, U.P., Bagh Gunge Nawab, Police station Kaiserbagh, Lucknow.

2/1. Mohd. Siddiq alias Hafiz Mohd. Siddiq, aged about 26 years, s/o late Haji Mohd. Ibrahim, resident of Lalbagh, Moradabad, General Secretary, Jamaitul Ulemai Hind, Uttar Pradesh, Jamait Building, B.N. Verma Road (Katchehry Road), Lucknow.
Added vide Court's order dated 18.12.91 Sd/- 19.12.91

~~3. Haji Mohammad Ehiram Ali, aged about 70 years, son of Munshi Mohammad Fatisham Ali, deceased, resident of Khayaliganj, Police Station Kaiserbagh, City Lucknow~~ (*Struck off under Court's order dated 14.3.70 Sd/-*)

4. Molvi Mohammad Faiq aged about 55 years, son of Haji Ramzan R/o Mohalla Tehri Bazar, Ajodhiya, Pargana Haveli Avadh, District Faizabad.
Deleted vide court's order dated 9.12.91 Sd/ 9.12.91

5. Molvi Mohammad Naseer aged about 58 years. Son of Ashiq Ali, resident of village: Ponthar, Pargana Tanda Tahsil Tanda, District Faizabad.
Deleted vide court's order dated 16.11.92 Sd/- 16.11.92

6. Shahabuddin aged about 42 years, son of Haji Munny Sahib, resident of Angoori Bagh, City Faizabad.
Deleted vide Court's order dated 9.12.91 Sd/- 9.12.91

6/1 Ziauddin aged about 46 years, son of Haji Shahabuddin (deceased) resident of Mohalla Angoori Bagh, Pergana Haveli Oudh, City and District Faizabad.
Amended as per court's order dated 23.8.90 Sd/- 31.8.90

7. Mohammad Hashim aged about 40 yeas, Son of Karim Bux, resident of Mohalla Kutya, Panji Tola, Ajodhiya Pergana Haveli Avadh, Distt. Faizabad.

8. Vakiluddin aged about 55 years son of Ismail, resident of Madarpur, Pargana and Tahsil Tanda, District Faizabad.

8/1 Maulana Mahfoozurahman, aged about 52 years, son of late Maulana Vakiluddin, Resident of village Madarpur, Pargana and Tahsil Tanda, District Faizabad.
Amended added as per court order dated 9.5.95 Sd/- 9.5.95

9. Mahmud Ahmad, aged about 30 years son of Ghulam Hasan, resident of Mohalla Rakabganj, City Faizabad.
Added under court's order dated 4.2.63

10. Zahoor Ahmad, S/o Noor Mohd. Syed about R/o Mohalla Naugazi Qabar, Ayodhya District, Faizabad.
Deleted vide court's order dated 9.12.91 Sd/- 9.12.91

10/1 Farooq Ahmad, son of Shri Zahoor Ahmad, R/o Mohalla Naugazi Qabar, Ayodhya City, Ayodhya, Distt. Faizabad. . . . Plaintiffs.
Added vide court's order dated 9.12.96 Sd/- 9.12.91

Versus

~~1. Shri Gopal Singh Visharad, aged about 53 years, son of Thakur Girdhari Singh, resident of Sargaddwar, Ajodhiya District Faizabad.~~
Deleted vide Court's order dated 9.12.91 Sd/- 9.12.91

2. Sri Paramhansa Ramchandra Das, resident of Ajodhia, Faizabad.

3. Nirmohi Akhara situate in Mohalla Rama Ghat City Ajodhiya, District Faizabad, through ~~Mahant Raghunath Das Chela Mahant Dharam Das Mahant Raghunath Das Chela Mahant Dharam Das Mahant Raghunath Das Chela Mahant Dharam Das~~ Mahant Rameshwar Das, Mahant Sarbarkar, resident of Nirmohi Akhara Mohalla Ramghat, City Ajodhiya District, Faizabad.
~~Mahant Prem Das Chela Mahant Gobardhan Das~~
Substituted under Court's order dated 23.7.66

4. ~~Mahant Raghunath Das Chela Mahant Dharam Das Mahant and Sarbarakhar Nirmohi Akhara Mohalla Ram Ghat City Ajodhiya, District Faizabad.~~
Substituted under Court's order dated 23.7.66

5. The State of Uttar Pradesh throught Chief Secretary to the State Government, U.P.
Corrected under
Court's order
Dated 30.1.62
Amended u/c order Dated 8.7.67 Sd/- 20.7.67

6. The Collector, Faizabad

7. The City Magistrate, Faizabad

8. The Superintendent of Police, Faizabad

9. B. Priya Dutt, son of R.B. Babu Kamlapat Ram, resident of Rakabganj, Faizabad.

10. President, All India Hindu Maha Sabha, Read Road, New Delhi.

11. President, ~~All India~~ Arya /~~Samaj, Delhi~~ Maha Pradeshik Sabha, Baldan Bhawan, Shradhanand Bazar, Delhi.
Added under Court's order dated 20.3.63

12. President, All India Sanatan Dharam Sabha, Delhi.
Added under Court's order dated 20.3.1963

13. ~~Abhiram Das age 54 years, Sadhak Shesh Shri Baba Sarein Das, R/o Hanuman Garhi, Ayodhya.~~
Deleted vide Court's order dated 9.12.91 Sd/- 9.12.91

13/1 Dharam Das alleged Chela Baba Abhiram Das, R/o Hanuman Garhi, Ayodhya, Faizabad, (Sd/- 27.1.92)
Added under Court's order dated 26.4.68 Sd/-

14. Pundarik Misra, age 33 years, s/o Raj Narain Misra, R/o Balrampur Sarai, Rakabganj, Faizabad.

~~15. Baba Bajrang Das, Chaila Baba Ram Dharan Das, R/o Hanuman Garh, Ayodhya, Faizabad.~~

~~15. Ram Lakhan Saran, member, Ramjanmabhumi Seva Samiti, Faizabad.~~

15. Shri Ram Dayal Saran, Chela of late Ram Lakhan Saran, resident of town Ayodhya, District Faizabad.
Substituted under order of Court dated 14.2.89

16. ~~Shab Narain Das Chaila Baba Badri Das Ji Sankatwali, R/o Shri Hanuman Garhi, Ayodhya, Faizabad.~~
Deleted vide Court's order dated 9.12.91 Sd/- 9.12.91

17. Ramesh Chandra Tripathi aged about 29 years, son of Shri Parsh Rama Tripathi, Resident of village Bhagwan Patti, Pargana Minjhaura, Tahsil Akbarpur, District Faizabad.
Added under Court's order dated 30.4.69 Sd/- 12.5.69

18. Mahant Ganga Das aged about 45 years, Chela of Mahant Sarju Das R/o Mandir Ladle Prasad, City Ayodhya, Faizabad.
Do-

19. Shri Swami Govindacharya, manas martant putra Balbhadar Urf Jhallu, R/o Makan No. 735, 736, 737, Katra Ayodhya, Pargana Haveli Audh Tahsil and Zila Faizabad.
Do-

20. Madan Mohan Gupta, convener of Akhil Bharatiya Sri Ramjanmabhumi Punarudhar Samiti, E-7/45 Bangla T.T. Nagar, Bhopal.
Amended vide order dated 27.1.92 Sd/- 27.1.92
Added by Court's order dated 8.12.89

21. Prince Anjum Qadar, President All India Shia Conference, Registered, Quami Ghar, Nadan Mohal Road, F.S. Chowk, Lucknow.
Amended vide Court's order dated 27.1.92 Sd/- 27.1.92
Added by Court's order dated 8.12.89

22. Umesh Chandra Pandey, son of Shri R.S. Pandey, R/o Ranupalli, Ayodhya, District Faizabad.
Defendants
Added vide Court's order dated 20.1.92 Sd/- 23.1.92
Claim for declaration and recovery of possession.

The plaintiffs named above beg to state as under:

1. That in the town of Ajodhiya, Pargana Haveli Oudh there exists an ancient historic mosque, commonly known as Babri Masjid, built by Emperor Babar more than ~~460~~ 433 (*Amended vide Court's order dated 30.9.2002*) years ago, after his conquest of India and his occupation of the territories including the town of Ajodhiya, for the use of the Muslims in general, as a place of worship and performance of religious ceremonies.

2. That in the sketch map attached herewith, the main construction of the said mosque is shown by letters A B C D, and the land adjoining the mosque on the east, west, north and south, shown in the sketch map attached herewith, is the ancient graveyard of the Muslims, covered by the graves of the Muslims, who lost the lives in the battle between Emperor Babar and the previous ruler of Ajodhiya, which are shown in the sketch map attached herewith. The mosque and the graveyard is vested in the Almighty. The said mosque has since the time of its construction been used by the Muslims for offering prayers and the graveyard has been used as graveyard. The mosque and the graveyard are in Mohalla Kot Rama Chander also known as Rama Kot town, Ayodhya. The *khasra* number of the mosque and the graveyard in suit are shown in the schedule attached which is part of the plaint.
Corrected under Court's order dated 2.1.62 Sd/- 3.1.62

3. That for the upkeep and maintenance of the mosque and other connected expenses, a cash grant used to be paid from the Royal Treasury which was continued by the Emperors of Delhi and by Nawab Saadat Ali Khan, the Nawab Wazir of Oudh.

4. That after the annexation of Oudh, the British Government also continued the case Nankar till 1864, in which year instead of cash Nankar grant of revenue free land in village Sholapur and Bahoranpur, in the vicinity of Ajodhiya, was made by the British Government.

5. That in the mosque, but outside the main building of the mosque, there was Chabutra 17' x 21' on which there was a small wooden structure in the form of a tent which is still there.

6. That in 1885, one Mahant Raghubar Das alleging himself to be the Mahant of Janmasthan instituted a suit (Original Suit No. 61/280 of 1885) against the Secretary of State for India in Council and Mohammad Asghar, *Mutawalli* of the Babri Mosque, for permission to build a temple on the Chabutra 17' x 21' mentioned in para 5 above in the Court of the learned Civil Judge, Faizabad which was dismissed and an appeal from the said decree was also dismissed by

the learned District Judge. Faizabad (Civil Appeal No. 27 of 1885). In the sketch map filed along with the plaint in Suit No. 61/280 of 1885 the entire building, with the exception of the Chabutra 17' x 21' was admitted to be mosque and was known as such.

Paras 6A, 6B, 6C, 6D, 6E & 6F are added by the Court's order dated 22.12.62 Sd/- 2.1.63

6A. That the cause of action for the suit in Suit No. 61/280 of 1885 in the Court of the Civil Judge, Faizabad, arose on the refusal of the Dy Commissioner of Faizabad on the representation of some Muslims to grant permission to Mahant Raghubar Das, Mahant of Janam Asthan for the construction of a temple for the ground that a temple could not be permitted to be built on land adjoining the mosque (meaning thereby the Babri Masjid).

6B. 'In that suit Regular Suit No. 61/280 of 1885 of the Court of Civil Judge, Faizabad Mahant Raghubar Das was suing on behalf of Himself, on behalf of Janam Asthan, and on behalf of the whole body of persons interested in Janam Asthan and Mohd. Asghar, Mutawalli of the Babri Masjid was made a defendant.'

6C. Mohammad Asghar, Defendant *mutawalli* of Babri Masjid contested the suit inter-alia on the ground that the land on which the temple is sought to be built is not the property of the plaintiff or of the Asthan, that the said land lies within the Ahata of Babri Masjid and is the property of the Masjid.

6D. That in the suit mentioned above the matter directly and substantially in issue was:

i. the existence of the Babri Masjid.

ii. the right of the Hindus to construct a temple on land adjoining the Masjid.

The existence of the mosque was admitted by the plaintiff in that suit and the suit of the plaintiff was dismissed on the further ground of public policy.

6E. If the building was not a Masjid but a temple as alleged in the present suit the matter might and ought to have been pleaded by Mahant Raghubar Das in the former suit (suit No. 61/280 of 1885 mentioned above) and shall be deemed to have been a matter directly and substantially in issue in that suit and the plea that the building is not a Masjid but a temple cannot be raised in the present suit. For the reasons mentioned above the decision in the former suit operates as res-judicate in the present suit.

6F. That on the admission contained in the plaint of Regular Suit No. 61/280 of 1885 mentioned in the preceding paragraphs it must be taken as an established fact that the building now claimed by the Hindus as the temple of Janmasthan was and is a mosque and not a temple.

These paragraphs are added by the order of the Court dated 22.12.62 Sd/- 4.1.63.

7. That the suit mentioned above was a sensational case, in which the entire Hindu public and more specially all the Mahants of Ajodhiya and other respectable Hindus of Ajodhiya and Faizabad were deeply interested.

8. That in 1934 during a communal riot in Ajodhia, portions of Babri Mosque were damaged. The damaged portions, were however, rebuilt and reconditioned at the cost of the government through a Muslim Thekadar.

9. That in 1936 the U.P. Muslim Waqfs Act XIII of 1936 was passed and under the provisions of the said Act, the Commissioner of Waqfs made a complete enquiry and held that Babri Masjid was build by Emperor Babar who was a Sunni Mohammadan and that the Babri Mosque was a public waqf. A copy of the Commissioner's report was forwarded by the State Government to the Sunni Central Board of Waqfs and the Sunni Central Board of Waqfs published the said report of the Commissioner of Waqfs in the Official Gazette dated 26.2.1944.

10. That, no suit, challenging the report of the Commissioner of Waqfs was filed by the Hindus or by any person interested in denying the correctness of the report of the Commissioner of Waqfs, on the ground that it was not a Muslim Waqf or that it was Hindu temple.

11. That the Muslim have been in peaceful possession of the aforesaid mosque and used to recite prayer in it, till 23.12.1949 when a large crowd of Hindus, with the mischievous intention of destroying, damaging or defiling the said mosque and thereby insulting the Muslim religion and the religious feelings of the Muslims, entered the mosque and desecrated the mosque by placing idols inside the mosque. The conduct of Hindus amounted to an offence punishable under sections 147, 295 and 448 of the Indian Penal Code.

11a. That assuming, though not admitting, that at one time there existed a Hindu temple as alleged by the defendants representatives of the Hindus on the site of which emperor Babar built the mosque, some ~~460~~ 433 (*Amended vide Court's order dated 30.9.2002*) years ago, the Muslims by virtue of their long exclusive and continuous possession beginning from the time the mosque was built and continuing right up to the time some mischievous persons entered the mosque and desecrated the mosque as alleged in the preceding paragraphs of the plaint, the Muslims perfected their title by adverse possession and the right, title or interest of the temple and of the Hindu public if any extinguished.
Added under Court's order dated 29.11.63 Sd/- 4.12.63

12. That the incident stated in the preceding paragraph was immediately reported by the constable on duty (Mata Prasad) to the police station Ajodhiya and the Sub-Inspector registered the report and proceeded to the spot for making enquiries in the matter.

13. That the City Magistrate, Faizabad-cum Ajodhiya started proceedings under section 145 Criminal Procedure Code and by his order dated 29.12.1949 attached the said mosque and handed over possession of the same to Shri Priya Dutt Ram defendant no. 9 as Receiver, who still continues in possession and the Muslims are deprived of their legal and constitutional right of offering prayers in the said mosque.

14. That the above action, taken by the City Magistrate, Faizabad, is not

only illegal but is fraught with injustice to the plaintiffs, and has the effect of depriving a large section of Muslim citizens of India from exercising their legal rights guaranteed by the Constitution of India.

15. That on 16.1.1950 defendant no. 1 filed Regular Suit No. 2 of 1950 in the Court of Civil Judge, Faizabad, in his personal capacity, for declaration and injunction, on the false allegation that the building in suit was a temple and thus deities are installed in it.

16. That sometime after, defendant no. 2 filed Suit No. 25 of 1950 in the Court of Civil Judge, Faizabad against the same set of defendants, and for identical reliefs, with this difference that while the first suit was filed without notice under section 80 C.P.C. to the State Government and its officers, Suit no. 25 of 1950 was filed with notice to them.

17. That a third Suit No. 26 of 1960 has been filed by Nirmohi Akhara and Mahant Raghunath Das, defendants 3 and 4 against defendants nos 5 to 9 and certain Muslim Community under Order 1 rule and C.P.C. The suit purports to be for the removal of defendant no. 9 from the management of building which the Hindu public call 'Temple of Janam Bhum' and for its delivery to Mahant Raghunath Das, defendant no. 4.

18. That on the application of the plaintiff in Suit no. 2 of 1950 temporary injunction was served restraining the defendants of that Suit from removing the idols from the mosque in dispute, and from interfering with *puja* etc. of the Hindus. The result of the injunction order of the learned Civil Judge is that while Hindus are permitted to perform *puja* of the idols, placed by them in the mosque, the Muslims are not allowed even to enter the mosque, are deprived of their just and legal rights and are not allowed even to enter the mosque, which was constituted about 460 years back and has been declared to be a public waqf and has been used by generations of Muslims since then, as a mosque, for reciting prayers therein. The order of injunction is fraught with injustice, hence the necessity of the institution of suit on behalf of Muslim public under order 1 rule 8 C.P.C. against the Hindu public so that the decision in the case may be binding on the Hindu community at large.

19. The present suit is filed by the plaintiffs on behalf of and for the benefit of the entire Muslim community and an application for necessary permission under / ~~for which necessary permission of the Court~~ (*Corrected under Court's order dated today Sd/- 21.12.61*) order 1 r. 8 C.P.C. is filed along with the plaint. Similarly, the defendants are sued as representing the entire Hindu community ~~for which the~~ an application for necessary permission under Or. 1 r. 8 C.P.C. is filed ~~requisite permission of the Court has been obtained~~ along with the plaint. *Amended under Court's order dated today. Sd/- 21.12.61*

20. That the building in suit claimed by the plaintiffs as Muslim waqf is in the possession of Receiver holding for the real owner and would be released in favour of the plaintiffs in case the plaintiffs Suit succeeds but if for any reason in

the opinion of the Court, a suit for possession is the proper relief to be claimed, the plaintiffs in the alternative pray for recovery of possession.

21. That two months notice of the suit under section 80 of the Code of Civil Procedure has been given to the defendants 5 to 9 by Registered Post on 19.6.1961. The notices were delivered to the defendants 5 to 8 on 20.6.1961 and defendant no. 9 refused to take the delivery of the notice on 23.6.1961. The two months' period from the service of the notice has expired, but no reply has been received.
Amendment/Addition made as per Court's order dated 25.5.95 Sd/- 7.8.95
21A, 21B, 21C – added under Court order dated 25.5.95

'21A.: That in violation of the orders of the Hon'ble Supreme Court, dated 15 November 1991 passed in three Writ Petitions and in violation of the orders of this Hon'ble Court dated 3.2.1986, 14.8.1989 and 7.11.1989 etc. the Babri Masjid was demolished on 6 December 1992. The idols wrongly placed in the premises of the Babri Masjid between the night of 22nd– 23 December 1949 were removed by the destructors of Babri Masjid and thereafter an illegal structure was created on 7 December 1992 in violation of all the orders of the Courts mentioned above and the undertakings given in the Hon'ble Supreme Court. These acts of demolition and destruction of the mosque were carried out by the miscreants and criminals with the connivance of the then State Government of the BJP. As the demolition and change in the position of the spot was made in defiance and flagrant violation of the various orders of this Hon'ble Court and the Hon'ble Supreme Court, the Plaintiffs are entitled for the restoration of the building as it existed on 5.12.1992.

21B: That under the Muslim Law mosque is a place where prayers are offered publicly as a matter of right and the same neither requires any structure and nor any particular mode of structure is provided for the same. Even the open space where prayers are offered may be a mosque and as such even after the demolition of the mosque building by the miscreants, the land over which the building stood is still a mosque and Muslims are entitled to offer prayers thereon.

21C.: That by means of ordinance No. 8 of 1993 promulgated on 7 January 1993, the land of the mosque and the entire land appurtenant thereto including the land in suit was sought to be acquired and the said Ordinance was later on substituted by an Act of Parliament, namely, Act No. 33 of 1993. However, in the cases challenging the said Ordinance and the Act, the Hon'ble Supreme Court by its judgement dated 24 October 1994, has held the Union of India to be the statutory Receiver of the land covered by the said mosque and has further provided that the land of the appurtenant and adjacent area will be provided for the enjoyment of the crucial area of mosque portion as per requirement in accordance with the judgement of the suits. The Commissioner, Faizabad Division, Faizabad, is presently working as Authorized Person on behalf of the Government of India.'

22. That the valuation of the suit for purposes of jurisdiction and payment of Court-fees is Rs 22,000 as follows:

Valuation of the mosque Rs 21,000 and that of graveyard is Rs 1,000 on which a Court fee of Rs 2,057.50 is paid.

23. That cause of action for the suit against the Hindu public arose on 23.12.1949 at Ajodhiya District Faizabad within the jurisdiction of this Hon'ble Court when the Hindus unlawfully and illegally entered the mosque and desecrated the mosque by placing idols in the mosque thus causing obstruction and interference with the rights of the Muslims in general, of saying prayers and performing other religious ceremonies in mosque. The Hindus are also causing obstructions to the Muslims going in the graveyard, (*Gan-Shahidan*) and reciting *fatiha* to the dead persons buried therein. The injuries caused are continuing injuries and the cause of action arising therefrom is renewed *de die indiem* and as against defendants 5 to 9 the cause of action arose to the plaintiffs on 29.12.1949 the date on which the defendant No. 7 the City Magistrate Faizabad-cum-Ajodhya attached the mosque in suit and handed over possession of the same to Shri Priya Dutt Ram defendant no. 9 as the receiver, who assumed charge of the same on 5 January 1950.

The State Government and its officials defendants 6 to 8 failed in their duty to prosecute the offenders and safeguard the interests of the Muslims.

24. The plaintiffs claim the following relief.

(a) A declaration to the effect that the property indicated by letters A B C D in the sketch map attached to the plaint is public mosque commonly known as 'Babri Masjid' and that the land adjoining the mosque shown in the sketch map by letters E F G H is a public Muslim graveyard as specified in para 2 of the plaint ~~commoly known as Ganja Shahidan~~ may be decreed. (*Corrected under Court's order dated 2.1.62 Sd/- 3.1.62*)

(b) That in case in the opinion of the Court delivery of possession is deemed to be the proper remedy, a decree for delivery of possession of the mosque and graveyard in suit by removal of the idols and other articles which the Hindus may have placed in the mosque as objects of their worship be passed in plaintiff's favour, against the defendants.

(bb) That the statutory Receiver be commanded to hand over the property in dispute described in the Schedule 'A' of the Plaint by removing the unauthorized structures erected thereon.
Amendment/Addition made as per Court's order dated 25.5.95 Sd/-

(c) Costs of the Suit be decreed in favour of the plaintiffs.

(d) Any other or further relief which the Hon'ble Court considers proper may be granted.

Faizabad Dated:
18.12.1961

Plaintiffs.
Sd/- 16.12.1961

Verification:
I, Mohammad Faiq, Plaintiff no. 4 do hereby verify that the contents of the plaint set forth in paragraphs 1-6-8-10, para 11 from the beginning of the para up to inside the mosque, and paras 12, 13, 14, 15, 16, 17, 18, 19, first part of para 20

and para 21, are true to my knowledge through information received and inspection of the records and those of paras 7, last para 11, para 14, second part of paras 20, 22, 23, and 24, are believed by me to be true.

Signed and verified this plaint this 6 day of December 1961 at Ayodhia Distt. Faizabad.

Sd/-

Plantiff No. 4

Schedule 'A'

Details of the Nazul Khasra numbers of the mosque and the grave yard in suit are as follows:

Nos 238, 579, 580, 581, 582, 583, 584, 585, 586, 587, 588, 590, 593, 594, 595, 603, 606, 607, 610, 619, 620, 621, and 628 Situate in Mohalla Kot Rama Chander also known as Rama Kot City Ayodhya (Nazool estate District Faizabad.)

Corrected under the Court's order dated 2.1.62 Sd/-

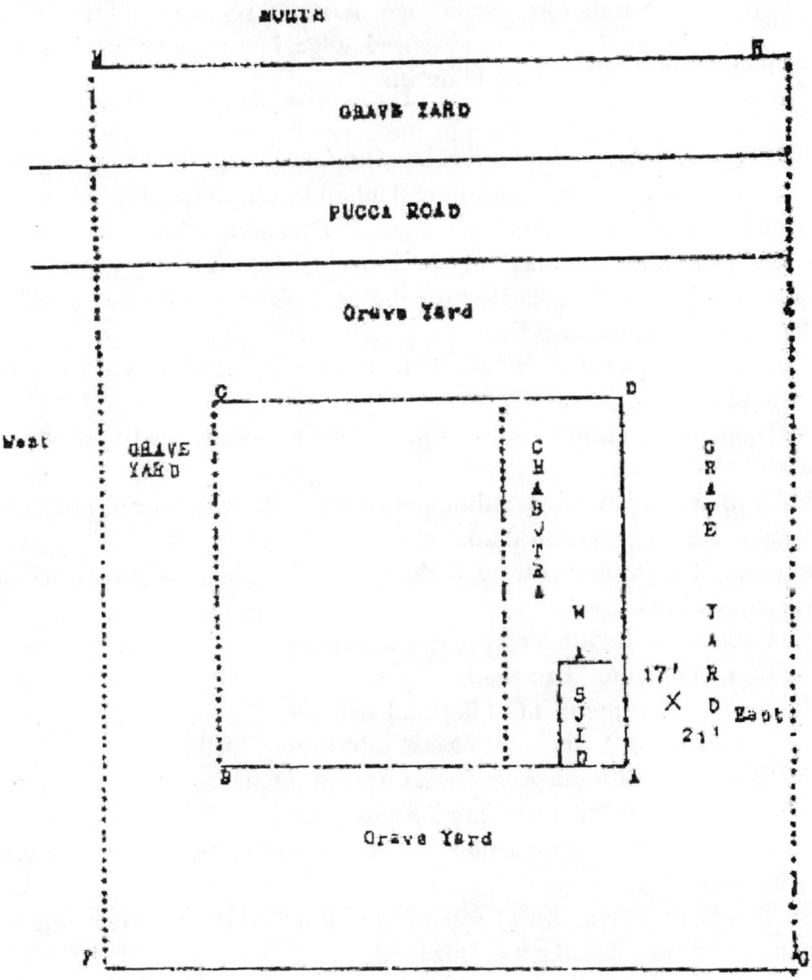

3. Plaint in suit filed on behalf of the deity in 1989 in supersession of four suits filed in 1950, 1959 and 1961

In the Court of the Civil Judge Faizabad
Plaint of Original Suit
(Under Order VII, Rule 1, of the Code of Civil Procedure, 1968)
Original Suit No. 236 of 1989

1.Bhagwan Sri Rama *Virajman* at Sri Ramjanmabhumi, Ayodhya, also called Bhagwan Sri Rama Bala *Virajman*, represented by next friend, Shri Deoki Nandan Agarwala, Senior Advocate and retired Judge High Court, 56, Dilkusha, New Katra, Allahabad.

2. Asthan Sri Ramjanmabhumi, Ayodhya, represented by next friend, Shri Deoki Nandan Agarwala, Senior Advocate and retired Judge High Court, 56, Dilkusha, New Katra, Allahabad.

3. Shri Deoki Nandan Agarwala, aged about 69 years, son of the late Shri M.L. Agarwala, Senior Advocate and retired judge, High Court, resident of 56, Dilkusha, New Katra, Allahabad, Plaintiffs.

Versus

1. Shri Rajendra Singh, Adult, son of late Shri Gopal Singh Visharad, at present residing at Gonda, care of the State Bank of India, Gonda Branch, Gonda.
2. Paramhansa Mahant Ramchandra Das of Digambar Akhara, Ayodhya.
3. Nirmohi Akhara, Mohalla Ram Ghat, Ayodhya, through its present Mahant Shri Ram Kawal Das, Chela Gopal Das, resident of Nirmohi Akhara, Mohalla Ram Ghat, Ayodhya.
4. Sunni Central Board of Waqfs, U.P., having its office at Moti Lal Bose Road, Lucknow.
5. Shri Mohammad Hashim, Adult, son of Shri Karim Bux, resident of Mohalla Sutahti, Ayodhya.
6. Shri Mohammad Ahmad, Adult son of Shri Ghulam Hasan, resident of Mohalla Rakabganj, Faizabad.
7. State of Uttar Pradesh, through the Secretary, Home Department, Civil Secretariat, Lucknow.
8. The Collector and District Magistrate, Faizabad.
9. The City Magistrate, Faizabad.
10. The Senior Superintendent of Police, Faizabad.
11. The President, All India Hindu Mahasabha, New Delhi.
12. The President, All India Arya Samaj, Dewan Hall, Delhi.
13. The President, All India Sanatan Dharma Sabha, Delhi.
14. Shri Dharam Das, Adult, Chela Baba Abhiram Das, Resident of Hanuman Garhi, Ayodhya.
15. Shri Pundarik Misra, Adult son of Shri Raj Narain Misra, resident of Bahampur Sarai, Rakabganj, Faizabad.

16. Shri Ram Dayal Saran, Adult, Chela Ram Lakhan Saran, resident of Ramacharitamanas Bhavan, Mohalla Ramkot, Ayodhya.
17. Shri Ramesh Chandra Tripathy Adult, son of Shri Paras Ram Tripathi, resident of Village Bhagwan Patti, Pargana Minjnaura, Tehsil Akbarpur, District Faizabad.
18. Mahant Ganga Das, Adult, Chela Sarja Das, resident of Mandir Lalta Prasad, Ayodhya.
19. Swami Govindacharya Manas Martand, Adult, son of Shri Balbdadar, alias Jhallu, resident of Ayodhya.
20. Shri Umesh Chandra Pandey, Adult, son of Shri Uma Shankar Pandey, Advocate, resident of Ranopali, Ayodhya.
21. Sri Ramjanmabhumi Nyas, a Trust, having its office at Sankat Mochan Ashram, Sri Hanuman Mandir, Rama Krishna Puram, Setor VI, New Delhi, through Shri Ashok Singhal, Managing Trustee.
22. Shia Central Board of Waqfs, U.P., Lucknow.
23. Shri Javvad Husain, Adult, resident of Village Sahanwa, P.O. Darshan Nagar, District Faizabad.
24. Prince Anjum Quder, President, All India Shia Conference, Qaomi Ghar, Nadan Mahal Road, Lucknow.
25. All India Shia Conference, through Shri S. Mohammad Hussain Abdul, Honorary General Secretary, Qaomi Ghar, Nadan Mahal Road, Lucknow,

Defendants

Suit for declaration and Injunction

The Plaintiffs above named beg to state as under:

1. That the Plaintiffs Nos 1 and 2, namely, Bhagwan Sri Rama *Virajman* at Sri Ramjanmabhumi, Ayodhya, also called Sri Rama Lalla *Virajman*, and the Asthan Sri Ramjanmabhumi, Ayodhya, with the other Idols and places of worship situate the rest, are juridical persons with Bhagwan Sri Rama as the presiding Deity of the place. The Plaintiff No. 3 is Vaishnavite Hindu, and seeks to represent the Deity and the Asthan as a next friend.

2. That the place Sri Ramjanmabhumi is too well known at Ayodhya to need any description for purposes of identification of the subject matter of dispute in this plaint. However, for greater precision, two site plans of the building premises and of the adjacent area known as Sri Ramjanmabhumi, prepared by Shri Shiv Shankar Lal, pleader, in the discharge of his duty as a Commissioner appointed by the Court of Civil Judge, Faizabad, in Suit No. 2 of 1950. Shri Gopal Singh Visharad *versus* Shri Zahur Ahmad and others: along with his report dated 25.5.1950, are being annexed to this plaint and made part of it as Annexures I, II and III, respectively.

3. That the said suit No. 2 of 1950 was filed on 16.1.1950, by Shri Gopal Singh Visharad against (1) Zahoor Ahmad, (2) Haji Pheku, (3) Mohammad Faiq, (4) Mohammad Shami, (5) Mohammad Achhan Mian, (6) Uttar Pradesh State,

(7) Deputy Commissioner, Faizabad, (8) City Magistrate, Faizabad, and (9) Superintendent of Police, Faizabad. The Plaintiff of that suit died recently and his name has been substituted by that of his son, who has been impleaded as Defendant No. 1, in this suit. Of the Defendants, the first five Muslim individuals are dead and their names have been struck off under the orders of the Court. They have, therefore, not been impleaded as Defendants in this suit. The Defendants Nos 6 to 9 of that suit have been impleaded as Defendants Nos 7 to 10, respectively, in this suit also.

4. That the relief claimed in that suit (No. 2 of 1950) was a declaration that the Plaintiff was entitled to perform the *puja* and to have *darshan* of Sri Bhagwan Rama Chandra and others *Virajman* at Asthan Janmabhumi without any hindrance, dispute or interruption, and that the Defendants had no right to interfere in the Plaintiffs a exercise of his said rights. A permanent injunction restraining the Defendants and their successors from ever removing the Idols of Sri Bhagwan Rama Chandra and others *Virajman* at Asthan Janmabhumi, from the place where they were, or closing the entrance gate or other passages of ingress and egress, and from interfering or disturbing the *puja* or *darshan* in any manner whatsoever, was also claimed.

5. That an identical suit, being Suit No. 25 of 1950, was filed a few months later, after serving a notice under section 80 of the Code of Civil Procedure, 1908, by Paramhansa Ramchandra Das, who is now the Mahant of Digambar Akhara, Ayodhya. He has been impleaded as Defendant No. 2 in this suit. The same five Muslim individuals were Defendants Nos 1 to 5 in that suit, and on their death their names were also struck off under the orders of the Court. Of the remaining Defendants of Suit No. 2 of 1950, Defendants Nos 8 and 9, namely, the City Magistrate and the Superintendent of Police, Faizabad, were not impleaded in Suit No. 25 of 1950, and the only surviving Defendants therein are the Uttar Pradesh State and the Deputy Commissioner, Faizabad, who have been impleaded as Defendants Nos 7 and 8, respectively, in this Suit.

6. That a third suit being Suit No. 26 of 1959 was thereafter filed in the Court of the Civil Judge, Faizabad, by the Nirmohi Akhara, Ayodhya, who has been impleaded as Defendant No. 3 in this suit, claiming the relief of removal of Babu Priya Dutt Ram, Defendant No. 1 thereto, from the management and charge of the temple of Janmabhumi with the Idol of Lord Ram Chandra and others installed therein, at Asthan Janmabhumi, whereto he had been appointed as Receiver in the year 1950 by the City Magistrate, Faizabad, in a proceeding under section 145 of the Code of Criminal Procedure, 1898. The other Defendants were (2) State of Uttar Pradesh, (3) Deputy Commissioner, Faizabad, (4) City Magistrate, Faizabad, (5) Superintendent of Police, Faizabad, (6) Haji Pheku, (7) Mohammad Faiq, and (8) Mohammad Achhan Mian. The said Defendants Nos 2, 3, 4 and 5, are respectively Defendants Nos 7, 8, 9 and 10 in this suit. The other Defendants have died and their legal representatives have not been brought on the record obviously because the cause of action did not survive against them.

7. That a fourth suit, being Suit No. 12 of 1961, was thereafter filed by the

Sunni Central Board of Waqfs, U.P., and eight other Sunni Muslims on 13.12.1961 in the Court of the Civil Judge, Faizabad. The reliefs claimed were: (a) A declaration that the property indicated by the letters A B C D in the sketch map annexed to the plaint is a 'public mosque commonly known as 'Babri Masjid', and that too land adjoining the mosque shown in the sketch map by letters E F H G is a public Muslim graveyard in suit by removal of the idols and other articles which the Hindus may have placed in the mosque as objects of their worship. The Sunni Central Board of Waqfs, U.P., is being impleaded a Defendant No. 4 in this suit, and of the remaining Plaintiffs of that suit, the legal representatives of Defendants Nos 1, 13 and 15, who have been impleaded therein, are being impleaded as Defendants Nos 1, 14 and 16 respectively in this suit. The surviving Defendants Nos 2, 3, 5, 6, 7, 8, 10, 11, 12, 14, 17, 18 and 19 of that suit, are being impleaded as Defendants Nos 2, 3, 7, 8, 9, 10, 11, 12, 13, 15, 17, 18 and 19 respectively, herein. Remaining Defendants Nos 4 and 16 have died and have been left out.

8. That it needs to be stated that by an order dated 8.8.1962 of the Court of the Civil Judge, Faizabad, in Suit No. 12 of 1961, the Plaintiffs thereof were permitted to sue, on behalf of the entire Muslim community, the Defendants Nos 1 to 4 therein as representatives of, and for the benefit of the entire Hindu community. Of them, Defendant No. 4 has since died. Defendants 10 to 19 were impleaded therein later, on their own request. Of them also, Defendant No. 16 has since died. Their legal representatives have not been impleaded in that suit. They have, therefore, been left out in this suit.

9. That it also needs to be stated that by an order dated 4.8.1951, suits Nos 2 and 25 of 1950 were consolidated together, and by an order dated 6.11.1964, all the four suits were consolidated, and suit No. 12 of 1961 was made the leading case.

10. That it must also be stated that in suit No. 2 of 1950, an *ad interim* injunction was issued on 16.1.1950, in the terms prayed for, but on an application made by the Defendant District Magistrate, the *ad interim* injunction was modified on 19.1.1950 to read as under 'The parties are hereby restrained by means of temporary injunction to refrain from removing the Idols in question from the site in dispute and from interfering with *puja* etc., as at present carried on'.

The aforesaid *ad interim* injunction was confirmed by order dated 3.3.1951, after nearing the parties, in the following terms. The interim injunction order dated 16.1.50 as modified on 19.1.50 shall remain in force until the suit is disposed off. A First Appeal from that order, being F.A.F.O. No. 154 of 1951, in the High Court at Allahabad, was dismissed by judgement dated 26.4.1955. The interim injunction continues to remain in force, ever since down to the present day.

11. That the issues were framed in all the four suits more than twenty-five years ago, but their nearing has not yet commenced. The *sewa* and *puja* of the Plaintiff Deities has in the meanwhile been looked after by a Receiver, to begin with by Babu Priya Dutt Ram, appointed by the City Magistrate in the proceedings under Section 145 of the Code of Criminal Procedure, 1898, and later by Shri

K.K. Ram Verma, who continued to function as such from 1970 onwards, pending the passing of final orders by the Civil Court, in suit No. 12 of 1961. He was discharged by the Court of the 111 Additional District Judge, Faizabad, by order dated 25.8.1988. Shri L.P.N. Singh was appointed Receiver. He functioned up to 22.11.1988, when by an order of that date Ṣhri Jamuna Prasad Singh was appointed as Receiver.

12. That when issues were framed, and the suits were consolidated, more than twenty-five years ago, the expectation was that the suits would be disposed off soon thereafter. But for one reason or another, they continued to remain pending, and still continue to remain pending, with a dim prospect of their immediate hearing. Although the *sewa* and *puja* of the plaintiff Deities was being conducted regularly and properly, yet *darshan* was allowed only from behind a barrier. It is true that in the temples in the southern parts of India, the devotees are not permitted to go near the deities for their *darshan* and *puja*, and must do so from behind a barrier, but that is not the custom in the northern parts of India, and it was hoped that after the decision of the suits, the devotees would be able to have a closer *darshan* of the Plaintiff Deity No. 1.

13. That because of the indefinite delay in the disposal of the said suits, on an application made by Defendant No. 28, herein, in the interest of the worshippers, with the prayer for allowing a closer *darshan*, the Court of the Munsif Sadar, Faizabad, refused to pass orders but on appeal therefrom, the Court of the District Judge, Faizabad, by an order dated, 1.2.1986, directed the authorities to remove the barrier by opening the locks on the gates O and P on the map, which is annexed here to as Annexure 1.

14. That the Plaintiff Deities and their devotees are extremely unhappy with the prolonged delay in the hearing and disposal of the said suits, and the deteriorating management of the affairs of the temple, particularly the way in which the Receiver has been acting. It is believed that a large portion of the money offered by the worshippers, who come in great numbers, is being misappropriated by the *pujaris* and other temple staff, and the Receiver has not controlled this evil. Further, the devotees of the Plaintiff Deities are desirous of having a new temple constructed, befitting their pristine glory, after removing the old structure of Sri Ramjanmabhumi Ayodhya.

15. That in order to improve the temple administration, and to reconstruct a new temple at Sri Ramjanmabhumi, the sacred duty of managing and performing the *sewa, archana* and *puja* of the Plaintiff Deities, and the task of protecting, renovating, reconstructing and developing the temple premises, in short, of managing all their estate and all their affairs, was entrusted, by unanimous public opinion, to Jagadguru Ramanandacharya Swami Shivaramacharya of Kashi, who was the head of the Ramananda *sampradaya* to which most of the *sadhus* and *vairagis* of Ayodhya belong. The Trust so reposed in him by the Hindu public was formally declared by him, by Deed of Trust dated December 18, 1985, and registered the same day with the Sub-Registrar, S.D. No. I, at Delhi, vide No. 16510 in Additional Book No. 4, Volume 1156, at pages 64 to 69. A copy of the

said Deed of Trust is annexed to and made part of this Plaint as Annexure IV.

16. That by the said Trust Deed, apart from declaring himself to be the First Trustee for life and the *pramukh* and *dharmakarta* of the Trust, which was named Sri Ramjanmabhumi Nyas, by Jagadguru Ramanandacharya Swami Shivaramacharya, the following others were appointed as Trustees for life, namely:

(2) Jagadguru Varishtha Sankaracharya Swami Shantananda Saraswati Ji Maharaj of Jyotishpeetha, Prayag.
(4) Mahant Nrityagopal Das Ji Maharaj of Maniram Chhaoni, Ayodhya.
(3) Gorakshapeethadhishwar, Mahant Avedyanata Ji Maharaj of Gorakhpur.
(5) Paramhansa Mahant Ramchandra Das Ji Maharaj of Digambar Akhara, Ayodhya, now the acting *pramukh* and *dharmakarta*, Defendant No. 2.
(6) Santpravar Prabhu Dutt Ji Brahmachari of Sankirtan Bhawan, Jhusi, Prayag.
(7) Mahant Ram Kewal Das Ji, Maharaj of Nirmohi Akhara, Ayodhya which is Defendant No. 3.
(8) Shri Vishnu Hari Dalmia, Tees January Marg, New Delhi.
(9) Shri Ashok Singhal, 16/10 Hashimpur Road, Allahabad.
(10) Shri Dau Dayal Khanna, Nanda Vihar, Civil Lines, Moradabad.

Of these Trustees, Shri Vishnu Hari Dalmia was named the Treasurer and Shri Ashok Singhal the Managing Trustee. In addition to the said to Trustees, power was given to the *marga darshak mandal* of the Vishwa Hindu Parishad to nominate four Trustees who are Mahatmas from different parts of India, and to its Governing Council to nominate ten Trustees from among eminent Hindu citizens of India, and in exercise of the said power the following further Trustees have been appointed by the Vishwa Hindu Parishad, namely:

a. From among the Mahatmas:
(1) Jagadguru Madhwacharya Shri Vishweshtirtha Ji Maharaj of Udipi, Karnataka.
(2) Bharata Gyan Jagat, Buddhist Bhikshu of Bodh Gaya, Bihar.
(3) Jagadguru Ramanujacharya Swami Purushottamacharya Ji Maharaj, Ayodhya.

b. From among Hindu citizens of India:
(1) Shri Justice Shiv Nath Katju, Retired Judge High Court, Allahabad.
(2) Shri Justice Deoki Nandan Agarwal, Retired Judge High Court, Allahabad, by whom this Plaint is being filed as the next friend of the Plaintiff Deities Nos 1 and 2, and as Plaintiff No. 3.
(3) Rajmata Smt. Vijaya Raje Scindia of Gwalior.
(4) Shri Shirish Chandra Dikshit, Retired Director General of Police, Uttar Pradesh, Lucknow.
(5) Shri Badri Prasad Toshniwal, Industrialist, New Delhi.

The Trustees so appointed hold office for four years, and half their number retire by rotation once every two years, but are eligible for reappointment.

17. The Sri Ramjanmabhumi Nyas is directly interested in the *sewa, puja* and other affairs of the Plaintiff Deities. It is being impleaded as Defendant No. 21 in this Suit.

18. That although the aforesaid suits have been pending trial for such an extraordinary long number of years, they are inadequate and cannot result in a settlement of the dispute which led to their institution or the problems arising therefrom, inasmuch as neither the presiding Deity of Bhagwan Sri Rama *Virajman* nor the Asthan Sri Ramjanmabhumi, the Plaintiffs Nos 1 and 2 herein, who are both juridical persons, were impleaded therein, although they have a distinct personality of their own, separate from their worshippers and *sewaks* and some of the actual parties thereto, who are worshippers, are to some extent involved in seeking to gratify their personal interests to be served by obtaining a control or the worship of the Plaintiff Deities. Moreover, the events which have occurred during these four decades, and many material facts and points of law require to be pleaded from the view point of the Plaintiff Deities, for a just determination of the dispute relating to Sri Ramjanmabhumi, Ayodhya, and the land and buildings and other things appurtenant thereto. The Plaintiffs have been accordingly advised to file a fresh suit of their own.

19. That it is manifestly established by public records of unimpeachable authority that the premises in dispute is the place where Maryada Purushottam Sri Ramchandra Ji Maharaj was born as the son of Maharaj Dashrath of the Solar Dynasty, which according to the tradition and the faith of the devotees of Bhagwan Sri Rama is the place where *he* manifested *himself* in human form as an incarnation of Bhagwan Vishnu. The place has since ever been called Sri Ramjanmabhumi by all and sundry through the ages.

20. That the place itself, or the Asthan Sri Ramjanmabhumi, as it has come to be known, has been an object of worship as a Deity by the devotees of Bhagwan Sri Rama, as it personifies the spirit of the Divine worshipped in the form of Sri Rama Lalla or Lord Rama the Child. The Asthan was thus Deified and has had a juridical personality of its own even before the construction of a temple building or the installation of the Idol of Bhagwan Sri Rama the rest.

21. That it may be here stated that the Hindus do not worship the stone or the metal shaped into the form of their *ishta devata*, or the stone of Saligram which has no particular shape at all. They worship the Divine, which has no quality or shape or form, but can be known only when it manifests itself in the form of an incarnation, and therefore, adopt the form of his incarnation as their *ishta devata*. For some, even that is unnecessary. They can meditate upon the formless and the shapeless Divine and aspire for a knowledge of him through his grace. It is the spirit of the divine which is worshipped by most Hindus, and not its material form or shape in an idol. The spirit of the divine in an Idol is invoked by the ritual of *pranapratishtha*. This spirit of the living is indestructible and ever remains present everywhere at all times for any one to invoke it in any shape or form in accord with his own aspiration. Different persons are at different levels of realization of the reality. Some find it helpful to pursue a particular set of

rituals for their spiritual uplift. A large section of Hindus follow their *bhakti marga*, and Bhagwan Sri Rama or Bhagwan Sri Krishna is their *ishta devata.*

22. That according to the faith of the devotees of Bhagwan Sri Rama Lalla, or Lord Rama the child it is the spirit of Bhagwan Sri Rama as the Divine child which resides at Asthan Sri Ramjanmabhumi and can be experienced by those who pray there and invoke that spirit for their spiritual uplift. The spirit is the Deity. An idol is not necessary for invoking the Divine spirit. Another example of such a Deity is that of Kedarnath. The temple of Kedarnath has no idol in it. It is the undulating surface of stone which is worshipped there as the Deity. Still another example of such a Deity is the Vishnupad temple at Gaya. That too has no idol in it. The place which is believed to have borne the footprint of Bhagwan Vishnu is worshipped as Deity. Similarly, at Ayodhya, the very Asthan Sri Ramjanmabhumi is worshipped as a Deity through such symbols of the Divine Spirit as the *Charan* and the Sita *Rasoi*. The place is a Deity. It has existed in this immovable form through the ages, and has ever been a juridical person. The actual and continuous performance of *puja* of such an immovable Deity by its devotees is not essential for its existence as a Deity. The Deity continues to exist so long as the place exists, and being land, it is indestructible. Thus, Asthan Sri Ramjanmabhumi is an indestructible and immovable Deity who has continued to exist throughout the ages.

23. That the books of history and public records of unimpeachable authenticity, establish indisputably that there was an ancient temple of maharaja Vikramaditya's time at Sri Ramjanmabhumi, Ayodhya. That temple was destroyed partly and an attempt was made to raise a mosque thereat, by the force of arms, by Mir Baqi, a commander of Babar's hordes. The material used was almost all of it taken from the temple including its pillars which were wrought out of *kasauti* or touch-stone, with figures of Hindu gods and goddesses carved on them. There was great resistance by the Hindus and many battles were fought from time to time by them to prevent the completion of the mosque. To this day it has no minarets, and no place for storage of water for *Vazoo*. Many lives were lost in these battles. The last such battle occurred in 1855. Sri Ramjanmabhumi, including the building raised during Babar's time by Mir Baqi, was in the possession and control of Hindus at that time. According to the 1928 Edition of the *Faizabad Gazetteer*, published by the Government Press, U.P.,

> Ayodhya is pre-eminently a city of temples. . . . It is locally affirmed that at the time of the Musalman conquest there were three important Hindu shrines at Ayodhya and little else. These were the Janmasthan temple, the Swargaddwar and the Treta-ka-Thakur, and each was successively made the object of attention of different Musalman rulers. The Janmasthan was in Ramkot and marked the birthplace of Rama. In 1528 Babar came to Ayodhya and halted here for a week. He destroyed the ancient temple and on its site built a mosque, still known as Babar-e-mosque. The materials of the old structure were largely employed, and many of the columns are in good preservation; they are of close-grained black stone, called by the natives

kasauti, and carved with various devices. Their length is from seven to eight feet, and the shape square at the base, centre and capital, the rest being round or octagonal. The mosque has two inscriptions, one on the outside and the other on the pulpit, both are in Persian and bear the date 935 *Hijri*. (p. 179)

And again according to the same *Gazetteer*:

> This desecration of the most sacred spot in the city caused great bitterness between Hindus and Musalmans. On many occasions the feeling led to bloodshed, and in 1855 an open fight occurred, the Musalmans occupying the Janmasthan in force and then making a desperate assault on the Hanuman Garhi. They charged up the steps of the temple, but were driven back with considerable loss. The Hindus then made a counter-attack and stormed the Janmasthan, at the gate of which seventy-five Musalmans were buried, the spot being known as the Ganj Shahidan or the martyr's resting place. Several of the king's regiments were present, but their orders were not to interfere. Shortly afterwards Maulvi Amir Ali of Amethi in Lucknow organized a regular expedition with the object of destroying the Hanuman Garhi; but he and his forces were stopped in the Bara Banki district (*Gazetteer of Barabanki*, p. 168). It is said that up to this time both Hindus and Musalmans used to worship in the same building; but since the mutiny an outer enclosure has been put up in front of the mosque and the Hindus, who are forbidden access to the inner yard, make their offerings on a platform which they have raised in the outer one. (p. 180)

24. That such a structure raised by the force of arms on land belonging to the Plaintiff Deities, after destroying the ancient temple situate thereat, with its materials including the *kasauti* pillars with figures of Hindu gods carved thereon, could not be a mosque and did not become one in spite of the attempts to treat it as a mosque during the British rule after the annexation of Avadh. Some salient points with regard thereto are noted below.

(a) According to the Koran Allah spoke to the Prophet thus:

> And fight for the religion of God against those who fight against you; but transgress not by attacking them first, for God loveth not the transgressors. And kill them wherever you find them; and turn them out of that whereof they have dispossessed you; for temptation to idolatry is more grievous than slaughter: yet fight not against them in the holy temple, until they attack you therein. . . .

(b) According to all the Muslim authorities and precedents and the decided cases also Allah never accepts a dedication of property which does not belong to the Waqf, that is, the person who purports to dedicate property to Allah for purposes recognized as pious or charitable, as Waqf under the Muslim law. By his acts of trespass and violence for raising a mosque on the site of the temple after destroying it by force, Mir Baqi committed a highly un-Islamic act. His attempt to convert the temple into a mosque did not, therefore, create a valid dedication of property to Allah, whether in fact or in law, and it never became a mosque.

(c) That in spite of all that Mir Baqi tried to do with the temple, the land always continued to vest in the Plaintiff Deities, and they never surrendered their possession over it. Their possession continued in fact and in law. The Asthan never went out of the possession of the Deity and His worshippers. They continued to worship Him through such symbols as the *Charan* and the Sita *Rasoi*, and the Idol of Bhagwan Sri Rama Lalla *Virajman* on the Chabutra, called the Rama Chabutra, within the enclosed courtyard of the building directly in front of the arched opening of its southern dome. No one could enter the building except after passing through these places of Hindu worship. According to the Muslim religion and law there can be no idol worship within the courtyard of a mosque, and the passage to a mosque must be free and unobstructed and open at all times to the 'faithful'. It can never be through a Hindu place of worship. There can be no co-sharing of title or possession with Allah in the case of a mosque. His possession must be exclusive.

(d) A mosque must be built in a place of peace and quiet, but near to a place where there is a sizeable Muslim population, according to the tenets of Islam, and as insisted upon by it, a mosque cannot be built in a place which is surrounded on all sides by temples, where the sound of music or conch shells or *ghanta-ghariyala* must always disturb the peace and quiet of the place.

(e) A mosque must have a minaret for calling the *Azan*. According to Baillie:

> 'When an assembly of worshippers pray in a masjid with permission, that is delivery. But it is a condition that the prayers be with *izan*, or the regular call, and be public not private, for though there should be an assembly yet if it is without *izan*, and the prayers are private instead of public, the place is no masjid, according to the two disciples' (Pt. 1, BK, IX, Ch. VII Sec. 1, p. 605).

Indeed, there has been no mosque without a minaret after the first half century from the *Flight*, (See P.R. Ganapathi Iyer, *Law Relating to Hindu and Mahomedan Endowments*, 2nd Edition, 1918, Ch. XVII, p. 388).

(f) According to the claim laid by the Muslims in their suit No. 12 of 1961, the building is surrounded on all sides by a graveyard known as '*Ganj Shahidan*'. There is a mention in the *Faizabad Gazetteer* also, quoted herein above, of the burial of 75 Muslims at the gate of the Janmasthan, and the place being known as *Ganj Shahidan*, after the battle of 1856. Although there are no graves anywhere near the building at Sri Ramjanmabhumi, or in its precincts, or the area appurtenant thereto, for the last more than fifty years, if the building was surrounded by a graveyard during the British times soon after the annexation of Avadh by them, the building could not be a mosque, and could not be used as a mosque, for the offering of prayers, except the funeral prayers on the death of a person buried therein, is prohibited in a graveyard according to the Muslim authorities.

(g) As already stated, there is no arrangement for storage of water for *Vazoo*, and there are the *kasauti* pillars with the figures of Hindu gods and goddesses inscribed thereon in the building.

25. That the worship of the Plaintiff Deities has continued since ever throughout the ages at Sri Ramjanmabhumi. The place belongs to the Deities. No valid Waqf was ever created or could have been created of the place or any part of it, in view of the title and possession of the Plaintiff Deities thereon. Allah, as conceived by the Muslims, never got any title or possession over the premises or any part of them. Nor has there ever been any person, living or juridical, who might have put forward any claim to ownership of the property or any part of it. Occasional acts of trespass or attempts to get into possession by the Muslims were successfully resisted and repulsed by the Hindus from time to time, and there was no blemish or dent in the continuity of title and possession of the Plaintiff Deities. No title could or did vest in Allah over any part of Sri Ramjanmabhumi by adverse possession or in any other matter. Neither Allah nor any person on his behalf had any possession over any part of the premises at any time whatsoever, not to speak of any adverse possession.

26. That at any rate no prayers have ever been offered in the building at Sri Ramjanmabhumi, which was recorded as Janmasthan Masjid, during the British times, and confined, after the annexation of Avadh, to the area within the boundary wall raised by them adjacent to the arch openings, in the courtyard which is now enclosed by what may now be described as the outer boundary wall. The domes of the building and substantial parts of it were destroyed by the Hindus in the year 1934 during the communal riots which occurred by way of retaliation to cow slaughter by some Muslims at Ayodhya. Although the building was re-built by the government, no one dared to offer *namaz* therein. No action was taken by anyone for its use or management as a mosque. Neither of the two Boards of Waqfs in U.P., namely, the Sunni Central Board of Waqfs and the Shia Central Board of Waqfs, created on the passing of the U.P. Muslim Waqfs Act in 1936, took any action or positive steps for the establishment of the building as a mosque, no one acted as a *Mutawalla,* or *Hussain,* or *Imam*, or *Khatib*, or *Khadim* of the building as a mosque.

27. That after independence from the British Rule, the *Vairagis* and the *Sadhus* and the Hindu public, dug up and levelled whatever graves had been left in the area surrounding Sri Ramjanmabhumi Asthan and purified the place by *Akhand Patha* and *Japa* by thousands of persons all over the area. Ultimately, on the night between the 22 and 23 December 1949, the Idol of Bhagwan Sri Rama was installed with due ceremony under the central dome of the building also.

28. That although there have been no Muslims residing anywhere near the place, and no resistance was offered by any Muslim to any of these acts, the local authorities found it difficult to get out of their old habits acquired under the British Rule; and a First Information Report was recorded by the Police on their own and proceedings were initiated by the Additional City Magistrate under section 145 of the Code of Criminal procedure, 1898, by recording a Preliminary Order dated 29.12.1949. The Magistrate did not identify any kinds of Muslim

individuals as parties to the dispute, and merely said that he was satisfied on information received from police sources and other credible sources 'that a dispute between Hindus and Muslims in Ayodhya over the question of rights of proprietorship and worship in the building claimed variously as Babri Masjid and Janmabhumi Mandir . . . is likely to lead to a breach of the peace'. That was merely a device to take over the administration of the Janmabhumi Mandir by the government by appointing a Receiver, namely, B. Priya Dutt Ram, who was appointed as such by the same order; and after his death in 1970 Shri K.K. Ram Varma was appointed in his place by the City Magistrate, although he had dropped the proceedings under Section 145 of the Code of Criminal Procedure, 1898, by order dated 30.7.1953, with the finding that there was no apprehension of the breach of peace any longer. Orders for appointment of Receiver have now been passed by the Civil Court, and Shri K.K. Ram Verma, who was functioning for more than fifteen years under stay orders, has been replaced by a Civil Court Receiver.

29. That the Plaintiff Deities were not made parties to any of the aforesaid proceedings in which the orders of appointment of Receiver have been passed, whether by the City Magistrate or the Civil Court. The powers of a Receiver are derived solely from the orders of the Court. The Receiver was not authorized to remove any person from the possession or the custody of the premises, and in fact the Receiver never interfered with the possession of the Plaintiff Deities. No party to proceeding could dispossess a third party, nor could the Receiver interfere with the possession of a person who is not a party to the proceedings. At the highest, the Receiver acted like a *Shebait*. He did not disturb the possession of the Plaintiff Deities. Their possession over the building premises in dispute ever since the installation of the first Plaintiff's Idol on the night between the 22 and 23 December 1949, is admitted by all the concerned parties. Thus, independently of the original title of the Plaintiff Deities which continued all along, the admitted position of their possession places the matter of their title beyond any doubt or dispute. Even if there had been any person claiming title to the property adversary to the Plaintiff Deities, that would have been extinguished by their open and long adverse possession, which created positively and affirmatively a proprietary title to the premises in the Plaintiff Deities.

30. That the Hindu Public and the devotees of the Plaintiff Deities, who had dreamed of establishing *Rama rajya* in free India, that is, the rule of *Dharma* and righteousness, of which Maryada Purushottam Sri Ramchandra Ji Maharaj was the epitome, have been keenly desirous of restoring his Janmasthan to its pristine glory, as a first step towards that national aspiration given to us by Mahatma Gandhi. For achieving this, they are publicly agitating for the construction of a grand temple in the Nagar style. Plans and a model of the proposed temple have already been prepared by the same family of architects who built the Somnath temple. The active movement is planned to commence from 30 September 1989, and foundation stone of the new Temple building, it has been declared, shall be laid on 9 November 1989.

31. That the Plaintiff Deities not being a party to any of the litigation pend-

ing in the Courts, and being thus not bound or affected by anything which may be decided or not decided in any of the four suits pending as aforesaid for the last so many years, the Plaintiff No. 3 felt that the tendency of the said suits may present a hindrance, inasmuch as a declaration has been sought, frivolously though, in Suit No. 12 of 1961 by the Sunni Central Board of Waqfs, U.P., that the building at Sri Ramjanmabhumi Ayodhya is a mosque known as 'Babri Mosque' and that the adjacent land is a Muslim public graveyard, known as *Ganj-Shahidan*, and the Court had permitted the Plaintiffs of that suit to sue the Defendants Nos 1 to 4 thereof as representatives of the entire Hindu community. The Plaintiffs of that suit cannot represent the entire Muslim community because they are all Sunnis, and thus only a segment of the Muslim population, who have wide ranging differences with other sects of Muslims, particularly the Shia. Nor were the Defendants, Nos 1 to 4 be competent or capable of representing the entire world of Hindus. The Defendants Nos 1 and 2 have categorically stated that they do not represent anyone else except themselves, and the defendant No. 3 has put forward a personal interest in the management of the worship of the Plaintiff Deities. Defendant No. 4 is already dead. Under the circumstances the Plaintiff No. 3 has been advised to file this suit as the next friend for and on behalf of the Deities, to remove whatever obstacle there may be in the path of the fulfilment of the aforesaid programme, against all the contending parties.

32. That according to the case taken up by the Defendants Nos 4, 5 and 6, and the documents filed by them or on their behalf, the 'Babri Masjid' was a Sunni Waqf but its Mutawallis, being the descendants of Mir Baqi, were Shia Muslims. A judgement dated 30.3.1946 of Shri S.A. Hasan, Civil Judge Faizabad, in suit no. 29 of 1945, of his Court, between the Shia Central Board of Waqfs, U.P., as Plaintiff and the Sunni Central Board of Waqf, U.P., as the Defendant, has been produced in this context, although the judgement has not been relied upon or referred to in the Plaint of Suit No. 12 of 1961, to show that the Waqf of the Babri Masjid was a Sunni Waqf and that its Mutawallis were Shias. This position seems to be incomprehensible in law, inasmuch as a Waqf created by a Shia Waqf would be a Shia waqf and could not be a Sunni waqf. Admittedly, according to their case, the 'mosque' was built by Mir Baqi and that he was a Shia, and that he being the Waqf his heirs were the *Mutawallis* one after the other. But the Shia Central Board of Waqfs, U.P., did not agitate the case any further, either because of negligence or collusion in those difficult days of communal conflict immediately before the Partition. At any rate this judgement is not binding. Further according to a report dated 10.12.1949 of Mr Mohammad Ibrahim, Waqf Inspector, and an office note signed by the Secretary of the Sunni Central Board of Waqfs, U.P., and dated 25.11.1948, Shri Javvad Husain, the *nambardar* of village Sahanwa, and in the line of descent from Mir Baqi, was the Mutawalli of the Waqf, although it appears, he was not acting as such and did not submit to the jurisdiction of the said Board of waqfs. The Shia Central Board of Waqfs, U.P., and Shri Javvad Husain are also being impleaded as Defendants Nos 22 and 23 in this suit. Prince Anjum Qadar, who is the President of the All India Shia

Conference and that body as representatives of the Shia Muslims, have also been impleaded as Defendants Nos 24 and 25 in the suit.

33. That the entire premises at Sri Ramjanmabhumi, Ayodhya, which contain, besides the Presiding Deity of Plaintiff No. 1, other idols and deities and the Rama Chabutra, the *Charan* and the Sita *Rasoi* etc., along with the yards, enclosures and buildings, including the Sita *Koop*, and all that, constitute one integral complex. They have a single identity. The claim by the Muslim represented by the Defendants Nos 4 and 5 and 6 is confined to the building and the area enclosed within the inner boundary wall, erected after the annexation of Avadh by the British. The rest of the area has not been claimed as 'Babri Masjid'. The claim that the surrounding area is a *Qabristan* known as *Ganj Shahidan* is vague and undefined. There are no graves anywhere for the last fifty years at least. The totality of the facts and circumstances set out above 'demonstrate the utter hollowness of the claim put forward by the Muslims represented by Defendants Nos 4, 5, and 6, who do not represent the entire Muslim community. Besides, although admitting that Defendant No. 23 is the present *Mutawalli* of the 'Babri Masjid' since before 1948, he was not joined as a Plaintiff or Defendant in the suit no. 12 of 1961, in spite of the well established position in law that only a *Mutawalli* of mosque can sue for its possession, and even where a worshipper sues in respect of an existing mosque he must sue for possession being delivered to the *Mutawalli* and that he cannot ask for possession being delivered to him.

34. That a sensible section of the Muslim community led by Prince Anjum Qadar, Defendant No. 24, does not approve of the course adopted by the Defendants Nos 4 to 6 and their like. Suggestions have been made from many quarters for ending the dispute by removal of the 'mosque' to a suitable place where it could serve the interest of its beneficiaries. Although the Plaintiffs do not admit for a moment that the building at Sri Ramjanmabhumi, Ayodhya, or any part of its precincts has ever been a mosque, they would not be averse to the proposal of removal of the materials of the building, except the *kasauti* pillars and the like, for the building will in any case have to be demolished for the construction of the new temple which they propose to construct at the place.

35. That the Muslims are as much the children of God as Hindus, and the Plaintiff No. 3, believes in the policy of living in amity and goodwill with all the several communities and religious denominations in free India. But having regard to the nature and significance of the Asthan Sri Ramjanmabhumi for the Hindus, its *situ* cannot be changed. On the other hand, under the tenets of Islam a mosque can be shifted under certain circumstances, and these circumstances are fully and entirely made out in the case of the 'Babri Masjid', if a mosque it ever was. The shifting of the so-called 'Babri Masjid' from its present site at Sri Ramjanmabhumi, would, therefore, appear to be the most sensible solution of the acrimonious dispute which has been raging for some time past and threatening the peace of this land of Sri Rama.

36. That the cause of action for this suit has been accruing from day to day, particularly since recently when the plans of temple reconstruction are being

sought to be obstructed by violent action from the side of certain Muslim communalists.

37. That the subject matter of dispute is situate within the limits of the territorial jurisdiction of the Court.

38. That the valuation of the suit for purposes of jurisdiction is placed at Rs 11,11,101, as the subject matter of the suit being inalienable is incapable of valuation in terms of money, and consequently that for payment of Court Fee it is Rs 2,22,220. The prescribed Court Fee of Rs 500 being the maximum, is being paid on the consequential relief of injunction.

39. That the Plaintiffs claim the following Reliefs:

(a) A declaration that the entire premises of Sri Ramjanmabhumi at Ayodhya, as described and delineated in Annexures I, II and III, belong to the Plaintiff Deities.

(b) A perpetual injunction against the Defendants prohibiting them from interfering with, or raising any objection to, or placing any obstruction in the construction of the new temple building at Sri Ramjanmabhumi, Ayodhya, after demolishing and removing the existing buildings and structures etc., situate thereat, in so far as it may be necessary or expedient to do so for the said purpose.

(c) Costs of the suit against such of the Defendants as object to the grant of relief to the Plaintiffs.

(d) Any other relief or reliefs to which the Plaintiffs may be found entitled.

Counsel for the Plaintiffs.
Dated: 1 July 1989

Plaintiff No. 3
For himself and for and on behalf of Plaintiffs Nos 1 and 2 as their next friend.
Verification
I, Deoki Nandan Agarwala, the Plaintiff No. 3, and Next Friend of Plaintiffs Nos 1 and 2, do hereby verify that the contents of paragraphs 1, 2, 12, 14, 15, 16, 17, 18, 19, 20, 21, 30, 31, 33, 34, 35, 36, 37, 38, are true to my own knowledge, and those of paragraphs 3, 4, 5, 6, 7, 8, 9. 10, 11, 13, 122, 23, 24, 25, 26, 27, 28, 29, 32 are true to my belief.
Signed and verified this 1st day of July 1989 at. . . .

(Deoki Nandan)
Plaintiff No. 3

4. Government of Uttar Pradesh's Application to the Allahabad High Court for transfer of title suits to Lucknow Bench

. . . 13. That one Shri Umesh Chandra Pandey made an application in R.S. No. 2 of 1950 for direction to the applicants unlocking the gates of the disputed premises and for restraining the applicants from placing any restrictions or hurdle in *darshan* and *puja* offered by Shri Umesh Chandra Pandey in particular and other members of Hindu community in general of the Idols of Bhagwan Rama Chandraji and others in the 'Sthan Janmabhumi Ayodhya'.

14. That upon the said application having been moved the learned Munsif, Faizabad by his order dated 28.1.1986 inter alia observed that since the suit no. 2 of 1950, 25 of 1950, 26 of 1959 and 12 of 1961 have been consolidated and since suit no. 12 of 1961 is the leading case and the records have been summoned in this Hon'ble Court in connection with F.A.F.O. No. 17 of 1977 and in absence of these records it would not be possible to pass any order on the application of Shri Umesh Pandey.

15. That the said Shri Umesh Chandra Pandey thereafter preferred Misc. Appeal No. 8 of 1986 in the Court in District Judge, Faizabad against the said order dated 28.1.1986 and the learned District Judge, Faizabad by his order dated 1.2.1986 allowed the appeal and directed the respondents in the appeal to open the locks of gates O and P forthwith and further directed that they shall not impose any restrictions or hurdle in *darshan* and *puja* of the applicant and other members of the community in general and permitted the respondents in the appeal to take independent decision to control any law and order problem according to the need of the situation and to regulate the entry of pilgrims.

16. That it is pertinent to mention that during the pendency of appeal one Shri Md. Hashim made an application for being impleaded as a party in the appeal as he claimed to be a necessary party. However, the learned District Judge, Faizabad by his order dated 1.2.1986 rejected the application moved by Shri Md. Hashim holding that any orders passed in the appeal preferred by Shri Umesh Chandra Pandey preferred writ petition No. 746 of 1986 on 3.2.1986 in this Hon'ble Court inter alia claiming the following reliefs:

(i) issue a writ, order or direction in the nature of certiorari or any other writ order or direction quashing the orders passed by the opposite party no. 1 dated 1.2.1986 contained in Annexures no. 5 and 6 of the writ petition.

(ii) Issue a writ of mandamus commanding the opposite parties no. 3 to 6 to maintain strictly the sanctity of the disputed premises and preserve the same prohibiting the opposite party no. 2, and others from disturbing the sanctity and preservation of the religious place.

19. That on 3.2.1986 this Hon'ble Court was pleased to pass the following interim order, 'Until further orders of the Court the nature of property in question as existing today shall not be changed. This interim order is operative.'

20. That during the pendency of the writ petition Shri Md. Hashim has made an application for amendment seeking to incorporate amendments in paragraphs 27A, 27B, 33A to 33J besides ground nos 16, 17 18 and 19 and has also claimed the following reliefs, '1A. to issue a writ in the nature of mandamus commanding the opposite parties 3 to 6 remove Idols wrongly and separately but inside the Mosque and restore the same to the petitioner and other members of the Muslim community for the purposes of their religious rites and offering *namaz*.'

21. That Sunni Central Waqf Board, U.P. Lucknow, also filed writ petition no. 3106 of 1986 against the orders dated 1.2.1986 passed by the learned District Judge, Faizabad in appeal filed by Shri Umesh Chandra Pandey. This writ petition was filed in this Hon'ble Court on 12.5.1986 when his Lordship Hon'ble Mr Justice K.N. Misra heard at length the counsel for the petitioner and directed him to file copies of certain documents. . . .

23. That in the writ petition No. 3106 of 1986 inter alia the following reliefs have been prayed by the petitioner:

(i) To issue a writ, direction or order in the nature of certiorari or any other writ, order or direction quashing the orders passed by the opposite party no. 1 dated 1.2.1986 contained in annexures nos 16 and 17 to the writ petition.

(ii) To issue a writ of mandamus commanding opposite parties nos 3 to 6 to maintain strictly the sanctity and original character of the disputed premises as a mosque and preserve the same prohibiting the opposite party no. 2 and also others from disturbing the sanctity and nature of the said religious place;

(iii) Any other appropriate writ order or direction which may be deemed just and proper in the circumstances of the case may also be passed and issued in favour of the petitioner and against the opposite parties; and

(iv) The writ petition be allowed with costs throughout. . . .

25. That on behalf of the applicants while steps were being taken for preparation of the counter affidavits in both the two writ petitions it was found that the dispute which was sought to be raised in the two writ petitions is identical with that which pending adjudication in the Trial Court in the four suits namely R.S. no. 2 of 1950, 25 of 1950, 26 of 1959 and 12 of 1961.

26. That the cause of action for filing the writ petitions appears to have arisen only on account of the orders dated 1.2.1986 passed by the learned District Judge in Misc. Civil Appeal No. 8 of 1986 Umesh Chandra Pandey *versus* State of U.P. and others but now during the pendency of the writ petition the efforts of the petitioners for the writ petition is to have the disputes pending in the Civil Court adjudicated by this Hon'ble Court.

27. That from a perusal of the allegations made in the writ petition No. 746 of 1986 and the affidavits filled by the parties in the writ petition as well as in the allegations made in the writ petition No. 3106 of 1986 it is evident that in event the disputes sought to be raised in the two writ petitions are adjudicated by this Hon'ble Court in proceedings under Article 226 of the Constitution of India and any observation made by this Hon'ble Court would affect the adjudication by the Civil Court in the four regular suits.

28. That as stated above all the four suits are ripe for final hearing and can be conveniently tried and decided by this Hon'ble Court.

29. That in view of the prevailing circumstances in the State and in public interest it is necessary that the hearing of the two writ petitions No. 746 of 1986 and 3106 of 1986 are deferred and the four suits namely R.S. No. 2 of 1950, 25

of 1950, 26 of 1959 and 12 of 1961 are expeditiously decided by this Hon'ble Court.

Wherefore, it is most respectfully prayed that this Hon'ble Court may graciously be pleased to defer the hearing of the writ petition No. 764 of 1986 Md. Hashim *versus* State of U.P. and others and writ petition no. 3106 of 1986 U.P. Sunni Central Waqf Board *versus* State of U.P. and others and be further pleased to withdraw for trial and disposal of the Regular Suit No. 12 of 1961 Sunni Central Waqf Board *versus* Gopal Singh Visharad alongwith three other connected Regular Suits No. 2 of 1950 Gopal Singh Visharad *versus* Zahoor Ahmad, R.S. No. 25 of 1960 Paramhansa Ramchandra Das *versus* Zahoor Ahmad and others R.S. No. 26 of 1959 Nirmohi Akhara *versus* Babu Priya Dutta Ram and others in this Hon'ble Court and for this purpose all the four suits may be withdrawn from the Court of Munsif Sadar, Faizabad by this Hon'ble Court and for which act of kindness the applicants shall ever pray as in duty bound.

Lucknow 10 December 1987
Counsel for applicants

5. The Problem of the Issues

The National Front government which has set high hopes on the judiciary resolving the Ramjanmabhumi–Babri Masjid dispute, might yet receive a nasty surprise from the proceedings of the Allahabad High Court.

Late last month, the Lucknow-based special bench of the Court framed the issues involved in the dispute. This is normal in civil suits but the problem arises because of the nature of the issues framed. Some of the issues are potentially so incendiary that when the contesting parties start adducing evidence, the frail thread of communal amity could well be strained.

This is because several of the forty-three issues framed by the Court on 25 May pertain neither to law nor any verifiable fact. Rather, those issues fall in the grey areas of history, mythology and religion.

Here is a sample: 'Is the property in suit the site of Janmabhumi of Sri Rama Chandraji?

'Whether the building and the graveyard stand dedicated to almighty God, as alleged by the plaintiffs (Sunni Waqf board)?'

'Have the Muslims been in possession of the property in suit from AD 1528 continuously, openly and to the knowledge of the defendants and Hindus in general? If so, its effect?'

'Whether any portion of the property in suit was used as a place of worship by the Hindus immediately prior to the construction of the building in question?'

'Whether the building has been constructed on the site of an alleged Hindu temple after demolishing the same? If so, its effect?'

'Whether even after the construction of the building deities of Bhagwan Sri

Rama *Virajman* and the Asthan Sri Ramjanmabhumi continued to exist on the property . . . and the said places continued to be visited by devotees for purposes of worship? If so, whether the property in dispute continued to vest in the said deities?'

The Judges—Justice S.C. Mathur, Justice Brijesh Kumar and Justice S.H.A. Raza—had to frame such intractable issues because of the constraints of the judicial process. Before the trial begins, the judges have to frame the issues on the basis of the written statements filed by all the parties to the suit.

But, while framing the issues, the judges do have some discretion to reject points which are extraneous to the dispute. And, in the Ayodhya case, the judges used their discretion to reject some contentions which would have had absurd political ramifications.

For instance, one of the parties, the Hindu Mahasabha, had proposed to following issue: 'Whether the division of India was unauthorized and unconstitutional and whether the U.P. Waqf Act was adopted by any lawfully constituted Government of India?' The judges, while declining to frame that issue, noted in their order that it was 'political' and, therefore, 'beyond the purview of Courts'.

But, as the issues enlisted earlier show, they had framed some that are purely matters of faith. The nature of the four suits that had been consolidated from the Faizabad district Courts and placed before this special bench of the High Court had apparently made such issues unavoidable.

The matter had earlier been with the district Court for almost four decades. The trial had never begun there because the district Court, apparently deterred by the religious conflicts involved in the dispute, stopped with framing the issues in the mid 1960s.

On the other hand, the Special Bench has, in less than a year, not only framed the issues afresh but also appointed a commissioner, Mr J.P. Srivastava, to make a survey of the disputed site and report by 16 July. The parties are scheduled to raise their objections, if any, to the report on 7 August, and the trial will begin thereafter.

The demand for setting up the special bench had been originally made by the Babri Masjid Movement Coordination Committee in response to the aggressive programmes chalked out by the VHP to 'restore' the Janmabhumi temple. But the VHP and the RSS had come out against the appointment on the ground that religious scriptures and beliefs could not be brought under judicial scrutiny.

Their opposition had evidently been influenced by the fact that the issues framed in the 1960s in the district Courts raised questions largely concerning Hindu scriptures.

But when the special bench had been set up, the VHP, had no option but to stand by the various Hindu parties embroiled in the suit. In a bid to redeem its position, the VHP had suggested in vain to the special bench to drop altogether one 'unprovable' issue framed in the district Court.

The issue was whether the disputed site was really the birthplace of Rama. The High Court's order dated 25 May records: Learned counsel, Shri V.K.S.

Chaudhary has objected to the above issue. According to him, this issue is not based on the pleading of any of the defendants. We are unable to agree with the submission of the learned counsel as the pleading is contained in paragraph 27 of the written statement filed on behalf of defendants 3 and 4 (Nirmohi Akhara and another Hindu party). Accordingly, the issue is retained.

But Mr Chaudhary subsequently turned the tables on the votaries of Babri Masjid by getting the High Court to frame issues concerning Islamic scriptures as well. Some of these, altogether new issues, which form part of the forty-three framed last month are:

If a portion of the disputed site was used as a place of worship by the Hindus immediately prior to the construction of the building in question, whether a mosque could come into existence in view of the Islamic tenets on the place in disputes?

Whether the building in question can be a mosque under the Islamic laws in view of the admitted position that it does not have minarets?

Whether the building in question can legally be a mosque as it is admittedly surrounded by a graveyard on three sides?

Whether the pillars inside and outside the building in the question contain images of Hindu gods and goddesses? If the finding is in the affirmative, whether on that account the building in question can have the character of mosque under the tenets of Islam?

These and other contentious issues framed in the Ayodhya case have never been decided before in the judicial history. It remains to be seen how the bitter claimants of the Ayodhya property will produce evidence for or against such issues. More importantly, how will the Special Bench pronounce a reasoned verdict on them?

[From *The Times of India*, 25 June 1990].

6. High Court's Order of 1 January 1993 on '*darshan*' of idols

. . . In this view of the matter when situations are changed to a large extent since the 6 December 1992, it has been the duty of the District Magistrate and the authorities to consider the question of relaxation of orders under Section 144 Cr.P.C. in the context of situation prevailing if some restraint is required the authorities can well make room to protect the rights of ordinary citizen to have *darshan* and could pass orders allowing the people, the devotees of Shri Rama Lalla to have *darshan* in regulated manner and under control and vigilance keeping in view the need and requirements of the situation. The restraint should be to such an extent and of such a nature as are only necessary and as such, the opposite parties including the State authorities are required to honour the fundamental rights of the petitioner and every peace loving Hindu and public at large in this regard who wishes to offer prayer and *darshan* before the deity at Shri

Ramjanmabhumi at Bhumi Asthan in the light of the orders contained in Annexures 1 and 2 to the writ petition. The *pujaris* of that temple, we have been informed, five in number are being allowed and three are being allowed to perform *puja* at a time. It is the duty of the State authority to see that to the best possible extent keeping in view the needs of the time as well as keeping in view the essential and necessary security measures and the least possible restrictions, the petitioners and the general Hindu public is allowed to have *darshan* in accordance with rituals and tenets of Vaishnav *Sampraday* and also to allow the *puja* and *Aarti* to be performed every day in accordance with the customs or religious scriptures and principles. The petitioners have further prayed that the opposite parties may be directed to collect and preserve debris, articles and materials which may furnish suitable evidence for being considered by the authorities deciding the disputed question of facts regarding the nature of old construction which existed prior to on or before 6 December 1992 either by the Full Bench or by the Supreme Court in case the matter is referred by the government as is alleged.

Thus, considering, the writ petitions are allowed to this extent only that the opposite parties are commanded by issuance of writ of mandamus directing them to allow the petitioners, the Hindus and devotees of Shri Rama Ji to have *darshan* in a meaningful manner at Ramjanmabhumi, Ayodhya from such a distance which may not be disproportionate and too far off, with reference to devotees and pilgrims view and the vision from outside but taking note of the security of the idol as well as the surrounding circumstances prevailing. . . .

[Judgement delivered on 1 January 1993 by Justice H.N. Tilhari and A.N. Gupta in Vishwa Hindu Parishad *versus* Union of India.]

7. Nani Palkhivala's critique of Presidential Reference to the Supreme Court

The Constitution of India provides for a just balance between the legislature, the executive and the judiciary. Each has a specific field to cover. The Court are there to maintain the most fundamental equilibrium of our society. They are the agency of a sovereign people to enforce the laws; to expound the Constitution and to ensure that its mandates are respected.

It is the primary duty of the executive, and of the executive only, to maintain order. . . . That freedom and order may coexist, it is essential that freedom should be exercised under authority and order should be enforced by authority. . . . Authority is vested solely in the executive, popularly known as the government.

Time and again the government has to make those hard decisions which are essential for the maintenance of order. The making of such decisions cannot be avoided by shifting the responsibility to the judiciary.

. . .The Courts can decide only questions of fact or of law. They cannot decide, and should never be called upon to decide, question to opinion or belief or political wisdom. It is not the Court's role to be an extended arm of the executive. Public opinion of public beliefs may weigh with the executive in shaping governmental policies. But it is not for the Court to decide whether there are cogent grounds for opinions or beliefs which the people may choose to entertain. . . .

It is true that many questions which arise before a Court can, in a sense, be regarded as political questions or questions of policy. But this is where perception and clarity of mind should come into play.

It is to my mind absurd to suggest that the highest Court in the country should be asked to decide questions of history or archaeology. But the government has now asked the Supreme Court to give its opinion under Article 143 of the Constitution, whether a temple existed centuries ago on the site where the Babri Masjid stood before its demolition. The correct position in law is that the Supreme Court should decline to entertain such a matter under Article 143, and emphatically state that it is not within the jurisdiction of the Court to hear the matter and not within the ambit of Article 143 to be asked to express an opinion on such an issue. Such strong attitude of the Supreme Court would prevent abuse of Article 143 in the years to come.

. . . Recent newspaper reports suggest that some Cabinet Ministers are of the view that the Supreme Court should be called upon to decide the following questions:

(i) Whether the devotees should be allowed to have *darshan* of Rama Lalla at the makeshift temple on the disputed site at Ayodhya.
(ii) Whether the government should rebuild the mosque which was dismantled.
(iii) Whether a mosque and a temple should both coexist at Ayodhya.

Is it the function of the Court to decide such questions?

Historians have expressed widely divergent views on the issue whether there was a pre-existing temple on the site on which the mosque was built by Babar. Much less are they agreed that Rama was born at that place. There is even a greater difference of opinion on the question whether Rama actually lived as a human being or whether he was the supramental ideal created by mythology to represent the perfect man. To ask the Supreme Court or the Allahabad High Court to decide such questions of mythology or history, or mixed questions of mythology and history, is to bear witness to the bankruptcy of our political institutions.

It is a measure of the degradation to which we have reduced our third-rate democracy that we have lost all sense of propriety, and are not only willing but eager to call upon the Courts to decide questions of opinion or belief, history, mythology, or political expediency. Never in the history of any country have Courts been approached to deal with the type of questions which are now suggested as fit to be referred to the Courts in connection with the incidents at Ayodhya.

The consequences of asking the Supreme Court or the Allahabad High Court to deal with the type of questions which are suggested for reference would be disastrous in the long run.

First, it would thrust upon the Court a task for which it is not qualified by training or experience. Courts can deal with questions of law or of fact. They are not qualified to deal with questions in other fields like archaeology or history. A judge can decide only upon documentary evidence or evidence given by a witness as to what he himself saw or heard. It is well established that hearsay evidence is inadmissible in a Court of law under the Indian Evidence Act.

Secondly, no government is entitled to shift the responsibility which the Constitution has squarely placed upon its shoulders, to any other agency of the State which was created for a wholly different purpose. Judicial pronouncements can never be a cover for inadequacy of government.

Thirdly, if the Court is pushed into the political arena, it would impair the image and undermine the status of the Court. . .

Fourthly, large organizations with millions of followers have officially and openly stated that they would not be bound by any verdict of the Court of law. The question is not whether they are right or wrong in adopting this attitude. The real point is that if a certain issue essentially involves a question of opinion or belief, the people are entitled to say that a Court of law cannot deal with the issue, and if it does its opinion would be without jurisdiction and not binding on the group which is adversely affected. . .

The blunt truth is that the failure of the political process can never be either concealed or supplemented by any reference to any Court.

The Supreme Court has to decide the issue whether there was a pre-existing temple on the disputed site before the mosque came into existence. Even a finding on this single point issue would leave at large various other questions which are bound to crop-up, irrespective of the Court's finding on the question referred for its consideration:

(i) If evidence is conflicting or non-existent that a temple stood on the site, should it be presumed that no such temple existed? Five hundred years of bloody history may efface marks and traces.

(ii) Should any religious place of worship be razed to the ground because a structure pertaining to another religion stood in its place before?

(iii) Archaeology is the study of the art, customs and beliefs of ancient times. It can afford a ground for a belief or an opinion but never for universal certainty. Cannot two minds come to different conclusions on the same archaeological evidence? How can a conclusion reached by a judge be binding on people whose opinions or beliefs go counter to those of the judge? Does it help in any way to confuse separate and distinct questions? Whether Rama was born at a particular place is wholly distinct and different from the issue whether a temple existed at that place. Therefore, are we in any way dislodging the beliefs of those who hold a certain spot to be the birthplace of Rama by saying that no temple existed there?. . .

There are times in a country's history when inaction and silence can be a culpable wrong, and we are living in such times. The nation is standing on the escalator of anarchy and chaos. At this perilous moment it is the duty of every right-minded citizen to raise his voice against the devious endeavour of politicians to relieve themselves of their own duty to make wise and strong decisions.

[From *Muslim India* 134, February, 1994.]

8. Supreme Court's Judgement on the President's Reference and on the acquisition of certain lands in Ayodhya Act, 1993

The Judgement of the Court were delivered by J.S. Verma, J. (*for Venkatachaliah, C.J., himself and Ray, J.*)

. . . 2. The constitutional validity of the Acquisition of Certain Area at Ayodhya Act, 1993 (No. 33 of 1993) (hereinafter referred to as 'Act No. 33 of 1993' or 'the Act') and the maintainability of Special Reference No. 1 of President of India under Article 143(1) of the Constitution of India are in question for decision herein. The background in which these questions are to be answered is contained in the facts stated in the White Paper at Ayodhya, February 1993, issued by the Government of India.

3. Certain undisputed facts emerging at the hearing may also have relevance for this purpose. These questions are answered on this basis eschewing facts which are in the area of controversy and have yet to be adjudicated.

Background

4. The Bill was introduced in Parliament leading to the above enactment and the said Reference to this Court was made in the historical background set out in the White Paper. Indeed, the two simultaneous acts are an indication of the legislative intent for enactment of the statute, the Reference being made as a part of the same exercise with a view to effectuate the purpose of the enactment. This is how they have to be viewed.

5. The 'Overview' at the commencement of the White Paper in Chapter 1 states thus:

> 1.1 Ayodhya situated in the north of India is a township in District Faizabad of Uttar Pradesh. It has long been a place of holy pilgrimage because of its mention in the epic *Ramayana* as the place of birth of Sri Rama. The structure commonly known as Ramjanmabhumi–Babri Masjid was erected as a mosque by one Mir Baqi in Ayodhya in AD 1500(?). It is claimed by some sections that it was built at the site believed to be the birthspot of Sri Rama where a temple had stood earlier. This resulted in a long-standing dispute.
>
> 1.2 The controversy entered a new phase with the placing of idols in the disputed structure in December 1949. The premises were attached under Section 145 of the Code of Criminal Procedure. Civil suits were filed shortly thereafter. Interim orders in these civil suits restrained in parties from removing the idols or interfering with their worship effect, therefore, from December 1949 till 6.12.1992 the structure had not been used as a mosque.

. . . On 6.12.1992 indicating an air of normalcy, around midday a crowd addressed by leaders of BJP, VHP, etc., climbed the Ramjanmabhumi–Babri Masjid (RJM–BM) structure and started damaging the domes. Within a short time, the entire structure was demolished and razed to the ground. Indeed, it was an act of 'national shame'. What was demolished was not merely an ancient structure; but the faith of the minorities in the sense of justice and fair play of majority. It shook their faith in the rule of law and constitutional processes. A five-hundred-year-old structure which was defenceless and whose safety was a sacred trust in the hands of the State Government was demolished. . . .

8. It may be mentioned that a structure called the Rama *Chabutra* stood on the disputed site within the courtyard of the disputed structure. This structure also was demolished on 6.12.1992. Worship of the idols installed on the Rama *Chabutra* by Hindu devotees in general, it appears, had been performed for a considerable period of time without any objection by the Muslims to its worship at that place, prior to the shifting of the idols from the Rama *Chabutra* to the disputed structure in December 1949. As a result of demolition of Rama *Chabutra* also on 6.12.1992, the worship by Hindus in general even at that place was interrupted. Thereafter, the worship of idols is being performed only by a priest nominated for the purpose without access to the public. . . .

10. Prior to December 1949 when the idols were shifted into the disputed structure from the Rama *Chabutra*, worship by Hindu devotees at the Rama *Chabutra* for a long time without any objection from Muslims is also beyond controversy. A controversy, however, is raised about use of the disputed structure as a mosque from 1934 itself and not merely from December 1949. The other side disputes the alleged disuse of the mosque for prayers prior to December 1949. The stand of the Uttar Pradesh Government in the suits was that the place was used as a mosque till 1949. . . .

In 1992 the Government of India said:

> The Government has decided to acquire all areas in dispute in the suits pending in the Allahabad High Court. It has also been decided to acquire suitable adjacent area. The acquired area excluding the area on which the disputed structure stood would be made available to two Trusts which would be set up for planned development of the area.
>
> The Government of India has also decided to request the President to seek the opinion of the Supreme Court on the question whether there was a Hindu temple existing on the site where the disputed structure stood. The Government has also decided to abide by the opinion of the Supreme Court and to take appropriate steps to enforce the Court's opinion. Notwithstanding the acquisition of the disputed area, the Government would ensure that the position existing prior to the promulgation of the Ordinance is maintained until such time as the Supreme Court gives its opinion in the matter. Thereafter the rights of the parties shall be determined in the light to the Court's opinion.

In pursuance of these decisions an ordinance named 'Acquisition of Certain Area at Ayodhya Ordinance' was issued on 7.1.1993 for acquisition of 67.703 acres of land in the Ramjanmabhumi–Babri Masjid complex. A reference to the Supreme Court under Article 143 of the Constitution was also made on the same day.

13. The acquisition of Certain Area at Ayodhya Ordinance, 1993 was replaced by the Acquisition of Certain Area at Ayodhya at 1993 (No. 33 of 1993).

14. The Ordinance, later replaced by Act No. 33 of 1993 and the Special Reference under Article 143(1) of the Constitution of India were made simultaneously the same day on 7.1.1993. The Statement of Objects and Reasons for the Act No. 33 of 1993 and the Special Reference under Article 143(1) of the Constitution read thus.

'Statement of Objects and Reasons

There has been a long-standing dispute relating to the erstwhile Ramjanmabhumi–Babri Masjid structure in Ayodhya which led to communal tension and violence from time to time and ultimately led to the destruction of the disputed structure on 6.12.1992. This was followed by widespread communal violence which resulted in large number of deaths, injuries and destruction of property in various parts of the country. The said dispute has thus affected the maintenance of public order and harmony between different communities in the country. As it is necessary to maintain communal harmony and the spirit of common brotherhood amongst the people of India, it was considered necessary to acquire the site of the disputed structure and suitable adjacent land for setting up a complex which could be developed in a planned manner wherein a Rama temple, a mosque, amenities for pilgrims, a library museum and other suitable facilities can be set up.

The Acquisition of Certain Area at Ayodhya Ordinance, 1993 was accordingly promulgated by the President on 7.1.1993. By virtue of the said Ordinance the right, title and interest in respect of certain areas at Ayodhya specified in the Schedule to the Ordinance stand transferred to and vest in the Central Government.

The Bill seeks to replace the aforesaid Ordinance.

S.B. Chavan

New Delhi
9 March 1993.'

'Special Reference

Whereas a dispute has arisen whether a Hindu temple or any Hindu religious structure existed prior to the construction of the structure (including the premises of the inner and outer courtyards of such structure, commonly known as the Ramjanmabhumi–Babri Masjid, in the area in which the structure stood in Village Kot Ramchandra in Ayodhya, in Pargana Haveli Avadh, in Tehsil Faizabad Sadar, in the District of Faizabad of the State of Uttar Pradesh;

And whereas the said area is located in Revenue Plot Nos 159 and 160 in the said Village Kot Ramchandra;

And whereas the said dispute has affected the maintenance of public order and harmony between different communities in the country;

And whereas the aforesaid area vests in the Central Government by virtue of the Acquisition of Certain Area at Ayodhya Ordinance, 1993;

And whereas notwithstanding the vesting of the aforesaid area is the Central Government under the said Ordinance the Central Government proposes to settle the said dispute after obtaining the opinion of the Supreme Court of India and in terms of the said opinion;

And whereas in view of what has been hereinbefore stated it appears to me that the question hereinafter set out has arisen and is of such a nature and of such public importance that it is expedient to obtain the opinion of the Supreme Court of India thereon;

Now, therefore, in exercise of the powers conferred upon me by clause (1) of Article 143 of the Constitution of India, I, Shankar Dayal Sharma, President of India, hereby refer the following question to the Supreme Court of India for consideration and opinion thereon, namely:

Whether a Hindu temple or any Hindu religious structure existed prior to the constitution of the Ramjanmabhumi–Babri Masjid (including the premises of the inner and outer courtyards of such structure) in the area on which the structure stood?

Sd/-
President of India

New Delhi;
Dated 7 January 1993.'

The Acquisition of Certain Area at Ayodhya Act, 1993 (No. 33 of 1993)
(3rd April 1993)

An Act to provide for the acquisition of certain area at Ayodhya and for matters connected therewith or incidental thereto.

Whereas there has been a long-standing dispute relating to the structure (including the premises of the inner and outer courtyards of such structure), commonly known as the Ramjanmabhumi–Babri Masjid, situated in Village Kot Ramchandra in Ayodhya, in Pargana Haveli Avadh, in Tehsil Faizabad Sadar, in the district of Faizabad of the State of Uttar Pradesh;

And whereas the said dispute has affected the maintenance of public order and harmony between different communities in the country;

And whereas it is necessary to maintain public order and to promote communal harmony and the spirit of common brotherhood amongst the people of India;

And whereas with a view to achieving the aforesaid objectives, it is necessary to acquire certain areas in Ayodhya;

Be it enacted by Parliament in the forty-fourth year of the Republic of India as follows:

Chapter 1
Preliminary

1. *Short title and commencement*: (1) This Act may be called the Acquisition of Certain Area at Ayodhya Act, 1993.
2. It shall be deemed to have come into force on the 7th day of January, 1993.
3. *Definitions*: In this Act unless the context otherwise requires,
   (a) 'area' means the area (including all the buildings, structures or other properties comprised therein) specified in the Schedule;
   (b) 'authorized person' means a person or body of persons or trustees of any trust authorized by the Central Government under Section 7;
   (c) 'claims Commissioner' means the Claims Commission appointed under sub-section (2) of Section 8;
   (d) 'prescribed' means prescribed by rules made under this Act.

Chapter II
Acquisition of the Area in Ayodhya

3. *Acquisition of rights in respect of certain area*: On and from the commencement of this Act, the right, title and interest in relation to the area shall, by virtue of this Act, stand transferred to, and vest in the Central Government.

4. *General effect of vesting:* (1) The area shall be deemed to include all assets, rights, leaseholds, powers, authority and privilege and all property, movable and immovable, including lands, buildings, structures, shops and whatever nature or other properties and all other rights and interests in, or arising out of, such properties as was immediately before the commencement of this Act in the ownership, possession, power or control of any person or the State Government of Uttar Pradesh, as the case may be, and all registers, maps, plans, drawings and other documents of whatever nature relating thereto.

(2) All properties aforesaid which have vested in the Central Government under Section 3 shall, by force of such vesting, be freed and discharged from any trust, obligation, mortgage, charge, lien and all other encumbrances affecting them and any attachment, injunction, decree or order of any Court or tribunal or other authority restricting the use of such properties in any manner or appointing any receiver in respect of the whole or any part of such properties shall cease to have any effect.

(3) If, on the commencement of this Act, any suit, appeal or the proceeding in respect of the right, title and interest relating to any property which has vested in the Central Government under Section 3, pending before any Court, tribunal or other authority, the same shall abate.

5. *Duty of person or State Government in charge of the management of the area to deliver all assets, etc.:* (1) The Central Government may take all necessary steps to secure possession of the area which is vested in that Government under Section 3.

(2) On the vesting of the area in the Central Government under Section 3, the person or State Government of Uttar Pradesh, as the case may be, in charge

of the management of the area immediately before such vesting shall be bound to deliver to the Central Government or the authorized person, all assets, registers and other documents in the custody relating to such vesting or where it is not practicable to deliver such registers or documents, the copies of such registers or documents authenticated in the prescribed manner.

6. *Power of Central Government to direct vesting of the area in another authority or body or trust*: (1) Notwithstanding anything contained in Sections 3, 4, 5 and 7, the Central Government may, if it is satisfied that any authority or other body, or trustees of any trust, set up on or after the commencement of this Act is or are willing to comply with such terms and conditions as that Government may think fit to impose, direct by notification in the Official Gazette, that the right, title and interest or any of them in relation to the area or any part thereof, instead of continuing to vest in the Central Government, vest in that authority or body or trustees of that trust either on the date of the notification or on such later date as may be specified in the notification.

(2) When any right, title and interest in relation to the area or part thereof vest in the authority or body or trustees referred to in sub-section (1), such rights of the Central Government in relation to such area or part thereof, shall, on and from the date of such vesting, be deemed to have become the rights of that authority or body or trustees of that trust.

(3) The provisions of Sections 4, 5, 7 and 11 shall, so far as may be, apply in relation to such authority or body or trustees as they apply in relation to the Central Government and for this purpose, references therein to the 'Central Government' shall be construed as references to such authority or body or trustees.

Chapter III
Management and Administration of Property

7. *Management of property by Government*: (1) Notwithstanding anything contained in any contract or instrument or order of any Court, tribunal or other authority to the contrary, on and from the commencement of this Act, the property vested in the Central Government under Section 3 shall be managed by the Central Government or by a person or body of persons or trustees of any trust authorized by that Government in this behalf.

(2) In managing the property vested in the Central Government under Section 3, the Central Government or the authorized person shall ensure that the position existing before the commencement of this Act in the area on which the structure (including the premises of the inner and outer courtyards of such structure), commonly known as Ramjanmabhumi–Babri Masjid, stood in Village Kot Ramchandra in Ayodhya, in Pargana Haveli Avadh, in Tehsil Faizabad Sadar, in the district of Faizabad of the State of Uttar Pradesh is maintained.

Chapter IV
Miscellaneous

Payment of amount: (1) The owner of any land, building, structure or other property comprised in the area shall be given by the Central Government, for the transfer to and vesting in that Government under Section 3 of that land, building, structure or other property, in cash an amount equivalent to the market value of the land, building structure of other property.

(2) The Central Government shall, for the purpose of deciding the claim of the owner or any person having a claim against the owner under sub-section (1), by notification in the Official Gazette, appoint a Claims Commissioner.

(3) The Claims Commissioner shall regulate his own procedure is receiving and deciding the claims.

(4) The owner or any person having a claim against the owner may make a claim to the Claims Commissioner within a period of 90 days from the date of commencement of this Act.

Provided that if the Claims Commissioner is satisfied that the claimant was prevented by sufficient cause from preferring the claim within the said period of 90 days, the Claims Commissioner may entertain the claim within a further period of 90 days and as thereafter.

9. *Act to override all other enactments:* The provisions of this Act shall have effect notwithstanding anything inconsistent therewith contained in any other law for the time being in force or any instrument having effect by virtue of any law other than this Act or any decree of order of any Court, tribunal or other authority.

10. *Penalties*: Any person who is in charge of the management of the area and fails to deliver to the Central Government or the authorized person any asset, register or other document in his custody relating to such area or, as the case may be, authenticated copies of such register or document, shall be punishable with imprisonment for a term which may extend to three years or with fine which may extend to ten thousand rupees, or with both.

11. *Protection of action taken in good faith*: No suit, prosecution or other legal proceeding shall lie against the Central Government or the authorized person or any of the officers or other employees of the Government or the authorized person for anything which is in good faith done or intended to be done under this Act.

12. *Power to make rules*: (1) The Central Government may in notification in the Official Gazette, make rules to carry out for provisions of this Act.

(2) Every rule made by the Central Government under this Act shall be laid, as soon as may be after it is made, before each house of Parliament, while it is in session, for a total period of thirty days which may be comprised in one session or in two or more successive sessions and if, before the expiry of the session immediately following the session or the successive sessions aforesaid, both Houses agree on making any modification in the rule or both Houses agree that the act should not be made, the rule shall thereafter have effect only is such modified form or be of no effect, as the case may be; so, however, its any such modification or annulment shall be without prejudice to the validity of anything previously done under that rule.

13. *Repeal and saving*: (1) Subject to the provisions of sub-section (2), the Acquisition of Certain Area at Ayodhya Ordinance, 1993 (Ord. 8 of 1993), is hereby repealed.

(2) Notwithstanding anything contained in the said Ordinance,

(a) the right, title and interest in relation to plot No. 242 situated in Village Kot Ramchandra specified against Sl. No. 1 of the Schedule to the said Ordinance shall be deemed never to have been transferred to, and vested in, the Central Government.

(b) any suit, appeal or other proceeding in respect of the right, title and interest relating to the said plot No. 242, pending before any Court, tribunal or other authority, shall be deemed never to have abated and such suit, appeal or other proceeding (including the orders or interim orders of any Court thereon) shall be deemed to have been restored to the position existing immediately before the commencement of the said Ordinance;

(c) any other action taken or thing done under that Ordinance in relation to the said plot No. 242 shall be deemed never to have been taken or done.

(3) Notwithstanding such repeal, anything done or any action taken under said Ordinance shall be deemed to have been done or taken under corresponding provisions of this act.

The Schedule

[See Section 2(a)]

Description of the Area

The Solicitor General made a statement in writing on behalf of the Union of India on 14.9.1994 as under:

> Government stands by the policy of secularism and of even-handed treatment of all religious communities. The Acquisition of Certain Area at Ayodhya Act, 1993, as well as the Presidential Reference, have the objective of maintaining public order and promoting communal harmony and the spirit of common brotherhood amongst the people of India.
>
> Government is committed to the construction of a Rama temple and a mosque, but their actual location will be determined only after the Supreme Court renders its opinion in the Presidential Reference.
>
> Government will treat the finding of the Supreme Court on the question of fact referred under Article 143 of the Constitution as a verdict which is final and binding.
>
> In the light of the Supreme Court's [*sic*] opinion and consistent with it, Government will make efforts to resolve the controversy by a process of negotiations. Government is confident that the opinion of the Supreme Court will have a salutary effect on the attitudes of the communities and they will no longer take conflicting positions on the factual issue settled by the Supreme Court.
>
> If efforts at a negotiated settlement as aforesaid do not succeed government is com-

mitted to enforce a solution in the light of the Supreme Court's opinion and consistent with it. Government's action in this regard will be even-handed in respect of both the communities. If the question referred is answered in the affirmative, namely, that a Hindu temple/structure did exist prior to the construction of the wishes of the Hindu community. If, on the other hand, the question is answered in the negative, namely, that no such Hindu temple/structure existed at the relevant time, then Government action will be in support of the wishes of the Muslim community.

Justice J.S. Verma said: 'The question now is whether the provision in Section 7 containing the mandate to maintain the status quo existing at the disputed site as on 7.1.1993 is a slant in favour of the Hindu community, intended to perpetuate an injustice done to the Muslim community by demolition of the mosque on 6.12.1993 and, therefore, it amounts to an anti-secular or discriminatory act rendering the provision unconstitutional. For this purpose it is necessary to recall the situation as it existed on 7.1.1993 along with the significant events leading to that situation. It is necessary to bear in mind the comparative use of the disputed area and the right of worship practised therein, by the two communities on 7.1.1993 and for a significant period immediately preceding it. A reference to the comparative user during that period by the two communities would indicate whether the provision in Section 7 directing maintenance of *status quo* till resolution of the dispute and the transfer by the Central Government contemplated by Section 6 is slanted towards the Hindu community to render the provision violative of the basic feature of secularism or the rights to equality and freedom of religion.

47. As earlier stated, worship by Hindu devotees of the idols installed on the Rama *Chabutra* which stood on the disputed site within the courtyard of the disputed structure had been performed without any objection by the Muslims even prior to the shifting of those idols from the Rama *Chabutra* into the disputed structure in December 1949; in one of the suits filed in January 1950, the trial Court passed interim orders whereby the idols remained at the place where they were installed in 1949 and worship of the idols there by the Hindu devotees continued; this interim order was confirmed by the High Court in April 1955; the District Judge ordered the opening of the lock placed on a grill leading to the sanctum sanctorum of the shrine in the disputed structure on 1.2.1986 and permitted worship of the idols there to Hindu devotees; and this situation continued till demolition of the structure on 6.12.1992 when Rama *Chabutra* also was demolished. It was only as a result of the act of demolition on 6.12.1992 that the worship by the Hindu devotees in general of the idols at that place was interrupted. Since the time of demolition, worship of the idols by a *pujari* alone is continuing. This is how the right of worship of the idols practised by Hindu devotees for a long time from much prior to 1949 in the Rama *Chabutra* within the disputed site has been interrupted since the act of demolition on 6.12.1992 restricting the worship of the idols since then to only by one *pujari*. On the other hand, at least since December 1949, the Muslims have not been offering worship at any place

in the disputed site though, it may turn out at the trial of the suits that they had a right to do so.

48. The communal holocaust unleashed in the country disrupting the prevailing communal harmony as a result of the demolition of the structure on 6.12.1992 is well known to require further mention. Any step taken to arrest escalation of communal tension and to achieve communal accord and harmony can, by no stretch of argumentation, be termed non-secular much less anti-secular or against the concept of secularism—a creed of the Indian people embedded in the ethos.

49. The narration of facts indicates that the acquisition of properties under the Act affects the rights of both the communities and not merely those of the Muslim community. The interest claimed by the Muslims is only over the disputed site where the mosque stood before its demolition. The objection of the Hindus to this claim has to be adjudicated. The remaining entire property acquired under the Act is such over which no title is claimed by the Muslims. A large part thereon comprises of properties of Hindus of which the title is not even in dispute. The justification given for acquisition of the larger area including the property respecting which title is not disputed is that the same is necessary to ensure that the final outcome of adjudication should not be rendered meaningless by the existence of properties belonging to Hindus in the vicinity of the disputed structure in case the Muslims are found entitled to the disputed site. This obviously means that in the event of the Muslims succeeding in the adjudication of the dispute requiring the disputed structure to be handed over to the Muslim community, their success should not be thwarted by denial of proper access to, and enjoyment of rights in, the disputed area by exercise of rights of ownership of Hindu owners of the adjacent properties. Obviously, it is for this reason that the adjacent area has also been acquired to make available to the successful party, that part of it which is considered necessary, for proper enjoyment of the fruits of success on the final outcome to the adjudication. It is clear that one of the purposes of the acquisition of the adjacent properties is the ensurement of the effective enjoyment of the disputed site by the Muslim community in the event of its success in the litigation; and acquisition of the adjacent area is incidental to the main purpose and cannot be termed unreasonable. The 'Manas Bhawan' and 'Sita ki Rasoi', both belonging to the Hindus, are buildings which closely overlook the disputed site and are acquired because they are strategic in location in relation to the disputed area. The necessity of acquiring adjacent temples or religious buildings in view of their proximity to the disputed structure area, which forms a unique class by itself, is permissible (see *M. Padmanabha Iyengar v. Government of A.P.* and *Akhara Shri Braham Buta v. State of Punjab*). We approve the principle stated in these decisions since it serves a large purpose.

50. However, at a later stage when the exact area acquired when it needed, for achieving the professed purpose of acquisition, can be determined, it would not merely be permissible but also desirable that the superfluous excess area is released from acquisition and reverted to its earlier owner. The challenge to acquisition of any part of the adjacent area on the ground that it is unnecessary for

achieving the objective of settling the dispute relating to the disputed area cannot be examined at this stage but, in case the superfluous area is not returned to its owner even after the exact area needed for the purpose is finally determined, it would be open to the owner of any such property to then challenge the superfluous acquisition being unrelated to the purpose of acquisition. Rejection of the challenge on this ground to acquisition at this stage, by the undisputed owners of any such property situate in the vicinity of the disputed area, is with the reservation of this liberty to them. There is no contest to their claim of quashing the acquisition of the adjacent properties by anyone except the Central Government which seeks to justify the acquisition on the basis of necessity. On the construction of the statute made by us, this appears to be the logical appropriate and just view to take in respect of such adjacent properties in which none other than the undisputed owner claims title and interest.

51. It may also be mentioned that even as Ayodhya is said to be of particular significance to the Hindus as a place of pilgrimage because of the ancient belief that Lord Rama was born there, the mosque was of significance for the Muslim community as an ancient mosque built by the Baqi in AD 1528. As a mosque, it was a religious place of worship by the Muslims. This indicates the comparative significance of the disputed site to the two communities and also that the impact of acquisition is equally on the right and interest of the Hindu community. Mention of this aspect is made only in the context of the argument that the statute as a whole, not merely Section 7 thereof, is anti-secular being slanted in favour of the Hindus and against the Muslims.

52. Section 7(2) of the Act freezes the situation admittedly in existence on 7.1.1993 which was a lesser right of worship for the Hindu devotees than that in existence earlier for a long time till the demolition of the disposed structure on 6.12.1992; and it does not create a new situation more favourable to the Hindu community amounting to conferment on them of a larger right of worship in the disputed site than that practised till 6.12.1992. Maintenance of status quo as on 7.1.1993 does not, therefore, confer or have the effect of granting to the Hindu community any further benefit thereby. It is also pertinent to bear in mind that the persons responsible for demolition of the mosque on 6.12.1992 were some miscreants who cannot be identified and equated with the entire Hindu community and, therefore, the act of vandalism so perpetrated by the miscreants cannot be treated as an act of the entire Hindu community for the purpose of adjudging the constitutionality of the enactment. Strong reaction against, and condemnation by the Hindus of the demolition of the structure in general bears eloquent testimony to this fact. Rejection of Bharatiya Janata Party at the hustings in the subsequent elections in Uttar Pradesh is another circumstance to that effect. The miscreants who demolished the mosque had no religion, caste or creed except the character of a criminal and the mere incident of birth of such a person in any particular community cannot attach the stigma of his crime to the community in which he was born.

53. Another effect of the freeze imposed by Section 7(2) of the Act is that it

ensures that there can be no occasion for the Hindu community to seek to enlarge the scope of the practice of worship by them as on 7.1.1993 during the interregnum till the final adjudication on the basis that in fact a larger right of worship by them was in vogue up to 6.12.1992. It is difficult to visualize how Section 7(2) can be construed as a slant in favour of the Hindu community and, therefore, anti-secular. The provision does not curtail practice of right of worship of the Muslim community in the disputed area, there having been *de facto* no exercise of the practice or worship by them at least since December 1949; and it maintains status quo by the freeze to the reduced right of worship by the Hindus as in existence on 7.1.1993. However, confining exercise of the right of worship of the Hindu community to its reduced form within the disputed area as on 7.1.1993, lesser than that exercised till the demolition on 6.12.1992, by the freeze enacted in Section 7(2) appears to be reasonable and just in view of the fact that the miscreants who demolished the mosque are suspected to be persons professing to practise the Hindu religion. The Hindu community must, therefore, bear the cross on its chest, for the misdeed of the miscreants reasonably suspected to belong to their religious fold.

54. This is the proper perspective, we say, in which the statute as a whole and Section 7 in particular must be viewed. Thus the factual foundation for challenge to the statute as a whole and Section 7(2) in particular on the ground of secularism, a basic feature of the Constitution, and the rights to equality and freedom of religion is non-existent.

55. Reference may be made to the statements of the Central Government soon after the demolition on 7.12.1992 and 27.12.1992 wherein it was said that the mosque would be rebuilt. It was urged that the action taken on 7.1.1993 to issue an Ordinance, later replaced by the Act, and simultaneously to make the Reference to this Court under Article 143(1) of the Constitution amounts to resiling from the earlier statements for the benefit of the Hindu community. It is sufficient to say that the earlier statements so made cannot limit the power of Parliament and are not material for adjudging the constitutional validity of the enactment. The validity of the statute has to be determined on the touchstone of the Constitution and not any statements made prior to it. We have therefore no doubt that Section 7 does not suffer from the infirmity of being anti-secular or discriminatory to render it unconstitutional.

56. We would now examine the validity of Section 6. Sub-section (1) of Section 6 empowers the Central Government to direct vesting of the area acquired or any part thereof in another authority or body or trust. This power extends to the entire acquired area or any part thereof. This is notwithstanding anything contained in Section 3, 4, 5 and 7. Section 3 provides for acquisition of the area and its vesting in the Central Government. It is, therefore, made clear by sub-section (1) of Section 6 that the acquisition of the area and its vesting in the Central Government is not a hindrance to the same being vested thereafter by the Central Government in another authority or body or trust. Section 4 relates to the effect of vesting and Section 5 to the power of the Central Government to secure

possession of the area vested, with the corresponding obligation of the person or the State Government in possession thereof to deliver it to the Central Government or the authorized person. Section 4(3) relating to abatement of pending suits and legal proceedings would be considered separately. Section 7 which we have already upheld, relates to management and administration of the property by the Central Government or the authorized person during the interregnum till the exercise of power by the Central Government under Section 6(1). Section 7 has been construed by us as a transitory provision to maintain *status quo* in the disputed area and for proper management of the entire property acquired during the interregnum. Thus, sub-section (1) of Section 6 read with sub-section (2) of Section 7 is an inbuilt indication in the statute of the intent that acquisition of the disputed area and its vesting in the Central Government is not absolute but for the purpose of its subsequent transfer to the person found entitled to it as a result of adjudication of the dispute for the resolution of which this step was taken, and enactment of the statute is part of that exercise. Making of the Reference under Article 143(1) simultaneously with the issuance of Ordinance, later replaced by the Act on the same day also is an indication of the legislative intent that the acquisition of the disputed area was not meant to be absolute but limited to holding it as a statutory receiver till resolution of the dispute; and then to transfer it, in accordance with, and in terms of the final determination made in the mechanism adopted for resolution of the dispute. Sub-section (2) of Section (6) indicates consequence of the action taken under sub-section (1) by providing that as a result of the action taken under sub-section (1), any right title and interest in relation to the area or part thereof would be deemed to have become those of the transferee. Sub-section (3) of Section 6 enacts that the provisions of Sections 4, 5, 7 and 11 shall, so far as may be, apply in relation to such authority or body or trustees as they apply in relation to the Central Government. The expression 'so far as may be' is indicative of the fact that all or any of these provisions may or may not be applicable to the transferee under sub-section (1). This provides for the situation of transfer being made, if necessary, at any stage and of any part of the property, since Section 7(2) is applicable only to the disputed area. The provision however does not countenance the dispute remaining unresolved or the situation continuing perpetually. The embargo on transfer till adjudication, and in terms thereof, to be read in Section 6(1), relates only to the disputed area, while transfer of any part of the excess area, retention of which till adjudication of the dispute relating to the disputed area may not be necessary, is not inhibited till then, since the acquisition of the excess area is absolute subject to the duty to restore it to the owner if its retention is found, to be unnecessary, as indicated. The meaning of the word 'vest' in Sections 3 and 6 has to be so construed differently in relation to the disputed area and the excess area in its vicinity.

57. Acquisition of the adjacent undisputed area belonging to Hindus has been attacked on the ground that it was unnecessary since ownership of the same is undisputed. Reason for acquisition of the larger area adjacent to the disputed area has been indicated. It is, therefore, not unrelated to the resolution of the dis-

pute which is the reason for the entire acquisition. Even though, *prima facie*, the acquisition of the adjacent area in respect of which there is no dispute of title and which belongs to Hindus may appear to be a slant against the Hindus, yet on closer scrutiny it is not so since it is for the larger national purpose of maintaining and promoting communal harmony and in consonance with the creed of secularism. Once it is found that it is permissible to acquire an area in excess of the disputed area alone, adjacent to it, to effectuate the purpose of acquisition of the disputed area and to implement the outcome of the final adjudication between the parties to ensure that in the event of success of the Muslim community in the dispute their success remains meaningful, the extent of adjacent area considered necessary is in the domain of policy and not a matter for judicial scrutiny or a ground for testing the constitutional validity of the enactment, as earlier indicated. However, it is with the caveat of the Central Government's duty to restore it to its owner, as indicated earlier, if it is found later to be unnecessary; and reservation of liberty to the owner to challenge the needless acquisition when the total need has been determined.

58. We find no infirmity in Section 6 also to render it unconstitutional.

59. The status of the Central Government as a result of vesting by virtue of Section 3 of the Act is, therefore, of a statutory receiver in relation to the disputed area, coupled with a duty to manage and administer the disputed area maintaining *status quo* therein till the final outcome of adjudication of the long-standing dispute relating to the disputed structure at Ayodhya. Vesting in the Central Government of the area in excess of the disputed area, is, however, absolute. The meaning of 'vest' has these different shades in Sections 3 and 6 in relation to the two parts of the entire area acquired by the Act.

60. The question now is of the mode of adjudication of the dispute, on the final outcome of which the action contemplated by Section 6(1) of the Act of effecting transfer of the disputed area has to be made by the Central Government.

61. Sub-section (3) of Section 4 provides for abatement of all pending suits and legal proceedings in respect of the right, title and interest relating to any property which has vested in the Central Government under Section 3. The rival claims to the disputed area which were to be adjudicated in the pending suits can no longer be determined therein as a result of the abatement of the suits. This also results in extinction of the several defences raised by the Muslim community including that of adverse possession of the disputed area for over 400 years since construction of the mosque there is AD 1528 by Mir Baqi. Ostensibly, the alternate dispute resolution mechanism adopted is that of a simultaneous Reference made the same day under Article 143(1) of the Constitution to this Court for decision of the question referred. It is clear from the issues framed in those suits that the core question for determination in the suits is not covered by the Reference made, and it also does not include therein the defences raised by the Muslim community. It is also clear that the answer to the question referred, whatever it may be, will not lead to the answer of the core question for determination in the pending suits and it will not, by itself, resolve the long-standing dispute relating to the disputed

area. Reference made under Article 143(1) cannot, therefore, be treated as an effective alternate dispute-resolution mechanism in substitution of the pending suits which are abated by Section 4(3) of the Act. For this reason, it was urged, that the abatement of pending suits amounts to denial of the judicial remedy available to the Muslim community for resolution of the dispute and grant of the relief on that basis in accordance with the scheme of redress under the rule of law envisaged by the Constitution. The validity of sub-section (3) of Section 4 is assailed on this ground.

62. To appreciate the stand of the Central Government on this point, we permitted the learned Solicitor General to make a categorical statement for the Union of India in this behalf. The final statement made by the learned Solicitor General of India in writing dated 14.9.1994 forming a part of the record, almost at the conclusion of the hearing, also does not indicate that the answer to the question referred would itself be decisive of the core question in controversy between to the statement, the Central Government proposes to resort to a process of negotiation between the rival claimants after getting the answer to the question referred, and if the negotiations fail, then to adopt such course as it may find appropriate in the circumstances. There can be no doubt, in these circumstances, that the Special Reference made under Article 143(1) of the Constitution cannot be construed as an effective alternate dispute-resolution mechanism to permit substitution of the pending suits and legal proceedings by the mode adopted of making this Reference. In our opinion, this fact alone is sufficient to invalidate sub-section (3) of Section 4 of the Act. [See *Indira Nehru Gandhi v Raj Narain.*[6]] We accordingly declare sub-section (3) of Section 4 to be unconstitutional. However, sub-section (3) of Section 4 is severable, and, therefore, its invalidity is not an impediment to the remaining statute being upheld as valid.

63. There is no serious challenge to the validity of any other provision of the Act except a feeble attack on Section 8. For Section 8, it was urged, that performance of the exercise of payment of compensation thereunder would be impractical in respect of the property of which ownership is in dispute. This argument itself does not visualize any such difficulty in respect of the remaining undisputed property. In the view we have taken that the vesting in the Central Government by virtue of Section 3 in relation to the disputed area is only as a statutory receiver, and Section 4(3) being declared invalid results in revival of the pending suits and legal proceedings, the application of Section 8 would present no difficulty. Section 8 is meant only for the property acquired absolutely, other than the disputed area, being adjacent to, and in the vicinity of the disputed area. The disputed area being taken over by the Central Government only as a statutory receiver, there is no question of payment of compensation for the same as it is meant to be handed over to the successful party in the suits, in terms of the ultimate judicial verdict of the power under Section 8, by the Central Government is to be made only then in respect of the disputed area, in accordance with the final judicial decision, preserving status quo therein in terms of Section 7(2) till then. No further discussion of this aspect is necessary. . . .

84. The result is that all the pending suits and legal proceedings stand received, and they shall be proceeded with, and decided, in accordance with law. It follows further as a result of the remaining enactment being upheld as valid that the disputed area has vested in the Central Government as a statutory receiver with a duty to manage and administer it in the manner provided in the Act maintaining *status quo* therein by virtue of the freeze exacted in Section 7(2); and the Central Government would exercise its power of vesting that property further in another authority or body or trust in accordance with Section 8(1) of the Act in terms of the final adjudication in the pending suits. The power of the Courts in the pending legal proceedings to give directions to the Central Government as a statutory receiver would be circumscribed and limited to the extent of the area left open by the provisions of the Act. The Central Government would be found to take all necessary steps to implement the decision in the suits and other legal proceedings and to hand over the disputed area to the party found entitled to the same on the final adjudication made in the suits. The parties to the suits could be entitled to amend their pleadings suitably in the light of our decision.

85. Before we end, we would like to indicate the consequence if the entire Act had been held to be invalid and then we had declined to answer the Reference on that conclusion. It would then result in revival of the abated suits along with all the interim orders made therein. It would also then result automatically in revival of the worship of the idols by Hindu devotees, which too has been stopped from December 1992 with all its ramifications without granting any benefit to the Muslim community whose practice of worship in the mosque (demolished on 6.12.1992) had come to a stop, for whatever reason, since at least December 1949. This situation, unless altered subsequently by any Court order in the revived suits, would, therefore, continue during the pendency of the litigation. This result could be no solace to the Muslims whose feelings of hurt as a result of the demolition of mosque must be assuaged in the manner best possible without giving cause for any legitimate grievance to the other community leading to the possibility of reigning communal passions detrimental to the spirit of communal harmony in a secular State.

86. The best solution in the circumstances, on revival of suits is, therefore, to maintain *status quo* as on 7.1.1993 when the law came into force modifying the interim orders in the suits to that extent by curtailing the practice of worship by Hindus in the disputed area to the extent it stands reduced under the Act instead of conferring on them the larger right available under the Court orders till intervention was made by legislation.

87. Section 7(2) achieves this purpose by freezing the interim arrangement for worship by Hindu devotees reduced to this extent and curtails the larger right they enjoyed under the Court orders, ensuring that it cannot be enlarged till final adjudication of the dispute and consequent transfer of the disputed area to the party found entitled to the same. This being the purpose and true effect of Section 7(2), it promotes and strengthens the commitment of the nation to secularism instead of negating it. To hold the provision as anti-secular and slanted in favour

of the Hindu community would be to frustrate an attempt to thwart anti-secularism and unwittingly support the forces which were responsible for the events of 6.12.1992.'

This tortuous reasoning was torn apart in the minority judgement delivered by Justice S.P. Bharucha on behalf of himself and Justice A.M. Ahmadi.

The obligation is cast in regard to the 'management' of the whole bundle of property and rights. This implies that the Central Government or the authorized person is required to continue with the puja that was being performed on the disputed site before 7.1.1993. This is provided for even though, by reason of Section 4(2), the orders of the Court in this behalf cease to have effect.

123. There is no provision in the Act which indicates in clear terms what use the whole bundle of property and rights, including the disputed site, will be put to by the Central Government. An indication in this behalf is provided by Section 6. Section 6 is an enabling provision. By reason of Section 6(1), notwithstanding the vesting in the Central Government of the whole bundle of property and rights, 'the Central Government may, if it is satisfied that any authority or other body or trustees of any trust set up on or after the commencement of this Act is or are willing to comply with such terms and conditions as that Government might think fit to impose direct . . . that the right, title and interest or any of them' in relation to the whole bundle of property or rights or any part thereof, instead of continuing to vest in the Central Government, shall vest in that authority or body or trustees of that trust. Thereupon, by reason of Section 6(2), the rights of the Central Government in the whole bundle of property and rights or such part thereof as has been vested under Section 6(1) shall, on and from the date of such vesting, be deemed to have become the rights of that authority or body or trustees of that trust. In other words, when the vesting takes place in respect of the whole bundle of property and rights or of any part thereof, all the rights of the Central Government in the whole bundle of property and rights or such part thereof as has been vested, shall be deemed to be transferred to the authority or body or trust in which it is vested.

124. The provisions of Section 6 apply to the whole bundle of property and rights; that is to say, they apply also to the disputed site. The disputed site may also be vested in an authority or body or trust that is willing to comply with the terms and conditions that the Central Government might think fit to impose. Those terms and conditions are not specified in the Act, nor is there any indication in that behalf available. The only restriction imposed upon such authority or body or trust, apart from the terms and conditions that the Central Government may think fit to impose, are those provided in Section 7. This is set out in Section 6(3). The provisions of Sections 4, 5 and 11 which are also mentioned in Section 6(3) are provisions that empower and protect the authority or body or trust.

125. Section 7 relates to the management and administration of the whole bundle of property and rights. Section 7(1) states that it shall be managed by the Central Government in this behalf; in other words, the authorized person. Section 7(2) obliges the Central Government or the authorized person, in managing the

whole bundle of property and rights, to ensure that 'the position existing' before the commencement of the Act in the area on which the disputed structure stood 'is maintained'. The Central Government or the authorized person is, therefore, obliged to maintain the 'position' in respect of the disputed site as it was before midnight on the night of 6.1.1993/7.1.1993, and it is required to do so in 'managing' the whole bundle of property and rights. This implies not only that the debris of the demolished structure must be maintained as it stands but also that the idols which had been placed on the disputed site after the demolition had taken place must be retained where they are and the *puja* carried on before them must be continued.

126. Since the Act does not spell out the use to which the whole bundle of property and rights is intended to be put and since the provisions of Section 7 are applicable even to the authority or body or trust in which the Central Government may vest the whole bundle of property and rights or any part thereof under the provisions of Section 6, it is possible to read the provisions of Section 7 as being of a permanent nature. The Act read by itself, therefore, suggests that the idols shall remain on the disputed site for an indefinite period of time and puja shall continue to be performed before them.

127. Section 8 gives to the owner of any land, building, structure or other property which is acquired compensation equivalent to the market value thereof. Claims in that behalf are to be entertained by a Claims Commissioner to be appointed by the Central Government. For the purposes of establishing his claim, the owner would have to establish his title to the property that has been acquired. The suits in then Allahabad High Court which abate by reason of Section 4(3) relate to the title of the disputed site. In other words, the forum for the adjudication of the title to the disputed site is shifted from the Courts to the Claims Commissioner.

128. The above is an analysis of the Act by itself. It is necessary to read it also in the context of its Statement of Objects and Reasons and the Reference.

129. The Statement of Objects and Reasons state that the acquisition of the whole bundle of property and rights is necessary for setting up a planned complex housing 'a Rama temple, a mosque, amenities for pilgrims, a library, museum and other suitable facilities'. The authority or other body or trustees of any trust willing to comply with such terms and conditions as the Central Government may think fit to impose would, under the provisions of Section to be vested with a part of the whole bundle of property and rights to construct and maintain a Rama temple and concomitant amenities. Another authority or body or trust so willing would be vested with another part of the whole bundle of property and rights to construct and maintain a mosque and concomitant facilities. So read, the provisions relating to the management and administration of the whole bundle of property and rights contained in Section 7 are interim provisions, to operate until vesting under Section 6 has taken place.

130. Having regard to the provisions of Section 6, the Statement of Objects and Reasons and the Reference, the acquisition of the disputed site and surrounding land is to hold the same pending the resolution of the dispute regarding the

disputed site. The resolution of the dispute is to take place in the manner stated in the Reference. Upon such resolution the disputed site would be handed over for the construction of a mosque or a Rama temple, as the case may be, and the surrounding area would house a place of worship of the other religion and ancillary facilities for the places of worship of both the Muslim and the Hindu communities. The validity of the provisions of Section 3, by reason of which the whole bundle of property and rights stands transferred to and vests in the Central Government, and, therefore, of the Act itself, depends upon the validity of the provisions that follow it, particularly, Section 4. . . .

132. As the White Paper shows, the demolished structure was built as a mosque in 1528. It was used as a mosque from 1528 until the night of 22.12.1949/ 23.12.1949, when the idols were placed therein. The idols continue is the disputed structure by reason of the orders of the Courts. Under the orders of the Court passed in 1986 public worship of the idols was permitted. This state of affairs continued until 6.12.1992, when the disputed structure was demolished.

133. The effect of Section 4 of the Act is that the Sunni Waqf Board, which administered the mosque that was housed in the disputed structure, and the Muslim community lose their right to plead adverse possession of idols remained in the disputed structure only under the orders of the Courts. Instead of judicial determination of the title to the disputed site on the basis of the law, the disputed site, along with surrounding land, has been acquired and a complex with a mosque and a temple thereon is planned. What is to happen to the disputed site is to depend upon the answer to the question used in the Reference and negotiations based thereon. The question posed in the Reference is: Whether a Hindu temple or any other Hindu religious texture existed prior to the construction of the disputed structure on the disputed site. The learned Solicitor General fairly stated that the Court should read the question as asking whether any Hindu temple or other Hindu religious structure stood on the disputed site immediately before the disputed structure was built thereon. The dispute, it will be remembered, was that a Rama temple had stood on the disputed site and it was demolished to make place for the disputed structure; the question posed, however, is: Was there 'a Hindu temple or any Hindu religious structure' on the disputed site? Secondly, the salient fact as to whether the temple, if any, was demolished to make place for the disputed structure is not to be gone into. The disputes as a title to the disputed site survive for consideration for the purpose of award of compensation. For this purpose title shall have to be established not before a Court of law but before a Claims Commissioner to be appointed by the Central Government, who is entitled to devise his own procedure. No right of appeal or reference to a Civil Court is provided for with the result that the decision of the Claims Commissioner would be final except for a remedy under Articles 226/227 of the Constitution. For the reasons aforesaid, the provisions of Sections 4 and 8 of the Act must be held to be arbitrary and unreasonable.

134. More importantly, the provisions of Section 4 of the Act, in as much as they deprive the Sunni Waqf Board and the Muslim community of the right to

plead and establish adverse possession as aforesaid and restrict the redress of their grievance in respect of the disputed site to the answer to the limited question posed by the Reference and to negotiations subsequent thereto, and the provisions of Section 3 of the Act, which vest the whole bundle of property and rights in the Central Government to achieve this purpose, offend the principle of secularism, which is a part of the basic structure of the Constitution, being slanted in favour of one religious community as against another. . . .

135. That secularism is a part of the basic features of the Constitution was held in *Kesavananda Bharati v. State of Kerala*[5]. It was unanimously confirmed by the nine-Judge Bench of this Court in *S.R. Bommai v. Union of India*[4].

136. The core provisions of the Act are Sections 3, 4 and 8. The other provisions of the Act are only ancillary and incidental to Section 3, 4 and 8. Since the core provisions of Sections 3, 4 and 8 are unconstitutional, the Act itself cannot stand.

137. The provisions of Section 7 are referred to in support of the finding that the Act is skewed to favour one religion against another.

138. The provisions of Section 7(1) empower the Central Government to entrust the management of the acquired area to 'any person or body of persons or trustees of any trust'. Section 7(2) states that 'in managing the property vested in the Central Government under Section 3 the Central Government or the authorized person . . . shall ensure that the position existing before the commencement of this Act in the area on which' the disputed structure 'stood . . . is maintained'. It is relevant to note that 'the position' is required to be maintained in the course of 'managing the property'. Before 'the commencement of this Act' the disputed structure had been demolished, the idols had been placed on the disputed site and *puja* thereof had begun. Section 7(2), thus, perpetuates the performance of *puja* on the disputed site. No account is taken of the fact that the structure thereon had been destroyed in 'a most reprehensible act. The perpetrators of the deed struck not only against a place of worship but at the principles of secularism, democracy and the rule of law' (White Paper, para 1.35). No account is taken of the fact that there is a dispute in respect of the site of which *puja* is to be performed; that, as stated in the White Paper, until the night of 27.12.1949/23.12.1949, when the idols were placed in the disputed structure, the disputed structure was being used as a mosque: and that the Muslim community has a claim to offer *namaz* thereon. . . .

140. The Preamble to the Constitution of India proclaims that India is a secular democratic republic. Article 15 in Part III of the Constitution which provides for fundamental rights, debars the State from discriminating against any citizens on the ground of religion. Secularism is given pride of place in the Constitution. The object is to preserve and protect all religions, to place all religious communities on a par. When, therefore, adherents of the religion of the majority of Indian citizens make a claim upon and assail the place of worship of another religion and, by dint of numbers, create conditions that are conducive to public disorder, it is the constitutional obligation of the State to protect that place of worship and to

preserve public order, using for the purpose such means and forces of law and order as are required. It is impermissible under the provisions of the Constitution for the State to acquire that place of worship to preserve public order. To condone the acquisition of a place of worship in such circumstances is to efface the principle of secularism from the Constitution.

141. We must add a caveat. If the title to the place of worship is in dispute in a Court of law and public order is jeopardized, two courses are open to the Central Government. It may apply to the Court concerned to be appointed Receiver of the place of worship, to hold it secure pending the final adjudication of its title, or it may enact legislation that makes it statutory Receiver of the place of worship pending the adjudication of its title by the Court concerned. In either event, the Central Government would bind itself to hand over the place of worship to the party in whose favour its title is found. . . .

149. The Act and the Reference, as stated hereinabove, favour one religious community and disfavour another; the purpose of the Reference is therefore, opposed to secularism and is unconstitutional. Besides, the Reference does not serve a constitutional purpose.

150. Secondly, the fifth recital to the Reference states that '*the Central Government proposes to settle the said dispute* after obtaining the opinion of the Supreme Court of India and *in terms of the said opinion*' (emphasis supplied). It is clear that the Central Government does not propose to settle the dispute in terms of the Court's opinion. It proposes to use the Court's opinion as a springboard for negotiations. Resolution of the dispute as a result of such negotiations cannot be said to be a resolution of the dispute 'in terms of the said opinion'. Asked to obtain instructions and tell the Court that the mosque would be rebuilt if the question posed by the Reference was answered in the negative, the learned Solicitor General made the statement quoted above. It leaves us in no doubt that even in the circumstance that this Court opines that no Hindu temple or Hindu religious structure existed on the disputed site before the disputed structure was built thereon, there is no certainty that the mosque will be rebuilt.

151. Thirdly, there is the aspect of evidence in relation to the question referred. It is not our suggestion that a Court of law is not competent to decide such a question. It can be done if expert evidence of archeologists and historians is led, and is tested in cross-examination. The principal protagonists of the two stands are not appearing in the Reference; they will neither lead evidence nor cross-examine. The learned Solicitor General stated that the Central Government would lead no evidence, but it would place before the Court the material that it had collected from the two sides during the course of earlier negotiations. The Court being ill-equipped to examine and evaluate such material, it would have to appoint experts in the field to do so, and their evaluation would go unchallenged. Apart from the inherent advisability of rendering a judicial opinion on such evaluation, the opinion would be liable to the criticism of one or both sides that it was rendered without hearing them or their evidence. This would ordinarily be of no significance for they had chosen to stay away, but this opinion is intended

to create a public climate for negotiations and the criticism would find the public ear, to say nothing of the fact that it would impair this Court's credibility. Ayodhya is a storm that will pass. The dignity and honour of the Supreme Court cannot be compromised because of it.

[Dr M. Ismail Faruqui and others *versus* Union of India and others (1994) 6 Supreme Court Cases 360.]

9. Soli Sorabjee's comment on the majority ruling

The majority judgement overlooks that the reason why the worship in the mosque had come to a standstill was the surreptitious entry into the mosque and the placing of idols there in a clandestine manner. Indeed that was the unequivocal admission of the State of U.P. in its written statement solemnly affirmed in the suit.

The real issue was not whether Hindus are offering worship in a reduced form but whether worship and *puja* of idols by one community should at all be permitted after the dastardly act of destruction, and for which in the ringing words of the majority 'the Hindu community must, therefore, bear the cross on its chest for the misdeed of the miscreants reasonably suspected to belong to their religious folds'.

The distressing part is that the majority judgement countenances a situation which was the outcome of an act of national shame. The minority community is understandably disappointed with the majority judgement.

[From *Minorities: National and International Protection*, Soli Sorabjee, Minorities Council of India, New Delhi, 1995, pp. 11–12].

10. Salient Points Regarding the Acquired Land at Ayodhya: A Local Muslim perspective by Khaliq Ahmad Khan, Convenor, Helal Committee

The Acquired Land at Ayodhya
(As per Ordinance 67.7 acres of land, as per Act 71.36 acres of land was acquired)

Salient Points regarding the Acquired Land

1. Vishwa Hindu Parishad (VHP) has no legal rights over acquired land.
2. Right, title and interest of the acquired land vest in the Central Government at present, vide Section 3 of the Acquisition Act 1993 (No 33 of 1993).
3. Apart from disputed plots, other Waqf properties comprising of mosques, graveyards, dargahs etc. are situated within acquired land. These are undisputed properties and Hindus have no claim over these properties.

4. Properties of several non-VHP trusts also exist in the acquired land that do not come under the VHP umbrella.

5. About 42.094 acres of land, acquired for Rama Katha Park is non-transferable to 'Sri Ramjanmabhumi Nyas' as per section 6 (1) of the Act 1993.

6. 2.7744 acres land acquired by the U.P. Government, 1991, under notification, does not have any legal value as it was quashed by Hon'ble High Court, Allahabad, Lucknow Bench on 11 December 1992.

The Acquisition of Land

The Acquisition of Certain Area at Ayodhya Ordinance, 1993 (No 8 of 1993), was promulgated by the President of India on 7 January 1993, covering 67.7 acres of land.

This ordinance was replaced by another 'The Acquisition of Certain Area at Ayodhya Act, 1993 (No 33 of 1993), 3rd April 1993'. This Act now covers 71.36 acres of land.

The Details of Plots Under Acquisition:

The acquired area encompasses 189 revenue plots spread over three localities:

1. Village Kot Ramchandar, Pargana Haveli Avadh, Tehsil Faizabad Sadar, District Faizabad, Uttar Pradesh	82 revenue plots	143 to 147, 158–162, (Babri Mosque was on Plot No: 159–160 and Nazul plot 583) 168–200, 204 to 239, 242, 244–246
2. Village Avadh Khas, Pargana Haveli Avadh, Tehsil Faizabad Sadar, District Faizabad, Uttar Pradesh	87 revenue plots	1104–1130, 1132–1136, 1143–1149, 1164–1206, 1210–1223, 1225–1243 and 1247–1259 1–19 and 27
3. Jalwanpur, Pargana Haveli Avadh, Tehsil Faizabad Sadar, District Faizabad, Uttar Pradesh	20 revenue plots	

Claims and Counter Claims Over The Acquired Land:

A. Muslim's Claim

i. Disputed Plots in Suit No 4 of 1989 (Regular Suit No 12 of 1961 of Sunni Central Waqf Board). Revenue Plots: 147, 159–160 (Plots over which Babri Mosque was situated), 162, 168, 169, 170, 172, 194, 197, 198 and 199
5 mosques (Babri and 4 Qanati mosques), and 13 grave yards existed in these plots.

ii. Undisputed Plots within acquired land

Kot Ramchandar	83*, 84*, 122B*, 147B*, 161, 171, 173, 174 and 177 (All plots are graveyards)
Avadh Khas	1130 (Dargah), 1136 (grave *pucca*), 1205* (graveyard)

*At the site these plots have been included in the acquired land, although these are not in the acquisition Act.

Source: 'The Acquisition of certain area at Ayodhya Act, 1993'.

B. Non-VHP temple trusts in the acquired land that do not come under the VHP umbrella:

a. Sita *Rasoi*, Janmasthan Mandir
b. Sakshi Gopal Mandir
c. Manas Bhawan (Secretary Radhey Shyam Agarwal, who has received compensation from Central Government)
d. Ram Khazana
e. Kohbar Bhawan
f. Anand Bhawan Mandir
g. Vishwamitra Ashram
h. Vatsalyakunj

C. Ram Katha Park, Encompasses 144 Plots (Revenue and Nazul Plots) 42.094 Acres of Land.

About 42.094 acres of land adjacent to disputed site was acquired in the mid-1980s, by Sripati Misra government for developing a Rama Katha Park.

The same was leased on a token amount of Re 1 per annum to the 'Sri Ramjanmabhumi Nyas' by an obliging Kalyan Singh, BJP Chief Minister of Uttar Pradesh, on 20 March 1992, for development of Rama Katha Park as per U.P. Government Scheme to provide amenities to tourists and promote tourism.

The land allotted to Rama Katha Park was in diverse plot locations (map attached), not meant for construction of Rama temple. The purpose was specifically mentioned as providing amenities to tourists and promoting tourism.

1. Details of Plots of 'Rama Katha Park'

Locality	*Plot Nos*	*Total plots*	*Area in acres*
Jalwanpur	1–15, 17–19, and 27	19	5.531
	16	1	0.273
Kot Ramchandar	173, 175, 176 (B), 191–93, 200, 206, 210, 212 (A), 212 (B) to 217, 219, 221, 221 (B), 226 to 230, 232–39	32	11.006
	188, 211 and 199	3	1.462
	180–83, 185, 186	6	1.728
Awadh Khas	1104, 1107, 1117, 1126, 1128 1133, 1134, 1136	8	2.179

Contd/-

Locality	*Plot Nos*	*Total plots*	*Area in acres*
	1219 to 1223, 1225–28, 1230, 1231, 1233, 1234, 1237 and 1239	15	2.993
	1135 and 1229	2	0.062
	569, 570, 668, 1107, 1110, 1114, 1116, 1117, 1124 to 1129, 1140 and 1141	16	
	494–98, 518, 519, 521, 545–51, 569, 570, 571, 573 and 574	22	
Kot Ram Chandar	221, 222, 227, 229, 590, 602, 604, 622, 628, 652, 661, 662, 663, 664, 666, 669, 683, 684, 687 & 689	20	16.86
	Total	144	42.094

Source: Details are taken from original lease papers.

2. Details Plots in the Rama Katha Park

The 42.094 acres of land encompasses some graveyards that were acquired against the Waqf Act 1995 (No. 43 of 1995).

List of Disputed Plots

Plots listed as . .	*Revenue Plot Nos*
Graveyard	173
Graveyard	194*
Graveyard	199*
Graveyard	1136

*Already claimed by Sunni Central Waqf Board in its regular suit.

D. Claim forwarded by VHP of undisputed plots within the acquired land:

S.No	*Undisputed Plot Nos within the acquired land as per VHP's claim*	*Total Plots*	*The fact as per government records*
1	171–78 180–90 VHP list claim these plots as Nazul plots	17	No such Nazul Plot numbers exist in the acquired area. If the numbers are assumed to belong to Revenue Plot numbering system, then most of these plots are disputed. 172 (Graveyard), 173 (Graveyard + RKP); 171, 174, 177, 178, 187–90 (not acquired for RKP); 175, 176, 180–86 (acquired for RKP)
2.	1334, 1335, 1338, 1339–42, 1344–46, 1376–81, 1386–88, 1349, 1390 94, 1396–98	28	No such Nazul Plot numbers exist in the acquired area. If the numbers are assumed to belong to Revenue Plot numbering system, then these

Contd/-

S.No	Undisputed Plot Nos within the acquired land as per VHP's claim	Total Plots	The fact as per government records
			plots exist outside the acquired area.
3.	Chak No. 1 and Chak No. 3 Plot Nos: 159, 160, 161, 169 and 170	5	Plot Nos 159, 160 encompass Babri mosque; 161-Manas Bhawan, now Central government property; 169–70 are graveyards claimed by Sunni Central Waqf Board.
4.	Chak No. 3 Plot Nos: 162 to 168	7	Plot Nos 162 and 168 are disputed plots; Plot Nos 163 to 167 are outside but adjacent to the acquired land.
5.	VHP list also includes some houses claimed as undisputed property within the acquired land: House Nos: 20/1/2; 20/1/6; 20/1/80; 17/3/3; 17/3/5; 17/3/6; 20/2/9		Municipal Board House numbers mentioned are about 1.5 km from the disputed site, and are outside the acquired land. They are situated at Thakur Rama Janki Jiwan Mandir, Gola Ghat, Ayodhya City

E. Acquisition of 2.77 acres land by the U.P. Government

The acquisition was done through Notification No. 3814/41-33/86 7 October 1991, followed by Notification No 3838/41-33/86, Lucknow, dated 10 October 1991.

Later, on 11 December 1992, deciding on Writ Petition No. 3541 (MB) of 1991, along with other Writ Petitions, Honorable High Court (Lucknow Bench) quashed the impugned Notifications.

The purpose of the said acquisition as per notifications was to provide amenities to pilgrims and drinking water, and for promotion of tourism, but the State Government of Uttar Pradesh, against apex court order, built cement concrete platform on the disputed plots. The Apex Court convicted the Chief Minister of BJP State Government, for contempt of Court, for his role in building the permanent structure (raised platform) at the disputed site opposite Babri Mosque (AIR 1995, SC 548, Mohd Aslam *versus* Union of India, Contempt Petition No-97 of 1992).

The said acquisition encompasses:

S.No.	Revenue Plot Nos	Area in Acres
1.	159 (Part)	0.3600
2.	160 (Part)	1.0706
3.	171 (Part)	0.4375
4.	172 (Part)	0.8063
	Total	**2.7744**

The transfer of land to Sri Ramjanmabhumi Nyas or VHP: disputed–undisputed or land of Rama Katha Park—Some legal aspects:

1. As per Section 6 (1) of the Acquisition of Central Area at Ayodhya Act 1993 (No 33 of 1993), after the matter is decided, the Central Government can transfer the surplus land to any authority, or other body or trustee of any trust set up on or after the commencement of this act.

Since the Sri Ramjanmabhumi Nyas and VHP both were established prior to the commencement of this act, the land cannot be transferred to them under the act.

2. The Rama Katha Park Land was acquired for promotion of tourism and development of 'Rama Katha Park' as per Uttar Pradesh Government Scheme.

Thus it cannot be transferred to 'Sri Ramjanmabhumi Nyas' or any other trust for constructing a 'Rama temple' over this land, against the acquisition act.

3. As per apex court's decision 1994, paras 52, 53 and para 60, regarding the acquired land, the undisputed land or adjacent excess land cannot be given to any one till the matter is sub-judice.

The justification given for acquisition of larger area including the property respecting which title is not disputed is that the same is necessary to ensure that the final outcome of adjudication should not be rendered meaningless by the existence of properties belonging to Hindus in the vicinity of the disputed structure.

Para-52, AIR 1995 SC 605

So under present circumstances full or any part of acquired land cannot be given to any one till the matter is sub-judice.

4. Adjacent to disputed site about 5.75 acres of land is Waqf property. (Kanati mosques, graveyards, graves etc.)

According to Waqf Act, 1995 (No. 43 of 1995), Section 51, alienation of Waqf property without sanction of Board is to be considered void.

Hence Waqf property cannot be transferred to 'Nyas' for Rama temple construction.

5. The acquired land comprises several undisputed temple trust properties that do not come under the VHP umbrella. The owner/controller of these temple trusts are fiercely against the VHP control.

a. Panch Ramanandi Nirmohi Akhara, Ayodhya, Faizabad, U.P., which is an actual party to the title suit of the disputed land (VHP or RJN is not a party to the suit), has challenged the *locus standi* of the RJN in a court case pending since 1.10.1993.
   Ref: Suit No. 386/93, in the Court of Civil Judge (Junior Divisions).
b. Another case which is against the temple demolition activity of RJN is also pending in the court.
   Ref: Ram Gopal Das *versus* Ashok Singhal, Suit No. 426/89 filed on date 1.11.1989, in the Court of Civil Judge (Senior Division).

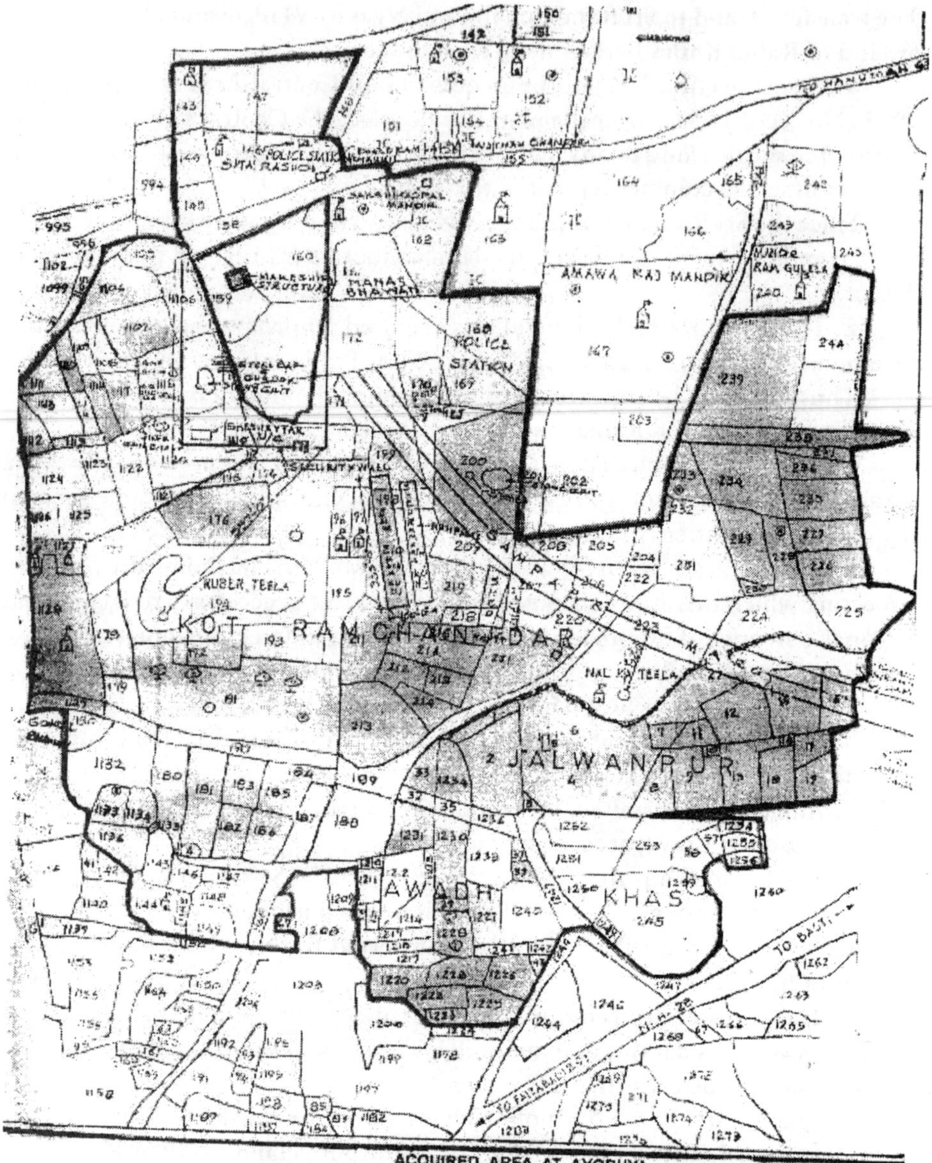

ACQUIRED AREA AT AYODHYA

(UNDER THE ACQUISITION OF CERTAIN AREA AT AYODHYA ACT, 1993 SHOWING REVENUE PLOTS)

ACQUIRED AREA

DISPUTED SITE

Plots were given to Ram Janam Bhoomi Nyas, on lease, for development of 'Ram Katha Park' (not for Ram Temple Construction) on 20 March 1992, by the State Government Uttar Pradesh

Plots claimed by Sunni Central Waqf Board, Suit No. 4 of 1989, (Regular Suit No. 12 of 1961).

2.7744 Acres Land Acquired by the U.P. Government. Notification No. 3814/41-33/86, Oct. 7, 1991. Followed by Notification No. 3838/41-33/86 Dt. Lucknow, October 10, 1991. Hon'ble High Court Quashed the Impugned Notifications. Decided on December 11 1992, Writ Petition No. 3541 (MB) of 1991. Alongwith Other Writ Petitions

Facts regarding Babri Masjid and adjacent Waqf properties

Our case regarding Babri Masjid, does not cover a single plot measuring 80' by 40' only, as popularly propagated by VHP. Our claim based on Court records, Nazul records and the Revenue Records, encompasses apart from the Babri Mosque, four more Qanati mosques, thirteen graveyards and an important dargah of Khwaja Hatti Ki Mazar, covering a total area of about 5.75 acres of land.

Facts regarding Babri Masjid and adjacent Waqf properties.

- Article 142 of the Indian Constitution Act, provides a maximum of twelve years period to file suit from the date of dispossession or discontinuance from a property.
- The only suit by Muslims in the 'Babri Masjid' case of Ayodhya, was filed just for days before the expiry of the twelve years stipulated period of dispossession from the mosque.
- This particular suit (Suit No. 12 of 1961, 18 December 1961), filed in the nick of time by Sunni Central Board of Waqfs and others, against Gopal Singh Visharad and others, is now being treated as the main representative suit for and on behalf of the Muslim Community.
- The relief in the instant suit is for declaration by court that 'the property in dispute, delineated in the site plan annexed to the plaint, is Babri Masjid and Muslim graveyards'. The additional relief sought from the court is for the delivery of possession, by the removal of the idols and other articles of worship.

The government connection

In 1991 State Government of Uttar Pradesh acquired 2.7744 acre land for the purpose of providing facilities to the pilgrims. This area had covered part of Plot Nos 159, 160, 171 and 172. These plots had excluded the area of the inner courtyard and the Babri Mosque, but had encompassed the land around it, including adjacent Muslim graveyards, all Waqfs property. After acquiring the land, the State Government in collaboration with VHP saints demolished the temples within this area and raised a cemented platform in front of the Babri Masjid.

The acquired land was declared illegal and void on 11 December 1992, by the Allahabad High Court.

The Allahabad High Court has now to decide four separate cases with claims on the Babri Masjid by different Hindu parties, and one representative suit by Sunni Central Waqf Board. Thus a total of five cases have to be decided for a final decision on this dispute.

The point to be emphasized here is that our case does not cover the Babri Masjid dispute only, covering a single plot measuring 80' by 40' as popularly propagated by VHP and believed by our average Hindu brothers.

The Court records, Nazul records and the Revenue Records tell us that the acquired area in Ayodhya encompasses apart from the Babri Mosque four more mosques (Kanati and others), thirteen graveyards and an important dargah of

Khwaja Hatti Ki Mazar, covering a total area of 5.75 acres of land.

The Sunni Central Board of Waqfs has in fact claims over twenty-three Nazul plots, situated in village Kot Ramchandra, Pargana Haveli Avadh, Tehsil Faizabad Sadar, District Faizabad.

The nos of these plots are: 238, 579, 580, 581, 582, 583, 584, 585, 586, 587, 588, 590, 593, 594, 595, 603, 606, 607, 610, 619, 620, 621, 628.

These Nazul plots overlap twelve Revenue plots as Revenue plots encompass a slightly larger area than Nazul plots. Serial No of these Revenue plots are: 147, 159, 160, 162, 168, 169, 170, 172, 194, 197, 198, 199.

According to Records:

- Babri Masjid existed at Plot No. 583.
- Four other mosques, including well-known Qanati Masjid, existed on Plot Nos 580, 590, 593 and 595.
- Thirteen Muslim graveyards owned by Waqfs existed on Nazul plots 580, 581, 582, 588, 590, 593, 194, 195, 606, 607, 610, 619, 620.
- Apart from these mosques and graveyards, other plots owned by Waqf Board are 'Waqf Ahade Shahi' Plot No. 586 (where *Shilanyas* was done) and Plot No. 628 which contains Khwaja hatti ki Mazar. This area has been renamed by the government as 'Kuber ka teela'.

Other non-VHP Temple Trusts in the acquired land

1. Sita *Rasoi* Janmasthan Mandir,
   Under the management of
   a. Sukhram Das
   b. Avadh Kishore Das
   c. Ram Shanker Das
2. Sakshi Gopal Mandir
   Under the management of
   Ram Kripal Das
3. Manas Bhawan Trust
   Secretary Radhey Shyam Agarwal
   (Compensation received from government)
4. Ram Khazana
   Lakshmi Niwas Mandir
   Prop: Shyam Bahadur Singh
5. Kohbar Bhawan
   Ram Janki mandir
   Owner: Rudra Pratap Singh
6. Anand Bhawan Mandir
   Owner: Ramanand Saran
7. Vishwamitra Ashram
   Owner: Ramsaran Das Ramaini
8. Vatsalya Kunj
   Yugal Kishore Pandey

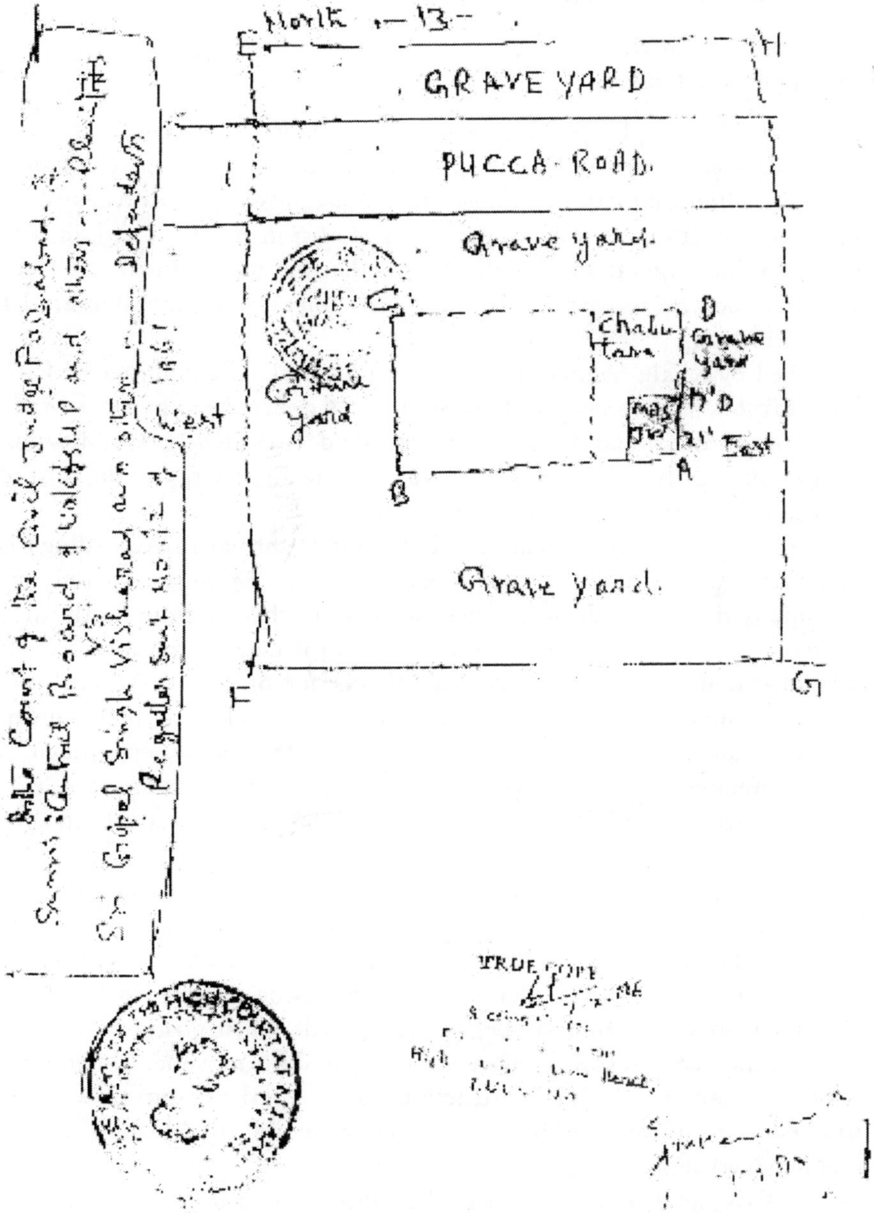
North
GRAVE YARD
PUCCA ROAD
Grave yard
West
Grave yard
TRUE COPY

Muslim Leaders cite Government Records to Back Claim

Babri had four satellite mosques
by Ambikanand Sahay

Ayodhya: The complicated Ramjanmabhumi–Babri Masjid legal battle has now taken a dramatic turn with a group of Muslim leaders, who have dug deep into tonnes of official papers, including rare manuscripts and court records, to come out with a startling revelation: the disputed area in Ayodhya had, in fact, four more mosques other than the Babri Masjid that was pulled down on 6 December 1992. Besides, there are thirteen graveyards and an important dargah, Khwaja Hatti Ki Mazar.

Led by Khaliq Ahmad Khan, convenor of Helal committee of Faizabad, these Muslim leaders say they have scrutinized government papers stored in the office of sub-divisional magistrate of Faizabad Sadar. Khan says Muslims were far too busy with Babri Masjid to find the time and energy to dig into official records all these years since the demolition.

He now wants to present the whole truth to the world. According to Khan and his associates, Babri Masjid on Nazul plot No. 583 is not the only place of worship that is under dispute. There were four other mosques in the area that were acquired by the State Government under the Land Acquisition Act in 1991 and the Union Government under the 'Acquisition of Certain Areas at Ayodhya Act' on 7 January 1993. These were all Kanati mosques. Kanats, better understood by tentwallahs, are pieces of thick, tough fabric used for making open air enclosures during ceremonies. Maybe that's why many people were not aware of the existence of these mosques. Nazul plot Nos 580, 590, 593 and 595 have been shown as mosques as per records.

The papers are now being sent to the All India Babri Masjid Action Committee. Chances are that these papers will be filed in court as further submission in the regular suit No. 12 of the Sunni Central Waqf Board, 1961.

What is significant is that far from preparing to negotiate with Vishwa Hindu Parishad, Muslims are beginning to harden their posture. They say they will win their case in Court and will then rebuild the mosque. Already, they are looking for land for storing construction material. If that happens, Ayodhya will have two busy camps—VHP's Karsewakpuram and 'the Muslims' mosque rebuilding workshop.

A five-member sub-committee has already been formed under BMAC in Faizabad to prepare for rebuilding the mosque. Mohammad Hashim Ansari, the only surviving plaintiff of the original suit, says money will pour in from all over the world. Haji Mehboob, joint convener of the BMAC unit in Faizabad, says the plan to rebuild the mosque is a direct consequence of VHP's temple building activity.

No mosque, no graveyard: VHP

New Delhi: VHP senior vice-president Acharya Giriraj Kishore has disputed the claims of Khaliq Ahmed Khan, convenor of Helal Committee of Faizabad. There were no mosques other than Babri Masjid at the disputed site, he said on Monday evening.

'These are wrong claims to create unnecessary controversy. Government records will prove that in 1992 when the structure was pulled down, there was only one so-called Babri Mosque. Even this was not a mosque because worship of Rama Lalla was going on unabated at the site since 1949 under a High Court order', he said.

Kishore claimed no trace of any graveyard was found when Babri Masjid was demolished.

'We have been visiting the site since 1983, we never saw any temporary structure or Kanati mosque there. We saw only this so-called Babri mosque', Kishore claimed.

[From *The Times of India*, 13 March 2001.]

Disputed Plots in suit No. 4 of 1989 (Regular suit No. 12 of 1961 of Sunni Central Waqf Borad

Name of Village	S. No.	Nazul Plot Nos	Description	Disputed Nazul Plots — Area: Bigha	Biswa	Biswansi	Kuch	Corresponding Revenue Plots — Revenue Plot Nos	Description	Area: Bigha	Biswa	Biswansi	Kuch.
Kotram	1	238	passage	...	...	...	...	147	Graveyard	05	08	00	00
Chandra	2	579	population	...	11	10	...	160	...	03	11	04	06
Pragna Haveli Avadh	3	580	Waqf (graveyard+ mosque	...	03	16	16	160	...	...	...	...	...
Tehsil Faizabad	4.	581	Passage (graveyard)	...	01	06	17	160	...	...	...	...	...
Sadar	5.	582	Waqf Ahad Shahi (graveyard)	...	05	15	14	160	...	...	...	...	...
District-Faizabad	6.	583	Waqf Ahad Shahi (Babri Mosque)	...	09	15	04	159 160	... ...	00 ...	13 ...	00 ...	00 ..
Uttar Pradesh	7.	584	vacant land	...	01	05	12	160	...	...	...	...	...
India	8.	585	passage	...	00	11	00	160	...	...	...	...	...
	9.	586	Waqf Ahad Shahi (*Shilanyas* site)	...	11	16	16	160	...	...	...	...	...
	10.	587	*pakka* wall, platform	...	01	06	16	160	...	...	...	...	...
	11.	588	Waqf Ahad Shahi (graveyard)	...	06	13	10	160 172	... graveyard	... 02	... 07	... 00	... 00
	12.	590	Waqf (graveyard+mosque)	...	14	07	07	172	...	...	...	...	...

Ahad Shah

Name of Village	S. No.	Nazul Plot Nos	Description	Disputed Nazul Plots: Area Bigha	Biswa	Biswansi	Kuch	Revenue Plot Nos	Corresponding Revenue Plots: Description	Area Bigha	Biswa	Biswansi	Kuch.
	13.	593	Waqf Ahad Shahi (graveyard+mosque)	2	05	15	04	169	graveyard	01	07	00	00
								170	graveyard	00	08	00	...
	14.	594	vacant land (graveyard)	00	06	12	00	162	...	01	08	00	00
	15.	595	Waqf Ahad Shahi (graveyard+mosque)	01	06	00	00	168	graveyard	00	08	00	...
	16.	603	vacant land	...	02	02	03	197	...	00	05	00	...
	17.	606	Waqf Ahad Shahi (graveyard)	...	...	19	17	198	...	00	03	00	00
	18.	607	Waqf Ahad Shahi (graveyard)	...	00	14	14	199	...	00	12	00	00
	19.	610	Waqf Ahad Shahi *pakka* (graveyard)	...	03	17	00	199	...	...	...	...	...
	20.	619	Waqf Ahad Shahi (graveyard)	...	07	00	00	194	graveyard	04	19	00	00
	21.	620	Waqf Ahad Shahi (graveyard)	...	03	12	00	197	...	00	05	00	00
	22.	621	vacant land	...	03	10	04	172	graveyard	02	07	00	00
	23.	628	Waqf Ahad Shahi (vacant)	01	10	08	00	194	graveyard	04	19	00	00

No. of Mosque - 5
No. of Graveyards - 13
Plot No 628 which contains Khwaja hatti ki Mazar. This area has been renamed by the government as 'Kuber ka teela'.

Undisputed Muslim Graveyards and other religious places of Muslims within acquired land-Ayodhya

Name of Village	*Revenue Plot Nos.*	*Description*	*Area*			
			Bigha	*Biswa*	*Biswansi*	*Kuch.*
Kotram Chandra	83*	graveyard	0	2	0	0
Pragna Haveli Avadh	84*	graveyard	0	2	0	0
Tahsil Faizabad Sadar	122 B*	graveyard	0	14	15	0
District-Faizabad	147*	graveyard	2	14	0	0
Uttar Pradesh	161	graveyard	0	18	0	0
India	171	graveyard	1	07	0	0
	173	graveyard	0	18	0	0
	174	graveyard	0	3	0	0
	177	graveyard	0	16	0	0
AVADH KHAS						
Pragna Haveli Avadh	1130	dargah	0	05	0	0
Tehsil Faizabad Sadar	1136	grave *pakka*	0	09	0	0
District-Faizabad	1205*	graveyard				
Uttar Pradesh						
India						

*Not acquired in the act but at the site acquired.

DISPUTED NAZUL PLOTS

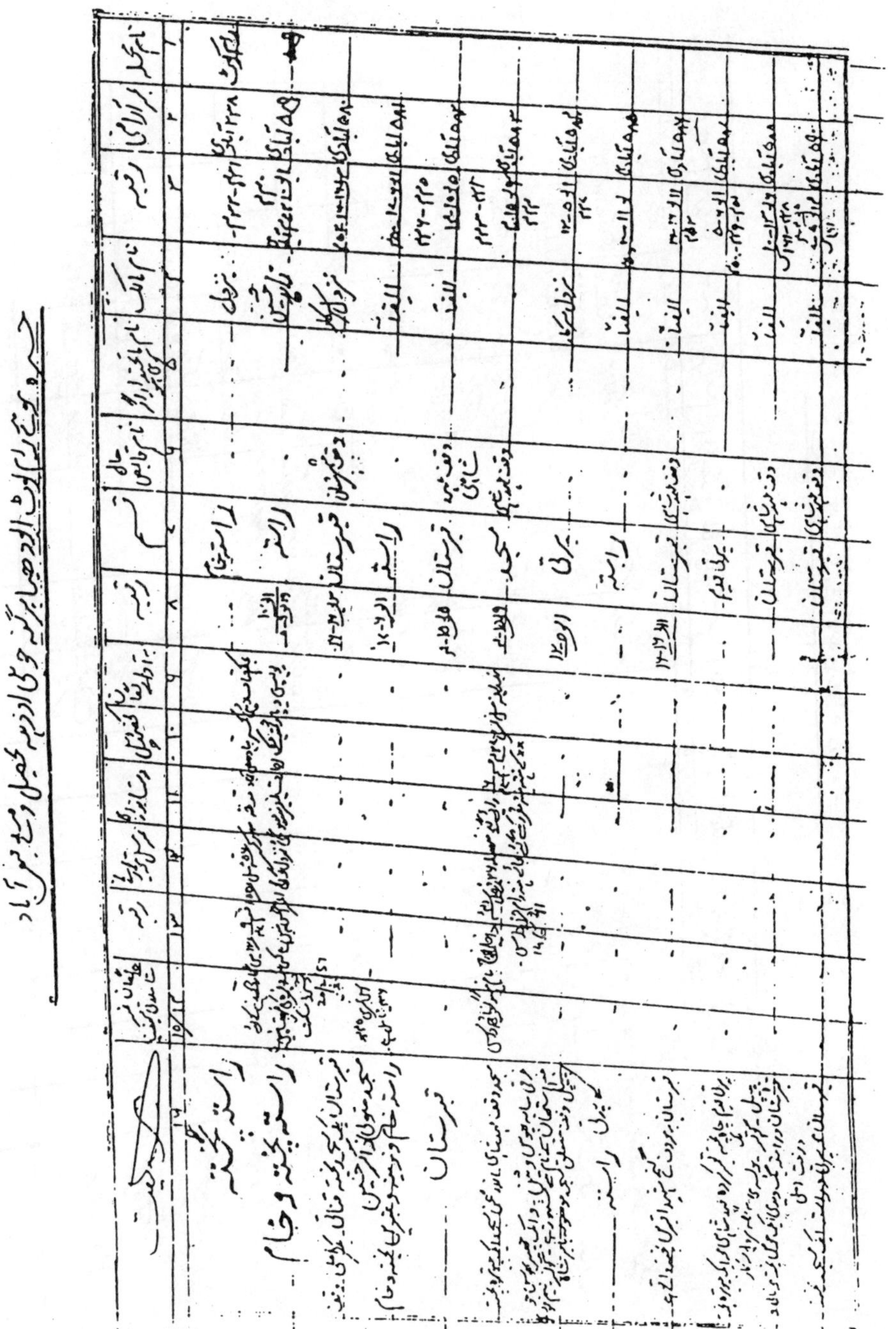

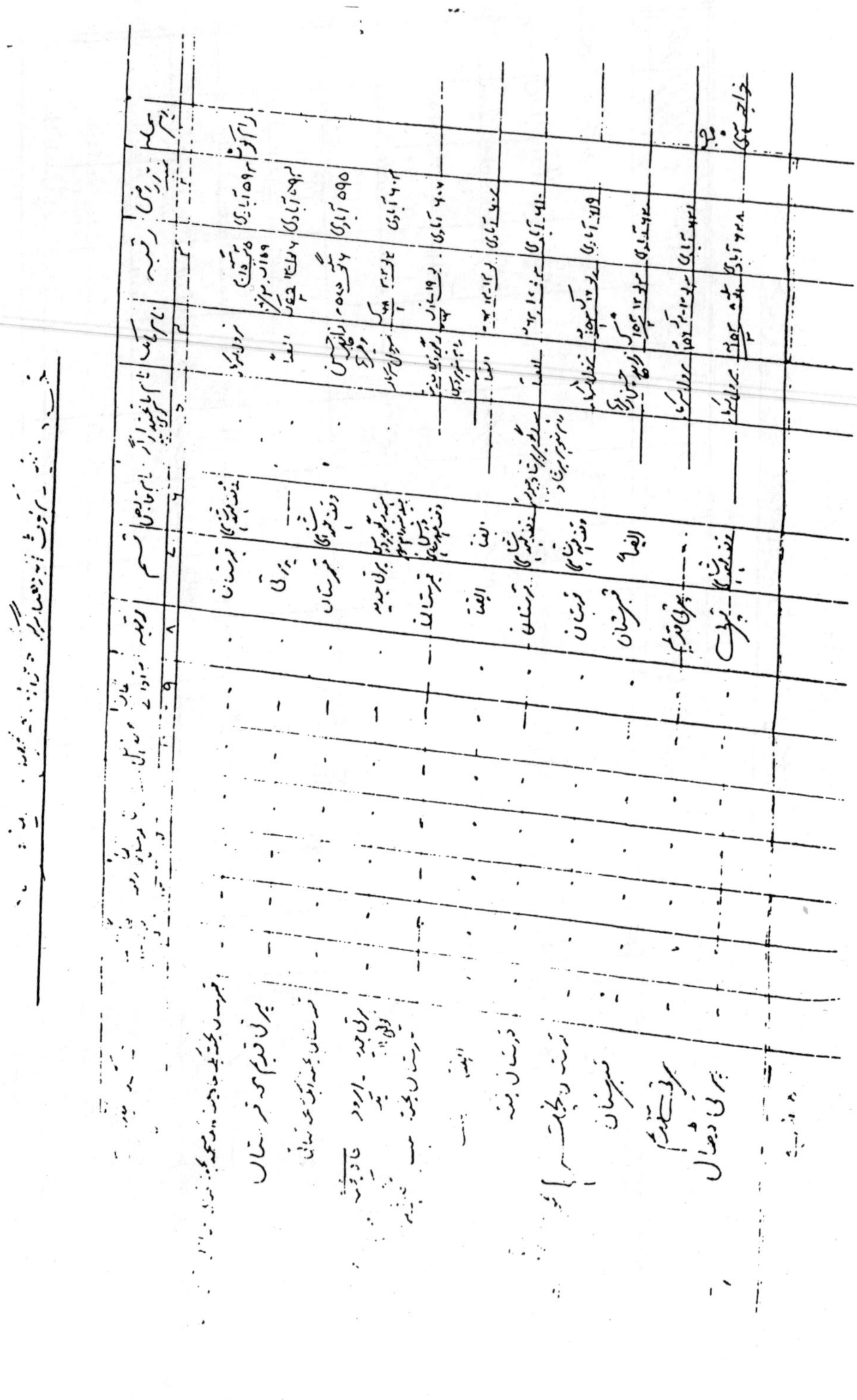

NAZUL PLOTS
BABRI MOSQUE, NAZUL PLOT NO. 583
RAM CHABOOTRA
NAZUL PLOTS CLAIMED BY SUNNI CENTRAL WAQF BOARD, SUIT NO. 4 of 1989, (Regular Suit No. 12 of 1961).

REVENUE PLOTS CORRESPONDING TO NAZUL PLOTS CLAIMED BY SUNNI CENTRAL WAQF BOARD.

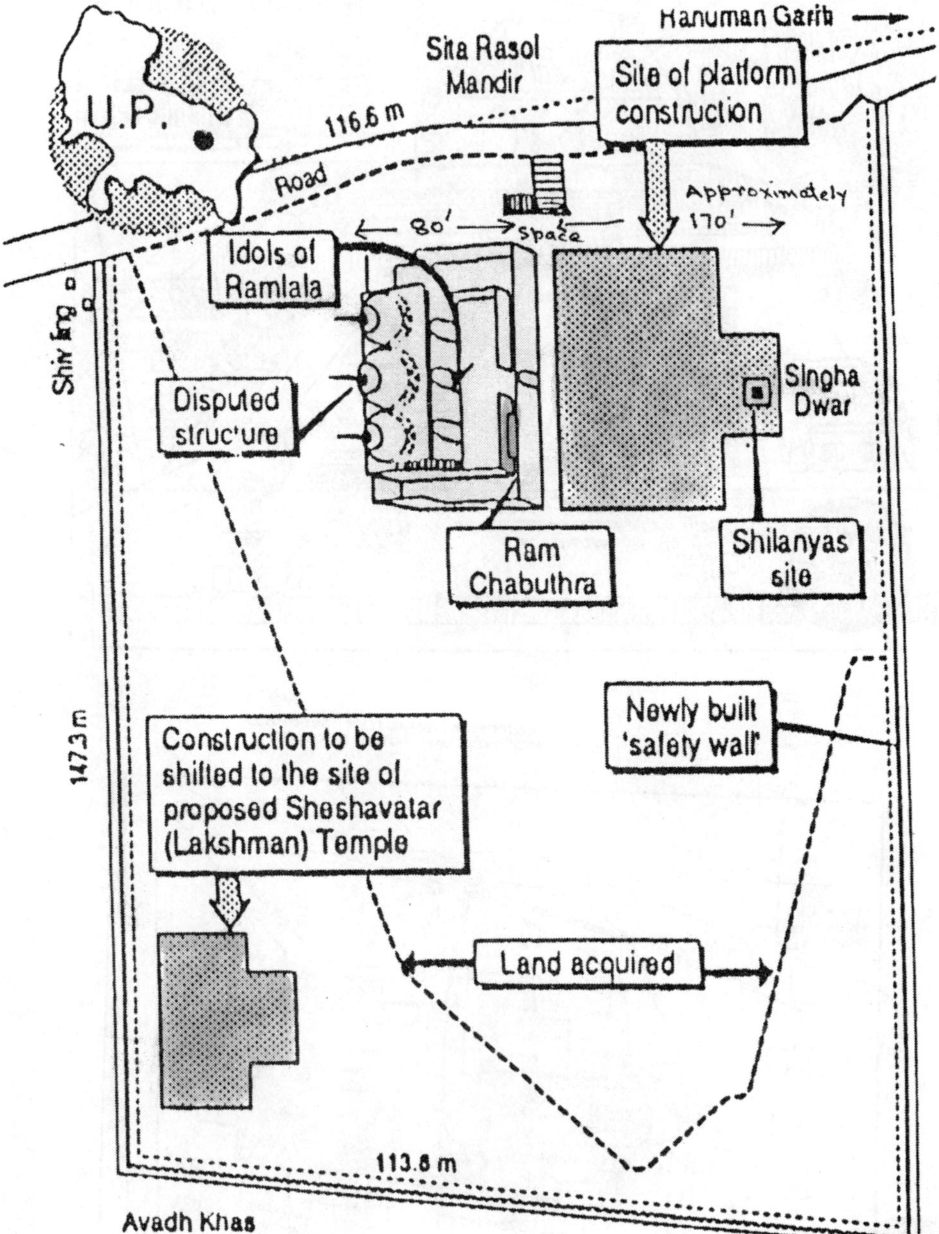
Hanuman Garh
Sita Rasol Mandir
Site of platform construction
U.P.
116.6 m
Road
Approximately 170'
80'
space
Idols of Ramlala
Shiv ling
Disputed structure
Singha Dwar
Ram Chabuthra
Shilanyas site
Newly built 'safety wall'
147.3 m
Construction to be shifted to the site of proposed Sheshavatar (Lakshman) Temple
Land acquired
113.8 m
Avadh Khas

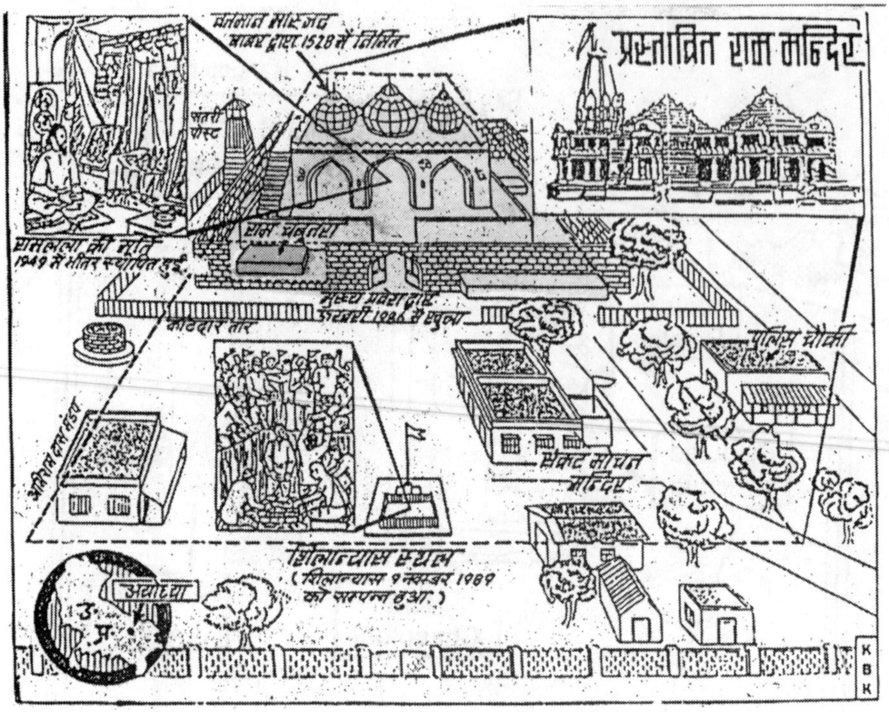

ACTUAL SITE PLAN OF PROPOSED RAM TEMPLE ON DISPUTED SITE COVERING ENTIRE BABRI MOSQUE AT AYODHYA

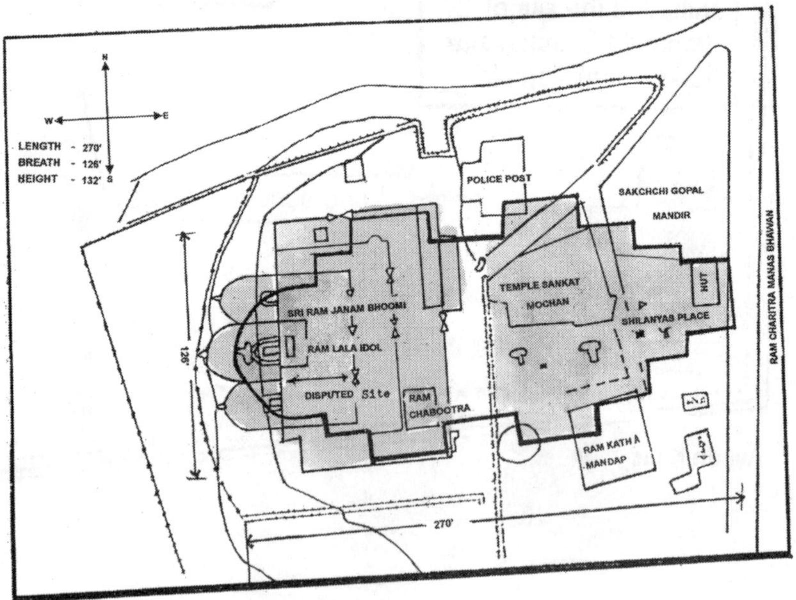

BABRI MOSQUIE

PLATFORM CONSTRUCTED OPP. BABRI MOSQUE

MAKESHIFT STRUCTURE

11. High Court's Judgement on 23 February 1996 on '*darshan*' of the idols

That directly confronts the Court with the petitioner's complaint in the context of amenities available to the Hindu devotees who visit, the improvised platform, erected at the disputed site shortly after the demolition of the Ramjanmabhumi–Babri Masjid structures on 6.12.1992, to have the *darshan* of the Child God Shri Rama Lalla *Virajman*. As would be evident from the averments raised by the contesting parties there are counter versions on the factual position which in the very nature of things can be determined only on recording of evidence and since the issue is being tried on the original side of this Court in relation to the title suits, therefore, we would not like to venture therein.

The pertinent point, however, is that some sort of *puja* practice is going on and in consultation with the Statutory Receiver the State has regulated the practice by putting some restrictions on the devotees' movements primarily on account of the 'threat perception', which according to the petitioner are highly derogatory, humiliating and unreasonable. . . .

It was contended that the maximum distance which the devotees were required to cover was around 394 meters (around 450 yards), that the passage was about 3 feet wide and that there was a proper facility for placement of the devotees' belongings including shoes which they normally collected on their return journey. Similarly it was urged that at a short distance from the disputed site a few improvized shops were permitted to sell the *puja* material and that there was no dearth of any other civic amenity.

There is no gain-saying that the issue requires appreciation against the back drop of the unfortunate events of 6 December 1992 when the Ramjanmabhumi–Babri Masjid structure was pulled down by some anti-social elements which, howsoever momentarily, not only disturbed the communal harmony of our plural society but also brought us all in ridicule of international community. The State's anxiety in imposing certain restrictions on the movements of the people and Statutory Receiver's responsibility to ensure the maintenance of *status quo* both on account of legislative as well as judicial mandate can in no way be minimized or over-looked. All the same the continuation of the *puja* practice as available on 7.1.1993, in its pith and substance, has also to be allowed in a meaningful and worthwhile manner. To be precise there has to be a constructive and functional synthesis of the rights and responsibility of the parties.

. . . These checkposts may be fitted with modern gadgets so as to minimize if not altogether avoid the breach of one's personal privacy. Similarly the frisking if required may also be confined to the male members barring, of course, a thorough frisking of suspect characters, but in no case the female devotees should be frisked by male guards.

On the complaint that the distance between the point from where one is required to have the *darshan* and the place where the idol of the Child God is installed is more than 15 meters which hinders the sight and visibility because of the small size of the idol; we are of the considered view that this distance can be easily halved if not reduced more, to facilitate a worthwhile *darshan* to the devotees without infringing the security aspect; as by the time a devotee reaches that point he/she must have passed through at least two checkposts.

In the same vein we also intend to remove another grouse of the petitioner relating to the reluctance of the *pujaris* in placing the devotees' offerings at the feet of the idol. There is no gain-saying that the *pujaris* are the employees of the Statutory Receiver. We think that no in-convenience is going to be caused to the respondents if the *pujaris* are required to symbolically and momentarily place the offerings near the feet of the deity.

[From Judgement delivered on 23 February 1996 in Deoki Nandan Agarwala *versus* The Commissioner Faizabad, by Justice I.P. Vasisth, A.P. Misra and C.A. Rahim.]

12. Supreme Court's Stay Orders of 10 May and 9 August 1996

Annexure: P/1

EM No. A and B Court No. 8 Section PIL and XI

Supreme Court of India
Record of Proceedings

87861

Contempt P. . . ./96 with IA Nos. . . . In W.P. (C) Nos. 972, 977/91 and 208/93 ad SPI. Ref. No.1/93

Mohd. Aslam Alias Bhure, Petitioner

versus

S.B. Chowhan and Ors, Petitioner
(For interim relief and directions with or and Item-B

IA No. 1: In petition(s) for Special Leave to Appeal (Civil) cc.2059/96 (From the judgement and order dated 23/02/96 in WP 3067/94 of the High Court of Allahabad, Lucknow Bench)

Mohammad Hashim, Petitioner(s)

versus

Deoki Nandan Agarwala and Ors, Respondent(s)
(with Appln(s). for permission to file SLP)
Date: 10.9.96. This petition was called on for hearing today.

Coram:
Hon'ble Mr Justice G.N. Ray

Hon'ble Mr Justice N.P. Singh
For the appearing parties: Mr M.K. Banerjee, Mc. Mr Altar Petitioner(s)
ASG, Rajiv
Mr Z. Jilani, MA Siddiqui, Mr Sahkil Ahmed Syed, Advs. Mr M.M. Kashyap, Mr S.K. Bandopadhyaya, Mr Dhan Singh Dogar, Adv.
For Respondent (s) M/s. A.K. Goel, R.B. Misra, S. Subhashini.
U.U. Lalit, A.M. Khanwilkar, Kamini Jaiswal, B.Y. Kulkarni, Anis Suhrawardy, A.K. Gupta, Dr S.K. Jain and P. Parmeswaran, Advs.
Upon hearing counsel the Court made the following:

In 1. No. 1 in SLP(C) . . ./96 cc 2059/98

Application for permission to file SLP is allowed.
In this special leave petition the order dated 23 February 1996, passed by the Special Bench, Allahabad High Court is under Challenge Inter alia contending that direction given by the Constitution Bench in Ayodhya matter has not been properly followed. We have been informed that review application was made before the Court against the said order and on 12 April 1996, the Court has already passed an order on that review application. Let the order passed on the review application also be filed. Place this matter two weeks after summer vacation alongwith other Ayodhya matters which have been directed to be listed on the said date. In the meantime, *status quo* as was prevailing on the date of the impugned judgement, namely, on 23 February 1996 will be maintained by the parties.
In Contempt P. . . ./96 with IA Nos . . . in WP(C) Nos. 972, 977/91, 208/93 and Spl. Ref. 1/93

List two weeks after summer vacation alongwith Item-B and other Ayodhya matters.
(S.A. Chandwani)
(Court Master)

EM No. B&D Court No. 8 Section XI

Supreme Court of India
Record of Proceedings

Petition(s) for Special Leave to appeal civil No. 11429/96 (From the Judgement and order dated 23/02/96 in WP 3067/94 of the High Court of Allahabad Lucknow Bench)

Mohammad Hashim, Petitioner
Versus
Deoki Nandan Agarwala and Ors., Respondent

(With Appln (3). for ex-Parte stay revocation of Court order) with SLP (Civil) No. 15109/96, SLP (Civil). CC 3656–3657/96 (with appln. for exem, from filing OT and permission to file SLP)

Date: 09/08/96 These Petitions were called on for hearing today.

Coram:
Hon'ble Mr Justice G.N. Ray
Hon'ble Mr Justice N.P. Singh
Hon'ble Mr Justice S.P. Bharucha

For Petitioner (s)	Mr S.S. Ray, Sr. Adv. M/s A. Mannam, Z. Jilania, MT Khan, advs. Mr Shakil Ahmad, adv.
In SLP 15109/96:	Mr A. Bhattacharjee, adv.
For Respondent (s)	Mr D. Nanilan Agarwala, Sr. Adv.
For Res. No. 1 in person in SLP 11429/96:	Mr A. Bhattacharjee, adv.

Upon hearing counsel the Court made the following order
Issue notice
Interim order passed in SLP No. 11429/96 on 10.05.96 will continue in the meantime.
List the matters after Diwali holidays.

Inder Pal
(Court Master)

13. Supreme Court's Order of 13 March 2002 and its modification on 14 March 2002

Supreme Court of India
Record of Proceedings

Writ Petition (Civil) No. 160/1002

Mohd. Aslam alias Bhure, Petitioner (s)

versus

Union of India & Ors., Respondent (s)
With Appln(s). for directions and intervention)
Date: 13.3.2002 This Petition was called on for hearing today.

Coram:
Hon'ble Mr Justice B.N. Kirpal
Hon'ble Mr Justice G.B. Pattanaik
Hon'ble Mr Justice V.N. Khare

Upon hearing counsel the Court made the following order

1. Rule returnable after ten weeks.
2. Counsel representing the Union of India All India Babri Masjid Action

Committee, All India Muslim Law Board, State of U.P., Union Lawyers Front and all other respondents present in Court accept notice.

3. Counter-affidavit be filed within four weeks. Rejoinder be filed within four weeks thereafter. List this matter before a larger Bench.

4. In the meantime, we direct that on the 67.703 acres of land located in revenue plot Nos 159 and 160 in village Kot Ramchandra which is vested in the Central Government, no religious activity of any kind by anyone either symbolic or actual including *bhumi puja* or *shila puja*, shall be permitted or allowed to take place.

5. Furthermore, no part of the aforesaid land shall be handed over by the government to anyone and the same shall be retained by the government till the disposal of this writ petition nor shall any part of this land be permitted to be occupied or used for any religious purpose or in connection therewith.

6. This is subject to further orders which may be passed in this case.

7. In all the IAs, issue notice.

(S.L. Goyal)
Court Master

Upon hearing counsel the Court made the following order
After hearing the learned Attorney General, as there was some ambiguity in para 3 of our order dated 13 March 2002, we correct para 3 of our order as follows:

In the meantime, we direct that on the 67.703 acres of acquired land located in various plots detailed in the Schedule to the Acquisition of Certain Area at Ayodhya Act, 1993, which is vested in the Central Government, no religious activity of any kind by anyone either symbolic or actual including *bhumipuja* or *shila puja*, shall be permitted or allowed to take place.

Kalyani

(S.L. Goyal)
Court Master

14. Union Government's Statements on 13 March 2002

The Minister of Law, Justice and Company Affairs (Shri Arun Jaitley)
Thank you, Madam. Madam, the Hon'ble Supreme Court has passed an interim order today in a Writ Petition filed by Shri Aslam Bhure *versus* Union of India. The Court has passed interim orders, directing the maintenance of *status quo* on the acquired land, and disallowing *puja* in any form. The government is fully committed to the implementation of the orders of the Hon'ble Supreme Court, and the same shall be fully complied with. The government had earlier taken a stand that a decision to allow *puja* or not, could depend on the orders passed by the Supreme Court in the hearing on 13 march 2002. The Attorney General of

India appeared on behalf of the Government of India, and, on being asked by the Court about the government's stand, stated: 'On the Government's reading and interpretation of the judgement in Farooqi's case temporary user of the undisputed land for performing a brief *puja* was not per se prohibited, if the *puja* was performed under well-defined conditions and restrictions. Such a *puja* would not violate the orders of the Supreme Court, which as per our understanding, restricted *status quo* to the disputed land.' He suggested several restrictions and safeguards that would be imposed. The Attorney General also informed that the security personnel in sufficient numbers were deployed to take care of any law-and-order situation. He also stated that it would be clarified that if the *puja* was permitted, the performance of *puja* would not create any right or interest in favour of anybody or person. The Supreme Court expressed the view that no religious activity of any kind or transfer of land to any person should be permitted, till the disposal of the petition. The government fully respects the orders and the same shall be fully complied with.

The Leader of the House (Shri Jaswant Singh): Madam, I have to add one more thing to what my Hon'ble Colleague has stated, because I had also asked the Hon'ble Attorney-General, as some comments were made, in this House or elsewhere—I cannot recollect exactly where they were made, whether any kind of affidavit was filed by the Attorney General on behalf of the government. I had sought this clarification from the Attorney General, because, as I said, I was not present in the Court, and I did not wish to say anything unless I had ascertained it. I have received from the Attorney General a confirmation—'No affidavit or written submission was filed on behalf of the government, by the Attorney General. It was only on being asked by the Court that I submitted the government's reading and interpretation of the Supreme Court's Judgement in the Farooqi case'—which the Hon'ble Law Minister has just pointed out. This, I had assured.

Madam, you were not there, my distinguished colleague—and he is a senior leader of the Congress Party—who raised it in this House in the morning. Quite rightly, he expressed his concern and asked, 'Did the Government file any affidavit or did we make any averment, which was a departure from what the Government has said?' Maintenance of the *status quo* is our commitment; one. Two, whatever the Court rules, we are bound by it, legally, maintenance of the *status quo*, which is the Farooqi case's interpretation. All that the Attorney General did was to give our interpretation, to maintain the *status quo*. If, however, the Court rules, 'No; nothing is to be permitted—disputed, undisputed; religious, irreligious, any kind of activity', fine. This is what I said in the morning, 'No activity shall be permitted, religious or irreligious'. But I cannot guarantee, Madam, that the municipal functions of cleaning the land will not take place. That might take place, but that is about all. I don't think there is any ambiguity, whatsoever, in the Government's position. We are bound by what we have said; we are bound by what the Court has ruled; we are bound to see to it that on the 15—which is cited by the Hon'ble Member as some kind of a defining date—there is no violation and no departure from this.

15. Supreme Court's Order of 21 February 2003

W.P.(C) No. 160 of 2002
Item No. 5 Court No. 1 Section PIL

Supreme Court of India
Record of Proceedings

I.A. No. 8 in Writ Petition (Civil) No. 160/2002
Mohd. Aslam alias Bhure, Petitioner(s)

Versus

Union of India and Ors., Respondent(s)
(for early hearing) (for directions)
Date: 21/02/2003 This Petition was called on for hearing today.

Coram:
Hon'ble the Chief Justice
Hon'ble Dr Justice A.R. Lakshmanan

Upon hearing counsel the Court made the following

Order

The present writ petition was filed on 7 March 2002 for different reliefs. On 13 March 2002, a Bench of three Judges, while entertaining the petition, issued rule returnable after ten weeks. The Court also passed an interim order on the said date which was modified on 14 March 2002. Subsequently, certain more parties were impleaded in the writ petition. When the matter was placed before Hon'ble Chief Justice on 3 September 2002, it was directed that the matter be posted before a Bench of five Judges. The matter was listed before the Court on 24 September 2002 but did not reach for hearing. Some time in October 2002, the Union of India filed a counter affidavit in the writ petition.

On 4 February 2003, the Union of India filed an application which was registered as I.A. No. 8/2003, inter alia, praying for vacation of the interim order dated 13/14 March 2002 and fixing an early date for hearing of the writ petition. A counter affidavit has been filed to this application by the petitioner wherein the prayer for vacation of the interim order has been opposed. However, there is an agreement between the parties to the effect that the case may be heard at an early date.

We are of the view that it would be just and expedient if the matter is heard and disposed of at an early date. We, accordingly, direct that the main writ petition be listed before a Bench of five Judges on 6 March 2003 to be nominated by the Hon'ble Chief Justice of India. In case, for some reason, the main matter is adjourned on that day, the Bench would consider the first prayer of the Union of India in I.A. NO. 8/2003 for vacation of the interim order.

The respondents in the writ petition and I.A. No. 8/2003, if they so choose, may file counter affidavit within one week from today and the rejoinder may be filed on or before 6 March 2003.

I.A. Nos 9 and 10 filed by Shri Raj Rajeshwari Shri Sitaram Waqf be also listed on 6 March 2003 at the time of final disposal of the main matter.

SP1
(D.P. Walia)
Court Master

(S. Krishnan)
Court Master

16. Supreme Court's Judgement on 31 March 2003

In the Supreme Court of India Civil Original Jurisdiction
Writ Petition Civil No. 160 of 2002

Mohd. Aslam alias Bhure, Petitioner

Versus

Union of India & Ors., Respondents

Judgement

Rajendra Babu. J.
In the Statement of Objects and Reasons in the Bill ultimately leading to the enactment of the Acquisition of Certain Area at Ayodhya Act, 1993 [hereinafter referred to as 'the Act'], it has been stated as follows:

> There has been a long-standing dispute relating to the erstwhile Ramjanmabhumi–Babri Masjid structure in Ayodhya which led to communal tension and violence from time to time and ultimately led to the destruction of the disputed structure on 6 December 1992. This was followed by wide-spread communal violence which resulted in large number of deaths, injuries and destruction of property in various parts of the country. The said dispute has thus affected the maintenance of public order and harmony between different communities in the country. As it is necessary to maintain communal harmony and the spirit of common brotherhood amongst the people of India it was considered necessary to acquire the site of the disputed structure and suitable adjacent land for setting up a complex which could be developed in a planned manner wherein a Rama temple, a mosque, amenities for pilgrims, a library, museum and other suitable facilities can be set up.

In the Preamble to the Act also, it has been mentioned as follows:

> An act to provide for the acquisition of certain area at Ayodhya and for matters connected therewith or incidental thereto.

Whereas there has been a long-standing dispute relating to the structure (including the premises of the inner and outer courtyards of such structure), commonly known as the Ramjanmabhumi–Babri Masjid situated in village Kot Ramchandra in Ayodhya in Pargana Haveli Avadh, in Tehsil Faizabad Sadar, in the district of Faizabad of the State of Uttar Pradesh;

And Whereas the said dispute has affected the maintenance of public order and harmony between different communities in the country;

And whereas it is necessary to maintain public order and to promote communal harmony and the spirit of common brotherhood amongst the people of India. And whereas with a view to achieving the aforesaid objectives, it is necessary to acquire certain areas in Ayodhya . . .

In M. Ismail Faruqui etc. *versus* Union of India & Ors. 1994 Supp. (5) SCR 1, the validity of the Act was challenged. This Court examined the scheme of the Act and held as under by majority of 3.2:

1(a) Sub-section (3) of Section 4 of the Act abates all pending suits and legal proceedings without providing for an alternative dispute-resolution mechanism for resolution of the dispute between the parties thereto. This is an extinction of the judicial remedy for resolution of the dispute amounting to negation of rule of law. Sub-section (3) of section 4 of the Acts, therefore is unconstitutional and invalid.

(b) The remaining provisions of the Act do not suffer any invalidity on the construction made thereof by us. Sub-section of Section 4 of the Act is several from remaining Act. Accordingly, the challenge to the constitutional validity of the remaining Act, except for Sub-section (3) of Section of, is rejected.

(2) Irrespective of the status of a mosque under the Muslim Law applicable in the Islamic countries the status of a mosque under the Mahomedan Law applicable in secular India is the same and equal to that of any other place of worship of any religion and it does not enjoy any greater immunity from acquisition in exercise of the sovereign or prerogative power of the State than that of the places of worship of the other religions.

(3) The pending suits and other proceedings relating to the disputed area within which the structure [including the premises of the inner and outer courtyards of such structure], commonly known as the Ramjanmabhumi–Babri Masjid, stood, stand revived for adjudication of the dispute therein, together with the interim orders made, except to the extent the interim orders stand modified by the provisions of Section 7 of the Act.

(4) The vesting of the said disputed area in the Central Government by virtue of Section 3 of the Act is limited, as a statutory receiver, with the duty for its management and administration according to Section 7 requiring maintenance of *status quo* therein under sub-section (2) of Section 7 of the Act. The duty of the Central Government as the statutory receiver is to hand over the disputed area in accordance with Section 6 of the Act, in terms of the adjudication made in the suits for imple-

mentation of the final decision therein. This is the purpose for which the disputed area has been so acquired.

(5) The power of the Courts in making further interim orders in the suits is limited to and circumscribed by the area outside the ambit of Section 7 of the Act.

(6) The vesting of the adjacent area, other than the disputed area, acquired by the Act in the Central Government by virtue of Section 3 of the Act is absolute with the power of management and administration thereof in accordance with sub-section (1) of Section 7 of the Act, till its further vesting in any authority or other body or trustees of any trust in accordance with Section 6 of the Act. The further vesting of the adjacent area, other than the disputed area, in accordance with Section 6 of the Act has to be made at the time and in the manner indicated, in view of the purpose of its acquisition.

(7) The meaning of the word 'vest' in Section 3 and Section 6 of the Act has to be so understood in the different contexts.

(8) Section 8 of the Act is meant for payment of compensation to owners of the property vesting absolutely in the Central Government, the title to which is not in dispute being in excess of the disputed area which alone is the subject-matter of the revived suits. It does not apply to the disputed area, title to which has to be adjudicated in the suits and in respect of which the Central Government is merely the statutory receiver as indicated, with the duty to restore it to the owner in terms of the adjudication made in the suits.

(9) The challenge to acquisition of any part of the adjacent area on the ground that it is unnecessary for achieving the professed objective of setting the long-standing dispute cannot be examined at this stage. However, the area found to be superfluous on the exact area needed for the purpose being determined on adjudication of the dispute, must be restored to the undisputed owners.

(10) Rejection of the challenge by the undisputed owners to acquisition of some religious properties in the vicinity of the disputed area, at this stage is with the liberty granted to them to renew their challenge, if necessary at a later appropriate stage, in case of continued retention by the Central Government of their property in excess of the exact area determined to be needed on adjudication of the dispute.

(11) Consequently, the *Special Reference No. 1 of 1993*, made by the President of India under Article 143(1) of the Constitution of India is superfluous and unnecessary and does not require to be answered. For this reason , we very respectfully decline to answer it and return the same.

(12) The questions relating to the constitutional validity of the said Act and maintainability of the Special Reference are decided in these terms.

In this proceeding, which is initiated as public interest petition, several reliefs were claimed but after the interested parties were impleaded and their pleadings were put forth what has crystallized is as to the manner in which the adjacent land should be preserved till the final decision in the title suit pending in the High Court of Allahabad. This Court, on 13.3.2002, while issuing the rule, made the following order:

> . . . in the meantime we direct that on the 67.703–acres of land located in revenue plot Nos 159 and 180 in village Kot Ramchandra which is vested in the Central Government no religious activity of any kind by anyone either symbolic or actual including *bhumipuja* or *shila puja*, shall be permitted or allowed to take place.
>
> Furthermore, no part of the aforesaid land shall be handed over by the Government to anyone and the same shall be retained by the Government till the disposal of this writ petition nor shall any part of this land be permitted to be occupied or used for any religious purpose or in connection on therewith.
>
> This is subject to further orders which may be passed in this case.

The aforesaid order was clarified by another order dated 14.03.2002 in the following terms.

> After hearing the learned Attorney General, as there was some ambiguity in para 3 of our order dated 13 March 2002, we correct para 3 of our order as follows:
>
> In the meantime we direct that on the 67.703 acres of acquired land located in various plots detailed in the Scheduled to Acquisition of Central Areas at Ayodhya Act, 1993, which is vested in the Central Government, no religious activity of any kind by anyone either symbolic or actual including *bhumipuja* or *shila puja*, shall be permitted or allowed to take place.

Subsequently after the pleading were completed an application was filed seeking for vacating the interim order and for final hearing of the petition. Instead of considering the interim application, we considered we should dispose of the main matter and hence we have finally heard the matter.

Learned counsel on both sides in the present case heavily relied upon the decision in M. Ismail Faruqui's case [supra].

The Act, as it was passed by Parliament, anticipated the settlement of the dispute after obtaining the opinion of this Court and in terms of the said opinion. However, the reference made to this Court having been returned to the President without any opinion thereto and the provisions of Section 4(3) of the Act by which the pending proceedings stood abated having been declared to be invalid, the suits and the other proceedings along with the interim orders stood revived. Therefore, the whole perception of the provisions of the enactment will have to be made in that light. While it is the contention of the petitioner that the decision of this Court in M. Ismail Faruqui's case [supra] clearly indicates that the purpose of the acquisition of the adjacent land is to meet the easement of necessity of proper enjoyment of the disputed land by its owner who is ultimately to be declared by the High Court of Allahabad and on consideration of the various observations made by this Court in the course of the judgement, particularly that the extent of the area required for carrying out the purpose of the Act would depend on the decision in favour of the Muslims or Hindus in respect of the disputed land and the scheme to be framed for purposes of developing a complex consisting of museum, library and other structures. All this cannot be done until the suits pending before the High Court of Allahabad are settled. Therefore, they pray that *status quo* as ordered by this Court in the interim order should be made absolute and an appropriate relief be granted in the aforesaid terms.

The Union of India and Others submit that the interim relief granted by this Court earlier goes beyond the scope of the decision rendered by this Court in M. Ismail Faruqui's case [supra] and the petition filed by the petitioner should be dismissed straightaway because he had filed a writ petition before the High Court of Allahabad which came to be dismissed and in this petition there is hardly any proper foundation laid for granting any relief. It is also pleaded that the allegations made in the petition are vague and do not contain the necessary details to appreciate the various contentions urged before the Court and several of the prayers made in the petition have already become infructuous.

On several occasions this Court has treated letters, telegrams or post cards or news reports as writ petitions. In such petitions, on the basis of pleadings that emerge in the case after notice to different parties, relief has been given or refused. Therefore, this Court would not approach matters where public interest is involved in a technical or a narrow manner. Particularly, when this Court has entertained this petition, issued notice to different parties, new parties have been impleaded and interim order has also been granted, it would not be appropriate for this Court to dispose of the petition on that ground.

Filing of the writ petition in the High Court of Allahabad or its dismissal will not come in the way of considering this petition. The scope of that writ petition filed in the High Court is different from what is urged in the present proceedings which is limited to maintaining *status quo* during pendency of suits before the High Court in respect of acquired land.

The Preamble to the Act itself discloses that the objective of the enactment is maintenance of harmony between different communities in the country and to maintain public order. If the acquisition has been effected on that basis not only of the disputed land but also of adjacent land, this thread will run through the entire proceedings and we must bear in mind that when the dispute is not yet finally resolved, maintenance of communal harmony and peace is absolutely needed. It is no doubt true that when passions run high, demands are made for several types of activities being carried on in the adjacent land. If any such activities are carried on in such land, even before the resolution of the dispute pending before the Court, it may affect the harmony and tranquility that has prevailed for so long.

Section 6(1) of the Act enables the Central Government to transfer its right, title and interest or any of them in the area or any part thereof to any authority or other body, or trusts on such terms and conditions as it may think fit to impose instead of continuing to retain the same itself. Sections 6(2) and (3) provide for certain arrangements of statutory transfer effected by Central Government by declaring that the transferee would step into the shoes of the Government acquiring the same right, title and interest in the area in question. As also that Sections 4, 5, 7, 11 so far as may be, would apply to such transferee as would apply to Central Government.

In the course of the discussion in M. Ismail Faruqui's case [supra], it has been observed as follows.

> The narration of facts indicates that the acquisition of properties under the Act affects the rights of both the communities and not merely those of the Muslim community. The interest claimed by the Muslims is only over the disputed site where the mosque stood before its demolition. The objection of the Hindus to this claim has to be adjudicated. The remaining entire property acquired under the Act is such over which no title is claimed by the Muslims. A large part thereof comprises of properties of Hindus of which the title is not even in dispute. The justification given for acquisition of the larger area including the property respecting which title is not disputed is that the same is necessary to ensure that the final outcome of adjudication should not be rendered meaningless by the existence of properties belonging to Hindus in the vicinity of the disputed structure in case the Muslims are found entitled to the disputed site. This obviously means that in the event of the Muslims succeeding in the adjudication of the dispute requiring the disputed structure to be handed over to the Muslim community, their success should not be thwarted by denial of proper access to, and enjoyment of rights in, the disputed area by exercise of rights of ownership of Hindu owners of the adjacent properties. Obviously, it is for this reason that the adjacent area has also been acquired to make available to the successful party, that part of it which is considered necessary, for proper enjoyment of the fruits of success on the final outcome to the adjudication. It is clear that one of the purposes of the acquisition of the adjacent properties is the ensurement of the effective enjoyment of the disputed site by the Muslim community in the event of its success in the litigation; and acquisition of the adjacent area is incidental to the main purpose and cannot be termed unreasonable. The 'Manas Bhawan' and 'Sita ki Rasoi' both belonging to the Hindus, are buildings which closely overlook the disputed site and are acquired because they are strategic in location in relation to the disputed area. The necessity of acquiring adjacent temples or religious building in view of their proximity to the disputed structure area, which forms a unique class by itself, is permissible (See M. Padmanabha Iyengar *versus* Government of AP., AIR 1990 AP 357, and Akhara Shri Braham Buta *versus* State of Punjab, AIR 1989 P&H 198). We approve the principle stated in these decisions since it serves a larger purpose.
>
> However, at a later stage when the exact area acquired which is needed for achieving the professed purposes of acquisition, can be determined, it would not merely be permissible but also desirable that the superfluous excess area is released from acquisition and reverted to its earlier owner. The challenge to acquisition of any part of the adjacent area on the ground that it is unnecessary for achieving the objective of setting the dispute relating to the disputed area cannot be examined at the stage but, in case the superfluous area is not returned to its owner even after the exact area needed for the purpose is finally determined it would be open to the owner of any such property to then challenge the superfluous acquisition being unrelated to the purpose of acquisition. Rejection of the challenge on this ground

> to acquisition at this stage, by the undisputed owners of any such property situated in the vicinity of the disputed area, is with the reservation of this liberty to them. There is no contest to their claim of quashing the acquisition of the adjacent properties by anyone except the Central Government which seeks to justify the acquisition on the basis of necessity. On the construction of the statute made by us, this appears to be the logical, appropriate and just view to take in respect of such adjacent properties in which none other than the undisputed owner claims title and interest.
>
> Acquisition of the adjacent undisputed area belonging to Hindus has been attacked on the ground that it was unnecessary since ownership of the same is undisputed. Reason for acquisition of the large area adjacent to the disputed area has been indicated. It is, therefore, not unrelated to the resolution of the dispute which is the reason for the entire acquisition. Even thought, *prima facie*, the acquisition of the adjacent area in respect of which there is no dispute of title and which belongs to Hindus may appear to be a slant against the Hindus yet on closer scrutiny it is not so since it is for the larger national purpose of maintaining and promoting communal harmony and in consonance with the creed of secularism. Once it is found that it is permissible to acquire an area in excess of the disputed area alone, adjacent to it, to effectuate the purpose of acquisition of the disputed area and to implement the outcome of the final adjudication between the parties to ensure that in the event of success of the Muslim community in the dispute their success remains meaningful, the extent of adjacent area considered necessary is in the domain of policy and not a matter for judicial scrutiny or a ground for testing the constitutional validity of the enactment. However, it is with the caveat of the Central Government's duty to restore it to its owner, as indicated earlier, if it is found later to be unnecessary, and reservation of liberty to the owner to challenge the needless acquisition when the total need has been determined.

From the observations quoted above, it is clear that the adjacent land, though vest in the Central Government, will have to be utilized in different manners depending upon the outcome of the litigation in respect of the disputed property. Thus the manner or extent to which the adjacent land could be used would depend upon the final outcome of the pending dispute in the High Court. The acquisition of larger extent of land is incidental to main purpose. Thus, the two acquired lands are intrinsically connected with one another and cannot be separated at this stage of the proceedings for different treatment during the interregnum. Further, it has also been made clear that if any land becomes superfluous such land will have to be returned to the owner who may have to initiate appropriate proceedings to challenge the validity of the acquisition as indicated in the course of the judgment of this Court in M. Ismail Faruqui's case [supra]. If land is transferred to any other body or trust as provided under Section 6 of the Act at this stage further complications may arise. Therefore, *status quo* will have to be maintained until suits are finally disposed of. We hold that the orders of this

Court made earlier are not beyond the scope of the decision in M. Ismail Faruqui's case.

Above all, *status quo* has been maintained from 1992 onwards and no activities as are set out in the course of the application have been required to be done so far. When for a long time, a particular state of affairs has prevailed—as in the present case for over a decade—and when the adjudication of the disputes which are pending before the High Court are reaching final stages, it will not be appropriate to disturb that state of affairs. It is well known that preservation of property in its original condition is absolutely necessary to give appropriate reliefs to the parties on the termination of the proceedings before the courts and, therefore, we do not think that this is one of those cases in which it becomes necessary to disturb that state.

On consideration of the entire matter, we are of the view that the order made by this Court on 13.3.2002, as modified by the order made on 14.03.2002, should be operative until disposal of the suits in the High Court of Allahabad not only to maintain communal harmony but also to fulfil other objectives of the Act. The writ petition shall stand disposed of accordingly.

Before parting with the case, we wish to put on record that all the learned counsel and the parties who appeared in person in arguing the matter thoroughly have presented their respective cases only on facts and law arising in the case without bringing into Court in any manner the passion raging outside whether religious or political. We greatly appreciate this stand of the Advocates and the parties in the Court.

S. Rajendra Babu
Syed Shah Mohammed Quadr
M.B. Shah
N. Santosh Hegde
Doraiswamy Raju
New Delhi
31 March 2003

17a. Babri Mosque Site

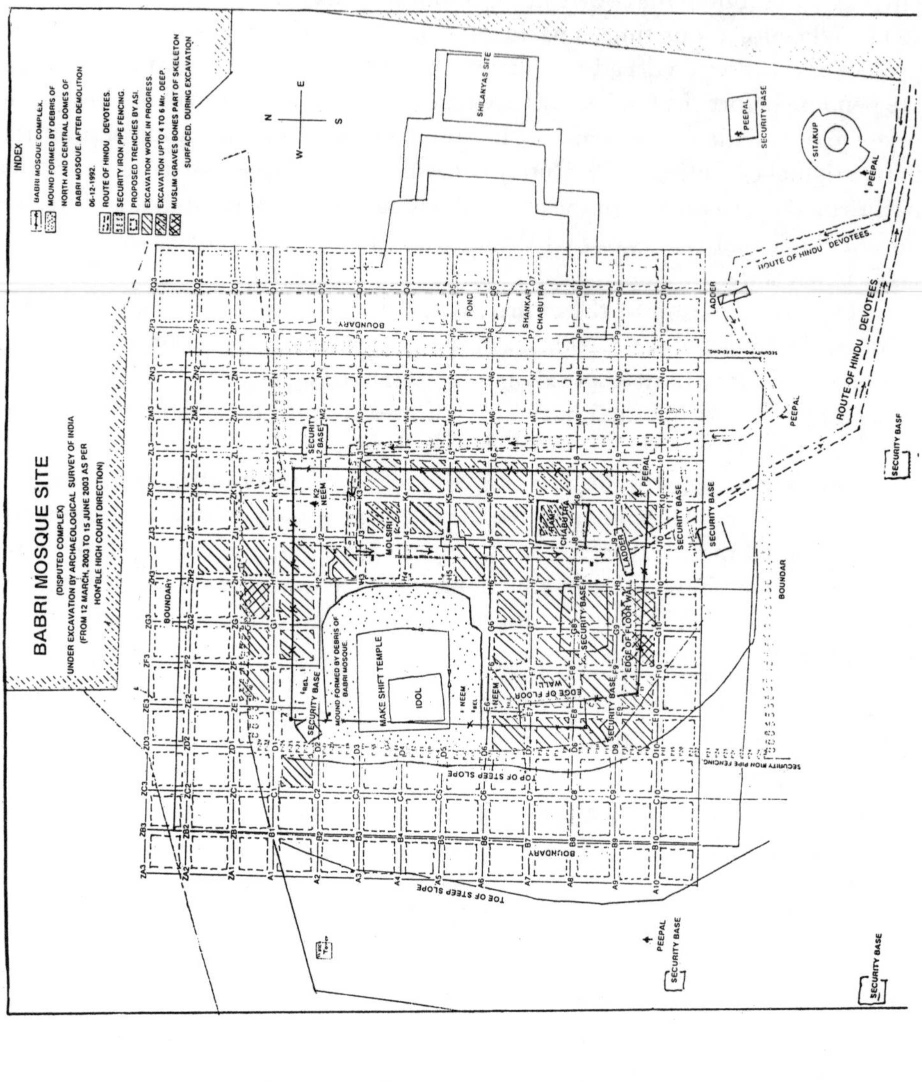

17b. The issues in the Title Suits

The issues framed by the special Court to decide the dispute is as far as follows:
In the High Court of Judicature at Allahabad
Lucknow Bench, Lucknow
Other original suite No. 4 of 1989
(Regular Suit No. 12 of 1961)
Sunni Central Board of Waqf.

and others. . . . Plaintiffs

versus

Gopal Singh Visharad and others. . . . Defendants

Issues as it stands now:

Issue No .1:
Whether the building in question described as mosque in the sketch map attached to the plaint (hereinafter referred to as the building) was a mosque as claimed by the plaintiffs? If the answer is in the affirmative.

(a) When was it built and by whom—whether by Babar as alleged by the plaintiffs or by Mir Baqi as alleged by defendant No. 13?

(b) Whether the building had been constructed on the site of an alleged Hindu temple after demolishing the same as alleged by defendant No. 13? If so. Its effect?

Issue No. 1-A:

Whether the land adjoining the building on the east, north and south sides, denoted by letters E F G H on the sketch map, was an ancient graveyard and mosque as alleged in para 2 of the plaint? If so, its effect? (deleted vide Courts order, dated 23.2.96)

Issue No. 1-B (a)

Whether the building existed at a Nazul plot No. 583 of the Khasra of the year 1931 of Mohalla Kot Rama Chandra known as Rama Kot, city Ayodhya (Nazul state? Ayodhya? If so its effect thereon)

Issue No. 1-B (b)

Whether the building stood dedicated to almighty God as alleged by the plaintiffs?

Issue No. 1-B (c)

Whether the building had been used by the members of the Muslim community for offering prayers from times immemorial? If so, its effect?

Issue No. 1-B (d)

Whether the alleged graveyard has been used by the members of Muslim community for burying the dead bodies of the members of the Muslim community? If so, its effect? (deleted vide Court order dated 23.2.96)

Issue No. 2 :

Whether the plaintiffs were in possession of the property in suit up to 1949 and were dispossessed from the same in 1949 as alleged in the plaint?

Issue No. 3:

Is the suit within time?

Issue No. 4:

Whether the Hindus in general and the devotees of Bhagwan Sri Rama in particular have perfected right of prayers at the site by adverse and continuous possession as of right for more than the statutory period of time by way of prescription as alleged by the defendants?

Issue No. 5 (a):

Are the defendants stopped from challenging the character of property in suit as a Waqf under the administration of plaintiff No. 1 in view of the provision of 5(3) of U.P. Act 13 of 1936? (This issue has already been decided in the negative vide order dated 21.4.1966 by the learned Civil Judge)

5 (b) Has the said Act no application to the right of Hindus in general and defendants in particular, to the right of their worship?

5 (c) Were the proceedings under the said Act conclusive? (This issue has already been decided in the negative vide order dated 21.4.1996 by the Learned civil judge.)

5 (d) Are the said provision of Act XIII of 1936 ultra-vires as alleged in written statement? (This issue was not pressed by counsel for the defendants. Hence not answered by the learned Civil Judge, vide his order dated 21.4.1996 by the Learned civil judge.)

5 (e) Whether in view of the findings recorded by the learned Civil Judge on 21.4.1966 on issue no. 17 to the effect that, 'No valid notification under section 5 (1) of the Muslim Waqf Act (No. XIII of 1936) was ever made in respect of the property in dispute', the plaintiff Sunni Central Board of Waqf has no right to maintain the present suit?

(f) Whether in view of the aforesaid finding, the suit is barred on account of lack of jurisdiction and limitation as it was filed after the commencement of the U.P. Muslim Waqf Act. 1960?

Issue No. 6:

Whether the present suit is a representative suit. Plaintiffs representing the interest of the Muslims and defendants representing the interest of the Hindus?

Issue No. 7:

7 (a) Whether Mahant Raghubar Das, plaintiff of Suit No. 61/280 of 1885 had sued on behalf of Janmasthan and whole body of persons interested in Jasa-Sthan?

7 (b) Whether Mohammad Asghar was the *Mutawalli* of alleged Babri Masjid and did he contest the suit for and on behalf of any such mosque?

7 (c) Whether in view of the judgement in the said suit, the members of the Hindu community, including the contesting defendants, are stopped from denying the title of the Muslim community, including the plaintiffs of the present suit, to the property in dispute? If so, its effect?

7 d) Whether in the aforesaid suit, title of the Muslims to the property in

dispute or any portion thereof was admitted by plaintiff of that suit? If so, its effect?

Issue No. 8:

Does the judgement of Case No. 6/281 of 1881, Mahant Raghubar Das *versus* Secretary of State and others, operate as res judicate against the defendants in suit?

Issue No. 9:

Whether the plaintiffs served valid notices Under Section 80 C.P.C. (deleted vide order dated May 22/25, 1990)

Issue No. 10:

Whether the plaintiffs have perfected their rights by adverse possession as alleged in the plaint?

Issue No. 11:

Is the property in suit the site of Janambhumi of Sri Rama Chandraji?

Issue No. 12:

Whether idols and objects of worship were placed inside the building in the night intervening 22 and 23 December 1949 as alleged in paragraph 11 of the plaint or they have been in existence there since before? In either case, effect?

Issue No. 13:

Whether the Hindus in general and defendants in particular had the right to worship the *Charans* and Sita *Rasoi* and other idols and other objects of worship, if any, existing in or upon the property in suit?

Issue No. 14:

Have the Hindus been worshipping the place in dispute as Sri Ramjanma-bhumi or Janmasthan and have been visiting it as a sacred place of pilgrimage as of right since times immemorial? If so, its effect?

Issue No. 15:

Have the Muslims been in possession of the property in suit from AD 1528 continuously, openly and to the knowledge of the defendants and Hindus in general? If so, its effect?

Issue No. 16:

To what relief, if any, are the plaintiffs or any of them, entitled?

Issue No. 17:

Whether a valid notification under section 5 (1) of the U.P. Muslim Waqf Act No. XIII of 1936 relating to the property in suit was ever done? If so, its effect? (This issue has already been decided by the learned Civil Judge by order dated 21.4.1966)

Issue No. 18:

What is the effect of the judgement of their lordships of the Supreme Court in Gulam Abbas and others *versus* State of U.P. and others. A.I.R. 1981 Supreme Court 2198 on the finding of the learned Civil Judge recorded on 21 April 1966 on issue no. 17?

Issue No. 19 (a):

Whether even after construction of the building in suit deities of Bhagwan Sri Rama Virajman and the Asthan Sri Ramjanmabhumi continued to exist on the property in suit as alleged on behalf of defendant No. 13 and the said places continued to be visited by devotees for purposes of worship? If so, whether the property in dispute continued to vest in the said deities?

Issue No. 19 (b):

Whether the building was land-locked and cannot be reached except by passing through places of Hindu worship? If so, its effect?

Issue No. 19 (c):

Whether any portion of the property in suit was used as a place of worship by the Hindus immediately prior to the construction of the building in question? If the finding is in the affirmative. Whether no mosque could come into existence in view of the Islamic tenets at the place in dispute?

Issue No. 19 (d):

Whether the building in question could not be a mosque under the Islamic Law in view of the admitted position that it did not have minarets?

Issue No. 19 (e):

Whether the building in question could not legally be a mosque as on plaintiffs own showing it was surrounded by a graveyard on three sides.

Issue No. 19 (f):

Whether the pillars inside and outside the building in question contain images of Hindu Gods and Goddesses? If the finding is in the affirmative, whether on that account the building in question cannot have the character of Mosque under the tenets of Islam.

Issue No. 20 (a):

Whether the Waqf in question cannot be a Sunni Waqf as the building was not allegedly constructed by a Sunni Mohammedan but was allegedly constructed by Mir Baqi who was allegedly a Shia Muslim and the alleged *Mutawallis* were allegedly Shia Mohammedans? If so, its effect?

Issue No. 20 (b):

Whether there was a *Mutawalli* of the alleged Waqf and whether the alleged *Mutawalli* not having joined in the suit, the suit is not maintainable so far as it relates to relief for possession?

Issue No. 21:

Whether the suit is bad for non-jointer of alleged deities?

Issue No. 22:

Whether the suit is liable to be dismissed with special costs?

Issue No. 23:

If the Waqf Board is an instrumentality of state? If so, whether the said Board can file a suit against the state itself?

Issue No. 24:

If the Waqf Board is state under Article 12 of the constitution? If so, the said

Board being the state can file any suit in representative capacity sponsoring the case of particular community and against the interest of another community.

Issue No. 25:

Whether after demolition of the disputed structure as claimed by the plaintiff, it can still be called a mosque and if not whether the claim of the plaintiffs is liable to be dismissed as no longer maintainable?

Issue No. 26:

Whether Muslims can use the open site as mosque to offer prayer when structure which stood thereon has been demolished?

Issue No. 27:

Whether the outer courtyard contained Rama Chabutra, *Bhandar* and Sita *Rasoi*? If so whether they were also demolished on 6.12.1992 along with the main temple?

Issue No. 28:

Whether the defendant No. 3 has ever been in possession of the disputed site and the plaintiffs were never in its possession?

18. High Court's Excavation Order of 5 March 2003

[Reproduced in full in Volume I, Chapter II, Doc. 25]

19. The Places of Worship (Special Provisions) Act, 1991

(Act No. 42 of 1991)

Contents

Sections

Statement of objects and reasons

1. In view of the controversies arising from time to time with regard to conversion of places of worship, it is felt that such conversions should be prohibited.
2. In order to foreclose any controversy in respect of any place of worship that

maintenance of the religious character of such place of worship as it existed on the 15th day of August 1947. As a consequence thereof, all the suits or other proceedings pending as on 11th day of July 1991 with respect to any such places of worship, may abate and also further suits or other proceedings may be barred.

3. However, since the case relating to the place commonly called Ramjanma-bhumi–Babri Masjid forms a class by itself, it has become necessary to exempt it entirely from the operation of this Act.
4. Moreover, in order to maintain communal harmony and peace, matters decided by Courts, tribunals or other authorities, or those settled by parties amongst themselves or through acquiescence, between 15th day of August, 1947 and the 11th day of July 1991 are also exempted from the operation of this Act.
5. The 11th day of July 1991 is proposed as the commencement date of the Act as on that day the President addressed the Parliament making such a declaration.
6. The Bill seeks to achieve the above objectives

—Gaz. of Ind., 23.8.1991, Pt. II, S. 2, Ext. p. 4 (No. 26).

[The] Places of Worship (Special Provisions) Act, 1991
(Act No. 42 of 1991)*
(18 September 1991)

An act to prohibit conversion of any place of worship and to provide for the maintenance of the religious character of any place of worship as it existed on the 15th day of August 1947, and for matters connected therewith or incidental thereto.

Be it enacted by Parliament in the Forty-second Year of the Republic of India as follows:

1. Short title, extent and commencement:

(1) This Act may be called the Places of Worship (Special Provisions) Act, 1991.
(2) It extends to the whole of India except the State of Jammu and Kashmir.
(3) The provisions of Sections 3, 6 and 8 shall come into force at once and the remaining provisions of this Act shall be deemed to have come into force on the 11th day of July, 1991.

2. Definitions: In this Act, unless the context otherwise requires:

(a) 'commencement of this Act' means the commencement of this Act on the 11th day of July, 1991;
(b) 'conversion', with its grammatical variations, includes alteration or change of whatever nature;
(c) 'place of worship' means a temple, mosque, gurudwara, church, monastery or any other place of public religious worship of any religious denomination or any section thereof, by whatever name called.

*Received the assent of the President on 18.9.1991 Act published in Gaz. of India; 19.9.1991 Part II-S. I, Ext. P. 1 (No. 55).

3. Bar of conversion of places of worship: No person shall convert any place of worship of any religious denomination or any section thereto into a place of worship of a different section of the same religious denomination or of a different religious denomination or any section thereof.

4. Declaration as to the religious character of certain places of worship and bar of jurisdiction of Courts, etc.:

(1) It is hereby declared that the religious char-acter of a place of worship existing on the 15th day of August 1947 shall continue to be the same as it existed on that day.

(2) If, on the commencement of this Act, any suit, appeal or other proceeding with respect to the conversion of the religious character of any place of worship, existing on the 15th day of August, 1947, is pending before any Court, tribunal or other authority, the same shall abate, and no suit, appeal or other proceeding with respect to any such matter shall lie on or after such commencement in any Court, tribunal or other authority provided that if any suit, appeal or other proceeding, instituted or filed on the ground that conversion has taken place in the religious character of any such place after the 15th day of August 1947, is pending on the commencement of this Act, such suit, appeal or other proceeding shall not so abate and every such suit, appeal or other proceeding shall be disposed of in accordance with the provisions of sub-section (1). . . .

(3) Nothing contained in sub-section (1) and sub-section (2) shall apply to:

(a) any place of worship referred to in the said sub-section which is an ancient and historical monument or an archaeological site or remains covered by the Ancient Monuments and Archaeological Sites and Remains Act, 1958 or any other law for the time being in force;

(b) any suit, appeal or other proceeding, with respect to any matter referred to in sub-section (2), finally decided, settled or disposed of by a Court, tribunal or other authority before the commencement of this Act;

(c) any dispute with respect to any such matter settled by the parties amongst themselves before such commencement;

(d) any conversion of any such place effected before such commencement by acquiescence;

(e) any conversion of any such place effected before such commencement which is not liable to be challenged in any Court, tribunal or other authority being barred by limitation under any for the time being in force.

5. Act not to apply to Ramjanmabhumi–Babri Masjid: Nothing contained in this Act shall apply to the place or place of worship commonly known as Ramjanmabhumi–Babri Masjid situated in Ayodhya in the State of Uttar Pradesh and to any suit, appeal or other proceeding relating to the said place or place of worship.

6. Punishment for contravention of Section 3:

(1) Whoever contravenes the provisions of Section 3 shall be punishable with

imprisonment for a term which may extend to three years and shall also be liable to fine.

(2) Whoever attempts to commit any offence punishable under sub-section (1) or to cause such offence to be committed and in such attempt does any act towards the commission of the offence shall be punishable with the punishment provided for the offence.

(3) Whoever abets, or is a party to a criminal conspiracy to commit, an offence punishable under sub-section (1) shall, whether such offence be or be not committed in consequence of such abatement or in pursuance of such criminal conspiracy, and notwithstanding anything contained in section 116 of the Indian Penal Code, be punishable with the punishment provided for the offence.

7. Act to override other enactments: The provisions of this Act shall have effect notwithstanding anything inconsistent therewith contained in any other law for the time being in force or any instrument having effect by virtue of any law other than this Act.

8. Amendment of Act 43 of 1951: In Section 8 of the Representation of the People Act, 1951), in sub-section (1):

(a) in clause (I), the word 'or' shall be inserted at the end;

(b) after clause (I), as so amended, the following clause shall be inserted, namely: '(j) section 6 (offence of conversion of a place of worship) of the Places of Worship (Special Provisions) Act, 1991'.

CHAPTER XII
Shri Krishna Janmasthan

1. Agreement of 12 October 1968 on the Sri Krishna Janmasthan

Translation of the Agreement between the Shahi Idgah Trust and Sri Krishna Janmasthan Seva Sangh, Mathura.

We, Shri Deodhar Shastri, U.P. *mantri* authorized by the Sri Krishna Janmasthan Seva Sangh, Mathura, *As First Party* and Shri Shah Mir Malih and Shri Abdul Ghaffar, Advocate, the Representative of the Shahi Masjid, Idgah Trust, Mathura, *As the Second Party.*

Under the Trust's Resolution No. 2, dated 8.10.1968.

In order to settle the longstanding disputes between the Sri Krishna Janmasthan Sangh and the Shahi Masjid Idgah Trust and the so-called *ghoshi* tenants and licencees of the second party, we, under the suggestion of the members of both Hindu and Muslim communities, have reached an agreement, henceforth, to settle our bilateral disputes and avoid cases against each other.

The following agreement agreed to by the Second Party, that is, Shahi Masjid Idgah Trust has the permission of the Uttar Pradesh Central Waqf Board *vide* their express letter no. 2876, 43 CIR dated 9.9.1968 and Shri Shah Mir Malih and Shri Abdul Ghaffar, Advocate have been authorized to get the Agreement implemented under their resolution No. 2 in the meeting of 8.10.1968.

Similarly the first Party i.e. the Sri Krishna Janmasthan Seva Sangh has also accepted the agreement at its meeting of 25.8.1968 and authorized Shri Deodhar Shastri to get the Agreement implemented.

Since the following agreement shall take some time for its full implementation we are therefore getting a written *Ikrarnama* registered. Hence, we the representatives of both the parties concerned, freely and after a full decision as well as by the Consensus of both the parties, that is, The Sri Krishna Janmasthan Seva Sangh and the Shahi Masjid Idgah Trust, are getting the *Ikrarnama* registered. Henceforth, we will have to abide by the following agreement and it will be our duty to implement the agreement.

1. The northern and southern walls of Idgah's *kuchchi kurshi* shall be

extended towards the eastern side, up to the Railway land. The expenses shall be borne by the Masjid Trust.

2. Outside the northern and southern walls the area occupied by Muslim *ghoshis* shall be evacuated on behalf of the Trust and handed over to the Janmasthan Seva Sangh. Thereafter, the Trust or the *ghoshis* shall not be entitled to claim the above-mentioned portion of the land.

Similarly, the portion of land lying inside the northern and southern walls shall be the Trust's property. Hence there shall be no claim on this land on the part of the Seva Sangh.

3. In the west-northern corner of Idgah *kuchchi kursi* a portion of land is occupied by the Seva Sangh (shown in the map A B C D). The Trust shall acquire the *kuchchi kursi* and it shall become the Trust's property.

4. The controversial debris of the stairs on the southern side, for which there are cases filed in the court, shall be cleared by the Trust by 15 October 1968. Thereafter the portion shall be the Seva Sangh's property.

5. The houses built by Muslim *ghoshis* out of the northern and southern walls under settlement with the Trust shall be evacuated on behalf of the Trust and handed over to the Seva Sangh. Only after the completion of evacuation, the Trust shall be entitled to get the walls constructed.

The Trust, moreover, shall not open doors, windows, *pinjars*, etc. nor any water outlets (drains) in the proposed wall, towards the Seva Sangh. The Seva Sangh too shall not do any such thing against the Idgah.

6. The outlets (*parnalas*) of Idgah flowing already westward of the Janmasthan shall be removed and turned towards Idgah by piping. The expenses shall be borne by the Seva Sangh. During the laying of the pipe, a representative of the Janmasthan shall be present.

7. A portion of the railway land in front of Idgah's northern and southern walls which is going to be acquired by the Janmasthan Seva Sangh, after acquiring the land, the Janmasthan Seva Sangh shall transfer that portion to the Trust which falls inside the north and south walls of the Idgah.

8. The portion of land in front of *kuchchi kurshi* towards the eastern side (shown in the map E F G H I J K L) and in the west-northern corner (shown in the map A B C D) which is left by the Seva Sangh in favour of the Trust is shown in oblique line in the map.

9. The cases against each other shall be withdrawn according to the above agreement.

10. Both the parties shall have the right to appeal to the court for having the agreement implemented if either party deviates from the agreement.

Hence this agreement reached in writing by the consent of both the parties.

Date of writing: 12 October 1968

Boundary of Masjid Idgah Shahi
East—Railway line
West—Chabutra Janmasthan
North—Ground Janmasthan
South—Ground Janmasthan banke katra, Keshaw—deve Mathura ton

Writer: Navnit Lal Sharma Shastri
Deodhar Shastri
Signature: Abdul Ghaffar: In English
Signature: Md Shah Mir Malih